Michael Praetorius

SYNTAGMA MUSICUM II

De Organographia

Parts III – V

with Index

Translated and edited
by
Quentin Faulkner

Zea Books
Lincoln, Nebraska
2014

ISBN 978-1-60962-050-9 paperback
ISBN 978-1-60962-051-6 ebook

English translation, notes, etc., copyright © 2014 Quentin Faulkner.

Design, layout, and composition, based on the 1619 edition, by Paul Royster.
Text set in IM Fell English Pro type, developed and furnished by
Igino Marini; display type in Diploma by Altsys Fontographer;
initials in Kanzlei Initialen designed by Dieter Steffmann.

The Fell Types
www.iginomarini.com

Zea Books are published by the University of Nebraska-Lincoln Libraries.

Available online: http://digitalcommons.unl.edu/zeabook/
Paperback orders: http://www.lulu.com/spotlight/unllib

Preface to the Translation

ichael Praetorius was born Feb. 15, 1571, and died Feb. 15, 1621. The fifty years of his life are distinguished by unremitting creative energy. Praetorius achieved distinction as a practicing musician: as organist and Kapellmeister at Wolfenbüttel, Dresden and Magdeburg, and (in his later years) by incessant travel to fulfill commissions at various central German courts. Amid his travels Praetorius found time to publish an impressive series of collections of musical compositions, in all more than a thousand works.

Praetorius's only literary publication, the three-volume *Syntagma musicum* (Musical Encyclopedia) belongs to the last years of his life.

Volume I, *Musicae artis analecta* (1614/15, in Latin), treats principles and practices of religious music, from a decidedly Lutheran perspective.

Volume II, *De organographia* (1619, in German) deals with musical instruments, in particular with the organ.

Volume III, *Termini musici* (1619, in German) explores the practice of music, both improvisation and composition.

The *Syntagma musicum* is the first comprehensive treatment of music in the German language. Looking back over the intervening 150 years, Jacob Adlung—himself a major figure in German musical scholarship—cites Praetorius constantly, and refers to him as the "primary book …."[1]

Volume I has not yet been translated into English. Volume III has been translated and edited by Jeffery Kite-Powell (Oxford University Press, 2004). The first two parts of Volume II, on all musical instruments except the organ, have been translated twice: by Harold Blumenfeld (Bärenreiter, 1962; reprinted by Da Capo Press, 1980), and by David Z. Crookes (Oxford: Clarendon Press; New York: Oxford University Press, 1986). The publication before you translates Volume II, Parts III-V on the organ.[2] Its belated appearance would have puzzled Praetorius, who declares the organ to be "a perfect (indeed one might also say "most perfect") musical instrument … which …

---

[1]. Jacob Adlung, *Musica mechanica organœdi*, (Berlin: Birnstiel, 1768), Vol. I, p. 12, §. 9. Facsimile and English translation: Lincoln, Nebraska: Zea E-Books, 2011; electronic edition: http://digitalcommons.unl.edu/zeabook/6/

[2]. It is intended to be used in tandem with either the Blumenfeld or the Crookes translation, both of which translate prefatory material, some of which is relevant to the chapters on the organ.

takes pride of place above all other musical instruments, most of which can be incorporated into this single instrument."[3]

Praetorius's writing style is at times fulsome, at times elliptical, and his spelling is neither standardized nor consistent; his text is peppered with imprecise colloquialisms. Therefore this translation is often forced to take on the character of a paraphrase. Despite the generous help I have received from scholars and organbuilders far more knowledgeable than I, there remain words and passages whose precise meaning remains elusive. They appear in the translation in red type, encouraging the reader to beware.

The word "lieblich" appears frequently in the text. In modern German it simply means "lovely." For Praetorius, however, it has a more specific meaning, for which a passage on pp. 99-100 provides the key: "... the instrument [at Halberstadt] could not produce the gentle (lieblich) higher tones, but only a deep, coarse, rumbling roar." Here Praetorius registers his preference for the more narrow scales and gentle, refined sounds of pipes in modern organs,[4] in contrast to the wider scales and loud, coarse sound of still extant older organs. The translation accordingly renders "lieblich" as "beautiful/lovely,"[5] "gentle/refined," or occasionally as "pleasing," depending on the context.

The translation incorporates Praetorius's corrections from the substantial list of errata on pp. 234-6.

---

[3]. pp. 117-18.

[4]. p. 143: "...every organbuilder ought diligently to pursue very narrow scales, since the narrower they are, the more gentle (lieblich) and charming they are."

[5]. See, e.g., the bottom of p. 127, "4. Klein Principal..."

Acknowledgements

 great number of people have graciously and generously offered me their expert help in understanding and interpreting the many challenges and puzzles this translation has presented. I am grateful to all of them for their time, their advice, and their patience.

If I have inadvertently omitted mentioning names of persons that should by right be in this list, I ask for their kind pardon, and assure them that the fault lies not in any ingratitude on my part, but rather in the scope of the project.

- Mr. Gene Bedient, organbuilder, for advice both practical and theoretical
- Prof. Konrad Brandt, Evangelische Hochschule für Kirchenmusik, Halle/Saale, Germany
- Prof. Anita Breckbill, Music Librarian, University of Nebraska-Lincoln
- Prof. Dr. Jürgen Eppelsheim, Ludwig-Maximilians-Universität, Munich, Germany, for many hours' wrestling with the most challenging passages.
- Dr. Mary Murrell Faulkner
- Prof. Kyriakos Gounaridou, Smith College, Northampton, Massachusetts
- Prof. Raymond Haggh, School of Music, University of Nebraska-Lincoln
- Frau Kettmann, Bibliothekarin, Evangelische Hochschule für Kirchenmusik, Halle/Saale, Germany
- Mr. Wayne Leopold and Ms. Christina Gogdill, for kindly preparing musical examples.
- Prof. George Ritchie, School of Music, University of Nebraska-Lincoln
- Mr. John Ross and other members of the Information Technology staff, University of Nebraska-Lincoln, for their kind and patient technical assistance.
- Prof. Paul Royster, Coordinator of Scholarly Communications, University of Nebraska-Lincoln Libraries, for his enthusiasm and creativity in preparing this digital publication.
- Prof. Pamela Starr, School of Music, University of Nebraska-Lincoln
- Prof. Harald Vogel, North German Organ Academy; Hochschule für Künste Bremen, Germany
- Herr Christian Wegscheider, organbuilder, Dresden, Germany
- Herr Rüdiger Wilhelm, Braunschweig, Germany
- Prof. Dr. Christoph Wolff, Department of Music, Harvard University; Director, Bach-Archiv Leipzig
- Marlene M. Wong, Head of Werner Josten Library, Smith College, Northampton, Massachusetts

Notice

Even with the generous, patient counsel I have received from those with particular expertise, I have all too often been unable to arrive at an incontestable translation of Praetorius's text. Questionable words and passages are indicated in dark red type in the electronic edition of the translation (http://digitalcommons.unl.edu/zeabook/), and appear in gray type in the printed version (available from http://www.lulu.com/spotlight/unllib). Among the advantages of electronic publishing is the opportunity it affords to alter and correct such words and passages. The translator and publisher would be grateful for suggested corrections and clarifications, but they reserve the right to accept or reject them as seems prudent.

Quentin Faulkner

SYNTAGMATIS MUSICI
MICHAELIS PRAETORII C.
TOMUS SECUNDUS
DE
ORGANOGRAPHIA.

Darinnen

Aller Musicalischen Alten vnd Newen / sowol Außländischen / Barbarischen / Bäwrischen vnd vnbekandten / als Einheimischen / Kurstreichen / Lieblichen vnd bekandten Instrumenten Nomenclatur, Intonation vnnd Eigenschafft / sampt deroselben Justen Abriß vnd eigentlicher Abconterfeyung:

Dann auch

Der Alten vnd Newen Orgeln

gewisse Beschreibung / Manual=vnnd PedalClavier / Blaßbälge / Disposition vnd mancherley Art Stimmen / auch wie die Regahl vnd Clavicymbel / rein vnd leicht zu stimmen: vnd waß in vberlieferung einer Orgeln in acht zu nehmen sampt angehengtem außführlichem Register befindlichen:

Nicht allein Organisten / Instrumentisten / Orgel= vnd Instrumentmachern / sampt allen den Musis **zugethanen gantz nützlich vnd nötig / sondern auch** Philosophis, Philologis **vnd** Historicis **sehr lustig vnd anmütig zu lesen.**

Benebenst einem außführlichem Register.

Gedruckt zu Wolffenbüttel / bey Elias Holwein Fürstl. Braunß. Buchtrucker vnd Formschneider daselbst. In Verlegung des Autoris.

Anno Christi. M. DC. XIX.

MuSIC ENCYCLOPEDIA
BY MICHAEL PRAETORIUS OF CREUZBURG

VOLuME TWO

Concerning

MUSICAL INSTRUMENTS.

In which may be found

The Name, Sound Properties and Structural Characteristics of Every Musical Instrument, ancient and

modern, both those that are foreign, barbarian, rustic, and
unfamiliar, as well as those that are indigenous, artful, gentle, and
familiar, together with a drawing of each to scale;

Furthermore,

A precise description of ancient and modern organs,

their manual and pedal keyboards, bellows, stoplists,
and various kinds of stops, as well as how to tune regals and
harpsichords easily and precisely; and what to consider when accepting
a [newly-built] organ, together with an appended detailed table;[1]

Not only useful and necessary for organists,

instrumentalists, organbuilders, instrument makers, and all who
are well-disposed toward the muses, but also to be read with
pleasure by philosophers, philologists, and
historians.

Together with a detailed Index.

Printed at Wolfenbüttel by Elias Holwein, Printer and
Woodcut-Engraver to the Prince of Brunswick.[2] Published by the author.

A.D. 1619

---

1. the *Universal Tabel* of organ stop names, bound between pp. 126 and 127.
2. Duke Heinrich Julius of Brunswick and Lüneburg, Praetorius's patron; see p. 139.

DE ORGANOGRAPHIA.

Dritter Theil
Dieses
TOMI SECUNDI.
Von den Alten Orgeln.

Darinnen
1. Von der dignitet vnd excellentz der Orgeln.
2. Wie lange sie im gebrauch/ vnd wer sie erstlich erfunden.
3. Von den allerersten vnd Kleinern Orgelwercken/ wie dieselben anfenglichen an Stimmen vnd sonsten gewesen.
4. Von den nechstfolgenden Mitlern Wercken.
5. Wie vnd wann das Pedall erfunden.
6. Von den gar Grossen alten Orgelwercken.
7. Von der Disposition der Claviren in den alten Orgeln: vnd was vor Harmony zu der zeit darauff zu wege gebracht/ vnd geübt worden.
8. Vom Thon der alten Orgeln/ vnd wie die Claves von Pfeiffen disponirt gewesen.
9. Von dero zeit Blasebälgen.
10. Von vnterschiedenen Nahmen der alten Orgeln.
11. Vom vnterschied der alten vnd jetzigen newen Orgeln.
12. Wie vnd welcher gestalt die Spring-vnd Schleiffladen erfunden:
13. Die Clavir: so wol
14. Die Stimmen vnd Pfeiffen geendert vnd vermehret/ vnd biß zu vnser jetzigen zeit alles zum bessern Stande bracht worden.

ℓ   Das I. Cap.

Third Part of VOLUME TWO.

Concerning Organs of the Past

Contents

1. The dignity and excellence of organs.
2. How long they have been in use, and who first invented them.
3. Stops and other characteristics of the earliest small organs.
4. Later instruments of medium size.
5. How and when the pedal was discovered.
6. Very large early organs.
7. The arrangement of the keyboards in early organs, and what sort of music they played.
8. The pitch of early organs, and how many pipes each key played.
9. The bellows at that time.
10. Various names for early organs.
11. The distinction between early and present-day organs.
12. The invention of spring- and slider-chests.
13. How the keyboards, as well as
14. The stops have been changed, increased, and improved up until the present.

Das I. Capitel.

Von der dignitet vnd fürtreffligkeit der Orgeln/vnd wie dieselbige alleine vnd sonderlich zum Kirchen-vnd Gottesdienst gerichtet/ allen andern Instrumenten vorzuziehen sey.

As etliche es dafür achten / das nechst der Theologia, der höchste locus, der Musicæ,(als einer schönen herrlichen Gaben Gottes/vnd die ein Vorbild vnd Gleichniß ist der himlischen Music/ wie die heiligen Engel Gottes mit dem gantzen himlischen Heer jhren Schöpffer/in einer lieblichen Harmonia stetigs ohn vnterlaß rühmen vnd preisen/ vnd das Sanctus, sanctus, sanctus Dominus Deus Sabaoth, singen) billig gegeben vnd zugeeignet werden solle: Ist vnter andern vielen derselben nutzbarkeiten/ Krafft vnd Wirckungen vielleicht diese nicht die geringste Vrsach / daß die Musica an jhr selbst mehr für ein Geistlich/ als Irdisch wesen zuhalten/ vnd dahero in der Menschen Hertzen eine innerliche Andacht deß Geistes/ GOtt den Allmechtigen mit schönen Psalmen vnd Lobgesängen desto inbrünstiger zu preisen/ erwecket. Darumb dann auch beyde Könnige/ David vnd Salomon / als sie den Gottesdienst im Tempel vnd Tabernackel zu Jerusalem auffs herrlichste vnd zierlichste anrichten wollen/ so viel Musicanten/ Singer vnd Instrumentisten/ mit grossen fleiß vnd vnkosten darzu bestellet/das Volck desto inbrünstiger vnd eyferiger zumachen. Zu welchem end auch David selbst seine Harpffen gebraucht/ vnd ohn zweiffel etliche herrliche Orgelwercke wegen grösse deß Tempels/fertigen vnd setzen lassen.

Darumb die Kirchen Musica, als ein Gottesdienst/auch noch heutigs Tags billig in Würden gehalten/vnd mit aller reverentz celebrirt werden soll: Dazu dann Kunstreiche berühmbte Organisten/welche die Zuhörer mehr auffmuntern/ als verdrossen machen/gehören: die auch selbst mit rechter Andacht/die Text oder Psalmen/so sie melodiren, im Hertzen vnd Gedancken Gott fürtragen. Wann man aber dieses nicht in acht nehmen/sondern einen jeden der nur ein Tänzlein machen kan / ohn vnterscheidt darzu auffstellen wil / so wird auch die Kirchen Musica leichtlich in verachtung kommen/vnd wegen solches mißbrauchs endtlich wol gar außgemustert werden/ wie die erfahrung bezeuget.

Vnd gemeiniglich wandert die Religion derselben nach / wie in Græcia auch geschehen/da vorzeiten die Musica zum höchsten floriret. Sieder dem aber der Machomet daselbst sein Zelt auffgeschlagen/hat sich die Music so gar verlohren/das man auch
fast

Chapter 1.

The dignity and excellence of organs, and how those designed especially for worship are superior to all other instruments.

here are those who believe it proper and right that, next to theology, the highest place should be accorded to music, since it is a beautiful and splendid gift of God,[1] and provides an image of music in heaven, where God's holy angels together with the entire heavenly host praise their creator without ceasing in gentle harmony, and sing "Holy, holy, holy is God, the Lord of Hosts."[2] Among its many merits, effects, and powers, perhaps not the least is that music is in its essence more a spiritual than an physical phenomenon, and thus awakens in human hearts an inner spiritual devotion, in order to praise Almighty God all the more fervently with beautiful psalms and hymns of praise. Thus both King David and King Solomon, when they wished to arrange worship in the Jerusalem Temple as magnificently and elegantly as possible, went to great effort and expense to appoint many musicians, both singers and instrumentalists,[3] with the intent of making the people more fervent and zealous. David himself used his harp for the same purpose, and doubtless had several splendid organs built and placed in the Temple,[4] because of its great size.

Thus church music, as a service to God, ought properly to be held in great esteem today as well, and to be celebrated with all due reverence. For this purpose skillful, celebrated organists are needed, who inspire rather than irritate their listeners,[5] and who make God present to hearts and minds, as they prelude upon a text or psalm with appropriate devotion. But when this purpose is not heeded, and due to indifference someone is appointed who can only play little dances, then church music will soon come to be held in contempt, and even be abolished due to abuse; experience has proven this to be true.

And religion itself is usually the next to go; this has indeed happened in Greece, where in the past music flourished at the highest level.[6] Since Mohammed

---

1. cf. Martin Luther's letter to Ludwig Senfl: "Music is a beautiful and glorious gift of God..." *Martin Luthers Schriften* (Erlangen: Carl Heyder, 1826-27, Vol. LXII), p. 309; English translation: Walter E. Buszin, *Luther on Music* (Lutheran Society for Worship, Music and the Arts, 1958), p. 8.
2. Praetorius provides a visual realization of this image in the frontispiece of the *Theatrum Instrumentorum*, the collection of illustrations at the end of this volume, following p. 236.
3. See I Chronicles 6: 31-48; 16: 4-42; 25: 1-31; cf. Luther, "One reads in the Bible that pious kings supported, maintained, and gave salaries to singers;" see Buszin, *Luther on Music*, p. 14. Here Praetorius's intention is in part to refute reformers such as Calvin and Zwingli who excluded instruments and elaborate polyphonic music from services of worship.
4. Praetorius may be referring to the *magrephah*, an instrument that the Talmud (Arachin tractate) reports as being found in the temple at Jerusalem and having pipes sounded by wind from a bellows. Nothing specific is known about it.
5. Friedrich Blume notes that "... [Lutheran] church orders sometimes mentioned that the organ must not impede congregational singing, ... perhaps directed against an overly elaborate practice of alternation or an egocentric accompaniment and embellishment of the chorale (Bach was reprimanded for this in Arnstadt);" *Protestant Church Music: A History* (New York: W.W. Norton, [trans. 1974]), p. 247.
6. Praetorius is probably referring to Plato's writings on music.

fast nichts mehr davon weis: Ja man ist deren so gram vnd entgegen worden/das nach art vnd Natur der wilden Leut/ mehr auff ein Satyrisch Pfeifflein vnd Päucklein/als auff ein recht geschaffene Musica gehalten wird. Inmassen verschiener Jahren Franciscus I. König in Franckr: dem Solimanno, Türckischen Käyser/die beste Musicos zugesendet/ der meinung grosse ehr damit einzulegen. Aber er hat die baldt wider abgeschafft vnd zurück geschickt/ mit dem bescheidt/das solche Music für sein Volck nicht dienet/sintemal sie die Gemüther nur weich vnd Weibisch mache. Welches der Griechen meinung (die da von keinem nichts gehalten/ noch jemandt zu fürnehmen Embtern kommen lassen/ der der Music vnerfahren/dieweil sie es dafür gehalten/ das man mores vnd gute Sitten daher erlerne/vnd an sich nehme) gantz zuwider.

Vnd gibts zwar auch die erfahrung/das die Musica nicht bleibt/an denen Orten da der Teuffel regieret/ dann die Gottlosen sind dern nicht werth.

Von der rechten Kirchen aber ist die Music zu jederzeit in hohem werth gehalten worden: Wie dann sonsten nirgendt von dergleichen Capellen gehört/als wie der König Salomon gehabt/vnd dieselbe im andern Buch der Chronica im 4. Capittel beschrieben ist.

Vnd ist gar gewiß/das zur selben zeit im Volcke Gottes die Music vielmehr floriret hat/als bey den Heyden. In dem die Jüden vber jhre blasende Instrumenta, als tubas, buccinas, tubas ductiles, tubas corneas, &c. auch besäittete Instr. als/ Psalteria, Decachorda, von 8. von 10. ja von 24. Sätten gehabt haben. Inmassen Hieronymus schreibt/welchs auch im vorhergehendem II. Theil/Num. 32. erjnnert worden/daß der Jüden Cithara, so man jetzo ein Harff nennet/von 24. Sätten gewesen sey. Do doch zu der zeit bey den Heyden vber drey Tetrachorda, das sind 11. claves oder Sätten noch nicht erfunden oder verhanden gewesen.

Ob man aber nun wol nicht so gar eben wissen kan/was für eine arth der Music domals gebraucht worden/so ist doch aus allen vmbstenden/ daran nicht zu zweifeln/das es eine herzliche Musica mus gewesen seyn: in sonderlichen betracht/ daß der heilig König David vnd Salomon / welche selbst auch der Music kündig vnd erfahren/dieselbe mit allem müglichstem fleiß angeordnet/ Sintemahl sie so grossen kosten auff den Tempel/welches doch nur ein todter Steinhauff gewesen/gewendet/ demselben ein Ruhm vnd Lob in der gantzen Welt zumachen: Vielmehr werden sie es in den Ceremonien bey den Opffern/ welchen GOTT selbst beygewohnet/ gethan haben.

Das sie aber so viel vñ mancherley Instrument vñ Gesäng zusamen gebraucht/ist anderst nit zuverstehen/dañ dz sie die Psal:Davids vieleicht in jren sonderliche Tonis,wie man noch an jtzo im Choral thut/in einer der fürnemüsten Stim̃ als im Baß gesungen/

L ij   darzu

has pitched his tent,[7] however, music has decayed so badly that it has all but disappeared. Indeed it is held in such low esteem that, just as among the barbarians, the panpipe and drum[8] are favored above decent and proper music. A number of years ago the King of France, Francis I, sent the Turkish Emperor Suleiman[9] the finest musicians, intending thereby to do him great honor. But the latter soon did away with them and sent them back, with the message that such music was inappropriate for his people, since it only made their spirits soft and effeminate. This is entirely contrary to the opinion of the [ancient] Greeks (who scorned anyone inexperienced in music, and never bestowed high office upon him, since they were of the opinion that experience with music developed good character[10]).

And experience proves that music cannot survive where the devil holds sway, since the godless are not worthy of it.

But the true church has always held music in high regard: there has never been a chapel[11] to equal that of King Solomon, as described in the fourth chapter of the second book of Chronicles.[12]

And at that time it was certainly the case that music flourished far more among the people of God[13] than among the heathen, since in addition to wind instruments such as tubas, buccinas, tubas ductiles, tubas corneas, etc., the Jews also had stringed instruments such as psalteries and decachorda of 8 to 10 and even 24 strings.[14] As has already been mentioned in Part II, No. 32,[15] Jerome writes that the Jewish cithara, now called a harp, had 24 strings. On the other hand, the heathen knew only three tetrachords, that is, 11 strings.

Although it is hardly possible today to know anything about the music of that time, the circumstances leave no doubt that it must have been splendid, especially considering that the saintly Kings David and Solomon, both well-versed in music, took great care in arranging for it. Since they spent great sums on the temple, which was after all only a lifeless pile of stones, in order to increase their own fame throughout the world, how much more effort must they have taken with the sacrificial rites at which God himself was present.

Since [the ancient Israelites] used so many different instruments and voices together, they obviously must have intoned the Psalms of David (perhaps in partic-

---

7. During the 7th-8th centuries Islam spread throughout the Middle East, North Africa, Spain, and the Caucasus. Over the course of the 15th-16th centuries the Ottoman Empire annexed Greece, the Balkans and present-day Hungary.
8. See *Theatrum Instrumentorum*, Plate 29.
9. In 1536 Francis I entered into an alliance with the Suleiman the Magnificent, ruler of the Ottoman Empire, against their commom foe, the Hapsburg Empire.
10. Cf. Plato, *The Republic*, trans. Paul Shorey (London: W. Heinemann, 1930), 401-2.
11. i.e., a body of musicians, both vocal and instrumental, that provides music for both secular and religious events at noble and royal courts.
12. Second Book of Chronicles 5: 12-14.
13. i.e., the Jews, as God's chosen people.
14. Wind and string instruments mentioned in the Old Testament, filtered through writers of antiquity as well as several layers of translation of the Bible.
15. p. 56, incorrectly numbered "54."

darzu alle andere Senger vnd Instrumentisten ad placitum sortisiret: sonsten hette es keine form oder art gehabt/ wann jede Partey eine besondere Melodey für sich genommen. Es bringts auch der Text mit sich/ darinn gemeldt wird/ das es nicht anders gelautet/ als wann einer allein trommetet oder sünge/ vnd als höret man eine Stimm/ zu loben vnd dancken dem HErrn.

Das aber dieselbe Musica nunmehr erloschen vnd vergessen/ auch in heiliger Schrifft nichts davon gefunden (ausser was im Titul der Psalmen gemeldet wird) in welchem Chor ein jeder sol gesungen werden/ das ist kein wunder. Dann gleich wie der Jüdische Tempel mit denselben Opffern vnd Ceremonien/ aus Gottes Rach/ gar zu grundt ist außgetilget worden/ also hat auch der Jüden Gesang vnd Musica erleschen müssen/ daß man dern nicht mehr gedencken sollen.

Wie dann die Jüden selber (als etliche jhres Mittels mich berichtet) jetzo keine Orgeln hören mögen/ in dem sie vorgeben/ das diese itzige vnsrige Orgeln allein ein Vmbraculum, vnd nichts gegen die Orgeln/ welche Salomon im Tempel zu der zeit hat setzen lassen/ zuachten vnd zurechnen seyn. Sintemahl Salomon/ als ein hochweiser König ohn allen zweiffel selbsten der fürnembste/ hocherfahrnester Orgelmacher/ Inventor vnd Angeber solches herrlichen künstlichen Instruments wird gewesen seyn: Vnd fürwar nach seiner Weißheit kein geringes/ sondern vortreffliches/ herrliches/ auß dermassen wolklingendes Werck vnd Orgel haben verfertigen/ vnd in den Tempel setzen lassen. Welches zwar so sehr nicht zuwidersprechen. Aber weil die Græci sich gar sehr der Music beflissen/ were es zuverwundern/ das sie nicht solche Invention vnd herrliches Instrumentum Musicum von den Jüden solten erlernet vnd nachgemacht haben. Das nun aber auff die Orgel oder Instrument aller Instrumenten/ in der Kirchen/ so ansehenlichen vnd trefflichen viel vnd groß gehalten wird: Daß macht die vnsägliche vnd überauß grosse Kunst die darinnen steckt vnd begriffen ist.

Denn das ist einmahl gar gewiß/ daß vnsere Vorfahren sonst auff kein Instrument so mercklichen grossen Fleiß gewendet haben/ als eben auff künstliche wolklingende Orgeln: Haben sie auch nicht alleine aus Ertz/ Silber vnd Goldt gemacht vnd gebawet/ sondern offt aus solcher wunderlicher seltzamen Materi/ das es einem fast vnmüglich zusein deuchtet/ wie sie doch jmmermehr dergleichen Materi darzu haben brauchen können.

Man siehet aller Stücken vnd Glieder/ welche zu dem gantzen Werck einer Orgel gehören/ so eine künstliche/ starcke/ vnd wolgeformirte zusammensetzung/ daß deroselben nicht alleine an der euserlichen/ vnd innerlichen gleichsam lebendigen gestalt nichts mangelt/ sondern es klingen auch alle Pfeiffen beydes groß vnd klein/ nach dem zusammen gestimbten angriff der Clavirn vnd Registerzügen baldt heller/ baldt

heim-

ular modes, just as with plainsong nowadays) in a given principal voice, such as the bass, augmented ad libitum by all the other singers and instrumentalists.[16] Otherwise [the music] would have had no form, if every part performed its own independent melody.[17] The text[18] relates that it sounded as if a single voice trumpeted or sang, praising and thanking the Lord.

It is no surprise, however, that this music exists no more, and that nothing further is found in Holy Scripture about the arrangement of choirs (except what is reported in the headings of the psalms). For just as God's vengeance obliterated the Jewish temple together with its sacrifices and ceremonies, Jewish music also had to be exterminated, so that no memory of it would remain.

The Jews themselves (as some of their number have told me) today have no desire to hear organs; they allege that our organs are only a pale reflection and nothing in comparison with the organs that Soloman had built for the temple in his day. They say that, since the most wise king Solomon must undoubtedly have been the highly skilled and competent builder who constructed that splendid, artistic instrument, in his great wisdom he never would have built an inferior instrument for the temple, but rather one that was excellent, splendid and pleasing to hear. And indeed that cannot be denied. Since the Greeks were so keenly interested in music, it is odd that they never learned from the Jews how to build such a splendid musical instrument.[19] It is due to its exceedingly, inexpressibly great art that the organ, the instrument of instruments, is held in such high regard in the church.

It is certain that our forebears never expended as much effort on any instrument as upon complex, melodious organs. They built them not only of brass, silver, and gold, but often out of other rare and marvelous materials as well; indeed, their inventiveness with new materials seems almost unbelievable.

All of the organ's many parts exhibit a wealth of artistry and careful construction, not only in their inner and outer form (which seems almost alive), but

---

16. This is all guesswork on Praetorius' part, and remains so today. He seems to be projecting a structure built on a cantus firmus (a compositional technique venerable but still well known to him) back onto a musical practice about which he could have known nothing.
17. Again, Praetorius is projecting a polyphonic texture back onto an unknown musical practice.
18. Second Book of Chronicles 5:13.
19. This comment is based on an erroneous assumption; see note 4 above.

DE ORGANOGRAPHIA. 85

heimlicher: vnd durch auff-vnd einblasung der Blaßbälge mit einem jmerwärendem vnd viel stärckerem Winde/als die andere Instrumenta,so durch Menschlichen athem müssen geregiret vnd geblassen werden.

Ja dieses vielstimmige liebliche Werck begreifft alles das in sich/was etwa in der Music erdacht vnd componiret werden kan/vnd gibt so einen rechten natürlichen klang/laut vnd thon von sich/nicht anders als ein gantzer Chor voller Musicanten, do mancherley Melodeyen/von junger Knaben vnd grosser Männer Stimmen gehöret werden. In summa die Orgel hat vnd begreifft alle andere Instrumenta musica, groß vnd klein/wie die Nahmen haben mögen/alleine in sich. Wiltu eine Trummel/Trummet/Posaun/Zincken/Blockflöt/Querpfeiffen/Pommern/Schalmeyen/Dolzian/Racketten/Sordounen/Krumphörner/Geigen/Leyern/ꝛc. hören/so kanstu dieses alles/vnd noch viel andere wunderliche lieblichkeiten mehr in diesem künstlichem Werck haben: Also daß/wenn du dieses Instrument hast vnd höret/du nicht anderst denckest/du habest vnd hörest die andern Instrumenta alle miteinander. Ich geschweige daß auff der Orgel offt ein schlecht erfahrner dieser Kunst/fürtreffliche Meister auff andern Instrumenten vbertreffen kan/ Sintemahl diesem Werck recht ins Maul zugreiffen/zugleich Hände vnd Füsse gebraucht werden. Vnd die Warheit zubekennen/so ist keine Kunst so hoch gestiegen/als eben die Orgelkunst: Denn der Menschen subtile Spitzfindigkeit vnd fleissiges nachdencken hat es dahin gebracht/daß sie nun gäntzlichen ohne einigen fernern zusatz/wol bestehen bleiben kan/vnd sich ansehen lest/daß zu jhrer perfection vnd vollkommenheit nichts weiter mangele/desideriret oder hinzu gesetzt vnd vermehret werden könne.

Dann was die Orgel vor ein vberaus fürtrefflich vnd/also zureden/gleichsam Göttliches Werck sey/bezeuget Hieronymus Diruta Italus in einer Vorrede: Welches eigene wort/aus dem Italianischen in daß Teutsche vertirt/also lauten:

†† Alle Künste vnd Wissenschafften (sagt er) so deß Menschen Vernunfft vnd Verstandt durch Gottes vnuberschwengliche Gnad vnd Gütigkeit/fassen begreiffen vnd verstehen kan/die referiren vnd ziehen sich auff ein principale intelligens,gleichsam als auff jhren Meister/der wegen seiner hohen fürtrefflichkeit von allen andern verstanden/geehret vnd gerühmet wird. Daher kompts/das wenn man in der Philosophia deß Philosophi allein erwehnet vnd gedencket/alßbald der Aristoteles, als der Philosophorum princeps dadurch verstanden wird: In der Medicina, Hippocrates: In der Poësi Kunst/ wird vnter den Lateinischen der Virgilius, vnd vnter den Italianern der Petrarcha mit dem Nahmen Poëtæ geehret.

L iij

in the variety of sounds, loud and soft, produced by all the pipes, both large and small, when the keys and stops are used well. This artistry is likewise evident in the operation of the bellows, that produce a constant, stable supply of wind, surpassing all other instruments, that have to be sounded by human breath.

This lovely instrument, with its many voices, indeed contains within itself everything that can possibly be conceived in music. It produces a genuine, natural sound, like a whole choir of musicians, with young boys and mature men singing different melodies together. In sum, the organ comprises within itself all other musical instruments, large and small, of whatever type. Whatever you want to hear—a drum, trumpet, trombone, cornett, recorder, traverse flute, pommer, shawm, dulcian, racket, sordun, krummhorn, violin, hurdy-gurdy—the organ has all of these, and many more beautiful things as well. When you listen to this instrument, you think you are hearing all of the other instruments sounding together. I hardly need mention that a less accomplished organist can often outshine a great master on another instrument, since both hands and feet are needed in order to make the organ do one's bidding. And to tell the truth, there is no art that has risen to such great heights as that of the organ. Thanks to subtle inventiveness and diligent reflection, the organ has reached such a state of perfection that it lacks nothing; it needs no further experimentation or development at all.[20]

In a preface[21] that I have translated into German, the Italian Girolamo Diruta[22] testifies to this excellent, one might almost say, divine instrument:

> All the arts and sciences that human understanding, thanks to God's boundless grace and favor, can comprehend, are related to a principal intelligence, a master who is praised and honored above all other intellects due to his great excellence. Thus it is understood that, when one speaks of "the philosopher," one means Aristotle, the prince of philosophers[23]; in medicine it is Hippocrates, in Latin poetry it is Virgil,

---

20. Cf. the final paragraphs on pp. 114 and 117.
21. i.e., Girolamo Diruta's *Il Transilvano*, vol. 1 (Venice: Vincenti, 1593), "L'Autore dell opera al prudente lettore." Praetorius has translated approximately the first half of Diruta's preface, freely and somewhat embellished.
22. c.1554-1610; Italian organist, teacher and music theorist. *Il Transilvano* is the earliest comprehensive treatise on playing the organ.
23. This identifies Diruta as a product of the Renaissance. In the Middle Ages, "the philosopher" would have been Plato.

Deßgleichen in der Theologia wird durch den Propheten der König David; vnd durch den Namen Apostel/ S. Paulus verstanden. Dann weil angeregte diese Männer in jhrer Kunst vnd geschickligkeit alle andere vbertroffen/ so ist jhnen auch der general Namen der vortreffligkeit billig gelassen vnd zugeeignet worden. Dieser gebrauch ist auch bey den Alten in der Musica vnd Singekunst gehalten worden/ in dem sie den höchsten vnd fürnembsten Titul vor allen andern Musicis, so jemals bey jhnen floriret/ dem Orpheo vnd Amphioni gegeben vnd zugeeignet haben.

Ebner massen gehet es noch heutiges tages zu / mit den Titeln in der Instrumentalischen Musica/ da dieses hievor offterwehnte Instrument wegen seiner vortreffligkeit/ Organum, (in welchem Griechischen Namen sonsten in genere alle Instrumenta, vnd Werckzeuge/ so vff der Welt verhanden / begriffen seyn) vff deutsch ein Orgel / genennet wird: Darumb/ das sie alle andere Instrumenta, wie die auch mögen Nahmen haben / in sich begreifft / gleichsamb vmbfenget vnd halten thut. Derhalben denn jtziger zeit/ bemelte Orgel gleichsamb vor einen König aller Instrumenten/ damit die Göttliche Mayest. in der Versamlung der Gleubigen gelobet/ gepreiset vnd geehret wird/ billich gehalten werden sol.

Aus ebenmessigen Vrsachen wird die Hand an deß Menschen Leibe/ Organum, ein Werckzeug aller Werckzeuge genennet/ darumb das sie im arbeiten mit allen pflichtschuldigen diensten/ so zu verrichtung seiner Gescheffte von nöthen sind/ seinem Ambt fürstehet/ vnd den andern Gliedern beyspringet.

Das aber daß wort Organum in seinem rechten natürlichen Verstande/ von allen nicht auffgenommen werde/ ist kein zweiffel. Denn jhr viel sind der meinung/ es werde durch diß wort Organum nur alleine eine Orgel/ welche mit Blaßbälgen geregiret/ vnd in den Kirchen vnd Choren zur ehre Gottes gebraucht wird/ verstanden: Davon im 150. Psalm stehet: Lobet den HErrn mit Harffen vnd Orgeln. Gleich wie aber die Lautte/ Harpffe / Geige/ vnd andere Säitenspiel / so durch die Säiten jhren klang bekommen/ eben so wol mit dem Namen Organi oder Instrumenti genennet werden/ weil der jenige/ der solche vnd dergleichen Instrumenta gebrauchet/ vnd darauff schlegt/ es zu dem ende thut/ das er seine Kunst im Geigen vnd schlahen damit an Tag geben vnd beweisen könne. Also thut die Orgel in jhrer schon erlangten hochheit gleichsamb mit jren vmbfang alle andere Instrumenta in sich einschliessen. Sie führet aber billich den Adelichen Titul vnd Nahmen der fürtreffligkeit/ dieweil sie zu der Menschlichen Stimme (durch den Wind vnd der Werckmeister hände regiret) am allernehesten kompt. Den die Pfeiffen repræsentiren oder stellen eigentlich für Augen/ deß Menschen Kehle oder Lufftröhre/ durch welche sie auch jhren Athem führet/ vnd den Thon/ Klang vnd Stimme formiret. Ja man könte wol sagen/ daß die Orgel ein künstlich gemachtes Thier sey/ welches durch

hülff

among the Italians Petrarch is honored as "the poet."

Similarly, in theology "the prophet" is King David, and "the apostle" is St. Paul. Since these men exceed all others in their respective fields in their skill and artistry, therefore their name rightly represents the entire endeavor. The ancients also adhered to this custom in music and singing, and bestowed this lofty title on the greatest musicians who ever flourished in their midst, Orpheus[24] and Amphion.[25]

Among all the instruments, it is likewise the organ, due to its excellence, that is granted this title in our time, the Greek word "organum"[26] signifying in general all the kinds of instruments and tools that are in the world; and for this reason, that it comprises in itself all other instruments, whatever their name. And thus the organ today, in that it praises the divine Majesty in the assembly of the faithful, is rightly considered the king of all instruments. For the same reason the human hand is called "Organum," the best of all tools, because it takes the lead when engaging in all the demanding tasks that require its services, and comes to the assistance of all the other limbs.

But of course not everyone would accept this definition of "organum," even though it is quite accurate. Many would understand this word to refer only to the organ, the instrument controlled by bellows, that is used in churches and choirs for the glory of God. Thus Psalm 150 says, "Praise the Lord with harps and organs."[27] The lute, harp, violin, and other instruments that produce their sound by means of strings are likewise called "organi" or "instrumenti,"[28] because players use them as tools to exhibit their performing skill. The organ, long established as the superior instrument, encompasses in its scope all the other instruments. It deserves its noble title "organum" because it comes closest to the human voice; both are controlled by wind and by the hands of their master. For the pipes actually represent the human throat, through which humans direct their breath to form the sound of their voice. One

---

24. A legendary Greek singer who rescued his wife Eurydice from the underworld by the charm of his singing.
25. A Greek mythological figure credited with being the first human to play the lyre.
26. Properly "organon;" Praetorius gives the Latin form of the word.
27. Psalm 150, vs. 4. The instrument indicated in the original Hebrew is uncertain; *organon* and *organum* stem from early translations, the Septuagint and the Vulgate.
28. Both of these words mean "tools" or "instruments," the first in Greek, the second in Latin.

„ hülff der Lufft oder Windes vnd Mänschlicher Hände/gleichsam rede/klinge/singe/ vnd modulire, werde auch mit allerhand zierligkeit/vñ so mercklichen grossen Vnkosten in die Kirchen gesetzt/dz sie einig vnd allein zu der ehre vñ lob Gottes bestimt/verlobet vnd versprochen sey/mit jrer Stim/Thon/laut vnd klang/die vnaußsprechliche Werck vnd Thaten der Göttlichen Majestet ohne vnterlaß zuruhmen vnd zupreisen.

Wird derowegen die Orgel wegen jhrer Hochheit nicht vngereumbt dem Menschlichen Leibe verglichẽ/welcher in verrichtung seines Ambts von der Seelen dirigiret vnd geleitet wird. Denn gleich wie die Orgel mit höchster belüstigung der Menschen Augen auff sich locket/vnd mit jren süssen Thon vnd lieblichen klang (durch hülff vnd zulassung deß Windes/welcher gleichsamb der Orgel Seele ist) die Ohren erfüllet vnd erweichet: Also auch der Mensch/in dem er anderer Leutte Augen auff sich ziehet/so nimbt er durch seine süsse vnd liebliche wolberedsamkeit der Zuhörer Ohren ein/vnd gibt mit den worten die innerliche Gedancken/so im Hertzen verborgen sind/zuerkennen. Ferner so referiren vnd zeigen die Blaßbälge die Lunge an; die Pfeiffen die Kehle oder Lufftröhre; die Clavier kommen gar fein mit den Zehnen vberein; der aber der Orgel den Thon künstlich gibt/ist an stat der Zungen/vñ weñ er mit der Hände artlichen bewegung vñ künstlichen geschwindigkeit darauff schlegt/vñ es lieblich lautent machet/so redet er gleichsam vffs zierlichste.

Derhalben wer sich auff diese löbliche kunst vnd studiũ begeben hat/der sol allen höchsten vnd müglichsten fleiß anwenden/damit er zu einer gründlichen vnd rechten volkomenen wissenschafft dieses Instruments/so durch dẽ Wind regiret wird/kommen möge. Wo aber das nit geschiehet/so wird die Hochheit vnd Würde dieses löblichen/fürtrefflichen Instruments abnehmen vnd geringschätzig gemacht werden/ vnd wird eben zugehen/wie mit einem Menschen/der zwar sonst von Leibe schöner vnd gerader gestalt ist/aber eine lispelnde vnd stammelnde Zunge hat/dardurch dañ das ander alles was an jhm ist/vollends deformiret vnd verstellet wird.

Ferner wie die schönen vnd künstlichen wolgemälten Bilder der anschawenden Augen an sich ziehen: eben also durchdringet auch die liebligkeit der süssen wolklingenden harmonia vnd concenten die heimliche Gedancken vnd affecten, wenn sie in der Zuhörer Ohren fellet. Derhalben hat die Orgel billich jhren Sitz in den Kirchen vnd Tempel Gottes/damit durch jhre anleitung Gottselige vnd andechtige Hertzen auffgemuntert/vnd durch jhren lieblichen resonantz, dem lobe/welches der hohen Göttlichen Majest. gesungen wird/zuzuhören/beyzuwohnen vnd außzuwarten/angereitzet vnd gleichsam genötiget werden.

Vnd bleibt wol war/das vnter allen/was Instrumenta können vnd mögen genennet werden/die Orgel die fürnemste vnd oberste stelle/præeminentz vñ würde habe/
„ alldieweil sie alle süssigkeit vnd liebligkeit/so die andern Instrumenta in sich haben/

oder

might indeed say that the organ is an artfully constructed living being, which, as it were, speaks and sings by means of wind and human hands. Organs are put in churches, at great expense and with elegant skill, to the glory of God and for the sole purpose of ceaselessly praising the inexpressible works of the divine Majesty.

Thus the organ in its grandeur is quite fittingly compared to the human body, that is controlled in its actions by the soul. For just as the organ attracts and pleases the sense of sight, and fills and melts the sense of hearing with its sweet, lovely sound (by means of wind, which is as it were the soul of the organ), so also the human being whose sweet eloquence communicates the hidden, inner meaning of words is the one others look to. Furthermore, the bellows represent the lungs, the pipes the throat, the keyboards correspond to the teeth; the one who makes the organ sound represents the tongue, and if he plays deftly and sweetly, he is as it were a most elegant speaker.

Therefore anyone who pursues this noble art should apply himself to it with the greatest industry, and thereby attain complete and perfect mastery of this instrument that is controlled by wind. Anyone who neglects this will diminish the majesty and dignity of this excellent instrument, just as a man with a handsome body but a lisping, stammering tongue gives a contradictory, distorted impression.

Furthermore, just as beautiful, skillful paintings attract the eye of the beholder, the lovely, sweet harmony penetrates the inner thoughts and feelings of the listener as it strikes his ear. Therefore the organ belongs in the church, the temple of God, to awaken holy, devout hearts, and through its lovely tone to encourage, yea, urge them to take part in the praise sung to the divine majesty.

It is indeed true that the organ holds pride of place above all other instruments, since it alone comprehends in itself all the sweetness and

oder zu wege bringen können/ ihr alleine zumisset vnd zuschreibet: Bevorauß/ weil sie solchen Grad der hochheit erreichet/ daß keine Musica oder Seytenspiel auff dem gantzen Erdboden ist/ dadurch der lieben heiligen Engel liebliche Harmonia vnd Gesang zu Gottes lobe/ eigentlicher repræsentiret vnd abgebildet werde/ als durch sie. Welches in dē Organo ad D. Petrum in Perusio gar fein außgetruckt vnd gegeben ist mit diesen Versslein: *Hæc si contingunt terris, quæ gaudia Cælo?* Weil dieses auff der Welt geschicht/ was wird allererst vor Frewde vnd lieblich Gedöhne im Himmel seyn? als wolte er sagen: Weil man vff dieser Erden so eine schöne/ liebliche wolklingende Musica haben/ vnd zuwege bringen kan; mein Gott/ was vor vnaußsprechliche Frewde/ Wonne vnd liebligkeit/ mus allererst seyn deß Engelischen Chors vnd der Gottseligen Seelen im Himmel? (Vnd so weit Hieronymus Diruta.)

Wer siehet nun nicht/ daß die Kirche zu der offentlichen außruffung/ außbreitung vnd erhaltung deß Nahmen Gottes vnd der Religion/ aus den andern Instrumenten allen miteinander/ allein dieses eintzige/ aus gnugsamen Vrsachen bestimpt/ gelobet vnd außerkohren habe.

Wann dann vff jetztbesagte weiß/ die vortreffligkeit dieses Wercks/ so hoch/ groß/ ja nicht gnugsam zurühmen ist: sollen billig alle Organisten/ solches in fleissige acht vnd betrachtung nehmen/ vnd dahin all ihr Sinn vnd Gedancken/ Händ vnd Füß täglich intendirn/ wie sie diesem herzlichen Werck im schlagen vnd regierung desselben/ ihr recht thun vnd geben mögen/ damit sie nicht für ignoranten gehalten/ vnd der Nahm deß Organisten τῆ ἀνυφέρειν ihnen zugemessen werde. Dann etliche werden zwar zu Organisten vocirt vnd promovirt, wenig aber bedencken/ wie sie ihrer vocation ein genügen thun/ vnd spartam quam nacti sunt, orniren wollen: Inmassen es die Erfahrung bezeuget vnd mit sich bringt/ daß mancher nicht das geringste Stück oder Motet applicirn, oder in vollem Chor einzuschlagen weiß: da er doch die gantze Musicam, vornemlich den Chorum Vocalem, durch hülffe der Orgel intra suos limites & cancellos coërcirn, daß er in suo certo modo vnd angestimbten Tono bliebe/ vnd nicht durch vbermässiges schreyen/ allzusehr in die höhe ascendirte, wie vnzehlich mahl geschicht/ sonderlich do viel Knaben/ oder aber in die tieffe dermassen descendirte, das die Concentores weder eins noch daß ander zuletzt assequirn, vnd mit der Stimm erreichen/ oder zu wege bringen können.

Diese vnd dergleichen Organisten aber solte zu grösserm fleiß vnd vbung antreiben vnd vermahnen.

1. Die

loveliness that all the other instruments can produce. This is especially so, since it has reached such a degree of excellence that there is no other music, either vocal or instrumental, in the whole world that can represent the lovely song the holy angels sing to the glory of God. This is well expressed by the following verse on the organ at St. Peter's, Perugia: Hac si contingunt terris, quae gaudia Coelo? — Since this can take place on earth, what joyful and lovely sound must there be in heaven? That is to say, since there is such lovely, beautiful, harmonious music on earth, my Lord, what inexpressible joy, bliss, and loveliness must there be with the choirs of angels and the blessed souls in heaven! (Here ends the quote from Girolamo Diruta.)

Anyone can see that the church has with good reason chosen and praised this instrument, above all others, for the preservation and public proclamation of religion in God's name.

If this instrument is thus great and excellent beyond all praise (as just stated), then all organists ought properly to keep this in mind, and daily to apply all their thoughts and senses, hands and feet, to do justice in performing on this splendid instrument. Thus they will avoid being considered ignorant and bringing the label $\tau\eta\omega\ \alpha\nu\tau\iota\Phi\rho\alpha\sigma\iota\nu$[29] [ten antifrasin] on the name 'organist.' For there are those who are indeed called and installed as organists, but never consider how they can live up to their vocation and become an ornament to their profession. Experience will testify that many of these cannot play the most insignificant piece or motet, or accompany a full choir. But what they ought to be doing is using the organ to keep the entire ensemble together, and especially choirs of singers, so that the singers maintain the right key, neither forcing their voices so that they go sharp (as happens over and over again, especially when many boy singers are involved), nor going so flat that the singers cannot do anything with their voices.

The following considerations however should impel such organists to more industrious practice:

---

29. Greek "an impostor."

1. Die vortreffligkeit deß Wercks/ davon in diesem Cap. I. weitleufftig gesagt vnd discurrirt worden.

2. Die weitberühmbten Meister dieser Kunst/ so vor wenig Jahren/ nicht allein in Italia, sondern auch in Germania nostra, bevorab in den Niederlanden gelebet vnd noch jtziger zeit/ beyder Orten sehr florirn, vnd celeberrimi befunden werden: Da dann diese Kunst von jhnen dermassen excolirt vnd augirt worden/ daß zu zweiffeln/ ob jhr auch noch etwas könne addirt werden?

3. Die jungen Knaben/ deren etliche solche specimina jhres profectus, heut zu tag von sich geben/ das auch langgeübte vnd Kunstreiche Organisten zum höchsten darüber in verwunderung gerathen/ vnd gedencken/ was doch künfftiger zeit noch zu hoffen/ weiln bey den Knaben solche Indoles vnd zuneigung zu dieser Knst sich ereuget?

Darneben aber were höchlich zu loben/ das auch Obrigkeiten an etlichen örtern vnd Städten das jhrige verrichteten/ vnd vff Mittel bedacht weren/ welcher gestalt/ jhre gute vnd fleissige Organisten/ in jhren Kirchen mit solchen vnterhalt versehen werden köndten/ damit jhnen jhre müh/ fleiß vnd saure Arbeit der gebühr nach recompensirt vnd belohnt würde. Dann es zubeklagen/ wie geringe solaria, auch an etlichen vornehmen örtern/ für jhre gutte vnd Kunstreiche Organisten deputirt seynd/ also das sie sich kümmerlich können erhalten/ ja bißweilen auch die Edle Kunst verfluchen vnd wündschen/ das sie an stat eines Organisten ein Kuhhirt oder sonsten nur ein geringes Handtwerck gelernet hetten. Welches gleichwol zuerbarmen/ vnd billig von dem Magistratu vnd Kirchen Inspectoribus ad notam genommen/ vnd vffs beste corrigirt werden köndte. Et tantum de I. Capite.

Das II. Capittel.

Zu welcher zeit ohngefehr/ vnd von weme die Alten Orgeln erfunden worden.

Autor Inventor.

Er aber der Autor vnd erster erfinder dieses wundersahmen zierlichen/ herrlichen Instruments sey/ wird (das wol zubeklagen) nirgends gefunden. Welches Polydorus lib. 5. Cap. 15. vnd folgends lib. 3. Cap. 18. höchlich beklaget:

†† Viel Musicalische Instrumenta, sagt er/ sind zu den Alten „ Zeiten erfunden worden/ deren Inventores vnd Erfinder gantz vnd gar vergessen „ sind/ vnter welchen auch dieses/ so aller verwunderung vnd lobes werth ist/ so man „ die Orgel nennet; Zwar sehr vngleich denen/ welche der Prophet vnd Jüdische

1. The excellence of the instrument, already discussed at length in this first chapter.

2. The renowned masters of this art who have lived during the past number of years, not only in Italy, but also in our own Germany (and formerly in the Netherlands[30]), and who still flourish as celebrities in both places.[31] They have cultivated their art to such a high degree that it is doubtful it could be improved in any way.

3. The young boys, some of whom are nowadays so proficient that even experienced and skillful organists have expressed their astonished admiration, commenting that, with the aptitude these boys are showing, the future is indeed full of promise.[32]

Furthermore, it would be a thing worthy of praise, if the authorities in some cities would also do their part, and seek the funds with which to pay the fine and diligent organists in their churches a proper salary for all their hard work. It is regrettable what paltry salaries even some prominent places pay their good and skillful organists; some of these musicians can barely support themselves. Indeed they sometimes curse their noble art, and wish they had become cowherds or petty laborers instead of organists. This is indeed lamentable, and needs to be noted and corrected by city and church officials. (This is the end of Chapter I.)

Chapter II.

At approximately what date and by whom the organ was discovered.[33]

The Inventor:

It is, sad to say, nowhere recorded who the inventor of this wonderful instrument was. Polydorus greatly laments this in Book 5, Chap. 15f. and Book 3, Chap. 18:[34] he writes: "Many musical instruments were discovered in antiquity, and it is completely forgotten who invented them; among these is the one called "organ," an instrument worthy of admiration and praise. It is indeed quite unlike the ones built by David, the Jewish King and Prophet, to whose

---

30. This is probably an oblique reference to the introduction of the Reformed faith during the second half of the 16th century, which severely curtailed the use of the organ and the employment of organists.
31. Praetorius has in mind such artists as Adriano Banchieri (1567-1634) and Girolamo Frescobaldi (1583-1643) in Italy and Jacob Praetorius (1586-1651) and Samuel Scheidt (1587-1654) in Germany.
32. Ironically, Praetorius made this observation on the eve of the 30 Years War (1618-48), from which all aspects of German culture, including music, did not fully recover for a half century.
33. The impressive number of sources that Praetorius cites in this chapter are due in part to his intelligence and diligence, and in part to the access he must have had to the ducal library at Wolfenbüttel, founded in 1572 and now known as the Herzog August Library. In the 17th century it was the largest library north of the Alps. The sources he cites differ greatly in their reliability.
34. Polydorus Vergilius, *De inventoribus rerum*, (1499); German translations appeared in 1537 and 1603. Praetorius seems to be unaware of antique sources that name Ktesibios (Ctesibius) as the organ's inventor; see: Jean Perrot, *The Organ from its Invention in the Hellenistic Period to the end of the Thirteenth Century* (London: Oxford University Press, 1971), pp. 7f.

DE ORGANOGRAPHIA.

„ König David gebawet hatte / darauff die Leviten jhre Hymnos, Psalmen vnd Geistliche Lieder sungen. Dergleichen Art sind auch die / so Monochordia, Clavicymbala, vnd sonst auff mancherley weise genennet werden / derer Inventores gleicher gestalt / mit grossem Verlust jhres herrlichen Nahmens / in der finstersten „ Nacht verborgen liegen.

Tempus. Wenn aber vnd zu welcher zeit / die **Orgeln** erstlich erfunden / vnd deroselben gebrauch in der Christlichen Kirchen auffkommen sey / darinnen stimmen die Chronicken vnd Historici gantz nicht vberein.

Man lieset bey Volat. lib. 22. an. 653. daß Babst Vitellianus vnter der Regierung Käysers Constantini deß dritten / den Gesang vnd die Orgel in den Kirchen angestellet habe. Polydorus lib. 6. Cap. 2. de invent. Vnd Cranzius lib. 2. Metrop. melden: Babst Vitalianus der I. habe die KirchenRegeln gemacht / vnd den Gesang angeordnet / auch dazu die Orgeln zu mehrer vollstimmigkeit vnd wollautung (wie etzliche wollen) gebraucht. Platina in Vitaliano setzet / welches auch Guil. Perkinsus Anglic. Theol. Acad. Cantab. in probl. de Catholicismo geschrieben vnd auffgezeichnet: Das die Instrumenta / so durch das Wasser oder den Windt getrieben / jhren Anfang vmb das Jahr Christi 660. oder vmb das Jahr 930. gehabt haben. Aimonius wil im Jahr 820. Genebrandus 997. Navarrus in lib. de Orat. & horis Canon. Cap. 16. spricht: das zur zeit Aquinatis die Orgeln noch nicht sein im brauch gewesen. Es ist aber Thomas von Aquino gestorben / vmb das Jahr Christi 1274. wie es Chytræus außrechnet.

Es ist aber zuvermuten / das die Orgeln viel Elter seyn / vnd das Vitalianus vmb das Jahr Christi 660. dieselbe nur allein approbiret vnd confirmiret habe. Denn wie es der H. Sethus calvisius Chronologus nostro tempore præstantißimus dafür helt / so hat man so baldt / als das viel singen in den Kirchen angeordnet / vnd in Choros getheilet worden / ohn zweiffel / wo man nicht zween Choros haben können / eine Orgel zuhülff genommen / welche den Choral alleine einfeltig moduliret hat / auch zu dem ende / das die Senger ein wenig haben ruhen können. So sind auch / durch hülff vnd vorschub der Orgeln / die tetrachorda antiquorum, so auch noch zu Boëthij zeiten (qui floruit Anno Christi 487. quo anno Romæ Consul fuit) gebreuchlich gewesen / abgeschafft / vnd die 6. voces Musicales erfunden / auch die scala Musicalis weit verbessert worden / wie bey dem Guidone (qui floruit plus quàm quingentis annis post Boëthium, circa Annum Christi 1026) zusehen: denselben wir es noch zudancken haben / das zwantzig Claves geordnet sind / da zuvor erstlich nur viere / hernacher sieben / baldt vierzehn / vnd endtlich 15. gewesen.

So ist auch durch die Orgeln / vnser figuralis Musica erfunden worden; denn die Musica harmonica apud veteres, ist gar durchaus anders gewesen / als vnser jetziger

accompaniment the Levites sang their hymns, psalms, and spiritual songs.[35] Of this same sort are the monochord, harpsichord, and others like them; the good names of their inventors are likewise hidden in obscurity, a great loss."

When the Instrument was Invented: Historians are not in complete agreement as to when the organ was first invented, and when it began to be used in the Christian Church.

Volat. lib. 22.[36] (653 A.D.) states that Pope Vitellianus[37] initiated both singing and the use of the organ in church, during the reign of Emperor Constantine III.[38] Polydorus,[39] (*de invent.*), Book 6, Chap. 2 and Cranzius, *Metrop*[*olis*], Book 2.[40] report that Pope Vitalianus I introduced rules for the church, regulated singing, and used the organ to gain a fuller, more harmonious sound. Platina in *Vitalianus*[41] writes that the instruments powered by water or wind originated around 660 or around 930 A.D.; Guil. Perkinsus, Anglic. Theol. Acad, Cantab., agrees with this in his *probl. de Catholicismo*.[42] Aimonius[43] sets the year at 820, Genebrandus[44] at 997. In his *Lib. de Orat. & horis Canon*, Chap. 16, Navarrus[45] says that at the time of Aquinas the organ was not yet in use; according to Chytræus,[46] Thomas Aquinas died in 1274 A.D.[47]

The organ is likely much older, however, and Vitalianus in 660 A.D. probably only approved and confirmed its use. According to the opinion of Mr. Seth Calvisius,[48] the most outstanding historian of our time, as soon as a great deal of singing, divided into choirs, became the rule in churches, then without doubt the organ was put to use wherever two choirs were not available. It performed the simple chant, monophonically, for the purpose of allowing the singers a bit of rest. And thus, with the help and support of the organ, the ancient tetrachord, still in use at the time of Boëthius[49] (who flourished around 487 A.D., in which year he was a Roman consul), was done away with, and the 6 church modes were invented. The musical scale was also greatly improved, as can be seen in Guido,[50] who flourished around 1026 A.D., more than five hundred years after Boëthius. We have Guido to thank for the expansion of the keyboard to 20 keys,[51] where there were previously only four, then seven, then fourteen, and finally fifteen.

It was also by means of the organ that figural music[52] was invented. For in ancient times musical harmony was far different from what we know as figural mu-

35. Though he is referring to the Old Testament, Praetorius's words echo the Apostle Paul in his letters to the Ephesians (5:19) and Colossians (3:16).
36. Raphael Volateranus (Raffaello Maffei of Volterra, Italy, 1451-1522), Commentariorum rerum urbanarum libri XXXVIII (Rome, 1506; Paris, 1516); Book 22 chronicles the lives of the popes.
37. The spelling in the next sentence is the correct one: Pope Vitalianus, r. 657-72
38. Constantine III r. 641; Constans II r. 641-68; Constantine IV r. 668-685
39. Polydorus Vergilius, De inventoribus rerum, (1499).
40. Albert Kranz (c.1450-1517), Metropolis, sive Historia de ecclesiis sub Carolo Magno in Saxonia (1548).
41. Bartholomaeus Platina, De Vitis Ac Gestis Summorum Pontificum Ad Sua Usque Tempora (1562).
42. William Perkins (1558-1602), Gvilielmi Perkinsi Problema de Romanæ fidei ementito Catholicismo (1604).
43. Aimon of Fleury (c960-c1010), Historia Francorum.
44. Gilbert Genebrard(?), (1537-97).
45. Doctor Navarrus (Martín de Azpilcueta)?, 1491-1586.
46. David Chytræus (1531-1600).
47. This is correct.
48. Sethus Calvisius (Seth Kalwitz) 1556-1615; from 1594 Cantor of the Thomaskirche, Leipzig. Praetorius engaged in professional correspondence with Calvisius, as documented in the quote from a letter on p. 100.
49. Anicius Manlius Severinus Boethius, c. 480-c524.
50. Guido of Arezzo (c991- after 1033)
51. The system of hexachords, Gamma ut - e la (G - e").
52. i.e. polyphony.

DE ORGANOGRAPHIA.

jziger Figural: wie in vorgedachten D. Calvisij Exercitatione secunda & tertia mit mehrerm zuvernehmen.

Vnd das die Claves chromaticæ oder die Semitonia sind erfunden worden/kompt ex tetrachordis veterum, welche tetrachordum Synnemmenon (das ist conjunctarum Clavium, als E f♮ a ♮ c d) haben/in welchen das b zwischen ♮ vnd a eingesetzet wird. Weil sie nun diesen clavem b gehabt vnd hinein bracht/hat sichs leichtlich weiter zu den andern extendirt, hat man anders mit den sex vocibus Musicalibus fortkommen wollen/vnd ist also das ♮ ohn zweiffel am nechsten erfunden worden/g a b c d ♮ etc.

Zu welcher zeit sie nun erstlich in Teutschlande vnd Franckreich auffkommen/vnd in Italia vnd anderßwo künstliche Orgeln gewesen seyn/kan man aus glaubwirdigen Historienschreibern zum theil ersehen vnd nachrechnen.

Aventinus in annalibus Bojorum lib. 3. hat auffgezeichnet/ daß Constantinus VI. Copronymus Leonis Sohn/welcher vmb das Jahr Christi 742. das Constantinopolitanische Käyserthumb gehabt/ Pipino der Francken Könige/ Käysers Caroli Magni Vatter/durch sonderliche Legaten (deren fürnembstes Haupt Stephanus ein Bischoff zu Rom gewesen) ein trefflich groß Instrument/vnd ein solch Werck/ das domals den Frantzosen vnd Teutschen noch gantz vnbekandt/vberschicket habe: vnd saget/das es mit Pfeiffen aus Bley zusammen gesetzt gewesen/vnd zugleich mit Blasebälgen auffgeblasen/ vnd mit Händen vnd Füssen geschlagen vnd eine Orgel genennet / vnd zum ersten in Franckreich gesehen worden sey. Lambertus Schafnab. vnd Marianus Scotus lib. 3. schreiben/das solches im Jahr 758. geschehen sey. Wiewol andere schreiben/ daß das Pedal in Orgeln zu Venedig erstlich sey erfunden worden. Daraus dann offenbahr/ das diese Art der Instrumentalischen Musica/welches wir heute zu Tage eine Orgel nennen/ nicht so gar alt sey in den Frantzösischen vnd Teutschen Kirchen.

Damit aber gleichwol beydes dem Aventino, (welcher sagt/das die Orgel zur zeit Pipini den Teutschen vñ Frantzosen noch vnbekandt gewesen) vnd auch dem Platinæ, (welcher wil/das die Orgel 300. Jahr vor Pipino, von Vitelliano in die Kirche gesetzt worden sey) glauben beygemessen werde : So mus es dahin verstanden werden/das Platina ohne zweiffel verstehe/das vngeschickte Instrument/welches 15. Pfeiffen hatte/ in welches der Winde durch 12. Blaßbälge eingelassen ward/ dergleichen eines zu Jerusalem in Oli veto vffm Oelberg gestanden/vñ einen Thon von sich gegeben/gleich als wenn es Donnerte: oder daß er sehe/auff das gar alte Instrument Hydravlicũ, so gemeiniglich eine Orgel geheissen ward/ wie Vitruvius l. 10. Architect. c. 13. anzeiget.

Wiewol aber diese beyde/ das Hydravlicum vnd vnsere Orgel/was die euserliche form belanget/ nicht wol zu vnterscheiden/ so ist gleichwol diß der vnterscheid ; daß deß

M ij Hydravlici

sic, as may be learned (among other places) in the abovementioned Mr. Calvisius's *Exercitatio secunda & tertia.*[53]

From the ancient tetrachord the semitones, the chromatic keys, were invented. They arose from the tetrachord of the ancients, the tetrachord Synemmenon (this is a linking of tones, such as E f g a b♭[54] c d) in which a b was inserted between b♮ and a. After the b♭ key was there, the other chromatic keys were quickly introduced. Otherwise it would never have been possible to extend the hexachord system. D♯[55] was undoubtedly the next note to be invented, which made g a b[56] c d d♯[57] possible.

From reliable historians it is possible in some measure to determine at what time these keys first appeared in Germany and France, and when highly developed organs were to be found in Italy and elsewhere.

In *Annales Bojorum*, Book 3, Aventinus[58] records that in 742 A.D.[59] Constantinus VI Copronymus, son of Leo and Emperor of Byzantium, dispatched legates (the foremost of whom was Stephen, a Roman bishop) to deliver quite a sizeable organ to Pepin, King of the Franks, the father of Charlemagne. Such an instrument was at that time still unknown, both to the Franks and to the Germans. Aventinus reports that it was made with pipes of lead, it was winded by bellows, it was played with hands and feet, it was called an organ, and that it was seen for the first time in the Frankish kingdom. Lambertus Schafnab.[60] and Marianus Scotus,[61] Book 3, report that this happened in the year 758. Others record that the pedal was first invented for an organ in Venice. Thus it is apparent that the kind of musical instrument that we today call the organ has not been in German and French churches very long.

In order to give credence, however, both to Aventinus (who says that in Pepin's day the organ was unknown either in France or in Germany) and also to Platina[62] (who asserts that the organ came into the church through Vitellianus, who lived 300[63] years before Pepin), one must realize that Platina is referring without doubt to the crude instrument that had 15 pipes operated by 12 bellows, the sort of instrument that stood on Mt. Olivet in Jerusalem and produced a noise like thunder.[64] Either that, or he is referring to the ancient hydraulis, commonly called the organ, described by Vitruvius, Book 10, *Architect.*, Chap. 13.[65]

Although both of these, the hydraulis and today's organ, are indistin-

---

53. Exercitationes musicae duae (1600), Exercitatio musica tertia (1609).
54. Praetorius prints a b♮, but this tetrachord requires a b♭.
55. i.e., e♭
56. This should be a b♭, not a b♮.
57. i.e., e♭. The e♭ yields the Dorian mode transposed to g, a very common mode in the sixteenth and early 17th centuries.
58. Johannes Aventinus (1477-1534) Annales Bojorum (Annals of Bavaria, 1554, 1580).
59. The correct date is 757; see: Jean Perrot, *The Organ from its Invention in the Hellenistic Period to the end of the Thirteenth Century* (London: Oxford University Press, 1971), p. 207ff.
60. Lampert of Aschaffenburg? (c.1024-c.1088).
61. (1028-1082/3), Chronicon (first printed in 1559), a purported universal history from the creation of the world until 1082.
62. Bartholomaeus Platina, De Vitis Ac Gestis Summorum Pontificum Ad Sua Usque Tempora (1562).
63. A glance at the dates Praetorius gives for Pipin and Vitellianus will quickly establish that this number is inaccurate. His observation is valid, though, since Vitellianus lived well before Pipin.
64. Perrot (Jean Perrot, *The Organ from its Invention in the Hellenistic Period to the end of the Thirteenth Century* [London: Oxford University Press, 1971]) records nothing about such an instrument.
65. Vitruvius Pollio, fl. 1st century BCE, De architectura, Book X.8.3-6.

Hydravlici Corpus mit den Pfeiffen aus Ertz zusammen aneinander geschmeltzet/ vnd gegossen worden/vnd nur ein einzige reige oder zeile Pfeiffen gehabt / auch vnterschiedlichen laut durch das eingegossene Wasser von sich geben. Dieses vnsers Organi Corpus oder Kasten aber/so aus Holtz künstlich zusammen gefügt wird/hat gar viel zeilen voller Pfeiffen/ vnd zerstrewet vnd zertheilet jhren Klang vnd Thon aus den Pfeiffen/fornen/hinden/vor der Brust auff der seyten vnd vnter den Füssen/ durch die Lufft vnd Windt/so jhr von den Blasebälgen zukompt.

Leander (welches auch Majolus erzehlet) Colloq. 23. schreibet / daß er zu Venedig ein sehr wolklingende Orgel aus lauterm Glase gemacht / gesehen habe. Es ist auch eine Orgel darin die Laden/Pfeiffen/Clavier/ vnd Blaßbälge von Alabaster (welcher Stein auff dem Volateranischen Acker in Italia wechset) gewesen/ gesehen worden: welche der Kunstreiche Meister von Neapolis, als er sie verfertiget/vnd vberaus wolklingendt zugerichtet/ dem Hertzog zu Mantua, Friderico gebracht/vnd sie jhme verehret. Leander in Thuscia bezeuget/daß er dieses aus dermassen wunderbarliches Werck selbsten gesehen habe. Dergleichen Positieffe/ da nicht allein das gantze Gehäuse vnd Clavier/sondern auch die Pfeiffen von eitel Glaß vnd Alabaster Stein gemacht/ seynd vor wenig Jahren in eine Churfürstliche Kunstkammer/als Newerfundene Wercke præsentirt worden. Das aber solche Invention allbereit alt/vnd vor dieser zeit verhanden gewesen/ist aus obgedachten Historicis gnugsam zuersehen.

Die fürtrefflichsten vnd berühmbtesten Musici vnd Erfinder newer Inventionen in Musica vnter den Christen sind gewesen: Georgius Sacerdos, von Venedig bürtig/ da er von Daldrico einem Vngerischen Graffen Ludovico Pio ist Commendiret worden/hat er diß Musicalische Instrument Hydravlicum, das sie eine Orgel heissen/ an dem Graneischen Wasser zusammen gegossen vnd gefertiget. (Aimonius l. 4. Cap. 113. de Francis. Aventinus l. 4. Annalium.

Gilbertus ein Prælat zu Rehms / welcher hernach Römischer Bapst vnd Sylvester II. ist genennet worden/hat durch hülff seiner Mathematica eine Orgel gebawet/welche durch die vngestühme Gewalt deß heissen Wassers jhren klang bekommen/Anno Domini 997. wie Erfordiensis, vnd Genebrandus bezeugen.

Boëthius, so zugleich auch ein guter Mathematicus, Philosophus, vnd außbündiger Poët gewesen/ wird vor den Erfinder deß Musicalischen Instruments Chiterini gehalten/(Bergomas vnd Genebrandus. Anno Domini 515.

Vnd das wir diß nicht vergessen/Sabellicus l. 8. Enn. 10. meldet/ das vmb das Jahr Christi 1470. Zu Venedig ein vberaus fürtrefflicher Man vor allen in der Musica gewesen.

Bernhar-

guishable in outward appearance, they nevertheless differ in that the pipes, made of iron, were fused with the body of the hydraulis; furthermore there was only one row of pipes, which produced different sounds because of the water that poured through them.[66] The body of our organ today, the case (Kasten[67]), skillfully constructed of wood, has however many rows full of pipes, and emits the sound from the pipes in front, in back, from the Brustwerk, on the sides, [and] beneath the feet, by means of wind supplied by bellows.

Leander writes in *Colloq.* 23[68] that he saw a very melodious organ in Venice made solely out of glass (Majolus[69] relates this as well). He also reports having seen an organ whose chest, pipes, keyboard, and bellows were of alabaster (a stone found in the field at Volterra in Italy); a skillful Neapolitan master, after having built it and voiced it exceedingly sweetly, presented it to Friderico, Duke of Mantua, to do him honor. Leander in his *Thuscia* testifies that he himself saw this exceedingly wonderful instrument. Such a positive, in which not only the entire case and keyboard, but even the pipes themselves were made entirely out of glass and alabaster, was exhibited several years ago in an electoral art collection as a newly invented instrument. But as the abovementioned historians indicate, such a invention was around long before our time.

Among Christians, the most distinguished and famous musical inventors have been: Georgius the Priest, born in Venice, whom a Hungarian count, Daldrico recommended to Louis the Pious,[70] cast and built in Aachen the musical instrument, the hydraulis, called an organ (see Aimonius, Book 4, Chap. 113, *de Francis*;[71] also Aventinus, Book 4, *Annales*[72]).

Gilbertus, Bishop of Rheims, who later was named Pope in Rome, as Sylvester II[73], built with the aid of his mathematical knowledge an organ that produced its sound by the violent power of boiling water; this was in 997 A.D., as Erfordiensis[74] and Genebrandus[75] both testify).

Boethius,[76] who was at once a good mathematician, a philosopher, and an exceptional poet, is considered to be the inventor of the musical instrument, the chiterini (see: Bergomas and Genebrandus[77]), in A.D. 515.

And lest we forget: Sabellicus, Book 8, Ennarratio 10,[78] reports that about the year 1470 A.D. there lived in Venice an exceedingly distinguished man, especially in music.

---

66. This statement rests on a misunderstanding propagated by medieval descriptions of the instrument.
67. The German word "Kasten" corresponds neither to the modern German word for "case" (Gehäuse) nor for "chest" (Lade); here the context seems to suggest the former.
68. Leandro Alberti, (Alberto, Albertus), 1479-c1552, Italian Dominican monk and historian.
69. Majolus, Abbot of Cluny? c906-994.
70. 778-840; son of Charlemagne; King of the Franks from 1814 until his death.
71. Aimon of Fleury (c960-c1010), Historia Francorum.
72. Johannes Aventinus (1477-1534) Annales Bojorum (Annals of Bavaria, 1554, 1580).
73. Gerbert d'Aurillac, c946-1003; reigned as Pope from 999.
74. Index I, p. 205, gives the name as "Henricus Erfordiensis" (Heinrich of Erfurt? Identity unknown).
75. Gilbert Genebrard(?), (1537-97).
76. Anicius Manlius Severinus Boethius, c. 480-c524; Roman senator and philosopher.
77. Gilbert Genebrard(?), (1537-97).
78. Marcus Antonius Coccius Sabellicus? (1436-1506), either Enneades sive Rhapsodia historiarum (a universal history, pub. 1498) or Historiae rerum venetarum ab urbe condita (a history of Venice, in Latin).

Bernhardus mit den Zunahmen Teutscher/ zur anzeigung deß Volcks/ davon er entsprossen/welcher der erste ist gewesen/der die Orgel verbessert vnd vermehret/das zugleich auch die Füsse/ durch anziehung der kleinen stricklein/ (nemlich im Pedall) zu mehrer wollautung vnd vollstimmigkeit helffen können. Sonsten aber/ob in der Griechischen/Italianischen/Asiatischen/oder Aphricanischen Kirchen/ die allerelteste Orgel sey/kan man nicht vor gewiß sagen/ oder eigentlich wissen.

Vnd ist freylich wol zubeklagen/das man nichts eigentliches noch gantz gewisses von dem Anfang vnd Erfindung der ersten Invention;so wol auch/wie alt die erbawung der eltesten Orgelwercke seyn möchte/haben kan. Welches aber wol zu wünschen vnd zu wissen nötig were:Sintemahl hieraus nicht alleine Gottes den Menschen verliehene Gaben/die Musicalische Instrumenta auff solche art zumachen/ zuersehen seyn/ sondern auch/ das vnserer lieben/ vnd für etlichen hundert Jahren verstorbenen alten Vorfahren fleissiges mühsehliges nachsinnen/(vnd wie sie gleichsamb ihren Nachkommen die Leyter/künfftig höher zusteigen/zurecht gesetzt/vnd den Weg fort vnd weiter zuwandern/gezeigt haben/) vns vnter Augen leuchten/ vnd auch zu derogleichen fleiß antreiben möchte/diese jtzige herrliche zeit/(da man alle dinge fast vffs höheste gestiegen seyn/vermeinet) in freyen Künsten so viel mehr ohn verdruß vnd nutzbarlicher/ zu Gottes ehren anzuwenden.

Welche vnvollkommene wissenschafft aber billich/ den kunst anbehörigen Organisten/ Orgelmachern vnd Meistern (so noch vor hundert/ mehr/ vnd weniger Jahren solche alte Werck/ ohn einiges nach-vnd zurückdencken/hinweg gerissen/vnd von deren domals befundenen Arten/ Inventionen/ in Schrifften/ wie fleissig man auch) darnach forschet vnd trachtet/nichts hin derlassen haben/)alleine zum verweiß zuzumessen.

Jedoch(damit wir alleine von denen Orgelwercken/darvon noch an jetzo vnd vor etlichen Jahren die rudera verhanden/in diesem opere etwas vermelden) so kan man aus gewisser Erfahrung vnd nachrichtung haben: das vor 600. Jahren/ Orgelwercke gebawet worden seyndt; wie dessen Zeugnuß vnd Jahrziffern vnter andern in Halberstadt vnd Erffurdt in den Paulinern Kirchen/vnd sonsten hin vnd wider annoch verhanden vnd zufinden seyn.

Das III. Capitel.
Von Art vnd Eigenschafft der allerersten Orgelwercken/ welche gar klein gewesen.

ES sind aber anfangs solcher Invention vnd erbawungen/ keine grosse/ sondern gar kleine Wercke/ so stracks an einem Pfeiler (als zu Magdeburg in

S. Jacobs

His name was Bernhardus, but he bore the surname "Teutscher" [i.e., "the German"] to indicate the people from whom he sprang. He was the first one to improve and expand the organ by stretching thin strings [from the keys] to the pedal, thus helping the organ sound fuller and more harmonious. But no one can say with certainty whether the first organs were in Greek, Italian, Asian, or African churches.

It is to be regretted that nothing can be known about the invention of the first organ, or when it was built. From that knowledge one could not only learn about the gift, given by God to men, of making this particular musical instrument, but also about our forebears' diligent, laborious thought several hundred years ago. They set a ladder in position, as it were, on which their descendants could subsequently climb ever higher; they illuminated for us the right way to proceed in the future. Their example could impel us to the same diligence in applying the liberal arts all the more effectively and usefully to the glory of God, in this marvelous age in which we live (when it appears that everything has risen almost to perfection).

Simply to tear down old instruments, some less than 100 years old, without a second thought, and to leave not a single description of them (despite an exhaustive search of the old records[79]): such a shoddy way of doing things is a blot on the reputation of those responsible for it—organists and organbuilders alike.

Nevertheless, on the basis of the remnants of organs that still exist (at least as of several years ago), which are to be described in this treatise, one can surmise certain things. Evidence, such as the dates on organs at Halberstadt and in the Paulinerkirche at Erfurt, among others, as well as other indications scattered here and there, suggests that organs were built as long as 600 years ago.

Chapter III
The characteristics of the earliest organs, which were quite small

hen organs first began to be built, however, they were not large, but quite small, attached directly to columns (one like this once stood in the Sankt Jacobi Kirche at Magdeburg), or as swallows nests, built

---

79. This remark attests to the diligence and effort Praetorius invested in seeking out primary source material.

S. Jacobs Kirchen eins gestanden/ oder in die höhe bey die Chor als Schwalbennester gesetzt/ vnd mit engen raum vnd vmbfange gemacht werden. So haben auch solche Wercklein anfangs/ nicht mehr als einen Laut/ ohn einige enderung gehabt vnd behalten: Welches anders nicht/ denn nach vnserm Gebrauch zureden/ eine Mixtur/ so mit 10. 15. vnd wol 20. Pfeiffen auff jedern Clave besetzet gewesen ist. Aus welcher disponirten Mixtur/ die grosse Pfeiff eines jeden Clavis, als das Fundament solcher Disposition, forne an nach der Ordnung/ wie wir jetzo vnser Principal setzen/ auch zum schein ist gesetzet worden: Haben scharff vnd starck geklungen vnd geschrien; Ihre Clavir aber sind also ohne Semitonia gewesen/ wie folget.

♮ c d e f g a ♮ c d e f
Etliche aber also/
c d e f g a b c d e f g a.

Allhier lest sichs ansehen/ als das sie zu den Orgeln anfangs nicht mehr als diese eilff claves, darinnen die Alten die drey tetrachorda comprehendirt, genommen haben; als/ 1. Tetrachordum ὑπάτων, von ♮ quadrato biß ins E. (♮ aber ist die grösste vnd eilffte chorda gewesen/ quam Timotheus Milesius excogitavit, tempore Philippi, patris Alexandri.)

2. Tetrachordum μέσων, vom E zum a.

3. Tetrachordum διεζευγμένων vom ♮ ins e.

♮ C D E F G A ♮ c d e

Aber baldt nach deß Timothei Milesij zeiten/ ist das 4. Tetrachordum ὑπερβολαίων e f g a a/ superiori loco erfunden/ vnd also XIV. Chordæ, zuletzt aber noch der vnterste Clavis A, extra ista Tetrachorda, tanquā fundamenti loco assumirt worden; ne Veterum Musicæ in hac re aliquid deesset: & ita in XV. Clavibus Cantus durus modulabatur. Wenn sie es aber in Cantum mollem sive transpositum bringen vnd haben wollen/ so haben sie das Tetrachordum συνημμένον darzu genommen vnd copuliret: de his vide Calvisium Exercit. 2. pag. 105.

Dieses alles ist nun/ wie gedacht/ zu Alexandri Magni zeiten/ noch vor Christi Geburt geschehen: die Orgeln aber/ deren Structuren noch vor wenig Jahren zu-

high above the choir, very compact and crowded together. At first these little instruments made only one unvariable sound, which was nothing other than a mixture (as we would describe it), composed of 10, 15, or even 20 pipes per key. In this mixture, the largest pipe of each key, the foundation pitch, stood in front, in the façade, where the Principal stands in today's organs. These instruments sounded powerful and penetrating; their keyboards had no semitones, like this:

b c d e f g a b♭ c d e f

Some, though, were like this:

c d e f g a b♭ c d e f g a

From this it is clear that in the beginning organs had no more than these eleven keys[80], which covered the compass of the three ancient tetrachords:

1. the tetrachord $υπατων$ [hypaton], from b♮ to E (b♮ is the last and lowest of the tones devised by Timotheus[81] during the reign of Philip,[82] father of Alexander [the Great]).

2. the tetrachord $μεσων$ [meson], from E to a.

3. the tetrachord $διεξευγμενων$ [diezeugmenon], from b♮ up to e.

B♮ C D E F G A B♮ c d e

Soon after the time of Timotheus Milesius the fourth tetrachord, $υπερβολαιων$ [hyperbolaion], was invented, the e f g a in the higher position; thus there were 14 tones. Finally the lowest key, A below the tetrachord, was added, as a bass tone, lest anything be lacking in the music of the ancients. Thus it was possible to play a Cantus durus[83] upon 15 tones. When they wanted to shift to the Cantus mollis or transpositus,[84] then they added the tetrachord $συννημμενον$ [synnemmenon]; in this regard, see Calvisius's Exercitium 2, p. 105.[85]

As already mentioned, all this happened at the time of Alexander the Great, before Christ's birth. The organs that still existed up until a few years ago,

---

80. i.e., the eleven tones listed below.
81. Timotheus Milesius (i.e., born in Miletus), c.450-360 BCE.
82. Philip II of Macedon, 382-336 BCE (reigned 359-336 BCE)
83. a melody based on G
84. a melody based on F, requiring a b♭.
85. Exercitationes musicae duae (1600)

ren zufinden gewest/ sind lang nach Christi Geburt allererst vnd gleichwol nicht mehr als mit XI. oder XII. Clavibus (wie zu deß vorgedachten Timothei Milesij zeiten/ nach den dreyen ersten Tetrachordis) gemacht worden.

Welches wol zuverwundern/ vnd vieleicht daher kommen/ das sie domals noch keine Experientz vnd vbung vff den Claviren gehabt/ vnd bey wenigen anfangen/ oder wie man sonsten zureden pflegt/ bey den Bäncken müssen gehen lernen/ biß sie immer von Tag zu Tage weiter kommen/ vnd die Claves vermehret. Wiewol der H. Calvisius vermeinet/ es komme daher/ weil die Mixtur so viel Octaven vber sich gehabt hat/ so habē sie es vor vnnötig geachtet/ mehr Octaven in den Clavibus zumachen: Zu dem so erfordert der Natürliche Ambitus in humana voce nicht viel mehr/ als eilff Claves, oder do sie höher gestiegen/ haben sie die Octav darunter genommen: so lang biß sie/ wie im 7.Cap. ferner meldung geschehen wird/ mehr Claves erfunden.

Das IV. Capitel.

Wie die erste Art der kleinen Orgeln vmb eine Octava ergrössert/ vnd zum Mittlern Werck gebracht worden.

Ey dieser Art vnd Verstande ist es sonder zweiffel (weil es/ als eine Newe Invention erst an Tag kommen/ vnd durch langwirige zeit einer den andern gelehret) viel Jahr beruhet/ ehe solches vnd damals newes wunder in der Welt bekandt/ vnd nur an vnterschiedlichen fernen Orten gebawet worden.

Als aber von derselben zeit an bey hundert vnd mehr Jahren/ diese Kunst deß Orgelmachens in gebrauch kommen/ vnd zu einer Lehr gedien/ damit man sonder zweiffel nicht wenig neidisch wird gewesen seyn; da hat man auch den Sachen allererst weiter nachgesonnen/ vnd **grössere Werck**/ noch eins so groß als die ersten zumachen angefangen. Wie dessen nicht allein hin vnd wider eigentliche vnd vernünfftige nachrichtung/ sondern auch in fürnehmen Städten/ Stifften vnd Klöstern der handtgreiffliche Augenschein noch anjetzo befunden wird.

Da ist denn eins aus dem andern entsprossen/ vnd hat sich vnter den Meistern ein Ingenium vor dem andern herfür thun wollen.

Es erscheinet auch aus jetzt gesetzten beyder Art Claviren (weil das eine b mol, vnd das ander ♮ dur) vornünfftig: daß man domals/ jedoch ohne gefehr bey hundert Jahren nach der ersten Invention, allbereit auff die Semitonia zuergrübeln buchstabirt hat; wie denn vor 400. Jahren etliche Semitonia in jhren Clavirn, sonderlich b fa in ♮ dur Clavir, vnd das in ♮ b moll, schon erfunden gewesen seyn.

Das V.Cap.

however, were built long after Christ's birth, and still had no more than 11 or 12 keys (encompassing the first three tetrachords), just like those built in the days of Timotheus Milesius.

This is quite astonishing. Perhaps it is because at that time they had as yet no experience with keyboard [instruments] and had to begin by taking their timid first steps ("holding onto the bench," as is said), improving with each try, until they finally increased the number of keys. Mr. Calvisius,[86] though, thinks it is because the Mixture had so many octaves, one atop the other, that it was considered unnecessary to increase the number of keys. Furthermore, the natural range of the human voice does not require many more pitches than the eleven keys produce; if the melody ascended beyond the compass of the keyboard, the octave beneath was played. This situation prevailed until more keys were invented, as reported more fully in Chapter 7.

Chapter IV.
How the earliest small organs were extended by an octave, and made into medium-sized instruments.

No doubt the matter remained like this for many years—progress being slow and protracted, as with any new invention—until this new and wonderful instrument became known, and was built at various widely separated places.

A hundred or more years ago, however, as the art of organ-building became more common and blossomed into a true discipline, envy doubtless began to play a role in the matter. For now builders became more and more clever, and they began to build larger instruments, twice as big as the first ones. There are not only reliable reports about this here and there, there are actual instruments still to be seen in important cities, collegiate and monastery churches.

One thing then led to another, and master builders vied among themselves in coming up with one ingenious idea after another.

From the two types of keyboards just mentioned above,[87] (since one had a b♭ and the other a b♮), it seems logical that, about 100 years after the instrument was invented,[88] someone had already devised semitones; 400 years ago various semitones began to appear in keyboards, especially the b♭ in the b♮ keyboard and the e♭ in the b♭ keyboard.[89]

---

86. Sethus Calvisius (Seth Kalwitz),1556-1615; from 1594 Cantor of the Thomaskirche, Leipzig.
87. p. 94.
88. i.e., about 400 years ago, according to Praetorius's report.
89. The hexachord beginning on b♭ requires the e♭.

Das V. Capitel.

Wie die Pedal erfunden/ vnd daher das erste vnd Oberste Clavir, welches sonsten keinen Namen gehabt/ Manual genennet worden.

B nun zwar die Orgelwercke an grösse vnd vielheit der Pfeiffen/ vnd vermehrung der Claviren zugenommen/ so ist es doch gleichwol bey der ersten Invention, das nicht mehr denn Principal vnd Mixtur (so doch zu der zeit noch nicht zertheilte/ sondern eine zusammenklingende Disponirte Stimme gewesen) geblieben; ohne allein/ das mehr Claves in die höhe gemacht/ vnd die Pedal auch allbereit vor 400. Jahren noch darzu erfunden seyn. Wie denn dasselbige der Augenschein der gar alten Structuren, wann man sonsten keine nachrichtung mehr finden köndte / anzeiget: Weil die beyden eussersten Seit Törme zum Pedal, vnd das mittel zum Manual ist disponiret gewesen.

Vnd wird allhier offtermelter vnser lieben Alten Vorfahren fleissige Speculation, vnd tieffes nachdencken mit allem Ruhm billig erwehnet/ das sie den Musicalischen klang/ auch mit den Fußtretten zubefördern erfunden haben.

Vnd wie Sabellicus schreibt/ auch in 4. Membro, Partis primæ, primi Tomi. c. 10. meldung geschehen/ so hat ein Deutscher mit Nahmen Bernhardus das Pedal, vmb das Jahr nach Christi Geburt 1470. aus Deutschlandt gen Venedig in Italiam gebracht.

Wiewol das Pedal in Italia, Engellandt vnd andern örtern mehr/ da doch die Orgelkunst jtziger zeit sehr florirt vnd excellirt, wenig vnd gar selten gebraucht wird. Vnd wollen etliche Scribenten, das die Musica in Italia, vorzeiten gar zergangen/ vnd von den Teutschen widerumb zu jhnen hat müssen gebracht werden.

Aus dieser ersten Invention deß Pedals/ (so anfenglichen nur 8. Claves, als ♮ c d e f g a ♮ gehabt) ist nach langwiriger zeit noch ein Manual Clavir, welches zwar zum Basse, an stad deß Pedals gebraucht/ gleichwol mit der lincken Handt geregiret/ wie es denn auch an der form vnd grösse dem Manual Clavirn gantz gleich/ erfunden worden. Inmassen denn auch aus dem ersten fundirten Manual Clavir noch eines erfolget ist/ darvon folgends sol gedacht/ vnd dessen disposition beschrieben werden.

Es sein aber nach dieser Pedal erfindung/ die allererste Clavir/ so wir jzt Manual nennen/ nicht Manual, sondern Discant genennet/ vnd daß Pedal bey seinem Nahmen

Chapter V.
How the pedal was invented, and thus the first and primary keyboard (previously without a name) came to be called "Manual"

lthough the organ had by this time increased in the size and number of pipes and in the number of keyboards, nevertheless when it was first invented the principals and the mixture were not yet split up, but sounded as one inseparable stop. The only alterations were in the increased number of notes in the treble and in the addition of the pedal, already invented 400 years ago. Although written records no longer exist, a glance at the layout of very old organs provides evidence of this: there are two side towers for the pedal, and the manual occupies the middle section.

Here it is only proper to acknowledge and to praise our forebears' profound thought and diligent inventiveness, in that they discovered how to produce musical sounds with their feet as well [as their hands].

In Vol. I, Chapter 10, Membrum 4, Pars I,[90] Sabellicus reports that a German by the name of Bernhardus brought the pedal from Germany to Venice in Italy.

The pedal is seldom used in Italy, England, and elsewhere as well, although the art of the organ is presently flourishing [in those places]. Some writers assert that in times past Italian music had totally perished, and that the Germans had to bring it there again.

A long time after the pedal (which originally had only eight keys: B♭, c, d, e, f, g, a, b♭) had been invented, another manual was devised, played by the left hand, to be used instead of the pedal as a bass. It was identical to the already existing manual in size and configuration. A second manual keyboard likewise grew out of the original manual keyboard; its layout will be described below.[91]

After the pedal was invented, the original keyboard that we have been referring to as "Manual," was called "Discant" instead of "Manual." The pedal was

---

90. Marcus Antonius Coccius Sabellicus? (1436-1506), either Enneades sive Rhapsodia historiarum (a universal history, pub. 1498) or Historiae rerum venetarum ab urbe condita (a history of Venice).
91. In Chapter VII, p. 98f., and the accompanying illustrations in the Theatrum Instrumentorum, Plates XXIV and XXV; Praetorius is thus describing an organ with three rows of keys to be played by the hands and one row to be operated by the feet.

Namen / Pedal geheissen worden; wie solches aus einer sehr alten Schrifft eines Münchs zuersehen gewesen/vnd auch die Vernunfft bezeiget; weil der Choral anfenglichen bloß mit einander Stim̄ gebraucht vnd geführet worden/daß das Clavir sonderzweiffel zu der zeit keinen Nahmen gehabt/weil es mehr ein Tenor deß Chorals, also zu sagen/ (welches auch die Clavir Buchstaben vnd disposition außweisen) gewesen ist. Aber hernacher / da die Pedal invention ans liecht kommen/ da sind die ManualClavir höher vnd jmmer von einer zeit zur andern/ mehr denn eine Octava erlengert/vnd mit kleinern Pfeiffen ersetzet/ daher es gegen dem Pedal, als denn billich / ein Discant genennet worden.

Solche DiscantClaves, oder Clavir seind zu der zeit auff solche ♃ vnd diese ♄ art (deren abriß in Sciograph. Col. XXIV. vnd XXV. zufinden) formiret / vnd so hart nieder zubringen gewesen/also das man dieselben mit einer vollen vnd zugethanen Faust hat niederdrucken müssen.

Vnd hat dasselbige Clavir, darin doch nur 9. Claves gewesen/ fast 5. oder 6. viertel einer Ellen an der breiten im raum eingenommen. Wie dann deroselben eigentliche grösse vnd lenge/ (welche in den dreyen vbereinander ligenden Claviren, am grossen Wercke im Thumb zu Halberstadt noch an jetzo zufinden seyn/vnd folgendes darvon weiter sol gesaget werden) in diesem Tomo / in der Sciographia Columna 24. abgerissen verhanden. Zu Magdeburg aber im Thumb sollen die Claves, wie etliche berichten/viereckicht/vnd fast 3. Zoll breit vnd an der zahl sechzehen gewesen seyn.

Bey derselben art Clavirn vnd invention ist es damaln/ aus gewisser nachrichtung bey 300 vnd wol mehr Jahren /(von anfang anzurechnen) geblieben/ vnd nicht mehr als nur ein Manual Clavir, (das sie/wie jetzt gedacht/ Discant geheissen/) doch auch mit ein Pedal, gearbeitet worden/darauff man endtlichen aus vbung ein trium hat zu wege bringen mögen.

Das VI. Capitel.

Von den gar grossen Alten Orgelwercken.

ES ist aber bey dieser Mitlern/ so wol bey der ersten kleinen Art Wercken/vnd ersten Invention keine verenderung deß klangs gewesen/ sondern stets vor voll/vnd ein wie allemahl/ doch wegen viel gesetzter Pfeiffen/eins noch gewaltiger als das ander zusammen geschrieben/ biß das die dritte Art/als grosse Wercke/ so abermahl eine Octava an allem grösser/ vnd mit mehrern Claviren, erfunden / vnd vor 250. Jahren nicht in gemeine/sondern in die vornembste grosse Münster vnd Thumbstifft Kirchen sind

N   gebawet

De Organographia.

then given the name "Pedal." This can be seen in an ancient monastic manuscript, and common sense confirms it as well. Here is the reason why: in the beginning the chant cantus firmus was performed monophonically, and so the keyboard doubtless bore no name since it was more or less an anchor for the chant;[92] the names and compass of the notes confirm this.[93] Subsequently however, after the pedal was invented, the manual keyboard gradually kept on adding smaller pipes in the treble, until it had added more than an octave to its range. In comparison with the pedal, therefore, it was rightly named "Discant."

The keys of this Discant manual were shaped like this ♃ or this ♃, (sketches of these may be found in the *Theatrum Instrumentorum*, Plates XXIV and XXV). They were so hard to depress that they had to be thrust down with a fully clenched fist.

Such a keyboard, with only 9 keys, was almost 1¼ or 1½ yards wide.[94] The *Theatrum Instrumentorum*, Plate 24, provides a sketch of keys of this actual size and length. They are to be found in the three keyboards, lying one atop the other, still extant in the large instrument in Halberstadt Cathedral; more will be said about them below.[95] Some reports say, however, that there were sixteen keys on the organ in Magdeburg Cathedral, each one rectangular and almost three inches wide.[96]

Reliable reports indicate that this sort of keyboard was in use for 300 years or more after its invention, and that during this time only one manual keyboard was built (called "Discant," as mentioned above) together with a pedal; with practice one might finally have been able to play a trio on such an instrument.

Chapter VI.
Concerning very large organs

ust like the small organs (the first ones to be invented), these medium-sized ones produced only one sound, an unchanging full organ. Because of their many pipes, these organs got louder and louder, until 250 years ago the third kind of organ was invented. It had several keyboards, and sounded an octave lower than the earlier ones. Such organs were not built in ordinary churches, but rather in large, eminent monastery and cathedral churches. The case of one such large cathedral

---

92. literally "because it was more a Tenor (Latin "holder") of the chant."
93. See above, Chap. III, p. 94.
94. The actual dimension Praetorius had in mind may perhaps be judged from the ruler he provided on the reverse side of the Theatrum Instrumentorum title page.
95. Chap. VII, pp. 98ff.
96. See the ruler on the reverse side of the Theatrum Instrumentorum title page. Theatrum Instrumentorum, Plate XXXV, provides a sketch of large keys at Magdeburg, similar to those at Halberstadt. Although they are not rectangular, it seems probable that they depict keys at Magdeburg Cathedral. On p. 98, in the course of discussing the Halberstadt organ, Praetorius mentions that "Another such instrument was recently removed from the cathedral at Magdeburg." On p. 105 Praetorius compares the two instruments, referring in particular to the number of their bellows.

gebawet worden: wie derer Structuren in den grossen Stifftkirchen/ sampt etwas von jhren eingebewde vnd etlichen Pfeiffen / vnter andern auch in der Halberstädtischen ThumKirchen noch heutiges Tages zubesehen/ vnd dergleichen newlichen aus dem Thum zu Magdeburg weggenommen worden ist. Welches grosse Werck im Thum zu Halberstadt vermöge seiner daran befindlichen eigentlichen Jahrzahl/ vor drittehalb hundert Jahren anfenglichen erbawet / vnd vor hundert vnd 20. Jahren erst renovirt worden. Vnd stehet diese nachrichtung an jetzo gedachten Wercke also beschrieben.

Anno Domini M. CCC. LXI. Completum in Vigilia Matthæi Apostoli, per manus Nicolai Fabri Sacerdotis.   Anno Domini. M. CCCC. XCV. renovatum est per manus Gregorij Kleng &c.

An diesem Orgelwercke vnd dergleichen befindet sich aber eine andere Art vnd höhere Invention, als an den vorbeschriebenen beyden Arten zuvor noch nicht gewesen ist. Daraus abzunehmen/ das man zur selben zeit allbereit den Sachen sehr fleissig nachgedacht/ vnd eben so wol/ als jetzt/ vnterschiedliche treffliche ingenia gefunden hat/ welche von zeit zu zeit/ nicht allein nach den Semitoniis (weil jhnen die Vernunfft/ als eine im Traum etwas fürgebildet wird/ noch ein anders vñ höhers dahinder zuseyn anleitung gegeben) gesucht vnd gegrübelt/ vnd auch endlich dieselbe ergründet haben; sondern auch allerley enderungen vnd Variationes deß klangs / gerne hören vnd haben wollen. Wie denn in diesem Orgelwercke/ als zu dero zeit newen invention, alles beydes befunden wird. Darumb denn von diesem vnd dergleichen Orgelwercken/ Manual vnd Pedal Claviren disposition vnd derselben gebrauch/ auch wie es balde nach derselben zeit/ als jhnen durch diese invention, weiter zukommen/ der Weg gezeigt worden/ mit gewalt in Orgelwercken also gestiegen ist / billich etwas außführlicher allhier mus angezeigt vnd berichtet werden.

Das VII. Capitel.

Von der Disposition der Claviren in den gar grossen Orgelwercken/ vnd sonderlich in jetztgedachter Alten Orgel zu Halberstadt/ vnd wie solche Clavir seindt gebraucht worden.

1. Das oberste Clavir, so zu der zeit Discant geheissen/ vnd zum vollen Wercke/ als nemlich den födern Præstanten vnd Hindersatz zugleich gebraucht worden.

organ, together with some of its interior components and pipes, can still be seen today (among other places) in the cathedral at Halberstadt.[97] Another such instrument was recently removed from the cathedral at Magdeburg. According to the date that actually appears on it, the large instrument at the Halberstadt Cathedral was first built 250 years ago, and was restored just 120 years ago. This is what is actually inscribed on this instrument:

> Completed on the Vigil of St. Matthew the Apostle[98] in 1361 A.D. by the priest Nicolas Faber.[99] Renovated in 1495 by Gregorius Kleng, etc.

Instruments such as this one exhibit a high level of achievement, to a degree not encountered in the two types described earlier. From this, one may deduce that by this time the undertaking had already been thoroughly thought through. Just as today, builders had devised and thoroughly explored various clever inventions; their imaginations gave them new and loftier insights, just as one visualizes something in a dream. Thus they eagerly sought out not only the semitones, but also all varieties of sound. Both of these innovations are already encountered in the organ at Halberstadt. It is only fitting to report here in greater detail about the construction and use of manual and pedal keyboards[100] in this instrument and others like it, and also about the rapid rise of the organ as these inventions soon pointed the way to further advances.

Chapter VII.

Concerning the layout of the keyboards in the very large organs, in particular in the abovementioned old organ at Halberstadt, and how such keyboards were used.

1. The uppermost keyboard, called at that time "Discant," controlling the full organ, the Prestant pipes in the front as well as the one large Mixture behind them.

---

97. For further information about this instrument, see: Karl Bormann, Die gotische Orgel zu Halberstadt, Berlin: Verlag Merseburger [c. 1966]. On p. 17 this publication provides a plate with an attempted reconstruction of the case, according to Praetorius's description.
98. September 20.
99. German "Nicolaus Schmidt." See Bormann, Die gotische Orgel zu Halberstadt, pp. 23, 111, & 113.
100. See Theatrum Instrumentorum, Plates XXIV and XXV,

DE ORGANOGRAPHIA.

♮ c ♯d ♮e f ♯g ♯ a♭♮c ♯d ♮ e f ♯g a

2. Ander Clavir/ so auch Discant genennet/ vnd zum Principal alleine gebraucht worden ist.

c ♯d ♮e f ♯g ♯ a b ♮ ♯ ♯d ♯ c f ♯ ...

3. Das drit/ist ein Baß Clavir, so vnter den vorigen beyden Claviren ordentlich gelegen/an aller gestaldt vnd grösse denselben gleich: Vnd obs zwar mit den Händen/oder aber/als etliche vormeinen/mit den Knien getrucket worden/so ist es doch an statt deß Pedals zu dem Principal oder grösten Baßpfeiffen / welche in den Seit-Törmen stehen / gebraucht worden.

♮ c ♯d ♮ e f ♯ g ♯ a ♭ ♮ c

4. Das vierte vnd vnterste PedalClavir, so mit den Füssen getretten/ vnd auch mit dem Obersten DiscantClavir zum gantzen vollen gepränge gebraucht ist.

♮ c ♯ d ♮ e f ♯ g ♯ a ♮

Dieses Pedal Clavir hat recht vnter den dritten / so nechst hieroben/in gleicher Einy gelegen/vnd mit demselben einerley außtheilung an der grösse/ aber nicht einerley Claves gehabt/wie solches in der Sciographia, Col. XXV. zusehen.

Aus dieser vier Clavirn Invention ist dieser nutz vnd gebrauch erfolget/ das man erstlich ein vnterscheit im klange machen vnd haben können/ vnd durch die beyden mittelsten Clavir(als nemlich das 2/vnd dritte (das Principal oder förderpfeiffen vor sich alleine hat können geschlagen werden/ Manualiter: vnd zwar mit der rechten Faust/welches sie den Discant genennet haben/auff den andern Clavir, vnd auff den dritten Clavir, ist mit der sincken Handt der Bass an statt deß Pedals, nicht mehr denn zu einem Bicinio oder Duum Vocum im Choral gebraucht worden. Die andern beyde/als das oberste vnd vnderste Clavir, sein zum gantzen Werck vnd vollem geschrey/ als der Mixtur,(so zu der zeit Hindersatz geheissen / weil es hinter den præstanten gestanden)neben vnd mit den præstanten gebraucht worden. Da denn das erste vnd oberste das Discant Clavir; vnd das vnterste das Pedal oder Baß Clavir gewesen ist/darauff man ein Trium hat können zu wege bringen. In solchem Hindersatz sein im Discant, nach eigentlicher befindung/32. 43. vnd 56. Pfeiffen auff vnterschiedlichen Clavibus disponiret gestanden; vnd im Bass oder Pedal Hindersatz nur 16.20.vnd 24.Pfeiffen/aber alles grober MixturArt/gesetzt wordē.

Welches dann wegen der grösse der præstanten,vnd weil sich jhre Manual Clavir, der wenigen Clavium halben/nicht in die höhe zur lieblichkeit begeben können/ ein solch tieffes grobes brausen vnd grewliches grümmeln; auch wegen vielheit der

Mixtur-

b♮ c c♯ d d♯ e f f♯ g g♯ a b♭ b c' c♯' d' d♯' e' f' f♯' g' a'

2. The second keyboard, also called "Discant," but used to play the Principal alone.

c c♯ d d♯ e f f♯ g g♯ a b♭ b c' c♯' d' d♯' e' f' f♯' g' a'

3. The third, a keyboard for the bass, lies directly under both the previous keyboards, and is like them in form and size.[101] And whether the keys were depressed with the hands or (as some assert) with the knees, it was used instead of the pedals for playing the great bass Principal pipes that stand in the side towers.

b♮ c c♯ d d♯ e f f♯ g g♯ a b♭ b c

4. The fourth and lowest keyboard, the pedal, is played with the feet, and is used together with the top Discant keyboard to play the full organ in all its splendor.

b♮ c c♯ d d♯ e f f♯ g g♯ a b [102]

This pedal keyboard lies directly under the third, described above, and is of the same size, but does not have precisely the same keys, as can be seen in Plate XXV of the *Theatrum Instrumentorum*.

The primary advantage these four keyboards provide is the possibility of achieving a difference in sound. The two middle keyboards (numbers 2 and 3) could have allowed the principal, the pipes in the façade, to be played alone with the hands, the right fist (then called the "Discant") playing on the second keyboard, and the left hand playing the bass on the third keyboard (instead of the pedal), thus producing nothing other than a bicinium, based on the chant. The other two keyboards, the top and the bottom, were for the powerful full organ, i.e., the mixture (called at that time "Hindersatz," since it stood behind the Principal (præstanten) sounding together with the praestant pipes. Since the uppermost keyboard was the Discant and the lowest was the pedal or bass keyboard, it would have been possible to perform a trio on them. According to my own observation, in the Discant there were 32, 43, or 56 pipes that sounded on various keys in the Hindersatz, but there were only 16, 20, or 24 pipes (large ones, like a low mixture) on the pedal or bass keys.

Since the praestants were quite large and the mixture had a great many pipes, all under considerable wind pressure, this instrument must have produced

---

101. Judging from the sketches of these keyboards (Theatrum Instrumentorum, Plate XXV), the sense of this remark seems to be that the keyboards were (more or less) alike in available pitches and in compass.

102. This highest note may have been a b♭ instead of a b♮, despite its position as a lower key. Both b♮ and b♭ were originally considered diatonic notes, and thus old organ keyboards (e.g., the instrument formerly at Norrlanda, on the island of Gotland, Sweden, dating c1370-1400, now in the National Historical Museum in Stockholm), have four "naturals" between g♯ and c♯: a, b♭, b♮, and c. Since the Halberstadt organ was not in playing condition when Praetorius examined it, he could not have known this; but a keyboard that already had a b♮ (here, as the lowest note) would likely have had a b♭ instead of another b♮. For this insight I am indebted to Prof. Jürgen Eppelsheim (Ludwig-Maximilians-University, Munich, ret.).

MixturPfeiffen/ein vberaus starcken schall vnd laut/vnd gewaltiges geschrey (darzu denn der geweste Windt rechtschaffen nachgedruckt hat) mus von sich gegeben haben.

Vnd dieses vmb so viel mehr daher/dieweil in solcher tieffen nichts mehr zwischen einer Octava, denn nur eine Quinta vnd auch terz perfect (sintemal zu jedem Manual Clave eine Handt oder volle Faust gehört hat) gegriffen werden können. Das demnach solches anzuhören/(wofern die disponirten Pfeiffen oder hintersatz nicht mit jhrem kleinen geschrey hindurch gebrochen/vnd einen vernemblichen Thon deß Chorals ins gehör gebracht) vnsern Ohren nachzureden/nicht sonderlich anmutig mus gewesen seyn.

Es sind aber die zwölff grosse Baß Pfeiffen oder Pedalia/ an die beyde Seit Thörme/vnd der Discant zwischen solchen hohen Thörmen jnnen nach der mensur geordnet gewesen.

Deß H. Galvisij meinung von dem Klang vnd Art der Alten Orgeln/vnd der alten Harmonia, ist diese; In dem er in quadam Epistola also an mich schreibet:

Nun ist die Frage/Ob man nicht noch vestigia der alten Harmoniæ finden könne? Dieselbige ist ohne zweiffel erhalten worden in den Kirchen. Wir haben noch zu vnser zeit zwey Instrumenta von der alten Musica, welche in stetem brauch sind; Als die Sackpfeiffe/vnd die Leyre; in denselbigen klingen besonders für vnd für eine Consonantia; auff der Sackpfeiffe nur eine Quinta; auff der Leyre aber wol drey oder vier Säiten / als Nemblich, eine Quinta, vnd Octava, zugleich durch drey Säiten: Vnd wird darnach vff andern Claviren welche die vierde Säite treffen vnd anrühren/etwas anders im füglichen Choral darin moduliret.

Solches ist ohne zweiffel stets in der Kirchen blieben/ vnd man hat vff den Orgeln/zu den Consonantiis eine andere sonderliche reige Pfeiffen haben müssen/in welchen man allezeit die Consonantias gezogen / welche sich zum Choral Clave schicken vnd reimen; wie auff der Leyre geschiehet ; als c g $\frac{1}{2}$ / oder d a $\bar{5}$ / oder e h $\bar{7}$ etc. Dieselbe Claves haben sie stets gehen vnd Thönen lassen/ vnd darnach einen Choral der aus dem c/d/oder e/gangen/vnd sein Fundament darinnen hat/ darein geschlagen/wie man auff dem Instrument ein Schäffertantz schlegt : Vnd dieses ist auff allen Instrumenten von anbegin der Welt die Musica gewesen/wie die Scriptores andeuten. Daraus denn leichtlich zuvernehmen/ das man zu der zeit zu solcher Music nicht so gar viel Claves, wie am ende deß 2. Cap. angezeiget worden/ vonnöthen gehabt.

Hernach aber/do etliche Ingeniosi Musici darzu kommen/haben sie privatim vnd sine arbitro sich weiter versucht/vn zu dem Choral, welchen sie in den acutioribus

bus

an exceedingly powerful sound. There was also a limited number of manual keys, and so the instrument could not produce the gentle higher tones, but only a deep, coarse, rumbling roar.

This must have been all the more so since, with such low pitches, nothing within the octave but fifths or major thirds could be played (each key requiring an entire hand, or rather, clenched fist). Listening to such an instrument must therefore not have been especially pleasant according to our taste, unless the higher pipes of the Hindersatz could penetrate through the mass of sound and allow the listener to hear the chant melody.

The twelve large pedal pipes stand in the side towers, and the Discant pipes are arranged between these two high towers progressively according to their height.[103]

Here is what Mr. Calvisius thinks about the sound of old organs and harmony in the past; this is what he wrote in a certain letter to me:

Here is the question: is it not possible to find vestiges of ancient harmony? Without doubt this harmony has been preserved in the church. Two musical instruments from the past are still in constant use today: the bagpipe and the hurdy-gurdy. Both of these continuously sound a consonance. With the bagpipe it is simply a fifth. In the hurdy-gurdy, though, there are three or four strings. Three of them simultaneously produce fifths and octaves; then there are keys that depress the fourth string, producing in contrast a true melody.

This sort of music has without doubt always been preserved in the church. In order to produce consonances on the organ, there had to be separate ranks of pipes that always sounded the consonances that fit with the pitches of the chant (just as happens on the hurdy-gurdy), e.g., c-g-c', or d-a-d', or e-b-e', etc. These notes sounded continuously, and then a chant whose final was c or d or e was played against them, just as one plays a shepherds' dance on a harpsichord.[104] Various authors indicate that this is how all instrumental music was performed, from the very beginning.[105] From this it is easy to see that, when this sort of music was current, not as many keys were needed as indicated at the end of Chapter 2.[106]

Later certain clever musicians made further private attempts to furnish consonances beneath the notes of the chant, which they transferred to a higher

---

103. Here the word "Mensur" means "the length of the pipes" (Praetorius specifically assigns it this meaning on p. 119 below). At other times, however, (such as in the first sentence under the entry "Schweitzerpfeiff," p. 128 below) the word clearly means what it means today: the relationship of the body's height to its width. In both instances "mensur" has to do with measurement, and Praetorius does not distinguish between the various senses of the word. Accordingly it has been translated as either "length" or "scale," depending on its context.
104. i.e., with a drone.
105. It is unclear whether Praetorius is actually quoting Calvisius, or simply paraphrasing him; but the following sentence suggests that the presentation of Calvisius's ideas ends here (if not indeed earlier).
106. Praetorius seems to be referring to his statement on the bottom of p. 90, that Guido d'Arezzo expanded the keyboard to 20 notes.

DE ORGANOGRAPHIA.

bus sonis geführet/vnten Consonantias versuchet/das man im rechten Manual zween Claves zusammen geschlagen/vnd endlich gefunden/wie sich der Choral füglich enden/vnd in einer Clausula zusammen kommen/vnd quiesciren köndte: Denn dieses ist das fürnembste gewesen. So baldt sie aber die Clausulas haben machen lernen/(welches ohn zweiffel/dieweil sie mancherleier Art/viel mühe gekostet) haben sie die andern Consonantias auch finden können/vnd zwo Stimmen in Contrapuncto simplici gesetzet/vnd also erstlich ein Bicinium erfunden: hernacher sind sie allemehlich weiter kommen/vnd ein Tricinium zuwege bracht/biß sie auch den floridum Contrapunctum funden.

Dieses aber ist langsam zugangen/denn es anfangs in den Consonantiis viel mühe gekostet/aus der Vrsach/das man die Tonos vnd Semitonia nicht rein hat Stimmen können; daher die Instrumenta oder Orgeln so rein nicht seynd gestimmet gewesen/als jetzunder: Haben auch nicht trawen dürffen/das die Tertien vnd Sexten Consonantiæ weren/dieweil die alten Musici alle miteinander nicht zugeben/das sie Consonantiæ sein sollen. Darumb denn keiner so vorschneppich seyn/vnd so klug sich düncken lassen wollen/daß er diß besser/als Ptolomæus, Boëthius, Euclides vnd andere fürtreffliche Musici, wissen wolte.

Ich bin der meinung/wenn man jetzo die alte Harmoniam gerne hören wolte/vnd wie die alte Music geklungen habe/so dürffte man nicht mehr/als das gantze volle Werck/(Nemblich die Principaln, Octaven, SuperOctaven, Quinten, Zymbeln, Mixturen, vnd SubBässe, vnd was sonsten mehr verhanden/so zum vollen Werck zuziehen gebreuchlich/vnd ein recht specimen der alten Mixtur ist) nehmen/vnd alßdann im Pedal mit beyden Füssen eine Quinta, als C. G. D. A; F. c; &c. zusammen halten/vnd führen den Choral eines Responsorij, Introitus oder Deutschen Gesanges/im Manual, allein in den vnvberstrichenen Buchstaben Clavir, c d e f g a ♮ ͞c (denn in den alten Orgeln kleinere Pfeiffen nicht verhanden gewesen (so wurde man der alten Art vnd Harmony zimlich nahe kommen: Wiewol sie es anfangs so gut nicht werden gehabt haben.

Das VIII. Capitel.
Vom Thon der Alten Orgeln.

ES befindet sich aber/daß desselben Orgelwercks Grösste Pfeiffe fornen an/nemblich das ♮ am obern Corpore ohne den zugespitzten Fuß/sechzehendhalb Ellen (das ist 31. Fuß lang) vnd 7 viertel einer Elln (das sind viertehalb Schuch) in der Circumferentz dicke ist. Vnd also wenn der gele-

pitch. They played two notes on the keyboard itself, and thus finally discovered how to bring the chant to a close properly, with a cadence. That was the most important thing. For as soon as they learned to make cadences (which was no easy matter, since there are various types of them), they were able to find consonances for the rest of the notes, and to play two voices in note-against-note counterpoint. Thus they discovered the bicinium. They continued to make progress until they produced a tricinium, and finally they invented florid counterpoint.

All of this, however, took a long time. It required a lot of effort to find the consonances, because organs were not tuned as accurately as today, and so the pitches, both naturals and chromatic tones, could not be tuned purely. For a long time musicians were not willing to accept thirds and sixths as consonances, since musical tradition would not permit this. For no one wanted to be considered impudent, or to present himself as more clever than Ptolemy, Boethius, Euclid or other eminent musicians.

If one should want to hear the kind of harmony found in early music, then in my opinion one need only draw the full organ: principals, octaves, superoctaves, quints, zimbels, mixtures, together with the subbass and whatever other plenum stops are available; this would be an accurate reproduction of an old mixture. Then one should sound a continuous fifth in the pedal with both feet (C-G, or D-A, or F-c, etc.), and play a chant responsory or introit, or a German hymn, as a cantus firmus on the manual—but in the tenor register, since there were no higher-pitched pipes in old organs. In this way one would come fairly close to the early way of making harmony—though in the past it would not have sounded so good.

Chapter VIII.
Concerning the pitch of old organs.

The body (not including the foot) of the largest praestant pipe in the Halberstadt organ, namely the b♮, is sixteen and one half ells, or 31 feet long, and 1 3/4 ells, or 4 1/2 feet, in circumference. Therefore if this principal is consid-

genheit nach/das Principal von 32. Fueß Thon gerechnet würde/ so stehet im hindersatz eine vnter Octava von 16. Fueß Thon; darnach eine grosse Octava von 6. Fueß-
Thon; vnd denn eine grosse Quint 6 Fueß Thon; hierauff etliche Octaven 4 Fueß-
Thon/vnd also fortan. Vnd ist die Dispositio eines Clavis ohngefehrlich also gewesen.

$$\text{Clavis, c,} \begin{Bmatrix} 2. \\ 3.\ 4. \\ 4.\ 5. \\ 6 \\ 7 \\ 8 \\ 10 \end{Bmatrix} \text{Pfeiffen von} \begin{Bmatrix} 8. \\ 4 \\ 3 \\ 2 \\ 1\tfrac{1}{2} \\ 1 \\ \tfrac{1}{2} \end{Bmatrix} \text{Fueß.}$$

Das also in diesem Hindersatz alle vnsere offene Stimmwerck Principaln-
Art verhanden. Welche sehr viele vberheuffte Pfeiffen in ihrer Mixtur, hernacher in
folgenden Jahren durch die Spring-vnd Schleiffladen in vnterschiedliche Stimmen vnd Register (wie hernacher sol gesagt werden) zertheilet worden; das man also
viel vnterschiedliche Stimmen aus der einigen Mixtur absonderlich brauchen kön-
nen/ vnd gleichwol noch Pfeiffen zur Mixtur vbrig blieben.

Es ist aber dieses vnd dergleichen Werck/ einen guten vnd baldt 1½ Thon höher gewesen/ als die vnsrige jtzige Chormessige Wercke stehen; Welches die vorange-
zogene grosse Pfeiffen leingde außweiset. Wie denn auch vermutlich/ das lange
zeit vorher alle Werck/ wie sie auch an vorbeschriebene grösse mögen gemacht seyn/
dieweil dieselben alle im Bapsthumb zu nichts anders/ denn zum Choral gebraucht
worden/ also in dem Thon vnd noch höher gestanden haben. Sintemahl letzlich die
Choral Werck/ welche nach vnserm Thon ein gantze Quart höher/ oder eine Quint
niedriger gemacht/ für die bequemsten erkandt/ vnd an solche Thon behalten worden.
Vnd ob schon an etlichen Wercken etwas mangelt/ das sie nicht Just in beschrie-
benen Thon einstimmen/ so ist doch solcher defect nicht denen Meistern/ welche die alten Choral Wercke/ so annoch im gebrauch anfenglich erbawet haben/ ihrem guten
willen vnd fleiß zuzumessen: sondern das man vieleicht zu der zeit noch keinen bestend-
digen Chöristen-oder Chor Thon/ darnach man sich richten mögen/ wie Gott lob
nunmehr im gebrauch/ erwehlt gehabt.

Auch seynd offt die Orgeln/ darnach gute Chorales vnd Schreyhälse zu sin-
gen/

ered to be at 32' pitch, then in the Hindersatz there is a sub-octave 16', a great-octave 8',[107] a great-quint 6', several 4' octaves, and so forth. This was the approximate distribution of pitches for one key:

$$\text{For the key c} \quad \left\{\begin{array}{c} 2 \\ 3\text{-}4 \\ 4\text{-}5 \\ 6 \\ 7 \\ 8 \\ 10 \end{array}\right\} \quad \text{pipes at} \quad \left\{\begin{array}{c} 8 \\ 4 \\ 3 \\ 2 \\ 1\,{}^{1}/_{2} \\ 1 \\ {}^{1}/_{2} \end{array}\right\} \quad \text{foot pitch}$$

Therefore in the Hindersatz there were all the varieties of today's open principal pipes. In succeeding years the great number of pipes in that mixture were divided into separate stops (to be described below) by means of spring- or slider-chests. Thus many different stops from this one mixture could be used separately, yet some pipes were still left together in a mixture.

This instrument, however, was a good step and a half higher than our present-day instruments at choir pitch, as the length of the abovementioned large praestant pipe demonstrates. Long ago all instruments, no matter how large or small, probably stood at that pitch, or even higher, since before the Reformation they were used for nothing but to accompany chant. It appears that chant-organs that were built a perfect fourth higher or a fifth lower than our present-day pitch[108] were finally recognized as being the most suitable, and so that pitch was adopted. And if there is some pitch discrepancy between various old organs that are still in use, it should not be attributed to a lack of good will and diligence among the masters who first built them, but rather perhaps to the absence of a standard choir pitch for them to use as a guide—something that we, praise God, have today.[109]

Organs that were installed in churches to accompany fine choirs of men

---

107. Praetorius has " 6' "; the context indicates that this is an error.
108. As the subsequent paragraph demonstrates, Praetorius is here referring to chamber pitch, a step (sometimes even a step and a half) below choir pitch. Since the Halberstadt organ stood one and a half steps above choir pitch, it would have been approximately a fourth higher (or a fifth lower) than chamber pitch.
109. Elsewhere, however (p. 116) Praetorius asserts: "Regarding pitch ... there has never been a universal standard observed by all builders."

gen/an dem Ort bestalt vnd verhanden gewesen/ baldt ein Thon höher vnd wol niedriger intoniret, vnd auch offte durch vieles renoviren vnd stimmen / noch mehr von jhrem anfenglichen Stande in die höhe gebracht worden. Sonsten aber wird obbeschriebener Thon /als/der eine Quart höher vnd Quint niedriger (nach vnsrigen jtzigen gewöhnlichen Thon / sonsten CammerThon genandt / zureden) für den richtigsten behalten / vnd in den vornehmen Stifft Kirchen noch also befunden.

Wiewol ausser deme auch viel Wercke gefunden werden / welche vmb eine Secund niedriger oder höher/ etzliche vnd deren nicht wenig auch vmb ein Semitonium höher intoniret vnd gemacht worden.

Das IX. Capitel.

Von Art dero zeit Blaßbälgen.

An muß aber zur selbigen obberührten zeit/vor drithalb oder dreyhundert Jahren (als solche grosse Werck/wie das zu Halberstadt/ davon jetzo gehandelt wird/ gebawet worden) noch geringe Inventiones vnd nachdencken auff Blaßbälge gehabt haben; Sintemahl an diesem Domwercke zu Halberstadt/ 20. vnd an deme zu Magdeburg/ 24. gar kleine Bälge/ (nach Ordnung vnd gestalt/ wie in der Sciograph. Col. XXVI. zubefinden) vorgeleget worden. Welche vnsern jtzigen Schmiedebälgen an grösse vnd Proportz nicht sehr vngleich gewesen: Sintemahl sie nicht durch bleyern oder steinern gewichte/ sondern eben durch solch ein Mittel regiert worden/ das man allzeit zu zweyen Bälgen eine Person zum tretten gebraucht/ vnd wann mit einem Fueß der eine Balck durch die schwere deß Calcanten nieder getretten ist/der ander mit dem andern Fueß wider in die höhe gezogen worden; das also zu 20. Bälgen/ zehen Personen/ vnd zu 24. jhrer zwölffe nothwendig haben verhanden sein müssen.

Vnd hat man sich nun billig zuverwundern/ weil gedachte vnsere liebe Alten/ in andern Sachen dieser Invention an Orgeln so weit kommen seyn/ das sie nicht auch auff andere weise vnd bequemere Manier/wegen deß Windes (mit formierung der Bälge/ so bessern vnd richtigern Windt geben können/ vnd auch deß trettens halben/ weil ja nicht allzeit gleiche starcke vnd schwere Personen solche Bälge zutreten vnd zu regieren/ nach dem Gewichte abgewogen werden können) besser nachgesonnen vnd darauff speculiret haben.

Inmassen

and boys were at times tuned a step higher (or even a step lower), and their pitch was often raised even further from the original due to repeated tuning and rebuilding. As a rule, though, the abovementioned pitch—a fourth higher or a fifth lower than our usual pitch (i.e., chamber pitch)—was considered the right one, and is still found in the important cathedral- and monastery-churches.

But many instruments can also be found that are a step higher or lower,[110] and also quite a few that are built about a half-step higher.

Chapter IX.

About the kind of bellows found at that time.

At the time mentioned above (250 or 300 years ago) when large instruments such as the one at Halberstadt were built, less thought must have been given to the bellows. Twenty little bellows are laid out in the Halberstadt Cathedral organ, and there were twenty four very small ones in the one at Magdeburg, in the size and order depicted in the *Theatrum Instrumentorum*, Plate XXVI. In their size and proportions they were not unlike our present-day blacksmith's bellows. They were not depressed by lead or stone weights, but by assigning one person to tread every two bellows. When the treader's weight depressed one bellows with one foot, the other foot drew the other bellows upward. Thus twenty bellows must have required ten people to operate, and twenty-four must have required twelve.

One must indeed wonder why our forebears back then, since they were so advanced in other aspects of organbuilding, never contrived a more convenient way of supplying wind, by designing the bellows to provide more adequate wind, and by devising a better way of treading them (since all people are not of uniform size and weight).

---

110. (presumably) than the pitch Praetorius has just been discussing (a fourth higher than choir pitch).

Inmassen dann einem nicht ohn Vrsach seltzames nachdencken einkommen möchte/ wie es sich doch im accordiren vnd stimmen/mit solchem vngleichen gepreſtem Winde müsse geartet haben; Sintemahl nichts anders in jhrer dispoſition, denn ein Mixturwerck/so von Octaven, Quinten vnd Quarten, vnd viel æqualen, vom gröſten biß zum kleinſten diſponiret zubefinden iſt.

Welches/so es den jtzigen Orgelmachern/wie ich ſelbſten gehört vnd geſehen/ bey guten gedyenen richtigen Winde im Werck accort zumachen vnd rein einzuſtimmen/schwer ankömpt/wie mus es denn offtgedachten vnsern lieben Alten mühſam vnd beſchwerlich vorgefallen ſeyn? zugeschweigen der mühſeligkeit/ welche die Calcanten in ſolchem ſtettigen tretten vnd bewegungen außſtehen müſſen. Dieſes iſt aber meines erachtens jhr beſter Vortheil geweſen/ das ſie ſolche Wercke nicht auff die proba/auch nicht durch ſonderliche Concordanten ſtimmen dürffen: Sintemahl keine Compoſition mit vielen Stimmen/ſondern nur der schlechte Choral einfältig darauff gemacht worden.

Darümb haben ſie auch fürnemlich nur jedem Clavem (Jedoch gleichwol nach jhren vorher geſtimmeten Præſtanten, die ſie domals alleine ziehen könten) in ſich ſelbſt rein/nach Mixtur Art vngezweiffelt ſtimmen müſſen. Vnd were zu wündſchen/das man jetzo ein ſolch Werck widerumb lautendt vnd klingendt machte/ damit man doch derſelbigen Art/gegen der vnsrigen jtzigen vnterſchiedlich hören vnd obſerviren möchte.

Das X. Capitel.

Von vnterſchiedenen Nahmen der Alten Orgeln.

Eil nun allhier von dreyerley gröſſe vnd Manieren der Elteſten vnd Alten Orgelwercken Bericht geſchehen/vnd zu vnterſchiedlicher langwiriger zeit im gebrauch zu bawen geweſen ſeyn:

So iſt dennoch auch aus gedachter vngleichen gröſſe/eine Frage/ damit jedem Wercke in ſolcher Art ein gewiſſer Name gegeben würde/entſtanden; Nemlichen/welches doch ein gantz/ halbes/ oder viertheil Werck ſey/ oder genennet werden könne? Nun iſt dieſe Frage nicht alleine vor etlichen hundert Jahren bey vnsern Vorfahren im gebrauch/ſondern auch damals recht vnd nötig fürgefallen; ſintemahl man zu der zeit/ von keiner Diſpoſition oder enderung der Stimmen gewuſt/vnd als die gar Groſſen Werck an Tag bracht worden; ſo hat man

Surely the tuning difficulties occasioned by such unsteady wind pressure must have made someone pause to reflect, since the organ was only one mixture, made up of octaves, fifths, fourths, and many unison ranks, from low to high.

Since today's organbuilders, as successful as they are in building instruments with stable winding (as I have observed), have difficulty tuning organs perfectly, how difficult and tiresome it must have been for our forebears! Not to mention the hardship such ceaseless movement imposed on the treaders. The only relief that [organbuilders] had was not having to tune such instruments by specific consonant intervals and by tests,[111] since [organists] never played polyphonic compositions, but only the plainchant melody.

Therefore, after tuning the praestant pipes (which by that time could be drawn separately), all that remained was to tune the pipes of each key pure according to the praestant, as with a mixture. I wish that someone would restore such an instrument, so that one could compare that sort of instrument with our modern ones.

Chapter X.

Concerning the various names of old organs.

ere I will describe the three sorts and sizes of the earliest organs that were in use for long periods at various times. The question that arose with these different sizes is this: which instruments should be given the name "whole," "half," or "quarter," in order to distinguish one type from another? This question was not merely current among our forebears several hundred years ago; it seems actually to have been right and necessary. For back then there was no variety in stops. So when really large instruments began to be built, it was thought necessary to call them "whole

---

111. Praetorius explains this tuning procedure on p. 153ff. below.

man nothwegen/dieselb vor ein GantzWerck; die Mitler Art aber vor ein Halbes/vnd also die kleine / welches die allererſten vnd elteſten/ vor ein Viertelwerck halten / vnd nennen müſſen: Vnd iſt alſo ein Nahme aus dem andern/gleich wie ſie vngleicher gröſſe vff vnd nacheinander erfolget ſeyn / entſtanden.

Vnd zwar hat man zun ſelben zeitten die Groſſen Werck billig jhrer Art nach Gantz geheiſſen; Weil dieſelbige von ſolchen groſſen Pfeiffen/ biß zu den kleineſten/ als eine gantze vollkommene Mixtur diſpoſition, diſponiret worden; daraus eine ſolche zahl der Pfeiffen auff einem Clave nacheinander geſtanden; Auff welche groſſe menge Pfeiffen dann ein gewaltiges gethöne vnvmbgenglichen erfolgen müſſen; Welches in der Mitlerart Wercken nicht geſchehen mögen. Jmgleichen habens die Erſten Kleine Wercklein/den Mitlern auch in der Art nicht nachthun können. Vnd iſt alſo/wie jetzt gedacht/zu der zeit ſolche Frage vnd Antwort/ die Wercke damit zu vnterſcheiden/recht nötig geweſen. Wie dann bey vnſer zeit noch wol ſolche Fragen von gemeinen Biederleuten vnd Alten Organiſten vorlauffen.

Vnd ſeynd etliche in der meinung geſtanden / das ſolche Namen / als Gantz/ Halb/ etc. Von der Zahl der Bälge jhren Vrſprung haben ſollen: Welches aber nicht ſein kan: Denn wenn man nur die beyden angezogene Dohm Wercke (anderer dergleichen zugeſchweigen) als zu Magdeburg vnd Halberſtadt anſihet; ſo hat das Magdeburg. 24. das Halberſtetiſche aber nur 20. Bälge/ vnd in allen beyden gleicher gröſſe gehabt: Weil ſie aber ſonſten an der gröſſe vnd diſpoſition gantz gleich/ können ſie vmb der Bälge willen am Nahmen gantz nicht vnterſchieden werden. Darumb iſt es zu den zeiten recht nach der gröſſe der Structuren vnd förder Pfeiffen/ Gantz/ Halb/ vnd Viertheil/ aus einfalt/ genennet worden.

Gleich wie jetzt ebener maſſen/ die Wercke nach jhren Principaln genennet/ vnd auch nur dreyerley Art Namen haben. Als wenn ein Orgelwerck/im Manual ein Principal von 16. Fueß Thon/vnd ein Octava von 8 Fueß Thon hat: ſo wird es ein groß PrincipalWerck genennet; Bey den Alten aber iſts ein Gantz Werck genennet worden / darinnen aber gemeinlich das F im Pedal von 24. Fueß nachem Chormaß zurechnen/ vnd eine Mixtur darbey geweſen: Wenn gleich ſonſten gar keine Stimme mehr vorhanden.

Wenn aber ein Orgelwerck im Manual ein Principal von 8. Fueß/ vnd ein Octav von 4. Fueß Thon; wird es ein AEqual Principal Werck/ von den Alten aber ein Halb Werck genennet.

Hat nun ein Werck ein Principal von 4. Fueß Thon im Manual, ob es wol noch eine andere gedackte oder offene Stimme vff 8. Fueß Thon im Pedal, bißweilen auch im Manual, ſo heiſſet man es doch nur nach ſeinen förder Pfeiffen / dem anſehen

instruments;" then the medium-sized ones were called "half-instruments," and the small ones, which were the earliest, were called "quarter-instruments." And so each name originated from the one before it, just as each size originated from an earlier, smaller one.

At that time the large instruments were appropriately given the name "whole," because they were constituted as one entire, complete mixture, from the largest pipes to the smallest. The inevitable result of such a great number of pipes sounding with each key was a mighty, thundering sound, which middle-sized instruments were incapable of. The earliest, smallest instruments, in turn, could not emulate the sound of the medium-sized ones. So labelling the instruments in this way was necessary to distinguish one from another. Older organists and ordinary citizens still make such distinctions among organs today.

Some are of the opinion that names like "whole," "half," etc., arose from the number of bellows. But this cannot be so. One need only consider both of the cathedral instruments discussed above, at Magdeburg and Halberstadt (to say nothing of others like them); Magdeburg had 24 bellows, while Halberstadt had only 20, and yet both of them were of the same size. Since they were of the same size and constitution, the distinction between them could hardly be drawn on the basis of the number of bellows. Back then the simplest way to designate them as "whole," "half," and "quarter" was according to the size of their structure and their praestants.

In the same way today, instruments are labeled according to the size of their principals, and have only one of three names. If an organ has a 16' Principal and an 8' Octave on the Hauptwerk, it is called a "Gross Principal-Werk." In former times, however, a "whole instrument" was usually one whose lowest pedal note was a 24' F. It was only a single mixture, having no separate stops.

If an organ has an 8' Principal and a 4' Octave on the Hauptwerk, it is called an "Aequal-Principal-Werk" (in the past, however, it was called a "half-instrument").

If an instrument has a 4' Principal on the Hauptwerk, regardless of the fact that it has an 8' stopped or open register in the pedal (or sometimes even in the Hauptwerk), it takes its name from the size of its praestants, and is called, accord-

hen nach ein Octav- oder Klein Principal Werck, wie im folgenden Theil von Newen Orgeln mit mehrerm sol angedeutet werden.

Vnd mögen die Orgelwercke deß vnterschieds halben / auch nicht besser mit Namen beschrieben werden / Sintemal allhier keine Zahl der Bälge / oder vielheit der Stimmen (weil darauß kein gewisser schluß entspriessen oder erfolgert werden mag) dem Kinde den Nahmen geben kan.

Das XI. Capitel.
Vom vnterscheidt der Alten / vnd vnserer jtzigen Orgeln.

WEnn wir allhier ein wenig innhalten / vnd der lieben Alten jhren anfang vnd invention / mit der vnsrigen jtzigen zeit Conferiren vnd besehen wollen; so wird man befinden / das / was die Haupt Invention der Orgeln / nebenst allem was darzu gehört / betreffen thut / der vnterscheid so gar oberauß groß nicht sey. Vnd billig zuverwundern stehet / wie es im anfang also baldt so weit kommen / das hierin biß an jetzo von keinem nit viel höher oder weiter hat können speculiret, noch durch andere mittel ein mehrers außgesonnen werden: Ohne das man numehr durch langwirige vbung vnd observirung; alle dasselbige / was die Alten erfunden / etwas natürlicher / bequemerer / zierlicher vnd lieblicher an tag bringen kan.

Vnd ist in den Eltesten Wercken ebener massen zubefinden / das dieselben auch / wie die vnsrigen / durch den Windt vnd Blaßbälge regiret / vnd zum klang gebracht worden seyn: Item / das die Bälge eben dieselben mittel / nemlich die Windtklappen oder Ventiel, dardurch der Windt in auß dem Balg geführt wird / gehabt haben; vnd mit ledder vberzogen vnd beschlagen worden seyn.

Weiter das man Canal oder Windtröhren gebrauchet / damit der Windt von den Bälgen zum Werck geleittet: Deßgleichen das auch Structuren mit vnterschiedenen formen disponiret gewesen / In welche die Windtladen (so inwendig alles an Cancellen, Ventilen, Stöhnfedern etc. als wir es noch brauchen / gehabt / vnd darauff das Pfeiffwerck gesetzet /) geleget / vnd mit Wellbretern / Angehenge / Pedal vnd Manual Claviren gemacht worden. Wie sie denn auch die Principalen, welche sie hernacher Præstanten, vnd auch vff den Grundt gesatzt genennet / fornen an zum zier gebracht vnd polliret / (auffn grundt gesatzt heist / dieweil diese Pfeiffen stracks vffs blosse Fundament / als nemlich vff die Windtladen / weil allda weder Register noch vfflagen verhanden / gesetzt sind.) Haben auch im Vollen Werck / welches damals jhre

Mixtur

ing to its appearance, an "Oktav-Principal-Werk" or a "Klein-Principal-Werk." Further information about such new organs will be given below.

There is no better way to distinguish by name the various sizes of organs. The number of bellows or of stops is insufficient to make a distinction,[112] since no valid conclusion can be drawn from these.

Chapter XI.

Concerning the distinction between old organs and those of today.

If we pause here and reflect, comparing organs of the past with those of today, we find that in all essential ways the difference is not so great. It is actually quite astonishing how quickly the instrument attained a degree of excellence that even present-day inventiveness and new materials have hardly improved upon. Lengthy experimentation has only succeeded in making the inventions of long ago somewhat more natural, convenient, elegant, and gentle.

Just like our modern instruments, the oldest ones already were operated by wind and bellows. The bellows, also overlaid with leather (like ours today), had the same wind valves or ventils through which wind entered and left.

There were also conduits or wind ducts to carry the wind from the bellows into the instrument, likewise structures in various shapes that held the windchests. Their interior parts were laid out just like those still in use, with channels, pallets, pallet-springs,[113] etc., upon which the pipes were set. There were rollerboards and trackers, as well as pedal and manual keyboards. There were principals, which they later called praestants, "uff den Grundt gesaßt," polished and in the façade for show ("auffn grundt gesaßt" means that these pipes were set directly on the windchest, there being no sliders or tables). The full organ, like ours, had a series

---

112. Literally, "to name the child."
113. German "Stöhnefeder" ("stöhnen" means "to groan" or "to moan"). The organbuilder Christian Wegscheider of Dresden offers the following explanation for this curious usage: for organbuilders, pallet springs are among the most troublesome parts of an organ; they constantly require adjustment or replacement. In order to avoid ciphers, builders often made these springs quite stiff (or put two or more on each pallet); the result was a heavier key action. Thus both builders and organists had good reason to groan about them!

DE ORGANOGRAPHIA. 107

Mixtur oder Hindersatz gewest/auff einander folgende Octaven, Quinten, Super-Octaven,&c.gehabt vñ disponiret, ohn das es alles auff einmahl angangen vn resoniret hat. Vñ ist billig zuverwundern/dz das Pfeiff vñ Flöt Werck/durch alle solche mittel/wie sie noch heutiges Tages nach allen vmbständen gemacht werden/vnd auch anders zuerfinden vnmüglich/zum klange hat können gebracht/ vnd anfanges auff speculiret werden. Vnd das man auch also baldt solche richtige vnd wolklingende (jedoch vnterschiedliche) Principal mensuren der Pfeiffen gehabt hat.

Ob aber zwar derselben Art Pfeiffen zu der zeit nur einerley/ als nemlich offen Stimwerck gewesen; so sind doch jhrer Principaln etliche am klange oder resonantz gewisser mensur vnd sauber Arbeit/ bey 200. Jahren hero / dergestalt beschaffen befunden/das man sich nicht alleine vber solchen jhrem vomats geübten vnd scharffgesuchten fleiß deß Zirckels/ gar wol bedechtig verwundern mus/ sondern auch etliche Orgelmacher zu vnser zeit mit ernst vnd fleiß von solchen Pfeiffen noch etwas zulernen sich nicht schemen dürffen. Wie dann derer Art Principaln, so aus den Päbstischen Alten Orgeln/in vnsere jetzigen Wercke versetzet vnd transferiret worden/ noch an jetzo an vnterschiedenen Orten zufinden seyn.

Das XII. Capitel.

Wie nun jetzo zu vnserer zeit die verbesserung der Laden/ verenderung vnd vormehrung der Claviren, auch der Stimmen vnd Pfeiffen/ aus der Alten Orgeln invention hergeflossen/ vnd eins aus dem andern erfolget sey.

Vnd erstlich:

Welcher gestalt die Springladen/so wol auch die Schleiffladen anfangs herfür kommen.

He aber die Invention der Schleiffen/ (darvon oben im 7. Cap. meldung geschehen) recht offenbahr worden/ist diese Art der Laden/so noch bey vnser zeit Springladen genennet werden/mit grossem mühseligen nachsuchen erfunden/ vnd in Niederlandt vnd Brabandt gemacht vnd gebraucht worden: Welche eigentlich (wie solches vorstendige Orgelmacher bekennen) aus

O ij   der

of octaves, quints, superoctaves, etc., except that it was all one mixture or "Hindersatz," and so all the pipes sounded all the time. It is quite amazing how the old builders were able to devise flue pipes and get them to sound, with all the same materials and according to all the same methods available today; also how they were able to devise the correct scales (though they were not uniform) to achieve a good tone.

Although there was only one kind of pipes back then, open flues, nevertheless some of the principals 200 years ago were tonally of such precise scale and fine workmanship that one must admire such a skillful and highly developed use of the compass. Some of today's organbuilders would do well to study these pipes seriously and diligently; they could indeed learn something from them. Such principals can still be found in various places, transferred from old, pre-Reformation organs into modern instruments.

Chapter XII.

Progress and development up to our day: improvement to chests, change and increase in number of keyboards and pipes.

First:
A description of the early spring and slider chests.

he type of chest known today as the spring chest, invented with much effort and thought, and used in the Netherlands and Brabant, was the first improvement upon the Blockwerk (described above in Chapter 7), and was invented before the slider chest came into general use. The reason for its invention (as the foremost organ-

der Invention/do man die vielheit der Pfeiffen voneinander hat absondern wollen/ (davon im 13. Cap. meldung geschehen sol) jhren Vrsprung haben. Darumb dann auch diese Art oder erfindung der Springladen kein newes/wie etzliche sich bedüncken lassen/sondern aus der eltesten Invention hergeflossen/vnd bey zweyhundert Jahren allbereit im gebrauch gewesen.

Wie dann im Bisthumb Würtzburg in einem Münche Closter/ noch vor wenig Jahren eine solche Springladen von einem Orgelmacher Timotheus genandt/aus einem sehr alten Werck/so ein Münch gemacht/genommen/vnd an deren statt/hinwiderumb eine newe Lade mit Schleiffen/darinn geleget worden ist.

Es hat aber in dieser Springladen eine jede Stimme jhre sonderliche Ventiel vnd viel Arbeit/doch wegen dessen/daß es also nicht hat können zusammen lauffen vnd durchstehen/sehr gut: Welche Ventiel dann mit eim eintzigen Register zugleich vffgezogen/vnd doch darbeneben in der Laden zu einen jeden Clave sondere Ventiel/welche mit dem Clavir nidergezogen werden/ verhanden.

Wie dann die Nieder-vnd Holländer von solchen Springladen mehr als von den Schleiffladen gehalten: Vnd solches darumb/das der Windt reiner/ohne vitia vnd sonderbahre mängel/vnter den Pfeiffen hat mügen behalten werden; auch in enderung deß Gewitters/wegen deß Schleiffwercks/welches sonsten nicht geringe defecten seyn/beftendig blieben.

Als man sich aber auch in diesen Landen die Schleiffladen Iust vnd perfect zumachen mit grosser mühe beflissen/ vnd die Nidder-vnd Holländer in Sachsen kommen vnd gesehen/das durch derselben vortheil eben so wol auch die Schleiffladen perfect zufertigen müglich; sind sie nachgefolget/ vnd sich deren anzumassen angefangen. Wie denn M. Fabian Peters von Schneeck/ zu Rostock/ Stralsundt vnd andern ortern dergleichen gemacht haben sol.

Vnd mus gewißlich nicht ein geringes Werck seyn/die Springladen (als ich von verstendigen Orgelmachern gehört vnd selbst vernünfftig erachten kan) Iust zumachen/wiewol auff den Schleiffladen mehr wünderlicher enderungen in Stimmwercken mit den abgesönderten Bässen/holtz verleitungen vnd sonsten zuerhalten vnd zu wege zubringen seyn/ als auff den Springladen dergestaldt nicht geschehen kan. Jedoch seynd alle beyde Inventiones/ wie denn auch beyderley Art von Spän vnd Ledder bezogenen Blaßbälgen/auch gut vnd beständig; wenn nur ein jeder Meister die hellen an Tag gebrachten Gaben recht vnd mit höchsten fleiß in acht nehmen wolte: als leyder itziger zeit der mangel mit grossem schaden der armen Leute (die in Städten vnd Dörffern/dem HErrn der Heerscharen zu ehren ein Orgelchen/nach jhrer

Kirchen

builders admit) was the desire to separate the many ranks of pipes from each other (this will be described in Chapter 14). The spring chest, therefore, is not a new invention, as some like to think, but was one of the earliest developments, and was already in use 200 years ago.

It was only a few years ago that an organbuilder by the name of Timotheus took a spring chest out of a very old instrument (made by a monk) in a monastery in the diocese of Würzburg, and replaced it with a new slider chest.

In a spring chest, every stop has a separate ventil, drawn open with a stop. It requires a great deal of labor, but is very good, since it prevents bleeding and running. In this chest there is also a separate ventil for each note, which is operated from the keyboard.

The Netherlanders considered spring chests superior to slider chests, because they thought that it could hold the wind under the pipes more effectively and with fewer drawbacks, and also because it is less affected by changes in weather (a major shortcoming in a slider chest).

But after the German builders with great zeal and effort had learned to make precise and perfect slider chests, the Netherlands builders visited Saxony[114] and saw that it was possible to make a slider chest with just the same advantages. Then they followed suit, and began to adopt the new practice. Master Fabian Peters from Sneek[115] is reported to have built such chests at Rostock, Stralsund, and elsewhere.

It is no small accomplishment to build a proper spring chest (I have heard this from knowledgeable organbuilders and consider it an accurate assessment), even though the slider chest allows more remarkable variations, such as off-set pedal pipes, wooden conductors, and the like; the spring chest will not permit these. Yet both of these inventions are reliable, as are both types of bellows, wedge bellows and those that are covered with leather,[116] provided that every builder diligently observes the by now well-known building techniques. Nowadays one unfortunately finds shoddy building practices, to the great detriment of

---

114. This refers to all the Saxon lands, including the present German states of Sachsen-Anhalt and Niedersachsen as well as Saxony.
115. A city in the province of Friesland, Netherlands.
116. The distinction between the two is unclear. Perhaps Praetorius is distinguishing between wedge and multifold bellows (cf. Theatrum Instrumentorum, Plate IV).

DE ORGANOGRAPHIA.

Kirchen gelegenheit setzen vnd auffzurichten zum offtern nicht ein geringes kosten lassen) befunden wird.

Welches dann in liefferungen der OrgelWercke etliche Organisten theils aus Vnverstandt/ theils aus affecten, den Orgelmachern zugefallen vnd gemeiner Quintin halber contra honestatem & conscientiam stillschweigendt vorüber passiren/vnd die Kirchen nicht vmb ein geringes beschneiden vnd schmeutzen lassen.

Das XIII. Capitel.

Enderung vnd vermehrung der Clavirn.

Gleich wie man nun vor dritthalb hundert Jahren mit fleiß auff enderungen vnd zertheilungen der Stimmen bedacht gewesen / vnd durch Göttliches eingeben dasselbe erlanget: auch gleich wie aus den erst erfundenen Claviren vnd Pedaln, so bey vierthalbhundert Jahren fast bey einer Art im gebrauch geblieben/ die Invention der der Semitonien (deren Art oben im 6. Cap. angedeutet) herfür kommen: Also seind auch von itzgesetzter Jahrzeit her/ die Clavier inventiones immer verbessert/ vnd vnterschiedlichen geendert/ gekleinert vnd vermehret/ das endlich vorgedachter dieser Art ☙ Claves abkommen/ vnd vnsere jtzige Art sich allmehlich angefangen: Jedoch also/ das ein Clavis baldt 2½ Zoll/ das ist drey guter Finger breit/ vnd also noch einmahl so groß/ als einer der jtzigen vnsern/ gewesen; wie dergleichen Claves noch an jetzo in einer alten kleinen Orgel im Thumbstifft Minden ich selbsten abgemessen vnd abgezeichnet habe. Vnd were zuwündschen/ das eine Jahrzahl darbey zufinden gewesen.

Balde hernacher sind die Claves noch vmb etwas mehr erkleinert worden/ also das eine Quinta so weit zugreiffen gewesen/ als jtzunder eine Octava außtregt: wie in der Alten Orgel zu S. AEgidien in Braunschweig noch jetzo zusehen/ vnd derselben Abriß vnd grösse in der Sciograph. Colum. XXVII. vnd XXVIII. zufinden.

Die Carmina so noch vnter derselben Orgel geschrieben/ zufinden/ hab ich auch hiebey setzen wollen.

    Offert devota nunc Clauſtri concio tota,
    Organa facta piè Christo matriq; Mariæ.
    Bartholdus rexit tunc Abbas, acopifex sit.

Andreas

the poor people in cities and villages who occasionally have a modest organ built in their churches, often at no small cost, to honor the Lord of Hosts.

Then when the organ is delivered, some organists (in part due to ignorance, in part due to excitement) support the organbuilder, and for silly reasons let things pass in silence, disregarding honesty and their conscience, thus allowing the churches to be cheated badly.

Chapter XIII.

Changes to the keyboards and the increase in their number.

wo hundred and fifty years ago builders diligently pursued, and through divine inspiration achieved, the division into separate stops; they also invented semitones (as indicated above in Chapter 6[117]) at the same time keyboards and pedals were invented, and these have remained without substantial change for 350 years. From that time on, the design of the keyboards was changed in various ways and constantly improved. They increased in number and were made smaller until finally the sort of keys described above ⊙ became obsolete, and the kind we have today gradually came into use. But each key was still 2 1/2 inches wide (fully the width of three fingers), twice as large as today's.[118] I have measured and sketched just such keys as this in a small, old organ in the Cathedral at Minden. I only wish there had been a date on it.

Not long afterwards the keys were once again made somewhat smaller, so that it was possible to reach the interval of a fifth, about the same span as today's octave. This can still be seen in the old organ at St. Aegidius in Braunschweig; a sketch showing their shape and size may be found in the *Theatrum Instrumentorum*, Plates XXVII and XXVIII.

I have decided to include here the verse found inscribed beneath this organ.

> Offert devota nunc Claustri concio tota,
> Organa facta piè Christo matrique; Mariæ
> Bartholdus rexit tunc Abbas, acopifex sit,

---

117. p. 98; see also the end of Chapter IV, p. 95.
118. Refer to the ruler on reverse of the title page of the Theatrum Instrumentorum.

Andreas gnarus existensq́; artéq; rarus:
Vt tangant cœlos, resonant hæc organa melos,
Tempus ut annale noscas, sic accipe tale:
1456. M tunc completo, sic bis duo C retineto,
L eum bisternis, est factum quod modò cernis;
In quo jubilo psalle placens Domino.

Der anfang jhrer Clavir aber ist noch allzeit bey den ♭ geblieben; wie denn zur selben zeit/etwan vor 200 Jahren/vnter andern in Venedig zu S. Salvator ein Werck gemacht worden/ deß Pedal also;

♭ c ♯ d ♭ e f ♯ g ♯ a ♭

Vnd das Manual, welches sie den Discant genennet/ auff folgende manier gewesen ist:

♭ c ♯ d ♭ e f ♯ g ♯ a ♭ ♭♭ cc

Vnd eben so viel Claves im Pedal vnd Manual, hat vorgedachtes Werck in Thumb zu Minden. Deßgleichen in Nürnberg zu S. Sebald/ohngefehr vor anderhalb hundert Jahren von einem Meister/ Heinrich Traxdorff genandt/ ein groß Werck gemacht worden / Welches Pedal sich im A, so zu der zeit Are (wie es in Schulen gebreuchlich) genennet/angefangen/ vnd also disponiret;

A B ♭ c ♯ d ♭ e f ♯ g ♯ a b

Der Discant aber also:

♭ c ♯ d ♭ e f ♯ g ♯ a ♭ ♭♭ cc

Noch eins hat zur selben zeit dieser Heinrich Traxdorff in Nürnberg zu vnser LiebenFrawen ohne Pedal gemacht/ welches als eine Schalmey sol geklungen haben: Vnd ist dessen Clavir auff diese maß disponirt gewesen;

♭ c ♯ d ♭ e f ♯ g ♯ a

Es hat aber dieser Meister seine förder Pfeiffen oder Præstanten in vorerwehntem grossem Wercke zu S. Sebald/Flötten gnennet; auch noch eine Octava

darin

110   DE ORGANOGRAPHIA.

        Andreas gnarus existens arteq́; rarus:
        Ut tangant cœlos, resonant hæc organa melos,
        Tempus ut annale noscas, sic accipe tale:
1456.   M tunc completo, sic bis duo C retineto,
        L eum bis ternis, est factum quod modò cernis;
        In quo jubilo psalle placens Domino.[119]

The lowest note of the keyboard, however, was still always b♮ [below tenor c]. At this time, about 200 years ago, one instrument (among others) was built at San Salvator in Venice whose pedal had these notes:

               c♯   d♯   f♯   g♯
B♮   c   d   e   f   g   a   b[120]

and whose manual, called the Discant, was constituted like this:

    c♯   d♯   f♯   g♯   b♭   c♯'   d♯'   f♯'   g♯'   b♭'
B♮   c   d   e   f   g   a   b♮   c'   d'   e'   f'   g'   a'   b♮'   c''

The abovementioned instrument in the cathedral at Minden[121] had the same number of pedal and manual keys. About 150 years ago a builder by the name of Heinrich Traxdorff constructed a large instrument at St. Sebaldus in Nuremberg. Its pedal began with A [below tenor c], called (as was customary in the schools at that time) A re,[122] and was laid out like this:

      B♭   c♯   d♯   f♯   g♯
A   B♮   c   d   e   f   g   a   b

while its Discant looked like this:

    c♯   d♯   f♯   g♯   b♭   c♯'   d♯'   f♯'   g♯'   b♭'   c♯''
B♮   c   d   e   f   g   a   b♮   c'   d'   e'   f'   g'   a'   b♮'   c''   d''

This Heinrich Traxdorff built another organ at this same time in the Frauenkirche at Nuremberg, this one without a pedal, which is said to have made a sound like a schalmei. Its keyboard was laid out with this compass:

    c♯   d♯   f♯   g♯   b♭   c♯'   d♯'   f♯'   g♯'
B♮   c   d   e   f   g   a   b♮   c'   d'   e'   f'   g'   a'

This builder called the praestants, the façade pipes, "flutes," in the previously mentioned large instrument at St. Sebald. He also built an Octave stop in

---

119. "The entire monastic community devoutly offers this organ, now completed, to Christ and his mother Mary. At that time Barthold reigned as abbot, and the builder was Andreas, an expert master of rare skill. Let this organ's melodies now resound, that they may ascend to heaven! That you may learn the count of years, know this: 1000 [years], then twice 200, plus 50 and twice 3 (1456) having past, this thing which you should admire was built. Therefore be jubilant in psalms to please the Lord." (from a German translation, provided by Herr Rüdiger Wilhelm, from: Piekarek, Richard, Die Orgel der Aegidienkirche. Eine Historische Studie, Braunschweig (Selbstverlag), 1979.)

120. Perhaps this should be read "bb;" see note 106 above.

121. p. 109 above.

122. according to the medieval hexachord system (deriving from Guido d'Arezzo), which was still taught in some schools during Praetorius's time as a part of the quadrivium.

DE ORGANOGRAPHIA.

darin gemacht; vnd dann den Hintersatz/welchen er/als es noch zu der zeit geheissen worden/ bey vorerwehnten Namen bleiben lassen.

Nach diesem sind andere kommen/ die für vornehme Meister geachtet gewesen; als Friederich Krebs/ vnd Nicolaus Müllner von Wildenberg/ so ihre Pedal vom A biß zum a/ also.

A B ♮ c d D e f g k a

Vnd den Discant auff diese weise gefertiget haben: also.

♮ c d e f g k a ♮ c d e f g a ♮ c d ee ff

Inmassen denn zu solcher zeit noch ein Fürnehmer Orgelmacher/ welcher Conrad Rotenbürger/ der geburt aus Nürnberg eines Beckers Sohn allda/in Beruff vñ Preiß kommen; welcher das grosse Werck im Stifft Bamberg vnd das Werck zun Barfüssern in Nürnberg Anno 1475. gemacht hat: Ist aber eben bey solcher Art/vnd disposition der Clavir vnd Pfeiffwercken geblieben; biß Anno 1493 sind ohngefehr 18. Jahr hernacher/gedachter Conradus Rotenb: das vorgedachte Werck im Stifft Bamberg/welches auch nur im ♮ seinen anfang gehabt/ ergrössert/ vnd angefangen vnter sich mehr Claves vnd dieselben kleiner zumachen; also.

F G A B ♮ c d e f g k a b

Im Discant aber also:

F G A B ♮ c d e f g etc. biß ins ff g g aa

Hat zwar auch nur 8. Bälge gehabt/ aber in der renovation mit 18. Bälgen/ so zehen spannen lang/ vnd 3 spannen breit gewesen/ beleget.

Kurtz zuvor/ als nemblich Anno 1483. ist die grosse Orgel im Thumb zu Erffurt durch Magistrum Steffan von Breßla/ Caspar Melchior/ vnd Michael seine Söhne gefertiget worden: wie ich dann deuselben Dingzeddel vnd Brieff selbsten gesehen vnd gelesen.

Anno 1499. hat Heinricus Crantius die grosse Orgel in der Stiffi Kirchen S. Blasij zu Braunschweig gemacht.

Wie folgende Verß vnter derselben Orgel solches außweisen.

Sub

this organ. He continued to use the term "Hintersatz," however, which was still current at that time.

In subsequent years other builders appeared who were also considered eminent, masters such as Friederich Krebs and Nicolaus Mülner of Mildenberg.[123] Their pedalboards extended from A to a, like this:

$$\text{A} \quad \overset{B\flat}{B\natural} \quad \overset{}{c} \quad \overset{c\sharp}{d} \quad \overset{d\sharp}{e} \quad \overset{}{f} \quad \overset{f\sharp}{g} \quad \overset{g\sharp}{a}$$

and they built the Discant in this manner:

$$B\natural \; c \; \overset{c\sharp}{d} \; \overset{d\sharp}{e} \; \overset{}{f} \; \overset{f\sharp}{g} \; \overset{g\sharp}{a} \; \overset{b\flat}{b\natural} \; \overset{}{c'} \; \overset{c\sharp'}{d'} \; \overset{d\sharp'}{e'} \; \overset{}{f'} \; \overset{f\sharp'}{g'} \; \overset{g\sharp'}{a'} \; \overset{b\flat'}{b\natural'} \; \overset{}{c''} \; \overset{c\sharp''}{d''} \; \overset{d\sharp''}{e''} \; f''$$

At this same time there was another eminent organbuilder, Conrad Rotenbürger, a baker's son born in Nuremberg, who likewise gained an outstanding reputation. He built the large instrument in Bamberg Cathedral, and in 1475 the instrument at the Barfüsserkirche in Nuremberg. The keyboard and pipes of these instruments maintained the same layout.[124] But 18 years later, in 1493, Conrad Rotenbürger enlarged the instrument in Bamberg Cathedral, mentioned above (which had originally begun with b♮), and introduced the practice of making more and smaller keys, like this:

$$\text{F} \; \text{G} \; \text{A} \; \overset{B\flat}{B\natural} \; c \; \overset{c\sharp}{d} \; \overset{d\sharp}{e} \; f \; \overset{f\sharp}{g} \; \overset{g\sharp}{a} \; b\flat$$

and in the Discant thus:

$$\text{F} \; \text{G} \; \text{A} \; \overset{B\flat}{B\natural} \; c \; \overset{c\sharp}{d} \; \overset{d\sharp}{e} \; f \; \text{etc. up to } f'' \; \overset{f\sharp''}{g''} \; a''$$

It originally had only 8 bellows, but during the renovation it was furnished with 18 bellows, ten spans long and 3 spans wide.[125]

Shortly before that time, in the year 1483, the builder Steffan from Breslau, together with his sons Caspar, Melchior, and Michael, constructed the large organ in the cathedral at Erfurt. I myself have read the contract for this instrument.

In the year 1499 Heinrich Kranz built the large organ in the Collegiate Church[126] of St. Blasius at Braunschweig, as the following verse beneath the organ indicates:

---

123. There is a small village with this name north of Berlin, but Praetorius may be speaking here of the much larger and more significant town, Miltenberg on the Main River.
124. Presumably, as mentioned above.
125. In Praetorius's time, measures were far from standardized, but for the sake of comparison (admittedly unreliable), in Braunschweig one "Spann" was 0.220 meter.
126. "Stiftskirche," an endowed monastic or cathedral church. Such churches have often retained their title, although their status may have changed over the course of time.

Sub Organo maiori.

Quæ nos exuperet tabulatu Condita miro
　　　Ordine diverso, dulci sonoq́; modo,
Axe sub arctoo vix credimus Organa pandi,
　　　Inter terrigenas æmula cælicolûm.
Quisquis opus spectas, Hinricus Crantius, atque
　　　Gudenbergensis Hasso magister erat.
Sole quaterdecies Centum terris revoluto,
　　　Vndeciesq́; novem fert ubi Virgo Deum.

Sub minore.

Struxit Ioannes Thomas hæc Organa Christo,
　　　Dædaleo juvenis præditus ingenio.
Ergo Christe tui populi defendito cætum,
　　　ut resonet laudes hîc & ubiq; tuas.

Vnd in diesen jetztgedachten Orgeln seynd die ManualClavir den vnserigen itzigen fast an allem gleich gewesen: denn die Semitonia auch also/wie jetzo / zwischen den Clavibus jnnen gelegen/vnd schwartz oder vnterschiedlich an farben/ nur das sie etwas vnd fast eines Clavis grösser vnd weiter in den Octaven getheilet worden/also/ das sie schwer zugreiffen/tieff hinunter gefallen/vnd zehe zu schlagen gewesen.

Daß ich aber allhier etlicher Clavierdispositiones mit deroselben vberzeichen vnd doppelten Buchstaben/so wol etlicher Meister Namen gesetzet; ist darumb geschehen/damit vnserer Vorfahren Art vnd gebrauch / so dann auch / wie die Inventiones mit der zeit von Jahren zu Jahren zugenommen vnd gestiegen seyn/manchem dadurch desto besser bekandt vnd angenehmer seyn mögen.

Denn so viel den vnterscheidt der Buchstaben von Octaven zu Octaven belanget/ist die erste Octava für sich geblieben; die ander aber mit einem kleinen(⸗) vberzeichnet; vnd die dritte Octava mit doppelten Buchstaben angedeutet worden. Darmit/weil die Clavier anzahl der Clavium jmmer zugenommen / auch ein vernemblicher vnterscheidt observiret werden köndte; Welchen sie aber allzeit von ♮ zu ♮ angefangen haben. Warumb aber/vnd was jhre Gedancken vnd meinung in deme gewesen sein mag/kan man eigentlich nicht wissen.

Mehrge-

Under the larger organ.[127]

Quæ nos exuperet tabulatu Condita miro
  Ordine diverso, dulci sonoq́; modo,
Axe sub arctoo vix credimus Organa pandi,
  Interterrigenas æmula cælicolûm.
Quisquis opus spectas, Hinricus Crantius, atque
  Gudenbergensis Hasso magister erat.
Sole quaterdecies Centum terris revoluto,
  Undeciesq́; novem fert ubi Virgo Deum.[128]

Under the smaller organ.[129]

Struxit Iohannes Thomas haec Organa Christo,
  Dædaleo juvenis præditus ingenio.
Ergo Christe tui populi defendito cætum,
  Ut resonet laudes hîc & ubiq; tuas.[130]

  The manual keyboards in the latter organ are the same as ours in almost every respect. The semitones are located between the [natural] keys, as are today's, and are either black or some other contrasting color. An octave of keys, though, is about one key wider, the keyfall is deep, and the action is stiff, so the instrument is difficult to play.

  The reason I have recorded the layout of various keyboards, together with the pitches they sound (even up to the two-stroke octave), as well as the names of various master builders, is to make the practices of our forebears, and also the inventions that kept increasing year by year, better known and accessible to more people.

  Regarding the distinction between the letters in the various octaves, the first octave remains unaltered, the second has a small sign (') drawn above it, and the third is indicated with double letters.[131] The number of keys in each keyboard has constantly increased, and [over time] one can observe a considerable difference. But at first the octaves all commenced with b♮; it is impossible to know what reason they had for doing this.[132]

---

127. i.e., the main case.
128. "That an organ should appear upon the round earth that should surpass this one, built here in such a marvelous way, in its playing mechanism, stoplist and sweet sound, an organ among the earth's inhabitants that vies with the inhabitants of heaven: this we doubt greatly. Whosoever you may be who behold his instrument, the builder was Heinrich Kranz from Gutenberg [in Hesse?]. When the sun distanced itself from the earth for the 1400th and 99th time, reckoning from when the Virgin bore God."
129. i.e., the Ruckpositiv.
130. "Johannes Thomas, a young man talented as Daedalus, built this instrument for Christ. Come now, Christ, defend the assembly of your people, that they may let your praise resound, here and everywhere." (from a German translation in: Uwe Pape, Orgeldatenbank, 1/7/1997.)
131. These are indeed the indications that Praetorius uses, but this translation has rendered them in conformity with modern usage: C, c, c', c".
132. The earlier method of designating a pipe's octave often began with b♮, e.g. a, b♭, b', c', etc.

Mehrgedachtes Herrn Calvisij Meynung ist diese/ do er an mich also schreibet: Causa esse videtur, quod principium Clavium ex Clave ♮ producitur, & originem traxit ex veterum tetrachordis, quorum Hypate Hypaten, hoc est primum tetrachordum incipiebat ex Clave ♮. Clavis autem A dicitur proslambanomenos, hoc est assumta Clavis, Ita ut ♮ regulariter sit prima ab antiquo.

Das XIV. Capitel.
Von Verenderung vnd Vermehrung der Pfeiffen vnd Stimmen.

So viel nun der aller ersten Art Stimmen vnd Pfeiffen / nemblich / der offenen Principaln Mensur Variation (weil man auch noch vor 150. Jahren von nichts anders / denn von dieser einen Art gewust) an vnterschiedener tieffen vnnd höhe belangen thut; haben vnsere Vorfahren dieselbe (wie wir die jetziger zeit in vnterschiedlichen Stimmen vnd Registern haben) alle in dem einigen jhren grossen Hindersatz oder Mixtur disposition, offt in die 56. Pfeiffen starck vff einem Clave mit den præstanten zusammen gesetzt vnd geordnet. Wie droben im 7. Capitel etwas darvon berichtet worden.

Denn vnsere grosse Subprincipal von 32. Fuß (nach vnserm jetzigen Thon zu rechnen) vnd die grossen Principal 16. ff Thon; Item vnser AEqualPrincipal, oder grosse Octava 8. ff. Octava 4. ff. Quinta 3. ff. Superoctava 2. ff Thon / etc. Wie dann auch vnsere Mixturen; Alles mit einander zusammen / ist in jhrem Hindersatz gestanden / vnd (jedoch jhre Præstanten oder Principalen davon abgerechnet) disponiret gewesen. Wie dann auch / was wir an jetzigenennten einzeln stimmen / durch das erfundene Mittel der Spring- vnd Schleiffladen zum vollen Werck zusammen ziehen können / das haben sie damals durch ein general Canel oder Windführung / so jeder Clavis, dorauff die disponirte Pfeiffen gestanden / gehabt / auff einmal klingend machen / vnnd als eine einzige Stimme zusammen nehmen müssen.

Vnd hat zwar einen grossen Namen / daß man sagt / 56. Pfeiffen vff einem Clave: Wenn mans aber recht ansihet / vnd wir jetziger zeit nur 5. Claves / oder 5. Componirter voces, als ohngefehr g c e̅ g̅ auffm ManualClavir, vnnd im Pedal

The oft-cited Mr. Calvisius has written me about this matter; this is his opinion: "The reason why the earliest keyboards began with B♮ seems to rest with the ancient tetrachords, of which *Hypate Hypaten* (the first tetrachord) began with the note B♮. The note A is called "proslambanomenos," i.e., "added note;" thus from antiquity B♮ was normally the first note."

Chapter XIV.

Change and increase in the number of pipes and stops.

egarding the earliest sort of pipes, open ones of principal scale, large and small (150 years ago there was no other sort of pipe than this): instead of having various stops as we do today, our forebears arranged them all together in the form of one large mixture or "Hindersatz,"[133] often with up to 56 pipes on one note, together with the facade pipes, the praestants. Chapter 7 contains some information about this.[134]

Our large Subprincipal 32' (according to the way we reckon pitch today), the large Principal 16', our Aequal Principal or large Octave 8', then the Octave 4', Quinta 3', Superoctave 2', etc., as well as our mixtures: all of these, united with each other, stood in their Hindersatz (with the exception of their Praestant or (façade) Principal). All of the stops mentioned above that we now can draw together to produce the full organ (stops now separable due to the discovery of the spring and slider chests)—these were at that time placed on one common channel for each note; all sounded together as a single stop.

It sounds impressive to say that 56 pipes sounded on one key. One needs to view the matter in perspective, however. If we simply draw the full organ and play a five-note chord in the manual today, say, c g c' e' g', and add a C in the

---

133. This name may be translated "sitting behind" or "located behind."
134. See p. *99* above.

Pedal einem Clavem C, der denn noch allezeit mehr/ vnd seine absonderliche Baßstimmen/ zugleich in vollem gezogenem Werck nieder drucket/ vnd rechnet auff jedem Cláve, nur gemeiner weise zu reden/ in 4. Stimmen/ als Princ. Octava, Quint, Super Octav: (welche gemeiniglich in grossen vnd kleinern Orgeln zum vollen Wercke gezogen werden) 4. Pfeiffen/ vnd die Mixtur darzu etwan von 6. Pfeiffen/ (denn vnsere Mixturen seynd nur eine Zubusse zum gantzen Werck/ oder andern Stimmen: Doher werden sie offt nach Zimbeln Art repetiret, weil sie auch in den allervntersten grossen Clavibus nicht so gar groß/ sondern klein von Pfeiffen/ wie sie dann auch nicht grösser/ weil die grössern in den Octaven, Principalen, Gedacten vnd Quintadehnen, &c. allbereit vorhanden/ vnnötig seyn) das sind 10. Pfeiffen vff jedem Clave; Also thun gedachte sechs Claves 60. vnd wol 62. Pfeiffen an der Zahl/ die eben so wol zugleich respondiren, als wenn es alles vff einem Clave ohne Schleiffen oder Registern stunde. Wenn ich aber im Pedal mit zweyen Füssen das G vnd c; Im Manual bey der lincken Hand das e g c̄ ē; Vnnd mit der rechten das ḡ c̄ ḡ ē das sind 10. Claves nehme/ vnd rechne zu jederm Clave in den vier obgedachten Stimmen vier Pfeiffen/ vnd in der Mixtur vffs wenigste auch nur 6. Pfeiffen/ wie wol offtermals 10. 12. oder 14. Pfeiffen in der Mixtur vorhanden) so sind es zusammen 100. Pfeiffen/ die zugleich vff einmal intoniren.

Es hat aber vngefehr vor hundert Jahren fast gleich zu der zeit/ als der Herr Lutherus durch Gottes schickung die Christliche Evangelische Lehre/ vnd das reine Wort Gottes an Tag/ vnd herfür bracht/ auch durch sonderbahres eingeben GOttes diese Musicalische Invention sich rechtschaffen herfür gethan/ vnd zu GOttes Lob vnd Preiß so vollnkömmlich an Tag zu kommen/ angefangen/ derogestalt/ daß man/ wie die vnterschiedliche Arten des Klanges/ eine aus der andern zunehmen/ vnd wie dieselbigen auch durch ein gewisses darzu erfundenes Mittel der Spring- vnd Schleiffladen/ zum Variation mögen gebracht werden/ hat erkennen lernen. Vnd gleich wie die heilige Schrifft im Bapstthumb so lange zeit verborgen/ vnd nur einen gemeinen Larven gleich geblieben; Also auch die Musica, vnd derselben Instrumenta vnd Opera fast jmmer in einem schlechten vnnd bald nichtigen Stande beruhet hat; Biß daß sie/ wie jetzgedacht/ durch Gottes gnädigen väterlichen Willen erhaben/ vnd gleich aus einer schwartzen verdunckelten Wolcken wieder herfür kommen vnd erhellet/ vnd bey dieser vnser zeit von Tag zu Tage also hoch gestiegen vnd verbessert ist/ daß es nunmehr fast nicht wol höher wird kommen können.

Vnd ist nun die erste Enderung der Pfeiffen/ daß man die offene Pfeiffen oben zuge-

pedal (which has its own independent pedal pipes), and figure that each note has the usual 4 stops, Principal, Octave, Quint, and Superoctav, plus the mixture with, say, 6 ranks, that makes 10 pipes on each note. (Our mixtures are simply a complement to the full organ, or to other stops. Therefore they often repeat, in the manner of a Zimbel. Their lowest bass notes contain only small pipes; big ones are unnecessary, since they are already on hand in the Octaves, Principals, Gedackts, Quintadenas, etc.) Thus these 6 notes contain 60 or even 62 pipes. They all sound as if they were on one single key, without sliders or stops. Suppose that I play C and c in the pedal with two feet, however, and then play e g c e' in the manual with the left hand and g' c' g" e" with the right (a total of 10 keys). Figuring that 4 pipes sound with each key (as described above) plus at least 6 in the mixture (though there are often 10, 12, or 14), then there are 100 pipes sounding together.

About 100 years ago, however (at almost the same time that Mr. Luther through the providence of God expounded the Protestant Christian doctrine, the pure word of God), musical inventiveness began to distinguish itself mightily, through the extraordinary inspiration of God, and to perfect itself to God's praise. Organ builders learned how to separate the various types of sound one from another, and how to create a variety of sounds, specifically by means of the spring and slider chest. Just as the Holy Scriptures remained so long hidden in an insignificant, infantile state during the years of papal rule, so also the art of music, both its instruments and its compositions, remained mired in a wretched state, near extinction, until (as just mentioned) exalted by the grace of God it came radiantly forth as if out of a dark cloud. In our time it has risen to such a height of perfection that it can scarcely be improved upon.

zugedäckt vnd versucht hat/ was sie vor einen Klang vnd Laut von sich geben möchten; Daher die Art der Gedacten Pfeiffen entstanden.

Aus diesem ist stracks fort gefahren/ vnd die menge der vberaus vielen Pfeiffen in dem zuvor offt benandten Hindersatze zertheilet worden. Als daß man die Pfeiffen/ so eine Octava höher/ vber die præstanten oder förder Pfeiffen gewesen/ von der Mixtur heraus genommen/ auff ein absonderlich Register vnd Schleiffen gebracht / vnd Octavam genennet. Deßgleichen die Pfeiffen/ so eine Quinta höher/ Als diese Octava am Laut gestanden/ Auch also abgesondert/ vnd Quintam geheissen.

Ebenmessig die Rauschpfeiffen/ so sie anfangs dieser newen Invention für gar gut erachtet/ vnd von zweyen Pfeiffen/ als nemblich/ der jetztgedachten Quint, vnnd einer kleinen Octaven von 4. Fußthon zusammen gesetzet; Daß also diese zwo Pfeiffen (welche allwege eine Quartam, als / ut·fa, re sol, mi la, resoniren vnd von sich geben·) vff einem Clave gestanden: Welches dann/ wenn einer groben Art der offnen vnd Gedacten Stimmen dazu gezogen wird/ recht daher rauschet.

Vnd ist jhnen gleichwol jhre Mixtur, wegen vorangezogener Menge der Pfeiffen starck gnugsam verblieben/ also / daß sie zu der zeit die Mixtur gar alleine auff eine sondere Lade gesetzet / vnd den Wind durch den Ventil ab- vnd zugelassen; Vnnd zu derselben Mixtur nur das Principal alleine gezogen / welches denn das volle Werck genennet worden/ vnd auch gewesen ist: Aus Vrsachen/ dieweil die Mixtur ein Octav, Quint, Snperoctav, vnd ander mehr noch kleiner Stimmen in sich gehabt/ so hat man nicht mehr/ dann das Principal, als das Fundament dazu nehmen dürffen. Wann nun die Mixtur durch das darzugehörige Ventiel oder Windversperrung wiederumb darvon abgesondert; So hat man alsdenn vff der förder Schleiffladen die Verenderungen mit der Octaven, Quinten, Kleinoctav, Gedacten, Zimbeln vnd Rauschpfeiffen gehabt.

Wie denn gleichsfalls ordentliche Bälge mit rechtmessigem Winde vnnd Gewichte/ vorhundert vnd neuntzen Jaren ohngefehr auch zum Gebrauch erfunden worden seyn: Welche aber gleichwol/ noch wie vor etlichen hundert Jahren mit Lohegaren Roß- vnd Ochsenhäutten vberzogen gewesen/ vnnd alle fünff Jahr haben eingeschmieret werden müssen.

Vor neuntzig Jahren ist man den Sachen aber näher kommen/ vnnd seynd zwar die Mixturen auff jhrer abgesonderten Laden vnnd Sperr Ventil geblieben; Aber da seynd mehr Stimmen/ als nemlich die zugespitzte Pfeiffen/ so sie Spitz-

P ij   Flötten

Open pipes were first altered by stopping them at the top, to test what sort of sound they might then produce. That is how stopped pipes originated.

Builders then immediately turned their attention to separating the great number of pipes in the oft-mentioned Hindersatz. They removed from the mixture the rank of pipes that sounds an octave above the Praestant, and gave it its own separate stop and slider; this they called "Octave." They also separated off the rank of pipes that sounds a fifth above the Octave, and called it "Quint."

The same process produced the Rauschpfeife, recognized as excellent from the moment it was invented. It consists of two pipes per note, namely the Quint (just mentioned) and a higher Octave at 2' pitch,[135] together on the same stop. These two pipes always sound the interval of a fourth: ut-fa, re-sol, mi-la. When a lower open or stopped rank is drawn with it, it produces a pronounced rustling effect.[136]

Because it still had so many ranks of pipes, the mixture nevertheless remained large enough to keep it all alone on its own separate chest, with the wind turned on and off by means of a ventil. Only the principal was drawn with this mixture, and these two were then called "the full organ," because the mixture still contained Octaves, Quints, Superoctaves, and other smaller ranks; thus it was unnecessary to draw anything other than the Principal with it. When the mixture was shut off by means of its ventil, then a variety of stops was available on the front slider-chest: Octaves, Quints, Superoctave, Gedackts, Zimbels, Rauschpfeifen.

Proper bellows, with weights providing well-regulated wind, likewise came into use about 119 years ago, although these were still covered with tanned horse- and oxhides (as they had been already for hundreds of years). They had to be recoated every five years.

Further improvements were conceived ninety years ago. Mixtures were placed on their own separate chests with cut-out ventils. New stops were then dis-

---

135. Praetorius's text reads "von 4. Fußton," and there is no entry among the Errata to correct it; but on p. 130 Praetorius again describes the Rauschpfeife as consisting of a Quint 3' and an Octave 2', drawn together.
136. "Rauschpfeife" is translated "rustling-pipe."

Flötten genennet/ vnd etwas von Schnarrwercken erfunden: Vnd seynd auch Spanbälge gearbeitet worden.

So hat man auch zu der zeit die Invention der RückPositiffen speculiret; Wie deren grossen Orgelwercke vnter andern zu Leipzig in der Pauliner Kirchen an jetzo noch eins stehet/ welches Principal im Pedal von 16. ff. Thon /im Manual von 8: ff. Thon gewesen; hat Grobgedacht vff 8. ff./ Octava von 4. ff. Superoctava 2. ff. Quinta 3. ff. Rauschpf. Zimbeln/ Mixtur 12. Fach auff einer besondern Laden.

Im RückPositiff; Principal 4. ff. Mittel Gedackt 4. ff. Zimbeln/ klein Octävelein/ vnd ein groß Blechen Kälber Regal. Sein Manual Clavir vom D angefangen/ vnd in zweybestrichnem c̄ sich endet; Sein Pedal vom C zum c gemachet/ vnd mit 12. Spanbälgen belegt gewesen; hat auch in der Brust ein Messing Regall, vnd im Pedal Posaunen gehabt.

Zu der zeit sind dieser Art Wercke viel/ beydes klein vnd groß gebawet worden/ Wie denn zu S. Iohann in Göttingen auch ein klein Werck in der höhe schwebend gefunden/ vnd auch noch gebraucht wird/ welches feine liebliche Stimmwercke/ vnd auch gute Trommeten hat.

Inmassen zu Northausen in Sanct Blasij Kirchen/ Eins mit dreyen Manual-Claviren gestanden/ vnd newlich abgebrochen worden. Das eine Clavir hat das grosse Principal vnd Mixtur alleine gehabt: Die Mixtur hat man abziehen/ das Principal aber (ob es wol vor sich alleine/ wenn die Mixtur darvon abgezogen/ zu gebrauchen) gar nicht abgezogen werden können/ vnnd also stets im Klange blieben. Das andere Clavir hat auch seine eigene Lade/ darauff die andern Stimmen/ als die Gedackten/ Octav, Quint, Superoctav, Zimbeln/ etc. gesetzet gewesen. Das dritte Clavir ist zum Rückpositiff gebraucht worden.

Vnd also haben sie alsbald mit der Invention der Register vnd enderung der Stimmen/ wunderliche Meynungen anfangs/ versucht; Jedoch daß diese Meynung gar gut zum langem reinen Klange wehrhafft befunden worden. Es hat aber dieses Werck ein Principal von 16. ff./ vnd seine Clavir im F angefangen/ vnnd ist/ wie fast die meiste do mahlige Orgeln vmb einen Thon höher/ als vnser jetziger Cammerthon gestanden; Wie denn/ was den Thon belangend/ niemals etwas gewisses von jhnen in acht genommen worden.

Also ist diese Invention, daß die Mixtur jhre eigene Laden mit einer Windversperrunge/ vnd das ander Pfeiffwerck auch seine eigene Laden mit Schleiffen gehabt hat/ vnd also eins dem andern den Wind nicht nehmen oder rauben können/ Allezeit für gut vnd beständig befunden. Wie denn derselben Orgelwercke/ ob sie schon
vor

covered as well, namely the tapered pipes, called Spitzflöten, and various reeds. Wedge bellows were also built.

At that time someone conceived the idea of inventing the Ruckpositiv. One large organ (among others) from this time still stands in the Paulinerkirche in Leipzig; it has a Principal 16' in the pedal and 8' in the manual, as well as a Grobgedackt at 8', Octave 4', Superoctave 2', Quinta 3', Rauschpfeife, Zimbel, and a twelve-rank mixture on a separate chest.

In the Ruckpositiv it has a Principal 4', Mittelgedackt 4', Zimbel, little Octavlein, and a large Kälberregal[137] of plated metal. The compass of its manual keyboard is D - c", of its pedal C - c', and it is provided with 12 wedge bellows. It also has a Messingregal[138] in the Brustwerk, and a Posaune in the pedal.

Many instruments of this sort, both large and small, were built at that time. For example, at St. Johannes in Göttingen there is a small instrument suspended high up under the vaulting,[139] still in use, that has some elegant, gentle stops, and a good trumpet as well.

Another such instrument stood in the St. Blasius Church at Nordhausen, with three manuals; it has recently been torn down. The first manual had only the large Principal and the Mixture. It was possible to retire the Mixture, but not the Principal, which was always ready to sound (it could of course be used by itself when the Mixture was retired). The second manual had its own chest, on which the other stops were placed, such as Gedackt, Octav, Quint, Superoktav, Zimbel, etc. The third manual operated the Rückpositiv.

When they first started to experiment with varieties of stops, builders tried out some quite remarkable notions, but always with the goal of achieving a good, pure tone.[140] This instrument had a Principal 16' on the manual, which began at F. As with most organs of that time, it was tuned one step higher than our present chamber pitch. Regarding pitch, however, there has never been a universal standard observed by all builders.

Thus this innovation gained general approval, that the Mixture should have its own chest with a cut-off ventil, and the rest of the pipes should also have their own chest with sliders; thus one could not rob wind from the other. And so

---

137. "Calves-Regal" (because of the bleating sound it produced?)

138. "Brass-regal;" see Theatrum Instrumentorum XXXVIII, no.14, "Messing Regahl 8 foot."

139. i.e., a swallow's-nest organ

140. This seems to be a parenthetical remark that applies to all the instruments Praetorius is discussing. With the sentence following, he seems to return to describing the organ at Nordhausen.

vor 60. 70. vnd mehr Jahren gebawet worden/ doch an jetzo noch gar gut am Klang/ vnd beständig seyn/ vnd gebraucht werden.

Als/ daß annoch stehende alte kleine Werck im Dohm zu Magdeburg/ so eine Quarta höher/ denn das jetzt erbawte grosse newe ist.

Item zu Aschersleben; Vffm Hause Mansfelde/ etc. vnd derer mehr/ sogar schön vnd gut Pfeiffwerck vnd Laden dieser Manier haben/ vnd noch gut zu gebrauchen seyn.

Die besten aber/ so vnter dergleichen Wercken seyn/ hat ein Münch/ mit Namen M. Michael gebawet/ der denn das jetztgedachte Magdeburgische mit sonderlichem fleiß gemacht vnd verwahret hat/ darinn auch nur Principal vnd Mixtur zum vollen Wercke gezogen wird/ weil die Mixtur jhre grobe Fundament Stimmen/ als Octav, Quint, vnd Superoctaven in sich hat.

Von solcher Invention ist es nun gar auff die vnserige jetzige Art kommen/ also/ daß die Mixtur nun nicht mehr alleine/ sondern zugleich mit den andern Pfeiffwercken vff eine Laden geordnet/ vnnd andere Stimmen darzu genommen werden.

Hierüber sind nun vieler vnd mancherley Arten Stimmwercke an grösse vnnd kleine/ so wol an vnterschiedlichen Klange/ beydes im Flöt- vnd Schnarrwercken erfunden worden. Vnter andern aber die Gemshörner/ Rohrflötten/ vnd Quintadehnen/ die Sordunen, Rancketen vnd andere stille Schnarrwerck; Wie auch die Gedäcten vntersätze/ vnd dergleichen Stimmen mehr bey Menschen Leben an Tag gebracht. Jnmassen denn der Tremulant mit jetztgedachten newen Stimmen auch herfür kommen ist.

Man hat sich aber von 50. Jahren her sehr der Lieblichkeit beflissen/ sonderlich in den Niederlanden mehr/ als dieser Orter: Wie dann vnter andern ein Meister/ Gregorius Vogel vor 51. jaren noch gelebt/ welcher ein sehr lieblich Werck/ von offen vnd zugedäckten Pfeiffen/ vnd Schnarrwerck zu S. Johannes in Magdeburg/ vnd sonsten in der Marck/ Auch in Braunschweig zu S. AEgidien vnd S. Marten gefertiget hat; der denn sonderlich den Zirckel in Pfeiffen Mensur fundamentaliter muß verstanden haben.

Vnd ist also von einem Jahr zum andern die Kunst in verfertigung der Orgeln so hoch gestiegen/ daß sich billich darüber zu verwundern: Vnd Gott dem Allmächtigen vnd alleine weisen/ nicht gnugsam zu dancken/ daß er den Menschen solche grosse Gnade vnd Gaben von oben herab so gnädiglich verliehen/ die ein solch perfectum, ja fast perfectissimum opus vnd Instrumentum Musicum, als die Orgel ist/ (die da/ wie im anfang erwehnet/ fürnehmlich für allen andern Musicalischen Instrumen-

P iij

organs like this, even though they were built 60, 70 or more years ago, are still in use; they are still in good condition and produce a very fine sound.

One example of this is the small, old instrument still standing in Magdeburg Cathedral, that is pitched a fourth higher than the newly built large instrument.

Another is at Aschersleben in the residence of the Counts of Mansfeld, and there are yet others as well that have beautifully made pipes and chests of this type, and are still quite playable.

The best examples of this sort of instrument, however, were built by a monk by the name Master Michael; it was he who constructed the abovementioned instrument at Magdeburg with extraordinary diligence. This instrument's full organ consisted of only the Principal and the Mixture, because the Mixture contained all the basic ranks, such as Octav, Quint, and Superoctav.

These developments were the immediate precursors of the kind of instruments built today, but now the Mixture is no longer on a separate chest, but is arranged together with the other ranks on a single chest. Other stops[141] are also placed on this same chest.

Furthermore, by now all sorts of stops of various timbres, flues and reeds both large and small, have been invented. Up to now, these include among others the Gemshorn, Rohrflöte, and Quintadena, the Sordun, Ranket, and other quiet reed stops, as well as the stopped Untersatz. The tremulant also appeared at the same time as these new stops just mentioned.

Beginning 50 years ago, builders became very zealous in the pursuit of gentle, charming sounds, more so in the Netherlands than in this area. Among others there was a Master Gregorius Vogel, still alive 51 years ago, who built a very lovely instrument with open and stopped [flue] pipes and reeds at St. Johannes in Magdeburg, and at various places in the Mark (Brandenburg), as well as at St. Aegidius and St. Martini in Braunschweig. He must have had an especially thorough understanding of the use of the compass in determining pipe scales.

And so from one year to the next, the art of building organs has risen to such heights as rightly deserve to be admired. And the Almighty and Only-wise God can never be given sufficient thanks for granting men, out of his boundless grace, such a gracious gift as the ability to build such a perfect (indeed one might also say "most perfect") musical instrument as is the organ (which, as was men-

---

141. i.e. flutes and other ranks that are not part of the principal chorus.

strumenten, welche meistentheils in diesem einzigen Wercke können begriffen/ vernommen vnd gehöret werden/ billich gerühmet vnd herfür gezogen wird) dergestalt disponiren vnd verfertigen; Vnd die auch daſſelbige dergestalt tractiren, manibus pedibusq; zwingen können/ daß Gott im Himmel dadurch gelobet/ der Gottesdienst gelehret/ vnd die Menschen zur Christlicher Andacht bewogen vnd erweckt werden.

Vnd diß sey also von alten Orgeln gnug vor dißmal.

Vierdter

tioned at the outset, takes pride of place above all other musical instruments, most of which can be incorporated into this single instrument[142]), and to play it with hands and feet in such a way that God in Heaven may thereby be praised, His worship adorned, and human beings moved and inspired to Christian devotion.

𝔗his description of old organs will suffice
for the present.

---

142. See p. 85 above.

Vierdter Theil
dieses
TOMI SECUNDI:
Von unsern jetzigen newen Orgeln.

So begreifft in sich vier Capitel.

Im I. wird gehandelt.

Von den rechten Namen vnd Titul der Orgeln/ nach ihrer Proportion vnd grösse der Principaln.

Im II. Capitel.

Von allerley Art/ vnd mancherley Namen der Stimmen in den Orgeln/ wie dieselbe nach ihrem Laut oder Klang/ vnd dero sonderbaren Eigenschafft recht eingenommen vnnd verstanden: Auch wie solche Stimmen vnterschiedlich/ aus der länge jhrer Corporum generaliter, vnd in gemein nach den Füssen/ oder Zahl der Füsse in ihrem vnterschiedenen tieffern vnd höhern Thon gerechnet werden mögen: Mit mehrerm vmb fernerm Bericht/ was bey jeder Stimme in specie vnd besonders zu wissen von nöthen sey.

Als:

Von der Mensur oder lenge der Pfeiffen:

Auch wie die Pfeiffen von einander vnterschieden vnnd abgetheilet werden/ mit beygesetzter Vniversal Tabell.

Da

The Fourth Part of
VOLUME TWO:
Concerning today's new organs,[1]

Contains four
chapters

Chapter I deals with

the proper names and titles of organs, according to the sizes of their Principals.

Chapter II

treats all the various names of organ stops, how they are to be properly understood according to their particular tonal characteristics, as well as how the pitch levels of these stops may be calculated in general according to the length of their bodies, commonly referred to as their number of feet; it further reports on what is necessary to know specifically about each stop,
such as:
the scale,[2] or length of the pipes;
as well as how the different pipes may be categorized, together with an appended General Table.

---

1. *Theatrum Instrumentorum*, Plate II, depicts such a "new organ," with three manuals (one a Rückpositiv) and pedal.
2. See footnote 103, p. 100 above.

Da dann

1. Von offenen Stimmwercken/ so Principaln Art vnnd Mensur seynd.
2. Von Holtzflöitten vnd derselben Eigenschafft.
3. Von Gemßhörnern/ Plock= Spitz= vnd Flachflöitten.
4. Von Quintadehnen= Nachthorn= vnd Querflöitten.
5. Von Gedacten allerley Art.
6. Von Rohrflöitten.
7. Von offenen Schnarrwercken.
8. Von Gedackten Schnarrwercken.

Jm III. Capitel.

Vnterricht/ Wie man Schnarrwercke in den Orgeln/ So wol auch absonderlich die Regalwerck vnd andere Instrumenta, als Clavicymbeln, Spinetten vnd dergleichen von sich selbst recht vnd rein accordiren vnd einstimmen könne: Jm gleichen/ welcher massen die andern Pfeiffen nachzustimmen/ oder im stimmen nachzuhelffen.

Jm IV. Capitel.

Wie sich die Kirchen/ vnd die jenige/ so vnserm HErrn GOtt zu Ehren ein Orgelwerck in ihren Kirchen setzen vnd bawen lassen wollen/ wol fürzusehen haben/ daß sie sich erfahrnen vnd berühmten Orgelmachern vmbthun/ damit sie nicht vmb eines geringen Vortheils willen/ denn sie bey etlichen vnerfahrnen vnnd allererst anfahenden Orgelmachern zu erhalten vermeinen/ berückt: Auch beydes, den Erfahrnen vnnd vnerfahrnen wol vbersetzt/ vnd zuweilen gleichwol mit einem vnbeständigen wandelbaren Werck/ daran man jährlich zu flicken vnd zu stücken hat/ versehen werden.

Vom

and then
1. about open pipes, those of Principal scale
2. about the characteristics of the Hohlflöte
3. about the Gemshorn, Block-, Spitz- and Flachflöte
4. about the Quintadena-, Nachthorn- and Querflöte
5. about all the types of Gedackts
6. about the Rohrflöte
7. about open reed stops
8. about covered reed stops.

Chapter III

provides an explanation about how to tune organ reeds purely,[3] with a separate discussion about tempering Regals and other instruments such as harpsichords, spinetts, and the like, as well as how subsequently to tune the other pipes[4] by oneself.[5]

Chapter IV

tells how churches, and those who want to have an organ built in their churches to the glory of God, should take care to make inquiries about experienced and reputable organbuilders, so that they are not cheated by choosing inexperienced, novice builders, thinking they can get a cheaper price; also how to avoid being taken in by either experienced or novice builders, and nevertheless at times ending up with an unstable, unreliable instrument that needs mending and patching every year.

---

3. Praetorius is referring to setting a temperament within an octave of pipes.
4. i.e., how to transfer the temperament to the other octaves of pipes.
5. i.e., without an organbuilder.

Das I. Capitel.
Vom rechten Namen der OrgelWercke/ nach ihrer Grösse.

Jeweil folgends zum offtern der Fußthon gedacht wird: Als ist sonderlich Cantoribus in acht zu nehmen/ daß 8. ft. Thon/ die rechte Chormasse sey/ welche die natürliche höhe vnd tieffe hat. Vnd müssen nach diesem die andern also wol im dupliren als halbiren geachtet werden.

Denn so offt diese Zahl dupliret wird/ klinget die Pfeiffe eine Octav niedriger: So sie halbiert wird/ eine Octav höher.

Als zum Exempel 16. ft. Thon klinget eine Octav niedriger/ vnd 32. zwey Octaven niedriger/ als 8. ft. Thon oder Chormasse.

Im gegentheil 4. f. Thon klinget eine Octav: 2. ft. zwey Octav: 1. ft. drey Octaven höher denn Chormasse/ wie in folgenden Abrissen zu ersehen.

16. ft. Thon.   8. ft. Thon.   4. ft. Thon.   2. ft. Thon.   1. ft. Thon.

Ferner ist zu mercken/ daß die Orgelwercke nach Füssen genennet werden: Klein/4. ft. Thon: Dessen Principal vnterste Clavis im Manual vnd Pedal.

Mittel oder Chormässig von 8. ft. Thon: Dessen Principal vnterste Clavis im Manual vnd Pedal.

Groß

Chapter I
About naming organs properly
according to their size.

ince subsequently [in this treatise] pitch is often cited in feet, cantors need especially to note that 8' is the proper unison pitch that lies at the correct pitch level [for singing]. The other pitch levels have to be figured according to this one, both the lower ones that double in size and the higher ones that halve.

Whenever this number [8'] is doubled, the pipe sounds an octave lower; whenever it is halved, it sounds an octave higher.

For example, 16' pitch sounds an octave lower than 8' or unison pitch, and 32' two octaves lower.

On the other hand, 4' pitch sound an octave higher than unison, 2' two octaves higher, and 1' three octaves higher, as shown in the following diagram:

16' pitch   8' pitch   4' pitch   2' pitch   1' pitch

Moreover, take note that organs are named according to "feet:" a small one is at 4' pitch, and its lowest manual and pedal note sounds:

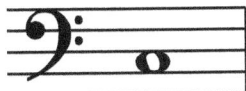

A medium or unison organ is at 8' pitch; its lowest manual and pedal note is:

Groß von 16. fi. dessen Principal vnterste Clavis im Manual vnd Pedal ist eine Octav von der vórigen tieffer. Wird aber eines Principalen von 2. fi. Thon gedacht/ dessen vnterste Clavis ist

Wo aber von 1. fi. 2.

32. fi. Thon aber ist eine Octav tieffer / denn 16. fi. aber eines gar vnnatürlichen vnd vnvernemblicher Soni vnd Klanges.

Welcher gestalt nun vnsere Vorfahren ihre Orgeln intituliret vnd genennet haben/ davon ist in vorhergehenden III. Theil von alten Orgeln gnugsamer Bericht geschehen.

Zu vnserer jetzigen zeit aber seynd fürnemblich dreyerley art Orgelwercke/ derer Namen recht zu nennen vnd zu gedencken seyn. Vnd solches dahero/ weil man dreyerley Principalen Art vnd grösse hat/ so fornen an ins Werck zum zierde gesetzet/ vnd die structuren oder gehäuse darnach proportioniret werden: Denn wie man sagt/ à potiori parte fit denominatio.

1. Vnd ist der ersten Art Name groß Principal; Welcher von den Orgelmachern wegen seines Corporis lenge vnd tieffen Lauts von 16. Fuß Thon genennet wird. In welchem Orgelwerck nu ein solchs Principal zum Manual zu gebrauche fornen an stehet/ dessen rechter Name wird ein groß Principalwerck genant: Vnd ist doselbsten die Großoctava von 8. Fuß Thon: Die Octava von 4. Fuß Thon. Vnd werden bißweilen in solchen Wercken im Pedal Subprincipal- oder Subgedacte Bässe von 32. Fuß Thon gefunden.

2. Der andern Art Name aber ist AEqual, oder wie es andere nennen mittel- oder Chor Principal: Welcher billich darumb also heisset/ dieweil solcher an der tieffe vnd höhe/ mit der Menschen Stimme vberein komme; Vnd werden dieselben Principal.

vmb

A large organ is at 16' pitch, and its lowest manual and pedal note is an octave lower than the one above. If however a Principal 2' is meant, its lowest note is:

If at 1' pitch, [the lowest note will be:]

32' pitch is an octave lower than 16', but it produces a very unnatural and imperceptible sound.

Part III above, about old organs has provided a sufficient report about how our forebears named their organs.[6]

Nowadays, however, there are three principal types of organs. They should be given their proper names, because there are three categories or sizes of Principals placed decoratively in the façade, according to which the case is proportioned. For as is said, *à potiori parte fit denominatio*.[7]

The first type of name is "large Principal," which organbuilders call "16' pitch" because of the length of its body and its low pitch. If such a Principal were to stand in the façade of a manual division of an organ, its proper name would be a "large Principal instrument." In such an instrument the Grossoctave is at 8' pitch and the Octave at 4' pitch. At times a Subprincipal or Subgedackt Bass 32' is found in the pedal of such instruments.

The name of the second type is "unison-" or, as others call it, "medium-" or "Chorprincipal." Its name is appropriate, because it corresponds in pitch to the hu-

---

6. Part III, Chapter X, pp. 104-6.
7. "Let the name be determined by the foremost part."

vmb jres Corporis Lenge vnd Lauts willen zu 8. Fußthon gerechnet. Wo nu etwan ein solch Principal zum Manual zu gebrauchen/ im Werck stehend gefunden/ wird dasselbige vngeachtet bißweilen auch ein GroßPrincipalbaß von 16. fi. Thon im Pedal, auch wol in den SäitThörmen verhanden seyn möchte: ein AequalPrincipalwerck geheissen/ vnd ist die Octava von 4. die klein Octava von 2. Fuß Thon.

Die dritte Art ist ein Octav- oder klein Principal, vnnd hat solches an seiner Corporis lenge vnd laut 4. Fuß am Thon. In welchen Wercken nun solcher Principal grösse gefunden wird/ dieselbige seynd billich der Mensur vnd Ordnung nach klein Principal Werck zu nennen; Vnd ist doselbsten die kleine Octava vor 2. Fuß/ vnd die Superoctav 1. Fuß Thon: Welche sonsten Siffloit genennet wird.

Vnd ob sich zwar ein Orgelmacher offte nach dem Ort vnd Raum richten/ vnd der grösse seiner Structuren zusetzen oder abbrechen muß; Daher denn vielmahl der Principalen gröste Pfeiffen nicht zum Gesichte/ weil es des Corporis grösse nicht leiden kan/ herfür gesetzt; Bißweilen auch geschicht/ daß die Principalen mit noch grösseren Pfeiffen/ jedoch allein pro forma ersetzet/ vnd der Gehäuse grösse damit erfüllet werden; So muß es doch bey obbeschriebenen dreyen Arten/ als 16. 8. vnd 4. Fuß Thon Principal bleiben vnd beruhen.

Es werden aber diese beschriebene Namen/ wie jetzt gedacht/ allein zu oder nach den ManualClaviren gerechnet: Sonsten seynd grosse PrincipalWercke zu finden/ welcher PedalPrincipal Baß/weil im Manual das Principal 16. Fuß Thon ist/schon 32. Fuß Thon gesetzet wird/ vnd dieses erfolget. Wenn die disposition der Structuren also/ daß die sonderlichen Bässe vff die Säiten neben das Manualwerck kommen/ geordnet werden. Vnd dieweil dann diese grösse SubPrincipaln nicht natürlich oder müglich im Manual zu gebrauchen/ sondern alleine ins Pedal zum Baß gehören/vnd von wenig Orgelmachern gearbeitet werden; Kan auch ein Werck nicht von solchem Basse im Pedal/ sondern vom Manual seinen gebürlichen Namen haben.

Ob auch etzliche gar kleine Wercklein/ derer Principal nur von 2. Fuß Thon gefunden werden/ so gehören doch solche nicht vnter der Orgelwercken Zahl der Namen/ sondern allein vnter die Disposition der Positiff: Aus Vrsachen/ weil sie gemeiniglich auch andere gröbere Stimmen zu ihren Fundamentis, als Gedact/oder Quintadehn von 4. auch wol von 8. Fuß Thon haben/ vnd dahero Groß- oder Kirchenpositiff/ auch klein Octaven Principal Wercklein genennet werden. Wie denn billich ein jeder Orgelmacher dahin sehen solte/ daß seine dispositiones, als an der geösse vnd Thon sein ordine disponiret würden/ damit man sich/ gleich wie in andern Instrumenten nach derer Namen Laut vnd disposition der Stimmen zu achten hette.

Q ij

man voice. This Principal is considered to be at 8' pitch due to the length of its body and its sound. Where such a Principal is found standing in the manual Hauptwerk, despite the fact that a large Principal at 16' pitch may sometimes stand in the pedal side towers, the instrument is called a "unison Principal instrument;" its Octave is at 4', and its small Octave at 2'.

The third type is an "octave-" or "little Principal," and is at 4' pitch, corresponding to the sounding length of its body. Instruments in which this size Principal are found are properly designated as "small-Principal instruments." In them are found a small Octave 2' and Superoctave 1', also called "Siffl[ö]it."

The situation and space often dictate that organbuilders must increase or diminish the size of the case. Thus the largest pipes of the Principal are often not placed in the façade, since it cannot accommodate their length. Sometimes it also happens that the Principal is augmented with even larger pipes, just to fill up the case, for the sake of proportion. Nevertheless there remain only the three types [of instruments] described above: 16', 8', and 4'.

The names that have just been described, however, are determined solely by the size of the manual Principals. For there are in fact large Principal instruments which have a 32' pedal Principal (since the Hauptwerk Principal is at 16'). This happens when the structural layout is such that the pipes especially designated for the pedal are arranged on either side of the Hauptwerk. Since such large Subprincipals are not suited for use in the Hauptwerk, but belong only in the pedal, to sound the bass notes, and since only a few organbuilders build them, an instrument cannot rightly take its name from them, but from the Hauptwerk [Principal].

There are also some very small instruments whose Principals are only of 2' pitch; however, these are not actually considered to be among those named "organs," but belong to the category of positivs.[8] The reason for this is that [such Principals] are normally undergirded by other lower stops, such as a Gedackt or Quintatön of either 4' or even 8' pitch, and so take the name "large-" or "church-positiv" or "little octave Principal instruments." Every organbuilder ought to see to it that his instruments are properly categorized according to the size and pitch [of their principals], so that they are always identified by the size and pitch of their stops, just like other instruments.

---

8. See *Theatrum Instrumentorum*, Plate I, an "old positiv with one set of pipes and three different stops, i.e., three separate voices at 2', 1 ½ ' [i.e., 1 ⅓'], and 1' pitch." Plate IV also depicts a small positiv.

Das II. Capitel.
Von allerley Art/ vnd mancherley Namen der
Stimmen in Orgeln/ wie dieselbe nach jhrem Laut oder Klang/ vnd dero sonderbaren Eigenschafft recht genennet: Auch wie solche Stimmen vnterschiedlich/ aus jhrer Corporum lenge/ generaliter nach den Füssen/ oder Zahl der Füsse in jhrem vnterschiedenem tieffern vnd höherm Thon gerechnet werden. Mit mehrerm Bericht/ was bey jeder Stimme in specie zu wissen von nöthen sey.

Es hier solte nun wol von der Mensur an den Pfeiffen nach der lenge der Corporum etwas gesagt werden: Weil aber solches vor die Orgelmacher allein gehöret/ist derselben allhier zu gedencken vnnötig.

Doch gleich wol kan dieses hierbey obiter angedeutet werden: Daß ein Principal vnd alles offen Pfeiffwerck am Corpore vnd der Mensur lenge/ (welche nicht von dem vnterfusse/ der nur eine Zuführung des Windes ist/ sondern von dem Labio oder Mundloche/ darvon das OberCorpus klingend gemacht wird/ jren anfang hat) fast allezeit gleich so viel Füsse hat/ als von Laut oder Thon gesagt wird. Wiewol derselben lenge auch vngleich/ vnd eine vor der andern/ wegen der vngleichen weiten/ vmb etwas (doch gar ein geringes/ also/ daß man es an den kleinen Pfeiffen kaum mercken kan) verkürtzer werden muß: Sintemal es die Vernunfft giebet/ daß/ wann einem dinge an der breite zugegeben wird/demselben an der lenge hinwiederumb etwas abgebrochen werden müsse/ also auch/ so an der weite abgebrochen wird/ muß an der lenge zugesetzt werden.

Mit den Gedacten Stimmwercken aber hat es nach dem Namen oder Zahl der Füsse eine andere Meynung vnd Verstand. Denn ob wol solche GedactePfeiffe juster Principalen weitte oder dicke im Circkel/ auch bißweilen vmb ein geringes weiter ist; So ist sie doch noch nicht gar halb so lang. Als zum Exempel: Die Principal-Pfeiffe ist 8. Fuß Thon/ vnd hat auch 8. Fuß an der Corpuslenge: Die Gedactpfeiff ist zwar auch 8. Fuß Thon/ vnd an der Corpus weitte/ (liceat sic loqui cum artifice) fast mit dem Principal gleichförmicht: Aber sie ist vnd hat nur 4. ß. vnd fast etwas ringer an der lenge; Vrsach/ weil sie gedäckt ist: Dann ein jede offene Pfeiffe/ so bald man sie zudecket/ wird vmb ein Octav oder Quint, oder Sext tieffer. Also ist es zwar auch mit der Quintadehnen Art/ nur allein/ daß sie viel lenger ist / als ein Gedact;

dackt;

Chapter II.

How the various and sundry names of organ stops
are to be designated correctly according to their sound and characteristic timbre; also, how such stops are variously classified in general according to their pitch in feet; with a further report concerning what is necessary to know about each stop in particular.

t this point something could be said about scaling pipes according to the length of their bodies. But because that is a matter for the organbuilder alone, it is unnecessary to treat it here.

But this much can be said in passing about the length of Principals and all open flue pipes (not including the length of their toes, which are only conduits for the wind, but beginning with the lip which sets the body above it into vibration), that they are almost always actually as tall as their designation in feet indicates. Even here, though, lengths are not precise, one or another of them having to be shortened because of varying widths (though only a little bit, hardly noticeable in the smaller pipes). Reason will tell you that when something gets wider, its length must diminish slightly, and vice versa.

With regard to stopped ranks, however, the designation in feet has another meaning. For although a stopped pipe is of the same or even of somewhat greater diameter than a Principal, nevertheless it is not even half as tall. For example: a Principal pipe of 8' pitch has a body that is 8' long; a stopped pipe, while it also produces an 8' pitch and has almost the same diameter as the Principal (technically speaking), is only 4' (or even a bit less) tall. The reason for this is that it is stopped; as soon as any open pipe is covered, it speaks an octave, or a fifth, or a sixth lower. Thus it is that a Quintaton pipe is much longer than a Gedackt, because it is only a bit wider

dackt; Denn sie vmb ein geringes weiter/ als ein Principal von 4. fi. do hergegen das Gedact so weit ist/ als ein MittelPrincipal von 8. Füssen.

Daß aber diese beyde zugedäckte Pfeiffwercke so vngleicher weiten sind/vnd dennoch nach der Fußlenge 8. fi. Thon am laut haben; daraus erfolget dieses/daß durch der Quinder Quintadehnen Engigkeit/ die in sich habende vnd lautende Quinta, darzu denn auch der Bart/ so vmb das Labium oder Mundloch herumb gehet/ vnd sonderlich der gar enge auffschnitt des Labij sehr helffen vnd befördern muß) heraus kan gebracht werden. Denn ohne diese beyde mittel/ (als nemblich/ daß die Quintadehn aenger als das Gedact/ vnd daß sie den uffenthalt des Windes/ nemblich den Bart darbey hat) kan keine Quinta von jhrem laut/ sondern nur eine bloß Gedacte Art allein vernommen werden.

Darmit aber auch im außsprechen der vnterscheyd vernommen werde: So saget man bey denen Stimmen/ da der Thon mit der Mensur vberein kömpt/ als in den offenen Pfeiffwercken/ es ist ein Principal von 8. fi. ein Octav von 4. Fuß Thon/etc. Bey den andern aber/ als in den Gedactens Arten/ do die Mensur dem Tono nicht respondiret, sagt man/ es sey ein Gedact oder Quintadehn uff 8. fi. ein Nachthorn/ uff 4. fi. ein Blockflöitlin/ uff 2. fi. Thon etc.

Aber hiervon uff dißmal gnug.

Diß ist aber anfänglich/ wol vnd mit fleiß in acht zu nehmen/ daß nur zweyerley Art/ Nemblich offene vnd zugedäckte Pfeiffen seyn/ daraus alle andere Arten vnnd Lautsenderungen erfolgen: Vnd ob schon mancher jnn duerun die Schnarr-Wercke allhier nicht mit eingerechnet haben wolte/ so befindet sich doch vnwidersprechlich/daß die enderung des Klanges in demselben eben so wol aus der enderung derer Corporum, (Jnmassen mit andern offnen vnd gedacten Pfeiffen geschicht) erfolget; darumb sie billich/ weil in jhnen noch viel wunderliche vnd mehr Variationes, als in andern Pfeiffwercken erwiesen vnd erfunden werden/ können vnd müssen mit eingeschlossen werden.

Vnd werden nu also 1. die Pfeiffen in Orgeln abgetheilet in Flöit- vnd Schnarrwerck.

2.

Das Flöitwerck ist oben an seinem Corpore entweder offen/ oder zugedäckt.

3.

Der offenen Flöitwerck etliche sind gleich aus Proportioniret, vnd haben

than a 4' Principal, while on the other hand a Gedackt is as wide as a medium Principal 8'.

These two stopped ranks have very different widths, and yet produce the same 8' pitch; the resulting narrow scale of the Quintadena, aided by the beard surrounding its lip and especially by the lip's very low cut-up, produces this stop's prominent fifth. Without both of these features, namely that it is narrower than the Gedackt, and that its beard confines the flow of wind, the Quintadena could never produce its strong fifth, but would merely sound like a type of Gedackt.

To express the distinction [between open and stopped ranks] clearly in words, one refers to those open stops whose size corresponds to their pitch as "Principal of 8' pitch," "Octav of 4' pitch," etc. With stopped pipes, however, in which the size does not correspond to the pitch, one says "Quintadena at 8'," "Nachthorn at 4'," "Blockflöitlin at 2' pitch," etc.

But enough about this for the present.

One should take careful note at the outset that there are only two types of pipes, open and stopped, from which all the various timbres are produced. Although some are against including reeds as a third type, yet it is undeniable that changes to their bodies result in modifications in their timbre (just as with other open and stopped pipes). Because they can produce as many or more remarkable varieties of tone as other types of pipes, it is only fitting to include them.

Therefore: 1. organ pipes are divided into flues and reeds

2.

Flue pipes are either open or stopped at the top.

3.

Some open flue pipes are cylindrical, and their bodies are of a uniform width; some, however, are conical.

haben gleichweite Corpora: Etliche aber sind nicht gleich aus weit proportioniret.

4.

Die gleichaus proportioniret seyn/ haben einstheils lange/ enge vnd schmale Corpora; Anders theils aber kurtze vnd weite Corpora, als die Holsflöitten allerley Art.

5.

Die nicht gleichaus proportioniret, deren sind auch zweyerley: Etliche vnten weit/ vnd oben enge/ als die Gemßhörner/ Spitzflöitten/ vnd Flachflöitten: Etliche aber oben weit vnd vnd vnten enge/ als der Dultzaen.

6.

Die zugedäckte Flöitwercke/ seynd entweder gantz zugedeckt/ als die Quintadehnen vnd Gedacten allerley Art: Aber seynd oben vffm deckel in etwas wiederumb eröffnet/ als die Rohrflöitten.

7.

Der schnarrwercken seynd auch zweyerley: Etliche offen/ als die Posaunen/ Trummeten/ Schalmeyen/ Krumbhorn/ Regall/ Zincken/ Cornett: Etliche zugedäckt/ als die Sordunen/ Ranckett/ Baerpipen/ Bombart/ Fagott/ Apffel vnd Köplinregal/ 2c. Wie in nachfolgender Tabell mit mehrerm zu ersehen.   Hieher gehört die Tabell.

Von offenen Stimmwercken/ so gleichaus

proportioniret vnd an ihret weite PrincipalMensur seyn. Als nemblich:
Principal, Octaven, Quinten, Rauschpfeiffen/ Schweizerpfeiffen/
Mixturen, Zimbeln vnd dergleichen.

Principal.

Dieser Name PRINCIPAL (welches die Alten/ vnsere liebe Vorfahren/ Præstanten genennet haben) ist nicht ohne gefehr/ oder nach geduncken solchem Pfeiffwercke zugeeignet worden. Dann dieweil dieselbigen nicht allein des Wercks Zierde vnnd Ornament seyn/ sondern auch das jenige/ was vor erwehnet/ vnd geliebter kürtz halber allhier nachmals zu gedencken vnnötig/

præ-

4.

Of those that are cylindrical, some have long, narrow bodies, while others, such as Hohlflutes of all kinds, have short and wide bodies.

5.

There are also two types of conical pipes: some, such as the Gemshorn, Spitzflöte, and Flachflöte, are wide at the bottom and narrow at the top; others, however, such as the Dulzaen, are wide at the top and narrow at the bottom.

6.

Stopped flue pipes, such as Quintadenas and Gedackts of all types, are either entirely covered; or they have some sort of opening in their cover, like the Rohrflöte.

7.

There are also two types of reed pipes: some, like the Posaune, Trummet, Schalmey, Krumbhorn, Regall, Zinck, and Cornett, are open; others, like the Sordun, Rancket, Baerpipe, Bombart, Fagott, Apffel- and Köplinregal, etc., are stopped. This is all depicted in the following Table of various and sundry stops. Here is where the Table belongs.[9]

About open Pipes that are cylindrical
and of Principal Scale, namely Principal, Octaves, Quints[10], Rauschpfeiffen, Schweitzerpfeiffen, Mixtures, Zimbels, and the like.[11]

Principal.[12]

"PRINCIPAL" (our forebears in former times called it "Praestanten") is a judiciously chosen, well-suited name for this kind of pipework. For these pipes are not only the ones that provide the instrument's ornamentation,[13] but are also (as has already been mentioned,[14] and for the sake of brevity need

---

9. In the original publication the Table was printed on an unnumbered fold-out double page, bound between pp. 126 and 127.
10. See *Theatrum Instrumentorum*, Plate XXXVII, no. 3.
11. Although it is not numbered as such, this title appears to mark the beginning of section I; section II begins on p. 131.
12. See *Theatrum Instrumentorum*, Plate XXXVII, no. 1.
13. i.e., the instrument's façade is normally composed exclusively of this kind of pipes.
14. Although Praetorius has previously mentioned Principals a number of times, and identified them as pipes standing in the façade, he has not specifically called them the most prestigious.

(NB. D

UNIVER

Darinnen der Vnterscheyd vnd Na
so dieser zeit in

(NB. Wo das M. vnd P. am rande verzeichnet befunden wird; muß man
do es dann/ Principal-Baß oder Gedact-&c. Baß genennet wi

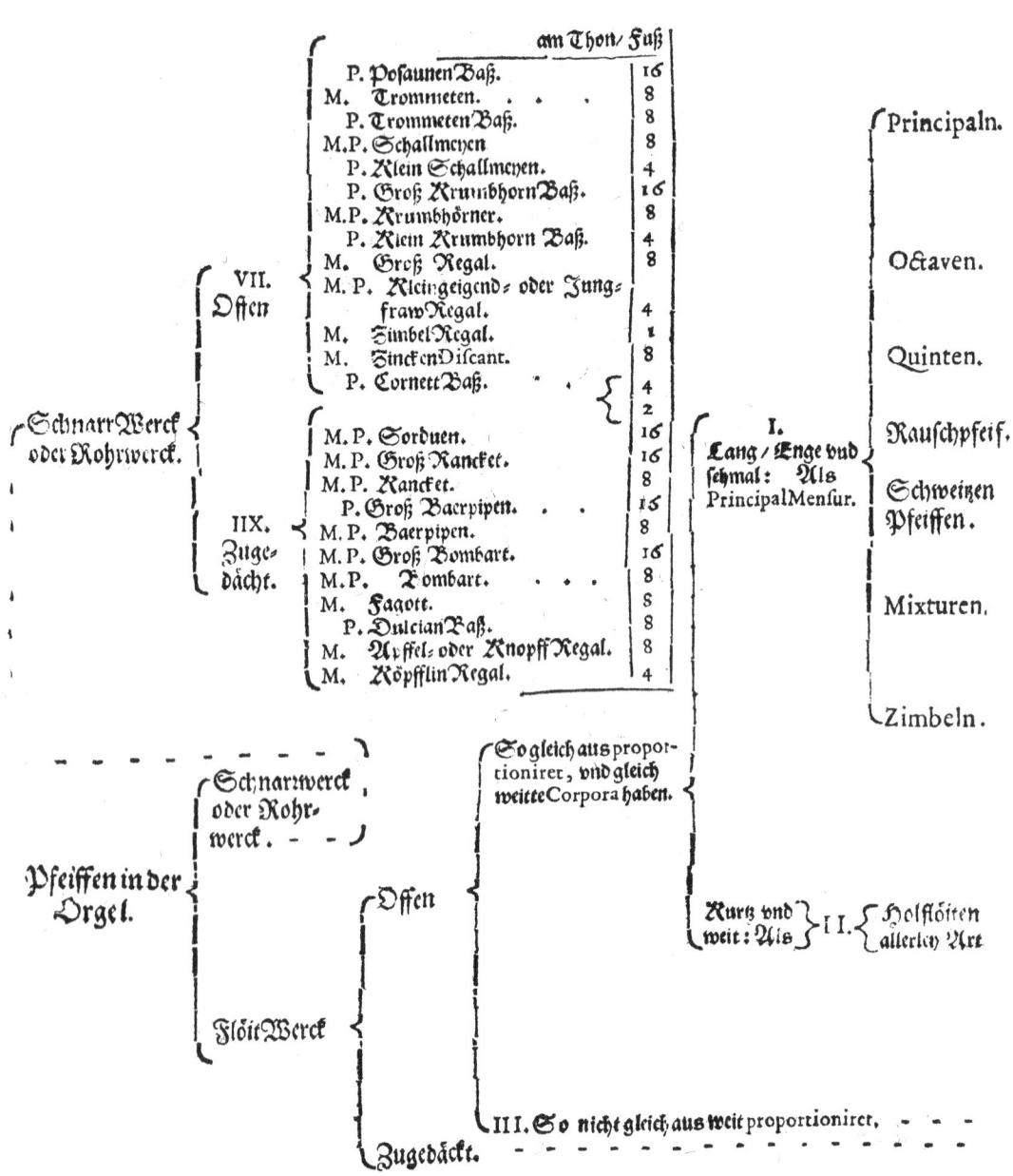

(dieſe Tabel gehöret ad fol. 126)

RSAL TABEL,

...men / Wo nicht aller / doch der meiſten Stimmen /
...Orgeln gefunden werden / begriffen.

...es alſo verſtehen / daß eine ſolche Stimme / beydes im Manual alleine / ſo wol im Pedal auch alleine /
...rd; Vnd dann auch im Manual vnd Pedal zugleich mit einem / oder zweyen abſonderlichen
...Regiſtern gebraucht werden könne.)

	am Thon / Fuß
P. Groß Sub Princip. Baſſ.	32
M. Groß Principal.	16
P.G. Pri. oder Pri. vnterſatz.	16
M. P. Princ. oder Preſtant.	8
M. P. Klein Principal.	4
M. Klein Princ. Diſcant.	4
M. P. Groß Octava.	8
M. P. Octava.	4
M. P. Klein Octava.	2
M. Super Octävlin. Sedetz.	1
M. P. Groß Quinta.	16
M. P. Quinta.	3
M. Klein Quinta.	1½

oder Rauſch Quint, Von { 3, 2 }

M. P. Groß Schweitz. Pfeiff.	8
M. Klein Schweitzer Pfeiff.	4
M. Klein Schw. Pfei. Diſc.	4
P. Klein Schw. Pf. Baſs.	1
M. P. Groſſe Mixtur.	
M. P. Mixtur 2. oder 1. fach.	
M. P. K. Mixtur oder Scharp.	4
M. P. Gröber Zimbel.	
M. P. Klingend Zimbel.	
M. P. Zimbel.	
M. Kleiner Zimbel.	
M. Repetirende Zimbel.	
P. Zimbel Baſs.	
M. P. Groß Holflöiten.	8
M. P. Hölflöiten.	4
M. Holpfeiffen Diſcant.	4
M. P. Hol Quint.	3
M. P. Kleine Holflöit.	2
M. K. Hol Qu. oder Qu. flöit.	1½
M. Swifflöitlin oder Sieffliit.	1
M. Waldflöitlin.	1½
P. Klein Flöitlin Baſs.	2
M. P. Groß Schwiegel	8
M. P. Klein Schwiegel.	4

Dieſer aller Abriß / iſt in Sciagraphia, oder Theatro Inſtrumentorum Col. XXXV. vnd XXXVI. zufinden.

{ Vnten weit vnd oben eng

			am Thon / Fuß
Gembßhörner oder Spillflöiten.	{	M. P. Groß Gembßhorn.	16
		M. P. Gembßhorn.	8
		M. P. Octaven Gembßhorn.	4
		M. P. Gembs Quinta.	3
		M. P. Klein- oder Super Gembßhörnlin.	2
		M. Klein Gembß Quinta. Naſat.	1½
		Spillflöiten.	4
Spitzflöiten.	{	M. Spitzflöit.	4
		M. P. Klein Spitzflöit	1½
		M. Spitz Quintlein.	
		Blockflöiten / oder Plockpfeiffen.	4
Flachflöiten.	{	M. P. Groſſe Flachflöit.	8
		M. P Flachflö ten	4
		M. P. Klein Flachflöit	2
		M. Klein Flachflöit Diſcant.	2

Oben weit: vnd vnten eng: als / der Dulzaen. 8

IV. Quintadeenen Menſur.			
Quintadeen.	{	M. P. Groß Quintadeen.	16
		M. P. Quintadeen.	8
		M. P. Klein Quintadeen.	4
Nachthorn.	{	M. P. Nachthorn.	4
		P. Klein Nachthorn Baſs.	2
Querflöit.	{	M. P. Groß Querflöit.	8
		M. P. Querflöit.	4

{ Die gantz zugedäckt ſeyn:

V. Gedacten: allerley Art.			
	{	P. Groß Gedackter Sub Baſs.	32
		M. Groß Gedact	16
		P. Gr Gedact Baſs, oder Gedact Vnterſatz.	16
		M. P. Gedact.	8
		M. P. Klein Gedact.	4
		M. Gedacte Quinta.	3
		M. Super Gedactlin.	2
		P. Bawerflöit Baſs.	1

{ Die zwar gedäckt / aber oben wiederumb in etwas eröffnet find.

VI. Rohrflöiten; allerley Art.			
	{	M. P. Groſſe Rohrflöiten.	16
		M. P. Rohrflöiten.	8
		M. P. Kleine Rohrflöite.	4
		M. Super Rohrflö tlin.	2
		P. Bawer Rohrflöitlin Baſs oder Rohrſchell.	1

(N.B.

UNIVE

Including the names and

prese

(N.B. "M." and "P." appearing before a name indicate that the stop in
Gedact-Bass, etc., or simultaneously in the manual

			pitch in feet
	P.	Posaune Bass	16
M.		Trompete	8
	P.	Trompete Bass	8'
M.	P.	Schalmei	8
	P.	Small Schalmei	4
	P.	Large Krummhorn Bass	16
M.	P.	Krummhorn	8
	P.	Small Krummhorn Bass	4
M.		Large Regal	8
M.	P.	Small Geigen- or Jungfrau Regal	4
M.		Zimbel Regal	1 [2?]
M.		Treble Zink	8
	P.	Cornett Bass	4 & 2
M.	P.	Sordun	16
M.	P.	Large Rankett	1
	P.	Rankett	16
	P.	Large Bärpfeife	16
M.	P.	Bärpfeife	8
M.	P.	Large Bombart	8
M.	P.	Bombart	8
M.		Fagott	8
	P.	Dulcian Bass	8
M.		Apfel- or Knopfregal	8
M.		Köpfflin Regal	4

Pipes in the Organ
- Reeds
  - VII. Open
  - VIII. stopped
- Flutes
  - Open
    - Cylindrical
      - I. Long & narrow, i.e. principal-scale
        - Principals
        - Octaves
        - Quints
        - Rauschpfeiffe
        - Schweitzerpfeifen
        - Mixtures
        - Zimbels
    - Short and wide-scale
      - II. Hohlflutes of all types
  - Stopped
    - III. Non-cylindrical

This table belongs after p. 126)

RSAL TABLE

categories of most, though not all stops
ently found in organs.

question appears only in the manual or in the pedal, in which case it is labeled Principal-Bass,
and pedal, with either a single rank or two independent ranks. either as one stop
or as two separate stops.)

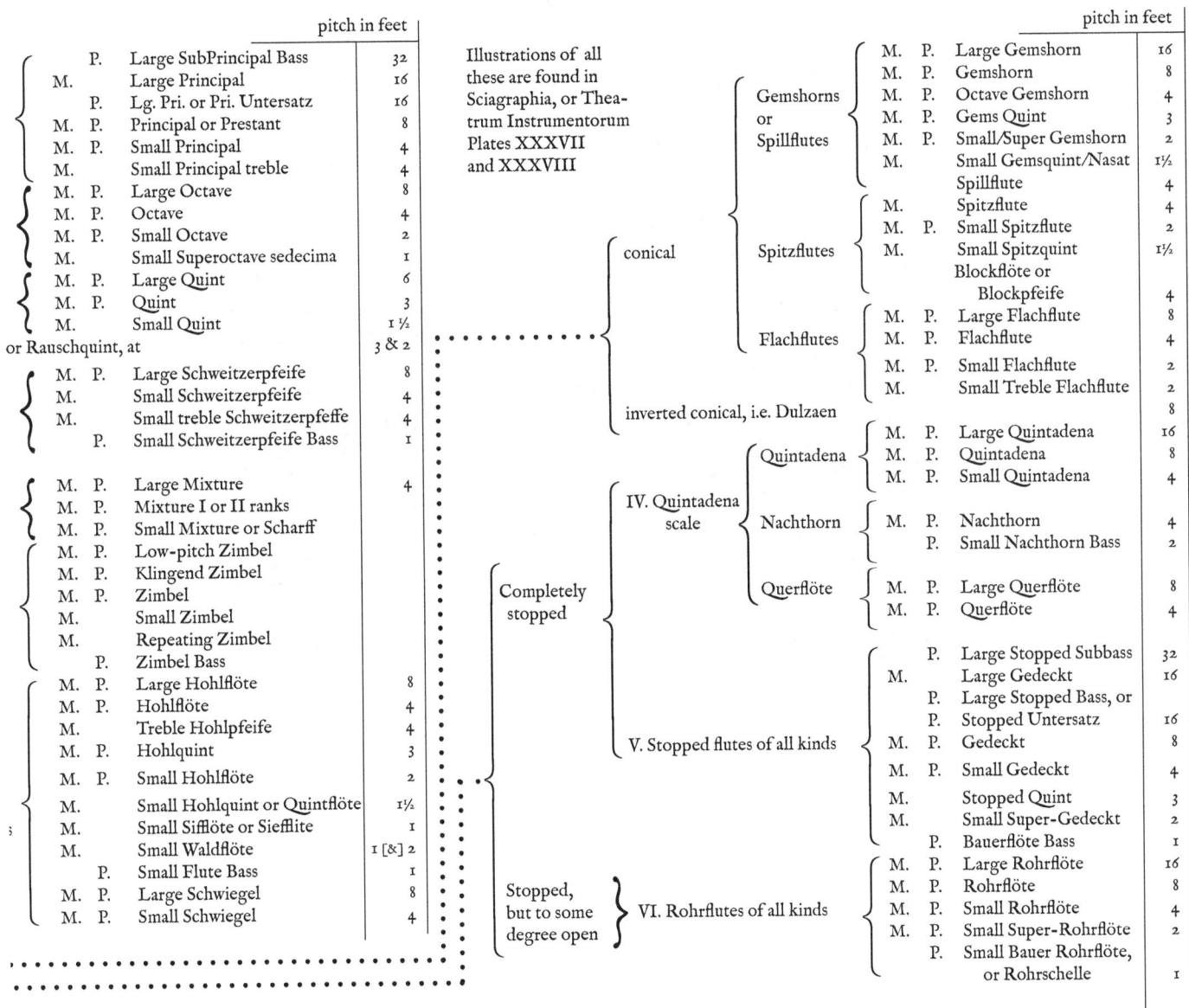

præstiren können/ werden sie recht/ wol vnd billich mit dem Namen Principaln in tituliret. Wiewol es von etlichen mit dem Namen Doeff genennet wird.

Es seynd aber derselben viererley Art:

1. Groß SubPrincipal Baß von 32. Fuß.

Diese Stimme kan nicht/ wie vorhergedacht/ zum Manual Clavier, sondern allein zum Pedal gebraucht werden; Darumb/ weil deroselben so gar tieffer Thon vnnatürlich ist/ daß wenn auch nur ein Clavis alleine/ als ein Baß respondiren sol/es mehr ein Windsausen vnd schnauben/ als ein rechter vernehmlicher reiner Thon zu hören ist; Was wolte denn/ wenn es Concordantenweise Manualiter geschlagen würde/ für eine grewliche vndeutlich vñ abschewliche Harmony erfolgen/ also/ daß es Organisten vñ Zuhörer bald satt werden/ vnd mit verdruß anhören würden: Darumb solche nur allein Pedaliter neben einer dazugezogenen Stimme von 16. Fuß sol vnd muß gebraucht werden.

2. Groß Principal von 16. Fuß.

Diese Stimme ist nun gebräuchlich/ vnd kan von derselben/ wenn sie aus rechter fundamentalischer Theilung an dem Corpore vnd Labien fleissig/ vnd just gemacht vnd Intonirt wird/ ein rechter vornemlicher Klang vnd Sonus erhöret/ auch Manualiter (wenn nur in der tieffen nicht zu grobe Concordanten mit Tertien vnd Quinten gegriffen) wol alleine geschlagen/ vnd lieblich vff einen langsamen Tact gebraucht werden; Aber noch besser/ wenn sie eine andere höhere Stimme/ wie folgen sol/ neben sich zur außbreitung des Klanges haben mag.

3. AequalPrincipal von 8. Fuß Thon.

Dieser Corpus grösse oder 8. füssiger Thon/ ist der allerlieblichste/ auch der Menschen Stimme/ vnd aller vornembsten Instrumenten ehnlichster Aequal Thon/ inmassen denn alle Stimmen die 8. Fuß Thon seyn/ zu Motetten vnd Choralconcordanten gantz bequeme/ ohne bedencken vnd Vitiis im Gehör/ nach rechter gesetzter Composition vnd præceptis gebraucht werden können vnd mögen. Darinnen auch eine sonderbare Geheimniß verborgen/ solcher 8. Fuß Thon/ aller anderer kleinen Stimmen/ ihre heimlich in sich habende vnreinigkeit auff vnd an sich nimpt/ zu seiner eigenen Reinigkeit vnd Ehren bringet/ vnd derselben sich theilhafftig machet: Davon auff eine andere Zeit/ geliebts Gott/ außführlicher geschrieben werden kan.

4. Klein Principal oder Octaven Principal 4. Fuß.

Ist zwar auch eine liebliche Stimme alleine zu gebrauchen/ aber dieweil sie für sich/ sonderlich in der höhe/ keine sonderliche Suavitet oder Liebligkeit hat/ wird in solchen Octav- oder kleinen Principalwercken/ als anfänglich gedacht/ gemeiniglich ein Fundamentstimme/ Quintadehn oder Gedact von 8. Fußthon dazu disponiret vnd gearbeitet.

In

not be repeated) the most prestigious, they are rightly given the name "Principal." Some,[15] however, call them by the name "Doeff."

There are many varieties of these:

1. Large SubPrincipal at 32' in the Pedal

As has already been mentioned,[16] this stop cannot be used in the manual, but only in the pedal, because its pitch is so very low and unnatural[17] that even when a single note is speaking in the pedal, it sounds more like a rush of wind than a clearly perceptible pitch. Imagine what a horrid, murky sound would result if it were played in chords in the manual; both organist and listeners would quickly tire of it, and become annoyed by it. Therefore this sort of stop must be used only in the Pedal, together with a 16' stop drawn with it.

2. Large Principal at 16'.

This stop is currently in common use. It can produce a clearly perceptible tone when it is built diligently and exactingly and with proper scaling of body and mouth. It can be played alone as a manual stop, as long as big chords with thirds and fifths are not played in the low register, and if it is played gently at a slow tempo. It is preferable, however, to draw a second, higher stop (as described below) with it, so the sound carries better.

3. Unison Principal at 8' pitch.

A body of this size, 8' pitch, is the loveliest of all, and corresponds to the unison pitch of the human voice and all the principal instruments. All stops at 8' pitch are well suited for use in accompanying motets and unison singing, according to the correct principles of composition,[18] without any fear of sounding offensive. A mysterious property lies hidden within such 8' pitch: it absorbs all the impurities that lie innate within all other higher stops, making them partakers in its noble purity. I will explain this in greater detail at another time, God willing.[19]

4. Little Principal or Octave Principal 4'.

This is likewise a stop that is lovely when used by itself, but since it is not especially sweet or gentle in the upper register, a foundation stop such as an 8' Quintadena or Gedackt is normally provided in Octave or Small Principal instruments, as mentioned earlier.[20]

---

15. In the Low Countries.
16. p. 122 above.
17. With reference to the human voice?
18. i.e., with proper spacing of intervals, without unpleasantly low thirds and fifths.
19. Praetorius seems never to have fulfilled this intention.
20. See pp. 122-123 above.

In etlichen AEqual Wercken / wird auch wol ein klein Principal Discant von 4. fi. gearbeitet / welches sich im vngestrichenen f von 1½. fi. Thon anhebet vnnd ascendiret, so weit das Clavier oben wendet: Wiewol sie sonsten nur im mittel C oder ♮ angefangen werden.

Schweitzerpfeiff.

Es ist aber noch eine Art Stimmwerck dieser Principalen art / aber gar enger Mensur, welche von den Nieder vnd Holländern Schweitzerpfeiffen genennet worden seyn; Vnd solches vielleicht darümb / weil sie so lang / vnd gegen der enge des Corporis im ansehen gleich der Proportion einer Schweitzerpfeiffen erscheinen: Haben gleichwol einen gar besondern / lieblichen / scharffen / vnd bald einer Violn Resonantz / welcher durch ihre Engigkeit entstehet; Seynd mit kleinen Seitdärlein vnd Vnterleplin / Als es die Orgelmacher nennen / gemacht / sonst wolten sie schwehrlich wegen der gar zu engen Mensur zur guten Intonation kommen. Wie man sie denn auch dieserwegen im Discant vnd kleinen Pfeiffen etwas weiter machen muß.

Es seynd aber derselben nur zweyerley:

1. Grosse Schweitzerpfeiff von 8. Fuß Thon.
2. Kleine Schweitzerpfeiff 4. Fuß Thon.

Aus dieser kleinen Schweitzerpfeiff wird von etlichen nur der Discant gearbeitet / vnd Schweitzerpfeiffen Discant genennet: Deßgleichen auch im Pedal allein von 1. Fuß Thon / vnd wird (3.) Schweitzerpfeiffen Baß / oder Schweitzer Baß genant.

Diese Stimmen aber sind nicht gemein / werden auch nicht leichtlich gearbeitet / denn sie ihrer schweren Intonation halber einen rechtschaffenen vnnd geübeten Meister suchen vnd haben wollen.

Die grosse Schweitzerpfeiff gibt im Pedal auch einen schönen lieblichen Baß / vnd gar einer Baßgeigen ehnlich / wenn sie zu stillen Stimmen gebrauchet wird. Es ist aber zu mercken / daß diese Stimme im Manual mit einem langsamen Tact vnnd reinem Griffen / ohne sonderbahre Colloraturen wegen ihres langsamen anfallens geschlagen seyn wil / sonsten sie zu ihrer Lieblichkeit vnnd Reinigkeit nicht kommen kan.

Some unison instruments are built with a small treble Principal at 4', beginning at 1½' in the tenor octave[21] and extending through the rest of the keyboard. Normally, however, it begins only with middle c or c♯.[22]

Schweitzerpfeiff.

There is yet another sort of Principal stop, though of very narrow scale, that the Netherlanders have named Schweitzerpfeiff. This is perhaps because its body is so long and narrow, and in its proportions it looks like a fife (Schweitzerpfeiff). As a result of its narrow scale, it has an unusual, gentle, keen timbre, rather like a violin. The mouths are provided with box beards, as organbuilders call them; otherwise it would be difficult, because of their very narrow scale, to make them speak well. For this reason the little pipes in the treble have to be built at a somewhat wider scale.

There are only two varieties of this stop:

1. large Schweitzerpfeiff at 8' pitch.
2. small Schweitzerpfeiff at 4' pitch.

Some builders construct the small Schweitzerpfeiff only in the treble range, and call it Schweitzerpfeiff Discant. The same stop is also found in the pedal, but at 1',[23] and is called Schweitzerpfeiff Bass or Schweitzer Bass.

These stops are not, however, in common use, and are not easy to build; because they are difficult to voice, they require an experienced master builder.

When it is used in the pedal against quiet [manual] stops, the large Schweitzerpfeiff also provides a beautiful, gentle bass, quite similar to a bass viol. One should also note that, when this stop is in the manual, it should be played in simple chords at a slow tempo, without rapid embellishments, due to its slow speech; otherwise it cannot achieve a pure, gentle tone.

---

21. i.e., at tenor g.
22. i.e., at 1'.
23. 'This is indeed identical with the variety described in the previous sentence; both begin at 1'.

Es findet sich auch noch eine andere Art von Schweizerpfeiffen/welche recht uff præstanten oder PrincipalMensur gerichtet/ oben aber gedäckt seyn; Vnd vngeachtet sie sich dahero nothwendig vberblasen müssen/ so fallen sie doch in rechtem Thon/ gleich/ als wenn sie offen/ vnd gar nicht gedäckt weren.

Octava.

Gleich wie nun von viererley Principalen Art jetzt gesetzt ist; Also folgen auch viererley Octaven aus derselben PrincipalMensur, als Octava/ Großoctava/ Octava/ klein Octava/ vnd Superoctävlin.

1. Großoctava ist von 8. Fuß Thon.

Diese Octava gehöret allein ins groß PrincipalWerck/ vnd ist an der Mensur vnd Klange nicht anders/ als ein AEqualPrincipal, Wie es denn von etlichen gegen das grosse Principal, klein Principal genennet wird. Weil aber im RückPositiff dasselbige kleine Principal von 4. Füssen/ zum vnterscheyd das von 8. Fuß Thon stehet: Vber diß auch die Principal mehrertheils von Zien/ die Octaven aber aus Bley oder halbwerck (das ist halb Zien vnd halb Bley gearbeitet/ vnd in die Orgelwercke hinein/ die Principal aber forn an gesetzt werden/ wird diese Stimme billich grosse Octava genennet.

2. Octava ist von 4. Fuß Thon.

Vnd gehöret in die AEqualWercke/ vnd heisset darumb also/ weil sie im Mittel mit ihrem Thon eine Octava höher/ als das AEqualPrincipal, vnd dergleichen 8. Fuß Thon Stimwercke ist; Auch ausser dem allein gebraucht werden kan/ vnd sich zu höhern vnd niedern Stimmen ziehen lesset.

3. Kleinoctava ist von 2. Fuß Thon.

Vnd wird sonst Superoctava genennet: Weil aber noch kleiner Octaven/ wie folget/ verhanden/ kan diese Stimme nicht recht Super- oder Supremaoctava heissen; Vnd gibts auch die Obergesetzte Ordnung/ Großoctava 8. Fuß Thon/ Octava 4. Fuß Thon sey/ darumb muß diese ja billich klein Octava 2. Fuß Thon/ vnd die folgende Superoctävlein 1. Fuß Thon genennet werden.

4. Superoctävlein ist von 1. Fuß Thon.

Heisset sonst Sedetze/ darumb/ weil es zwo Octaven vber der Octaven 4. Fuß Thon stehet: Aber weil die Octava 4. Fuß/ keine Fundament oder AEqualStimme

There is yet another type of Schweitzerpfeiff, of Principal scale but stopped at the top. Despite the fact that its design causes it to overblow, it nevertheless produces the same pitch as if it were an open pipe.

Octave

Just as four types of Principals have been described, so there are also four types of Octaves of the same Principal scale: large Octave, Octave, small Octave, and little Superoctave.

1. Large Octave is at 8' pitch

This Octave belongs only in large Principal instruments.[24] In its scale and sound it is nothing other than a unison Principal, and so some call it small Principal, as compared to the large Principal [16']. This stop is properly called large Octave, however, in order to distinguish it from the small Principal 4' already in the Ruckpositiv. Moreover, Principals are usually of tin and are in the façade, while Octaves are made of lead or pipe metal (i.e., half tin and half lead) and are inside the case.

2. Octave at 4' pitch[25]

This stop belongs in unison instruments,[26] and gets its name because it lies at a medium pitch level, an octave higher than a unison Principal and other stops of 8' pitch. It may be used by itself, or it may be drawn with higher and lower stops.

3. Little Octave at 2' pitch[27]

This stop is also called "Superoctave." But because there are also Octaves at higher pitches (described below), it is not proper to call this stop "Super-" or "highest Octave." Take note also of the order already established above: large Octave 8' pitch, Octave 4' pitch; thus the stop at 2' pitch must properly be called "little Octave 2'," and the octave above it "little Superoctave 1' pitch."

4. Little Superoctave at 1' pitch

This stop is also called "Sedetz,"[28] since it lies two octaves above the Octave 4'. But since the Octave 4' is not a stop at unison pitch, this stop cannot rightly be

---

24. For an explanation of this designation, see p. 122 above.
25. See *Theatrum Instrumentorum*, Plate XXXVII, no. 2.
26. See pp. 122-23 above.
27. See *Theatrum Instrumentorum*, Plate XXXVII, no. 4: "Klein Octava 2. Fuß."
28. In *Musica mechanica organœdi* (Berlin: Birnstiel, 1768, Vol. I, p. 117), Jacob Adlung states: "Sedetze is the same as Sedecima, the 16th; however, if I proceed upward 16 keys from c, then I arrive at d" rather than c". This cannot be the Superoktave, since [the Superoktave] is 15 tones higher than the Principal; ... this name is given to the Oktave even though it is not correct."

iſt/ kan dieſe nicht wol von derſelben anzurechnen/ Sedez genennet werden: Sondern behelt billich den Namen Superoctava, vnd gehöret vornemlich in die groſſen Poſitiff/ darinnen Principal von 2. Fuß Thon diſponiret ſeyn.

5. Hieher gehören auch die Quinten von 6. 3. vnd 1½. Fuß Thon/ vnnd dieſe letzte Art wird von etlichen Quindetz genennet/ aber vnrecht.

6. Item/ die RauſchPfeiffen/ welches ein Alter Name/ von den Alten erfunden. Do dann etliche dieſe zwo Stimmen vnd Regiſter/ Als Quint 3. Fuß vnd Superoctava 2. fſ. zuſammen gezogen: Etliche aber auff ein Regiſter zuſammen geſetzet/ vnd eine abſonderliche Stimme draus gemacht/ welche ſie mit dem Namen Rauſchpfeiff intituliret, gleich wie die Mixtur vnd Zimbeln einen Namen vnd Regiſter/ doch mehr als eine Pfeiffen haben: Etliche haben es auch Rauſchquinten genennet/ dieweil die Quinta gröber iſt/ als die Superoctava. Alſo haben ſie auch eine Rauſchpfeiffen Baß gehabt/ welcher jetzt noch im Gebrauch gefunden wird.

MixturZimbeln.

Nter oder aus dieſer Menſur werden nu die Mixturen vnd Zimbeln groß vnd kleiner diſpoſition genommen vnd gearbeitet/ vnd gehören dieſelbige billich zu den Principal vnnd Octav Stimmwercken/ dieweil ſie eben derſelben Menſur ſeynd/ vnd die Octaven vnd Quinten ohne das zur Mixtur vnd Zimbeln des vollen Wercks halben gezogen werdē. Vnd weil derſelben diſpoſitiones vnd Variationes von den Orgelnmachern mancherley/ nach Art vñ Gelegenheit der Wercke vnd Kirchen/ gemacht werden/ iſt hiervon in ſpecie nit zu ſchreiben: Nur allein das/ ob ſie wol allezeit eine einige Octaven hinauff ſteigen/ vnd denn alſo bald wieder repetiret werden/ doch dieſer vnterſcheyd hierinn verhanden: Daß einerley Art 1. groſſe Mixtur genennet wird/ welch die Alten in jhren Wercken/ (weil ſie domaln noch nicht von mancherley Art Stimmen/ wie jetzo gewuſt) geſetzet haben: Vnd wiebevor angezeigt worden/ offte von 30. 40. vnd mehr Pfeiffen ſtarck/ darunter die gröſte von 8. Füſſen geweſen: Jetziger zeit aber ſeynd die groſſen Mixturen allein von 10. 12. bißweilen doch gar ſelten 20. Pfeiffen ſtarck auff einem Chor/ vnd iſt die eine groſſe Pfeiffe im vnterſten Clave von 4. fſ. Thon.

2. Die andere Art heiſſet Mixtur, weil dieſelbige im mittel/ vnd nicht zu groß noch zu klein mit Pfeiffen beſetzet: Vnd iſt eben die/ welche jetzund in die AequalPrincipal, auch wol in die groſſe Principalwercke von 4. 5. 6. 7. 8. vnd 9. Pfeiffen oder Choren gemacht wird: Darinnen die gröſte Pfeiffe gemeiniglich von 2. oder 1. fſ. Thon iſt.

3. Die

named "Sedetz" figuring from the Octave. Rather the name "Superoctave" should be retained. It belongs principally in large Positiv organs that are based on a Principal at 2' pitch.

5. The Quints at 6', 3',[29] and 1 ½'[30] also belong under this heading. Some call the last of these "Quindetz,"[31] but this is incorrect.

6. The Rauschpfeiffe belongs here as well, an old name for a stop invented a long time ago. Some [builders] left the two stops Quint 3' and Superoctave 2' to be drawn together, while others put them both into a single, separate stop, and gave it the name "Rauschpfeiffe," just as each Mixture or Zimbel is one stop, but yet has more than one rank. Some called it "Rauschquinte," since the Quint is lower than the Superoctave. They also put a Rauschpfeiffe in the pedal, as is still found today.

Mixtur Zimbeln

Mixtures and Zimbels in sizes large and small are built at this scale.[32] They are properly considered in the same category as the Principal and Octave stops, since they are of the same scale, and furthermore the Octaves and Quints are drawn along with the Mixture and Zimbel to make the full organ. And because their make-up varies considerably, depending on the type and size of the instrument and the church, nothing specific can be said about them, with one exception: they always rise several octaves, and then begin to repeat frequently. These distinctions should be made, however: one kind is is called

1. large Mixture, which our forebears put in their instruments, since back then they did not have all the different kinds of stops known today. These Mixtures, as previously indicated,[33] often had 30, 40, or more ranks, the largest of which was at 8'. These days, however, large Mixtures have only 10 or 12 ranks, and very seldom as many as 20; their lowest rank is at 4' pitch.

2. The second kind is called Mixture, because it is of medium size, with neither too many nor too few pipes. This is the sort of Mixture that is now built into unison Principal instruments, as well as into large Principal instruments. It has 4, 5, 6, 7, 8, or 9 ranks, and its lowest rank is normally at 2' or 1' pitch.

---

29. See *Theatrum Instrumentorum,* Plate XXXVII, no. 3.
30. i.e., 5 1/3', 2 2/3', and 1 1/3'.
31. From Latin "quindecima," "fifteen."
32. i.e., as the pipes described under the previous heading, i.e., Principal scale.
33. E.g., p. *99* above.

DE ORGANOGRAPHIA.

3. Die dritte Art wird genennet kleine Mixtur, oder wie sie die Niederländer vor Jahren genennet haben/ Scharp: vnd nicht vnrecht/ denn es ist eine rechte scharffe Stimme/ vnd doch nur von drey Pfeiffen/ als f c̄ f̄/ etc. disponiret, vnd wird offt repetiret: Wol in grossen Wercken in die Brust/ oder im kleinen vor seine rechte Mixtur gesetzet vnd geordnet. Etliche nemen gar kleine/ subtile vnnd junge Pfeifflin darzu/ die gröste 3. Zoll lang/ als f f̄ c̄ f̄: oder drey oder vier Pfeifflin in unisono, vnd ein Octävlein/ aber keine Quint, vnd gehen von einer Octav zur andern: Dasselb heissen sie Scharp. (Repetirt heist/ zu etlichen malen in einem Clavir durch Octaven wiederholen/ als von einem c oder f zum andern/ vnd ist einerley/ derowegen dann die Mixturen vnd Zimbeln zum schlagen vor sich selbst alleine nicht können gebraucht werden.)

Zimbeln.

1. Grober Zimbel ist von 3. Pfeiffen besetzet.
2. Klingende Zimbel/ 3. Pfeiffen starck repetiret durch gantze Clavir in f vnd in c̄/ vnd wird also gesetzt f a c: welches die kunstreichste seyn sol.
3. Zimbel ist von 2. Pfeiffen/ vnd wird etlichmal mehrentheils per Octavas repetiret.
4. Kleiner Zimbel ist von einer Pfeiffen vnd offt repetiret.
5. Repetirende Zimbel ist von 2. vnd 1. Pfeiffen besetzet/ vnd repetiret sich fort vnd fort.
6. Zimbel Bässe seynd zwey- oder zum höchsten dreyerley Arten: Die grösten etwan ein halben Fuß Thon; vnd werden einmal repetiret: Die andern seynd etwas geringer/ werden zweymal repetiret, vnd doch alle durch Quarten vnnd Quinten disponiret.

II.
Holflöit.

Ist ein offenes Stimmwerck/ welchs viel weiterer/ doch etwas kürtzerer Mensur, als die Principaln, vnd gleichaus weitere Corpora hat: Vnd an ihrer weitten bald Gedacter Mensur seynd/ ohne daß sie engere Labia haben.

Vnd dieweil sie offen/ vnd so weit sind/ so klingen sie auch so hol/ daher ihnen dann der Name Holflöit gegeben worden.

R ij   1. Groß

3. The third kind is called small Mixture, or Scharp, as the Netherlanders started calling it years ago—not without reason, for it is a very penetrating stop, even if it is composed of only 3 ranks (e.g., f c' f'). It repeats frequently. It is also placed in the Brustwerk in large instruments, or in small instruments in place of the actual Mixture. It is sometimes built of very tiny pipes, the largest of which is 3 inches long (e.g., f f c' f"), or of three or four little pipes in unison, sounding only a unison pitch, and not a Quint. These break back every octave, and for this reason they are called "Scharp".[34] ("To repeat" means to repeat the same pitches at several octaves of a keyboard, e.g., several times always at c, or always at f. For this reason Mixtures and Zimbels cannot be played by themselves.)

Zimbeln

1. a low-pitched Zimbel has 3 ranks.
2. a Klingende Zimbel also has 3 ranks, and repeats at f and c throughout the keyboard. The most artistic way to build it is said to be as a chord, f a and c.
3. [an ordinary] Zimbel has 2 ranks, and repeats a number of times, mostly at the octave.
4. a small Zimbel has only one rank, which repeats often.
5. a repeating Zimbel contains 1 or 2 ranks, and repeats constantly.
6. Zimbels in the pedal are of two, three, or at the most, four kinds. The large ones are around ½' pitch, and repeat once. The other kinds are somewhat higher in pitch, and repeat twice. Both of these types are made up of fourths and fifths.

II.

Holflöit.

This is an open stop, of a scale much wider but somewhat shorter than a Principal. It has a cylindrical body. In its width it is almost the scale of a Gedackt, except that it has a narrower lip. Its being open and of such wide scale are what make it sound hollow, and that is how it got the name "Holflöit."[35]

---

34. i.e., "keen," "penetrating."
35. "hollow flute"; modern German spelling: Hohlflöte

1. Groß Holflöiten 8. Fuß Thon.

Es haben aber die alten Orgelmacher vor 60. vnd mehr Jahren in die Choral-oder Thumbkirchen Wercke solche Stimme ins Pedal, vnd so groß am Thon / als das Principal gemacht; Sintemal man domals von den vnterschiedenē Bässen oder Vntersätzen noch nichts gewust/ vnd solchen Baß/ Subbaß vnd Thunbaß/ auch Coppel geheissen / darumb daß er weit vnd Tohn endgeklungen/ vnd den Wercken/ weil sie eine Quinta tieffer/ als ChorThon gewesen/ eine besondere brausende Art/ in solcher Tieffe gegeben hat. Wie derer noch in vielen alten Thumb-Wercken gefunden werden/ daß ein vnwissender meynen solte/ es were wegen seines Thonens vnd erfüllens ein Vntersatz/ weil es an dessen Stadt nun vollen Wercke gebraucht worden/ dabey verhanden.

2. Holflöiten 4. Fuß Thon.
3. Holquinten 3. Fuß Thon.

Werden durchs Manual vnd Pedal/ wie man wil/ gebraucht: Vnd haben die Alten den Holquinten Baß gern in den ChoralWercken/ den SangMeister vnd die Chorales, bißweilen zur Schalckheit/ außm rechten Thon vnd anfang des Chorals zu verführen gehabt.

4. Kleine Holflöit 2. Fuß Thon.

Diese ist von etlichen auch Nachthorn genennet/ darumb daß es hol/ vnd fast als ein Hornklang sich im Resonantz Artet: Ist aber nicht gar recht nach jhrem klang genennet/ Sintemal sich die Quintadehnen Art viel besser darzu schicket.

5. Kleinflöitten Baß/ 2. fl. ist auch gar gut zum Choral zu gebrauchen.

6. Quintflöitten anderthalb Fuß Thon.

7. Suiflöit 1. Fuß Thon.
Das Suiflöt oder Siefflitt rechnen etliche vnter die PrincipalStimmen.

8. Waldflöitlin anderthalb Fuß Thon.

Welche Stimm in Seestädten anjetzo noch gebräuchlich/ vnd wird 2. oder 3. mal welles so kleine ist/ repetiret.

9. Klein Flöiten Baß ist 1. Fuß Thon.

Wird an statt / vnd wie die Bawrflöitlein disponiret, ist aber etwas heller vnd lauterer

1. large Holflöit 8' pitch

Sixty years ago or more, organbuilders [began] to build this stop in the pedal [of instruments] in monastery and cathedral churches, at the same pitch as the Principal, since having a variety of pedal or "Untersatz" stops was unknown at that time. Such a pedal stop was also called Subbass, Coppel, or Thunbass, because of its broad, ringing[36] sound. The fact that instruments back then stood a fifth lower than choir-pitch gave this stop a special sort of booming effect in its lower register. There are still examples of this stop found in many old cathedral churches; they replace the Untersatz in the plenum, and they sound so full and resonant that anyone who did not know better would think that there was actually an Untersatz there.

2. Holflöite 4' pitch[37]
3. Holquint 3' pitch

These may be used in either manual or pedal, as desired. In former times organists liked to have a Holquint in choir organs; they sometimes used them mischievously, to mislead cantors and singers as to the correct beginning pitch of the chant.

4. little Holflöit 2' pitch

Some also call this stop "Nachthorn," because it sounds hollow and has about it something of a horn-like timbre. Its timbre does not entitle it to this name; it is more appropriate to build this stop like a Quintadena.

5. Small Flöit in the pedal at 2' is well suited for playing a cantus firmus.

6. Quintflöit 1 ½' pitch

7. Suiflöit 1' pitch. Some reckon the Suiflöt or Siefflitt among the Principal stops.

8. Waldflöitlin 1 ½' pitch

This stop is still in use in the coastal cities;[38] because it is at such a high pitch, it repeats 2 or 3 times.

9. Small Flöit in the pedal, at 1' pitch,

is put there in place of the Bawrflöitlein, but the former has a somewhat brighter and louder sound.

---

36. "Thun-" = "Tönend-" in modern German.

37. *Theatrum Instrumentorum*, Plate XXXVIII, no. 5, depicts an "Offenfloit [Open flute] 4 foot."

38. i.e., the large Hanseatic cities on the North Sea and the Baltic, whose commercial ties promoted similar characteristics in their organs.

DE ORGANOGRAPHIA.

lautterer am Klange. Vnd sind nun diese kleine Stimmen/wenn dieselbe zu Aequal-Stimm Wercken mit vnd ohne den Tremulant gezogen werden/ gar gut vnd frembd am Klange zu hören.

Schwiegell.

Es hier ist noch eine besondere Art von Laut oder Resonantz vnd Namen/ die nicht so gar weiter Mensur, als diese Holtzflöten/verhanden/ welche von den Niederländern auch fast vor hundert Jahren/ wie aus des Sebastiani Virdungs Musica zuersehen/ Schwiegel (weil sie gegen ander enge Mensur Pfeiff Werck zurechnen auch hot/ vnnd doch sanffte/vnd am Resonantz den Querflöiten gar ehnlich klingen) genennet worden. Sie sind biszweilen vff Gemszhörner form gerichtet/ doch vnten vnd oben etwas weiter/ gleichwol oben wiederumb zugeschmiegt/ das Labium ist schmahl/ vnd sind stiller als Spilsflöitten. Es seynd aber derselben nur zweyerley Art: Als

1. Grosse Schwiegel 8. Fuß Thon
2. Kleine Schwiegel 4. Fuß Thon.

Woher aber solch sanffter Klang komme/ laß ich andere dessen verständige bericht geben. Vnd diß sey also von dieser Mensur vom Grösten biß zum Kleinesten genug gesagt.

III.
Offene Stimmwerck/ welche nicht gleichaus weite Corpora haben.

Es ist nun die andere Art der offnen Pfeiffen/ welche/ weil sie vnten ziemlich weit/ vnd oben zugespitzet/ vnd also mehr/ als halb zugedäcket seyn/ viel ein andern Resonantz/ als vorbeschriebener Principalmensuren Art an vnd in sich haben. Vnd werden dieselben darumb/ daß sie an der Proportz vnnd Resonantz als ein Horn klingen/ billich Gemszhorn genennet: Vnd sind derselben Art vnterschiedlich/als Gemszhorn/ Plockflöit/ Spitzflöit/ Flachflöit; Dultzian vnd dergleichen.

Gemszhorn.

DE ORGANOGRAPHIA.

These small stops produce a fine and unusual sound when they are drawn with stops of 8' pitch, with or without the Tremulant.

Schwiegell

There exists yet another separate sound category, not of such wide scale as the Holflöit. About 100 years ago the Netherlanders named it "Schwiegel" (one may see it in Sebastian Virdung's *Musica*[39]) because in comparison with other narrow-scale stops it sounds both hollow, yet gentle, much like the sound of a traverse flute. It is sometimes built in the shape of a Gemshorn, though somewhat wider both at the bottom and the top, and bevelled inward on top. The lip is narrow, and the stop is quieter than a Spillflöit.[40] There are only two varieties of this stop:

1. Large Schwiegel 8' pitch
2. Small Schwiegel 4' pitch

I will leave it to others to give a thorough report as to how this gentle tone is produced. This is enough to say about pipes of this scale,[41] from the largest to the smallest.

III.

Conical Open Pipes.

This is a second kind of open pipe that has a very different timbre than those of Principal scale described above, since it is cone-shaped[42] and thus more than half stopped. It rightly bears the name "Gemshorn," because its proportions give it a horn-like sound. There are various types of these, such as Gemshorn, Plockflöit, Spitzflöit, Flachflöit, Dulzain,[43] and the like.

Gemshorn

---

39. *Musica getutscht und ausgezogen* (Basel, 1511); see: Beth Bullard, trans., *Musica getutscht: a treatise on musical instruments*. Cambridge: Cambridge University Press [1993], p. 106. Virdung spells the name "Schwegel."
40. Praetorius does not describe the Spillflöit, but he provides an illustration of it in *Theatrum Instrumentorum*, Plate XXXVII, no. 11.
41. i.e., Hohlflöten.
42. Literal translation: "rather wide at the bottom and proceeding to a point at the top"
43. Here Praetorius spells this stop "Dulzian," but the stop is entitled "Dulzain" on p. 136. "Dulzian" is a reed stop; see p. 147 below.

1. Groß Gemßhorn ist am Thon 16. Fuß.

Dieses ist eine liebliche Stimme/ aber besser im Pedal als ManualClavir zu gebrauchen/ es sey dann/ daß eine andere Stimme von 8. oder 4. ff. Thon darzu genommen werde.

2. AequalGemßhorn ist am Thon 8. Fuß.

Vnd ist eine sonderbahre liebliche vnd süsse Stimme/ wenn sie aus rechter fundamentalischer Theilung nach allen jhren Vmbständen gemacht vnnd Intoniret wird/ zu hören; Gibt wunderliche enderungen mit andern Stimmen zu verwechseln: Möchte auch wol Viol de Gamba, weil sie solchem Instrument am Resonantz sehr nachartet/ wenn sie recht gemacht wird/ intituliret werden. Die Niederländer nennen es auch Coppelflöiten; vnd sind lenger als ein Gedact/ aber kürtzer als ein Principal.

3. Octaven Gemßhorn ist am Thon 4. Fuß.

Diese Stimme ist der nechst obgesetzten von 8. Fuß zu vielen lieblichen enderungen nicht vngleich zu gebrauchen: Vnd können beyde so wol in groß- als in klein Principalwercken gesetzt vnd gebraucht werden.

4. Klein Octaven Gemßhorn ist am Thon 2. Fuß.

Gehöret mehr ins Rückpositiff vnd klein OctavenPrincipal Wercklein/ als im grossen: Jedoch kan sie von andern vnd grossen dispositionen auch nicht außgeschlossen seyn; Denn sie doselbst eben so wol eine liebliche Art im Manual, vnd auch ein schönen Baß im Pedal zum Choral zu gebrauchen gibt/ vnd sich gar vernemblich vnd eigentlich hören lesset.

Es werden auch aus dieser Gembßhörnen Art Quinten disponiret: Als

5. Die grosse Gemßhorn Quinta 6. Fuß Thon.
6. Die Gemßhorn Quinta 3. Fuß Thon: Vnd denn
7. Die klein Gemßhorn Quinta anderthalb Fuß Thon:

Ist oben halb so weit als vnten: Das labium wird in fünff Theil getheilet/ ein Theil ist des Mundes breitte/ alsdann wird die helffte vffgeschnitten.

Vnd wird diese letzte Stimme sonsten nicht vnrecht NASATH genennet/ dieweil sie wegen jhrer kleine zu andern Stimmen gleichsam nösselt/ sonderlich wenn sie recht/ vnd nicht so scharff intoniret ist; Gibt auch einen schönen Discant in der rechten Hand/ mit andern darzugezogenen Stimmen zu gebrauchen. Etliche arbeiten das Nasath vff weit Pfeiffwerck Mensur, vnd enge labiret.

Etliche

1. **Large Gemshorn is at 16' pitch.**

This is a gentle stop, better used in the Pedal than in the manual, unless another stop at 8' or 4' pitch is drawn with it.

2. **Unison Gemshorn is at 8' pitch.**[44]

It is an especially gentle and sweet stop when all its dimensions are built according to the correct basic proportions, and when it is properly voiced. It creates unusual sounds when it is combined with other stops. It may also be called "Viol de Gamba," because when it is correctly built, its timbre closely resembles that instrument. The Netherlanders also call it Coppelflöit.[45] It is taller than a Gedackt, but shorter than a Principal.

3. **Octave Gemshorn at 4' pitch.**

This stop is quite similar to the abovementioned variety at 8' pitch, in that it can be combined with other stops to produce many lovely combinations. Both stops may appear in both large- and small Principal instruments.[46]

4. **Small Octave Gemshorn at 2' pitch.**

This stop belongs primarily in the Ruckpositiv or in small Octave Principal instruments,[47] rather than in large instruments. Yet it cannot be excluded from the stoplists of larger organs, where it may be used either as a gentle manual stop or as a beautiful pedal stop for playing the cantus firmus, since it can be heard clearly and distinctly.

The Gemshorn may also be built as a Quint stop:

5. The large Gemshorn Quinta at 6' pitch
6. The Gemshorn Quinta at 3' pitch, and finally
7. The small Gemshorn Quinta 1 ½' pitch.

The Gemshorn is half as wide at the top as at the bottom. The mouth is ⅕th the length of the circumference, and the cut-up is half the width of the mouth.

This stop is also called NASATH, and not without reason, since, due to its being so small, it adds a nasal quality when drawn with other stops, especially when it is voiced properly, i.e., not so keenly. It provides a beautiful treble solo when it is played with the right hand in combination with other stops. Some builders construct the Nasath as a wide-scale stop with a narrow mouth.

---

44. See *Theatrum Instrumentorum*, Plate XXXVII, no. 10: "Gemßhorn 8 foot."
45. *Theatrum Instrumentorum*, Plate XXXVIII, no. 2, depicts a "Coppelfloit 4 foot."
46. See pp. 122-3 above.
47. See p. 123 above.

DE ORGANOGRAPHIA.

Etliche heissen das Gemßhorn auch Spilfflöiten/ vnd daffelbige allein wegen der Gestalt vnd Proportion, daß solche Pfeiffen einer HandSpillen gar gleich vnd ehnlich anzusehen seyn.

Etliche nennen die Gemßhörner noch an jetzo Plockpfeiffen: Ist aber nicht recht getaufft. Denn Plockpfeiffen eine andere Gestalt vnd Klang haben/ vnd können die Spitzflöitten von 4. ff. Thon (darvon jetzt alsbald sol gesagt werden) wenn ihnen oben die rechte weite/ etwas weiter/ als den Gemßhörnern/ gegeben wird/ des Klanges halben billicher Plockpfeiffen oder Plockflöiten geheissen werden: Weil sie alsdann einen Resonantz/ natürlich als die andere blasende Instrumenta, welche Plockpfeiffen genennet werden/ von sich geben. Kleiner aber/ als von 2. Füssen/ werden dieser Art Stimmen von verstendigen Meistern nicht gearbeitet.

Etliche arbeiten die Plockflöiten fast vff Querflöiten Art/ also/ daß das Corpus noch eins so lang wird/ als sonsten die rechte Mensur mit sich bringt/ oben zugedäckt/ vnd daher sich in der Octav vbersetzen vnd vberblasen muß.

Spitzflöit.

ES sind noch andere vnd fast dieser Art Stimmen/ welche auch also zugespitzet seyn/ vnd Spitzflöiten genennet werden: Vnd dieser Art Mensur ist auch nicht gar lange vblich vnd im Gebrauch gewesen.

Es ist aber ein ziemlicher vnterscheid zwischen den Gemßhörnern/ vnd dieser Spitzflöiten; Weil dieselbe vnten im labio weiter/ vnd oben mehr zugespitzet wird/ als gedackte Gemßhörner: Darumb sie recht Spitzflöit geheissen. Vnd sind derselben nicht mehr/ als zweyerley an Grösse vnd Thon.

1. Spitzflöit 4. Fuß am Thon.
2. Klein Spitzflöit 2. Fuß Thon.

Auch habe ich Spitzflöiten Art funden/ welche oben gar wenig offen/ vnd vnten gar enge labiret seyn; Dahero einen aus dermassen lieblichen Resonantz von sich geben; Aber mit grosser Mühe zur reinen vnd rechten Intonation zu bringen seynd.

Flach-

Some also call the Gemshorn "Spillflöit," because the shape of these pipes closely resembles a hand spindle.

Some continue to call Gemshorns "Plockpfeiffen"; but that name is incorrect, since Plockpfeiffen have another shape and sound. The name "Plockpfeiffe" or "Plockflöit"[48] can more properly be applied to the 4' Spitzflöit (discussed immediately below), if it is built at the correct width (somewhat wider than a Gemshorn). Then this stop produces a timbre as natural as the sound of the actual wind instrument, the Plockpfeiffe.[49] Knowledgeable builders do not build this sort of stop smaller than 2'.

Some build the Plockflöite almost like a Querflöit,[50] i.e., with a body one and a half times as long as is appropriate for its scale, but capped. It is then forced to overblow at its octave.

Spitzflöit

There is another stop, very similar to the Gemshorn, that is likewise conical, called the Spitzflöit.[51] Stops with this scaling have not been in use very long.

There is a considerable difference between the Gemshorn and the Spitzflöit. The latter is wider at the lip and more tapered at the top than the abovementioned Gemshorn; it is therefore properly called "Spitzflöit.[52] They come in only two sizes.

1. Spitzflöit 4' pitch
2. Little Spitzflöit 2' pitch

I have also encountered a type of Spitzflöit that is almost completely closed at the top, and has a very narrow lip at the bottom. Thus it produces a truly gentle timbre; but it is very difficult to voice properly and cleanly.

---

48. See *Theatrum Instrumentorum*, Plate XXXVII, no. 12: "Plockfloit 2 foot."
49. i.e., the Blockflöte or recorder.
50. See p. 138 below.
51. See *Theatrum Instrumentorum*, Plate XXXVII, no. 9 (labeled "Grossgedact lieblich 8'," clearly an error.)
52. German "pointed flute."

Flachflöit.

Vn ist noch eine Art Stimme fast von dieser Mensur/ vnd werden Flachflöiten geheissen; Die seynd vnten im labio nicht gar weit/ mit einem engen niedrigen vffschnidt/ doch gar breit labieret, daher es auch so flach vnd nicht pompich klinget/ vnd seynd oben nur ein wenig zugespitzet/ wollen aber jhrer Intonation halben ein erfahrnen Meister haben; Klingen sonsten gar wol/ vnd etwas flacher/ als Gembßhörner/ drumb sie recht mit dem Namen/ Flachflöit getaufft seyn. Es ist aber dieselbe dreyerley Art am Thon vnd Fuß lenge.

Als
1. Groß Flachflöit 8. Fuß Thon.
2. Flachflöit 4. Fuß Thon.
3. Klein Flachflöit 2. Fuß Thon.

Seynd alle drey gar gut vnd nütze/ wenn viele Stimmen in einem Werck disponiret seyn/ zu lieblichen enderungen zu gebrauchen: Geben auch im Pedal schöne Bässe zu vornehmen/ denn sie etwas lauter/ jedoch frembder/ als die Gembßhörner am Klange seyn.

Mögen auch sonderlich die kleine Flachflöit/ wenn sie nach der Quinten Art disponiret ist/ im RückPositiff mit einer Zimbel vnd Quintadehn zu einem geigenden Discant gebraucht werden; denn es dem gar ehnlichen sich hören lest. Vnd so viel sey von dieser Art berichtet.

Dulzain.

Es ist noch eine Stimme/ die vngleicher weitten ist/ übrig/ oben weit/ vnten aber im labio vmb ein ziemliches enger: Solche stimme wird Dulzain genennet/ stehet zum Stralsond im newen Wercke/ vnd ist 8. Fuß Thon/ kan auch wegen der gar schwehren Intonation kleiner nicht gemacht werden: Klinget darumb dem Dulzian etwas ehnlich/ weil sich das Corpus oben aus/ gleich wie das Instrument Dulzain erweittert/ vnd im labio enger ist. Weil aber der Dulzian an jhm selbsten ein Rohr oder schnarrent Instrument bleiben muß/ vnd jetzt beschriebene Stimme vnter das Flöit oder Pfeiffwerck gehöret/ kan dieselbige dem

Flachflöit

There is yet another type of stop, with almost the same scale [as the Spitzflöit], called Flachflöit. The bottom of the pipe, at the lip, is not very wide, but the lip is quite broad and has a low cut-up. This is why it sounds so thin and not full. It is only slightly conical. Its voicing requires an experienced master. It has a pleasant timbre, somewhat thinner than the Gemshorn, and therefore it has rightly been dubbed "Flachflöit."[53] There are three varieties of this stop:

1. Large Flachflöit 8' pitch
2. Flachflöit 4' pitch[54]
3. Small Flachflöit 2' pitch

If there are many stops in an instrument,[55] all three of these are quite useful in creating gentle combinations. [The Flachflöit] also works well as a pedal stop, since it sounds somewhat louder, but more exotic than a Gemshorn.

In particular, the small Flachflöit built as a Quint stop[56] in the Ruckpositiv may be used in combination with a Zimbel and a Quintadena to produce a string-like treble [solo]; this registration does indeed sound very much like a stringed instrument. But enough about this type of stop.

Dulzain[57]

There is one final stop that is of conical construction, but it is wide at the top and considerably narrower below at the lip. This stop is called 'Dulzain.' It stands in the new instrument at Stralsund.[58] Since it is very difficult to voice, it cannot be built smaller than at 8' pitch.[59] It sounds rather like the instrument the Dulzian, because its body is narrow at the lip and gets wider as it lengthens out. But since the Dulzian is by nature a reed instrument, and the Dulzain is a flue pipe, the

---

53. German "flat flute" or "thin flute."
54. See *Theatrum Instrumentorum*, Plate XXXVIII, no. 3 (spelled "Flachfloit").
55. Praetorius writes "Werck," which may signify either an entire organ, or a single division of an organ.
56. i.e., 1 1/3'
57. See *Theatrum Instrumentorum*, Plate XXXVIII, no. 1, where this stop is called "Dolcan" (in the *Universal Tabel*, p. 126, it is called "Dulzaen"). Praetorius seems never to have seen this stop.
58. See Praetorius, *Syntagma musicum II*, p. 167; there the stop is called "Dolcian," at 8'.
59. The illustration in *Theatrum Instrumentorum*, Plate XXXVIII, no. 1, however, is labeled "Dolcan 4 foot."

ge dem RohrInstrument nicht gar gleich Stimmen. Man leſt es aber alſo bey deß Meiſters gegebenen Namen bleiben.

IV.
Von Gedacten Pfeiffen/ Vnd erſtlich von der Quintadehna/ Nachthorn vnd Querflöit.

Quintadehna.

ES iſt dieſe Stimme nicht lange/ ſondern etwa 40. oder 50. Jahr im Gebrauch geweſen/ wie ſie denn in alten Orgeln nicht gefunden wird; Vnd iſt eine liebliche Stimme (von etlichen Holſchelle genennet) darinnen zweene vnterſchiedliche Laut/ als die Quinta, ut, ſol, im Gehör zu vernehmen ſeyn; Daher ſie anfänglich Quinta ad una genennet worden; Sie iſt faſt/ jedoch ein ziemliches weiter/ an Proportz jhres Corporis/ als die Principal an der Menſur ſeyn; Vnd weil ſie gedäckt/ ein Octava tieffer als offene Pfeiffwerck gegen jhrer lenge zurechnen. Es ſeyn aber derſelben/ die aus einer Menſur vnterſchiedlichen nach dem Thon oder Füſſen gearbeitet werden/ nur dreyerley Art verhanden:

Als/
1. Groſſe Quintadeen 16. Fuß Thon.

Dieſe Stimme iſt Manualiter vnd Pedaliter, wenn eine andere Stimme von 8. fſ. daju genommen wird/ gantz lieblich zu gebrauchen vnd zuhören.

2. Quintadeen 8. Fuß Thon.

Dieſes iſt beydes im RückPoſitiff/ oder im kleinen Octaven PrincipalWerck zum Fundament. Wie denn auch im Pedal zum ChoralBaß gar bequem zu gebrauchen.

3. Quintadeen 4. Fuß Thon.

Iſt eine liebliche Stimme/ ſonderlich bey vnd zu gröſſern Stimmen in der Variation anzuhören; Kleiner aber wird ſie nicht gefunden/ wie ſie denn auch nicht geringer gearbeitet kan.

S Nacht-

latter cannot sound exactly like the reed instrument. Therefore it is best that it keep the name given it by its inventor.⁶⁰

IV.
Concerning Stopped Pipes, beginning with the Quintadena, Nachthorn, and Querflöit.

Quintadena

This stop has not been in use very long, only about 40 or 50 years; it is not found in old organs. It is a gentle stop (some call it "Holschelle"⁶¹) in which two distinct pitches can be heard, sounding a fifth, do-sol. Therefore it was initially named "Quint ad una."⁶² The dimensions of its body are as wide or even wider than those of a Principal. And since it is stopped, it sounds an octave lower than its length would indicate, or than open pipes of the same length. There are only three varieties of this stop, built with the same scaling but at different pitches, namely:

1. Large Quintadena 16' pitch.⁶³

This stop is found in both manual and pedal. It is a very useful and gentle stop, if another stop at 8' pitch is drawn with it.

2. Quintadena 8' pitch.⁶⁴

This stop may appear in the Ruckpositiv, or it may serve as the foundation stop for a small Octave Principal Instrument.⁶⁵ It is also well suited to playing a cantus firmus in the pedal.

3. Quintadena 4' pitch.

This is a gentle stop, especially well suited for use with lower stops, for variety. It does not appear any higher [than 4'], however, since it cannot be built any smaller.

---

60. The sense of the foregoing passage seems to proceed from the presumption that, because the names "Dulzain" and "Dulzian" are similar, their sounds also ought to exhibit some similarity. Since however their sounds are fundamentally dissimilar, being produced by entirely different means, it is best that they retain different and distinct names.
61. Translation: "little hollow tinkling/jingling bells".
62. Latin "fifth added to a unison."
63. See *Theatrum Instrumentorum*, Plate XXXVII, no. 6: "Quintadehna 16 foot."
64. See *Theatrum Instrumentorum*, Plate XXXVII, no. 7: "Quintadehna 8 foot."
65. See p. 123 above.

Nachthorn.

ES wird aber diese kleine Quintadeena von etlichen Orgelmachern an der Mensur, Jedoch vff gewisse masse erweitert/ vnd daher/ (weil sie aus solcher erweiterung einen Hornklang bekömpt/ vnd die Quinta etwas stiller darinnen wird) Nachthorn geheissen. Welcher Name auch recht ist. Es mag aber diese Art ebenmessig zu vielen andern Stimmen gar lieblich vnd mannigfaltig verendert werden.

Aus dieser Mensur oder Art kömmet auch der Nachthorn Baß/ beydes von 4 Fuß/ so denn auch von 2. Fuß Thonher/ vnd ist eine zierliche Stimme/ bevorab im Baß anzuhören.

Die Niederländer arbeiten das Nachthorn offen/ wie eine Holßöite/ doch obcit vmb etwas enger/ vnd brechen allmehlich jmmer etwas ab/ ist auch im Labio nicht so hoch vffgeschnitten/ als die Holßöite/ daher es einen sonderlichen Klang bekömpt/ gleichsam/ als wie einer zuchete oder schluggete.

Querflöit.

NOch ist aus dieser Invention der Quintadeen/ eine newe Art erfunden worden/ welche sich mit den Querflöiten/ wie sie denn auch Querflöit genennet wird/ gar ehnlich im Klange vergleichet vnd vereinbaret.

Es kömpt aber derselbe Klang nicht aus freywilliger natürlicher Intonation, sondern außm vbersetzen oder vbergallen; Das vbergallen oder vbersetzen aber daher/ weil das Corpus gegen seiner enge mehr als noch eines/ vnd fast noch anderthalb mal so lang ist.

Als zum Bericht; Wenn das c͞ 4. Fuß Thon seinen Klang hören lest/ so ist desselben Corpus an der lenge so lang/ daß/ ob es zwar wegen seiner lenge auff 12. Fuß respondiren solte vnd köndte/ so intoniret doch in denselben nur allein die Quinta, die vom vbersetzen oder vbergallen herrühret; Wie denn auch solch Corpus wegen der vnnatürlichen lenge gegen der enge/ anders nicht als Quinten kan.

Diese art der Querflöiten ist zwar gar gut/ vnd auch newer Invention; Aber die offener Mensur vnd an der Corpuslenge noch eins so lang seyn/ welcher Art denn auch in dem Fürstlichen newen hölzernen Orgelwerck/ (welches der Hochwürdige/ Durch-

Nachthorn.

Some organbuilders make the small [4'] Quintadena just mentioned above at a somewhat wider scale. Since widening the pipes gives them a horn-like timbre and somewhat weakens their innate Quint, its builders therefore call this stop "Nachthorn."[66] And this is an appropriate name for it. It may be combined successfully with many other stops to produce all sorts of gentle registrations.

The Nachthorn at both 4' and 2' in the pedal is of the same scale. It is an elegant stop, above all in the pedal.

The Netherlanders build the Nachthorn as an open stop,[67] like a Holflöit but becoming slightly conical as it rises. This variety does not have such a high cut-up at the lip as the Holflöit, and this gives it its characteristic unstable, fluttering sound.

Querflöit.

From the newly invented Quintadena sprang yet another innovation, which closely approximates the sound of the traverse flute. Thus it has been named "Querflöit."[68]

Its sound is however not the result of unforced, natural voicing, but of overblowing (ubersetzen oder ubergallen). The overblowing happens because the body is about three times too long for its narrow diameter.[69]

To explain further: if the pipe produces a sound at 4' pitch, then its body, even though it is 12' long and should produce a correspondingly low pitch, nevertheless sounds only its Quint,[70] which is the result of the pipe's overblowing. Because it is so unnaturally long in relation to its narrow diameter, such a pipe can do nothing else but overblow to its Quint.

This sort of Querflöit is quite fine, to be sure, and also up-to-date. But I find the variety that is open and of double length[71] more pleasing. This is the kind that the distinguished organ- and instrument-builder, Master Esaias Compenius, built[72] into the new organ with wooden pipes, which His Reverend, Serene, Noble Lord-

---

66. German "night horn;" see *Theatrum Instrumentorum*, Plate XXXVII, no. 8.
67. See *Theatrum Instrumentorum*, Plate XXXVII, no. 5.
68. German "traverse flute."
69. Literal translation: "...because its body in proportion to its narrow diameter is almost more than one and a half times twice its [normal] length." Thus, to produce a 4' pitch, the pipe would be 4' × 2 = 8' × 1½ = 12' long.
70. i.e., its second overtone.
71. See *Theatrum Instrumentorum*, Plate XXXVII, no. 13: "Offen Querflöit 4 foot."
72. From 1605-1610.

Durchleuchtige hochgeborne Fürst vnd Herr/ Herr Heinrich Julius/ Postulirter Bischoff zu Halberstadt/ Hertzog zu Braunschweig vnd Lüneburg/ Mein gnädiger Fürst vnd Herr hochlöblicher gedechtniß/ S. Fürstl. G. hertzl. Gemahl. vff deroselben Schloß zu Hessen durch den vornemē Orgel-vñ Instrumentmacher/ Meister Esaiam Compenium von 27. Stimmen/ mit dreyen Claviren in einem zierlichen Schappe/ dessen Disposition hinten im V. Theil zu finden/ setzen lassen) an jetzo von Holtz/ sonsten aber von andern hiebevor auch in Metall gearbeitet worden seyn/ gefallen mir besser; Denn es ist natürlicher/ daß es sich in der Octava vbersetzet/ als daß es noch weiter sich vbersetzen/ vnd ferner in die Quint fallen solte. Vnd sind dem natürlichen Querflöitenklang am Resonantz noch gleicher/ als die Gedacte/ derer Art auch in vor hochgedachter S. F. G. herrlichen grossen Orgel zu Grüningen/ von 8. vnd 4. Fuß Thon im Manual vnd Pedal verhanden seyn.

V.
Gedacten allerley Art.

Diese Stimme ist von den Alten in jhren Wercken nur allein schlecht mit dem Namen Flöitten genennet worden. Die Niederländer vnd etliche andere nennen sie Bordun/ sonderlich wenn sie enger Mensur sind: Etliche nennen sie auch Barem/ wenn sie gar still vnd linde intonirt wird. Es seynd aber der Gedacten oder gantz zugedäckten Stimmen nach jhrem Thon vnd Fuß gerechnet/ sechserley Arten.

1. Groß Gedact vff 16. Fuß Thon.

Diese Stimme wird mehrern theils ins Pedal gesetzt/ vnd groß Gedackter Vntersatz geheissen: Sie wird auch wol ins Manual herdurch geführet. Aber wegen jres thunen vnd stillen Klanges vnd jhrer Tieffe nicht so gar anmutig vnd vorstendlich zuhören/ wie die Erfahrung vnd Natur bezeuget. Vnd ob zwar diese gedackte Mensur, auch wol zu zeiten von 32. Fuß Thon im Pedal gesetzet/ vnd groß Gedacter SubBaß genennet wird/ so ist doch/ wie vorher vom grossen SubPrincipal berichtet worden/ darauß viel weniger/ als in offenen Pfeiffen ein rechter verständlicher Thon zu vernemen. Meines erachtens were vff 32. Fuß Thon keine bessere Art anzubringen/ als die Flachflöiten: Doch wil ich solches einem verständigen Orgelmacher zu probieren anheim gestellet haben.

2. Gedact am Thon 8. Fuß.

Dieses ist nu eine gemeine Stime im gebrauch/ wird auch wol in kleine OctavPrincipalwerck zum Fundament/ wie den auch in grosse Ruckpositiff gesetzt vñ disponiret.

3. Klein G:dact am Thon 4. Fuß.

Wird

ship, Lord Heinrich Julius, Bishop Postulate of Halberstadt, Duke of Brunswick and Lüneburg, my Gracious Prince and Lord of praiseworthy memory, and Her Princely Grace his wife, had built at her palace in Hessen.[73] This instrument has 27 stops and three keyboards,[74] enclosed within an elegant cabinet; its stoplist can be found in Part V below.[75] In that organ, Mr. Compenius built this stop out of wood, but others have previously built it out of metal. It is more natural for this stop to overblow at the octave, rather than to overblow further to the Quint. This variety produces a sound closer to an actual traverse flute than the stopped variety found at 8' and 4',[76] in the manual and pedal, in the great and splendid organ of His Princely Grace mentioned above,[77] at [the Palace at] Gröningen.[78]

V.
Gedackts[79] of all Varieties.

he old [organ builders] called this stop simply "Flöitten" in their instruments. The Netherlanders and some others call it "Bordun," especially when it is of narrow scale. Some call it "Barem" if it is voiced very quietly and gently. There are six varieties of Gedackts, that is, completely stopped ranks, according to their pitch and length.

1. Large Gedackt at 16' pitch.

This stop appears for the most part in the Pedal, where it is called great Gedackt Untersatz. It may also be carried up into the manual. But experience confirms that it does not sound very pleasant and clear, due to its quiet, booming tone. Although stopped pipes of this scale also appear at times at 32' in the pedal with the name 'great Gedackt Subbass,' yet they produce a far less perceptible pitch than open pipes (this same observation is made above[80] in connection with the large SubPrincipal). In my opinion there would be no better stop to put into the Pedal at 32' pitch than the Flachflöit. But I will leave that to a knowledgeable organbuilder to test.

2. Gedackt at 8' pitch.[81]

This stop is in common use, and serves both as the foundation stop in small Octave Principal instruments as well as in the Ruckpositiv in large instruments.

3. Small Gedackt at 4' pitch.

---

73. SE of Wolfenbüttel; its stoplist is found on p. 189 below
74. i.e., upper manual, lower manual, and pedal.
75. See p. 189. In 1616 the Duke's widow gave the organ to her brother, King Christian of Denmark. The instrument was placed the royal castle at Frederiksborg, where it survives today.
76. See *Theatrum Instrumentorum*, Plate XXXVII, no. 14: "GedacktQuerfloit 4 f."
77. "mentioned above" refers to "His Princely Grace," not to the organ at Gröningen.
78. The stoplist of this organ is found on pp. 188-89. Gröningen is a village about 10 miles NE of Halberstadt, Germany (not to be confused with the city in Holland of the same name.)
79. German "gedackt/gedeckt" means "covered" or "stopped."
80. p. 127.
81. See *Theatrum Instrumentorum*, Plate XXXVIII, no. 6: "Gedact 8 foot"; no. 4, identified as a "Klein Barduen [Bourdon?] 8 foot," appears to be quite similar.

Wird auch in gemein in allerhand dispositionen der Wercken vnd Positiffen gesetzet: Ist aber gut/ vnd gibt feine vnd mannichfaltige/ sonderlich mit Quintadehnen vnd Gemßhörnern vorenderungen.

Es ist ohngefehr vor 28. Jahren von einem domals jungen Meister E. C. eine seltzam Art erfunden/ nach dem derselbe ein gedackt 4. Fuß Thon/ mit zweyen labiis, die just einander gleich respondiren, gemacht/ also/ daß man die Pfeiffen durchsehen kan/ welche er Duiflöt genennet hat. Dieselbe verendert jhren Klang gar vor anderer Gedacten Arten. Ist aber noch zur zeit nicht gemein worden.

4. Supergedäcktlein ist 2. Fuß am Thon.

Ob dieses schon gleich ist/ so gibt es doch auch liebliche Variationes mit grossen Stimmwercken/ Wie von dem Suifflöit vnd andern mehr erwehnet worden; sonderlich aber/ wo ein guter Tremulant verhanden ist. Inmassen es dann/ wofern es juster Mensur, vnd reine gleichlautend intoniret, einen außbündigen guten Discant in der rechten Hand zu gebrauchen/ vnd einem kleinen Plockflöitlein gantz gleich vnd ehnlichen; Wie es denn auch zum grossen Rancket oder Sorduen von 16. Füssen einen frembden Klang vnd enderung gibt/ vnd mit Lust anzuhören ist.

5. Gedacte Quinta 3. Fuß Thon.

Diese Stimme ist von etlichen/ als Gregorio Vogel/ Pfeifferflöit/ welches eine Quinta vom ChorThon gestanden/ genennet worden.

6. Bawerflöit Baß/ oder Päurlin 1. Fuß Thon.

Von dieser Stimme wird bey vns in Deutschland/ sonderlich/ wenn man den Choral im Pedal führen wil/ gar viel gehalten: Die Italiäner aber verachten alle solche kleine Baßstimmen von 2. oder 1. Fuß Thon/ dieweil sie/ als eitel Octaven lautten/ vnd im Resonantz mit sich bringen.

VI.
Die zwar gedäct/ aber wiederumb oben
in etwas eröffnet seyn:
Als
Röhrflöiten.

Auß

This stop is commonly found in all sorts of stoplists, both in organs and in positivs. It is a fine stop, and produces a great variety of good combinations, especially when drawn with Quintadenas and Gemshorns.

About 28 years ago a then young master organ builder, E[saias] C[ompenius,] invented an unusual variant, by building a 4' Gedackt with two lips, one just opposite the other, so that one could peer through the pipe; he named it "Duiflöt." This construction makes it sound completely different from other Gedackts. But at this time it has not yet become a common stop.

4. Supergedacktlein at 2' pitch.

Although this is the same [as the 4' Gedackt], yet it too produces gentle combinations with lower stops, as has already been mentioned about the Suiflöit and other stops as well, especially when a good Tremulant is available. When it is of proper scale, and purely and evenly voiced, it is exceptionally fine when played in the treble by the right hand, and sounds quite similar to a little Plockflöit.[82] When combined with the large Rancket or Sorduen 16', it creates an unusual but pleasant sound.

5. Gedackte Quinta at 3' pitch.

Some builders, such as Gregorius Vogel,[83] call this stop Pfeifferflöit, a Quint at choir pitch.[84]

6. Bauerflöit or Päurlin in the pedal at 1' pitch.

We Germans hold this stop in high regard, especially for playing a cantus firmus in the pedal. The Italians, however, scorn all such high pedal stops at 2' or 1', since they merely reinforce octaves.

VI.
Pipes that are indeed stopped, but on the other hand open to some degree, such as the Rohrflöit.

---

82. It is unclear if Praetorius means the instrument the recorder, the organ stop the Blockflöte, or both.
83. See p. 117 above.
84. The final clause seems to refer specifically to Gregorius Vogel's work; such a stop likely stood in the organ at St. Johannes in Magdeburg, an instrument Praetorius seems to have been familiar with. See p. 117 above.

Als dieser Gedacten Mensur vnd Art ist nun eine andere erfunden/ welche durch gewisse mensurirte Röhrlein/ wiederumb in etwas eröffnet wird: dahero sie denn recht Rohrflöit heisset.

Dieser Art Stimmen aber werden vnterschiedlich gearbeitet. Etliche lassen die Röhren halb herausser/ vnd halb hinein gehen: Etliche gar hinein / daß man nichts sihet/ als oben das Loch / vnnd diese seynd zum beständigsten/ denn die Röhren können alsdenn nicht verbeuget werden: Dieselbige aber muß man alsdenn mit Deckhütten stimmen.

1. Grosse Röhrflöit 16. Fuß Thon.

Wann nun ja von solchen grossen Gedacten Stimmwercken eine durchs gantze Manual gehen solte/ so were diese grosse Rohrflöit wegen dessen/ daß sie lautter vnd reiner klingt/ weit besser/ denn die gantz Gedacte Art/ weil sie noch eine feine wolklingende Quintam darneben mit hören lesset.

2. Rohrflöit ist 8. Fuß Thon.
3. Kleine Röhrflöit ist 4. Fuß Thon.
4. *Super* Röhrflöitlein 2. Fuß Thon.

Diese sind alle gar füglich vnd lieblich zu aller Art Stimmen / sonderlich aber zur Quintadehnten zu gebrauchen.

5. Es gibt auch keine Art Stimmwerck ein besser Bawrflöit Bäßlin von 1. Fuß Thon/ als diese; Denn sie gar eigendlich solchen Klang / als wenn einer mit dem Munde pfiffe/in der höhe in sich hat / vnd dasselbige wegen des vffgesetzten Röhrleins. Ditz Stimmlein ist von etlichen/ weils eine helle Quint in sich hat/ vnnd hören lest/ Rohrschell/ Aber wenn seine Eigenschafft wol betrachtet wird/ nicht recht genennet worden.

Allhier solte auch wol das höltzern Pfeiffwercks gedacht werden; Dieweil aber dasselbige/ wegen allerhand Fundament Theilung/ wie ichs selbst gar fleissig mit angesehen/ so wol auch im Klange/ gantz eine andere Meynung davon zuschreiben hat/ vnd mit andern Orgelwercken an Laut vnd arbeit fast wenig zu vergleichen: Welches dann mit vorgedachtem Musicalischem vff dem Schloß Hessen stehenden OrgelWerck zu beweisen.

Dessen frembder/ sanffter/ subtiler Klang vnd Lieblichkeit aber im Schreiben so eigentlich nicht vermeldet werden kan: Als habe ich weitläufftigkeit zu vermeyden/ von solchen Pfeiffwerck vor dißmal allhie etwas mehr zu erinnern vnnd anzudeuten

From Gedackt pipes there developed another variety [of stop], which becomes slightly open due to precisely proportioned little tubes. Thus it is appropriately given the name "Rohrflöit."

This sort of stop is however built in various ways. Some builders set the tubes half inside [the pipe] and half outside. Others build it entirely inside, so that all there is to see at the top [of the pipe] is a hole. This latter kind is the most durable, since the tubes then cannot become bent; but it must then be tuned by means of its cap.

1. Great Rohrflöit at 16' pitch.

If such a large 16' capped stop were carried through the entire manual, this large Rohrflöit (in that it sounds louder and clearer) would be far better than a totally stopped Gedackt, since it sounds a harmonious quint as well as its basic pitch.

2. Rohrflöit at 8' pitch[85]

3. Small Rohrflöit at 4' pitch

4. Very small Super-Rohrflöitlein at 2' pitch

All of these are suitable and pleasing when combined with all sorts of stops, but especially with the Quintadena.

5. There is no better way than this to make a little Bauerflöit 1' in the pedal, for its higher pipes produce a sound that is just like someone whistling. This is caused by the little tube on top. Because it produces a prominent Quint, some builders call this stop Rohrschell.[86] But when one considers its characteristics, this name is inappropriate.

Here it would be appropriate to discuss pipes made of wood.[87] But this is a very different way of making pipes, due to a great variety of basic proportional and tonal differences (as I have personally witnessed), and little comparable to other organs,[88] either in tone or construction. The abovementioned[89] organ in the palace at Hessen demonstrates the truth of this statement.

The unusual, delicate, subtle timbre and gentleness of wooden pipes cannot really be described in writing. But since I must avoid wordiness, I consider it unneces-

---

85. See *Theatrum Instrumentorum*, Plate XXXVIII, no. 7: "Rohrfloit: or Holfloit 8 foot."
86. From German "Schelle," a little bell.
87. Praetorius here leaves off discussing the Rohrflöit, and moves to another topic, without providing a new heading.
88. i.e., those with pipes made of metal.
89. See pp. 138-9 above.

vor vnnötig erachtet. Es kan aber hiernechst vnd vielleicht bald von gedachtem Compenio selbsten von diesen vnd andern Sachen mehr fundamentaliter nach Geometrischem Bericht etwas außführlichers an Tag gegeben werden; Sintemal solches eigendlich meiner Profession nicht ist. Gleichwol wil ich meines Theils dieser Kunst Liebhabern zum besten solches mit fleiß zu befördern nicht vnterlassen; Inmassen denn auch billich von dem Monochordo, darauß alle Instrumenta Musicalia vnd Pfeiffwerck jhren Vrsprung/rechten Thon/vnd fundamentalische Theilung haben müssen/ vnd billich eine Mutter aller Instrumenten vnd der gantzen Music möchte genennet werden/auch dasselbige eintzig vnd allein aus dem Zirckel herfleust/vnd mit demselbigen bewiesen vnd demonstriret seyn wil/ daran jhrer viel mit grosser mühe/ aber doch vergeblich gearbeitet haben/ etwas erwehnung vnd Bericht ob Gott wil/ erfolgen sol. Vnd so viel von offen vnd zugedäckten Pfeiff- vnd Stimmwercken.

Folget von den Schnarrwercken.

VII.
Von offenen Schnarrwercken.

Weil die Schnarrwercke fast gemein vnd einem jeden bekant/ist vnnötig darvon allhier viel zu erinnern/ nur allein/ daß allezeit in der lenge vnd structur dieser offenen Corporum zu disponiren, der eine Meister ein andere Art hat/als der ander; In dem etliche die Posaunen/gleich wie sie am Resonantz 16. Fuß Thon halten/ also auch am Corpore, doch gar selten/ von 16. Füssen lang arbeiten: Etliche aber von 12. ff. daß es also von dem rechten Thon in die Quint abweiche/vnd das ist die beste art: Die gemeineste art ist von 8. ff. Mensur. Etliche arbeiten die Posaunen nur von 6. füssen. Etliche von 5. füssen lang/ oben etwas zugedäckt/ vnd ein loch/ als ein Spund vierecket drinn geschnitten/etc. Dieselbige aber/weil die Corpora so klein/ haben gar ein flachen vnd plattwegfallenden Klang vnd Resonantz. Wenn es aber pralen/prangen/ vnd gravitetisch klingen sol/ muß es von 12. füssen seyn. Vnd solche Variation wird auch in den andern succedirenten offenen Schnarrwercken gehalten: Also/

Wenn die Mensur der Posaunen von		So sind die Trommeten von		Schalmeyen von		Fuß.
	16. Fuß		8 Fuß		4	
	12		6		3	
	8		4		2	
	6		3		1½	

Daß aber so gar viel an der Mensur vnd lenge der Corporum in Schnarrwercken

sary to discuss this sort of pipework here. Since building organs is not my profession, perhaps Mr. Compenius, the gentleman mentioned above, will himself soon publish a more detailed report about this and other matters, discussing its basic geometrical aspects. I for my part will never cease diligently to promote this art[90] among organ-lovers, to the best of my ability. And, God willing, there will follow a report on the Monochord,[91] out of which all [stringed keyboard] musical instruments and pipework derive their proper pitch and basic temperament. This instrument might properly be called the mother of all [stringed keyboard] instruments, and of music in its entirety; it stems entirely from the compass, and needs to be demonstrated by the compass (many have occupied themselves with this matter, but in the end unprofitably). Enough about open and stopped pipes; let us turn to the reed stops.

VII.
About open reed stops.[92]

ince reeds are quite common and familiar to everyone, it is unnecessary to report extensively on them here. I will only mention that each builder has his own way of designing the length and structure of these open resonators. Some build a Posaune that produces a 16' pitch with a resonator that is 16' long, but that is quite rare. Some however build it 12' long, a fifth shorter than it actually speaks, and that is the best kind. The most common kind is 8' long. Some build the Posaune with a resonator only 6' long, some 5' long and partially covered on top, with a hole like a square stopper-hole in it. Since this variety's resonator is so small, however, its tone is dull and flat-sounding. If it is to crackle and strut, to sound weighty, the resonator must be 12' long. This proportion is likewise valid for the open reed stops that follow, thus:

If the length of the Po-saune is		Then the length of the Trompete will be		and the length of the Schalmei will be	
	16'		8'		4'
	12'		6'		3'
	8'		4'		2'
	6'		3'		1 ½'

The reason why not all that much depends on the length of the resonators is

---

90. i.e., of scaling pipes.
91. Although he provides an illustration of the Monochord (*Theatrum Instrumentorum*, Plate XXXVII, no. 15) as well as a diagram of its scaling (*Theatrum Instrumentorum*, Plate XXXIX), Praetorius seems never to have completed such a report.
92. See *Theatrum Instrumentorum*, Plate XXXVIII, no. 8: "Trommet."

cken nicht gelegen/ kömpt daher/ dieweil die tieffe oder höhe des Resonantzes nicht vom Corpore oder structur (welche aber gleichwol auch jhre richtigkeit vnnd rechte maß haben muß) sondern von den Mundstücken herrühret: Vnd ist diß dabey/ wenn die Mundstücke lenglicht vnd schmal seyn/ so geben sie viel ein lieblichern Resonantz/ als wenn sie kurtz vnd breit seyn: Welches denn auch in den andern Pfeiff vnd Flötiwercken sich gleichergestalt also befindet/ daß die weiter Mensur nimmer nicht so lieblich am Resonantz seyn/ als die enge.

Darumb sich billich ein jeder Orgelmacher der gar engen Mensuren befleissigen solte; denn je enger/ je lieblicher vnd anmutiger. Aber weil solche enge Mensuren zur rechten intonation zubringen/ nicht eines jeden Orgelmachers thun ist/ sintemal es guten verstand/ grossen fleiß/ vnd treffliche mühe erfodert: So bleiben die meisten/ welche faule Patres vnd etwas mehrers zu lernen verdrossen sind/ gemeiniglich bey den gewöhnlichen weiten Mensuren/ so dürffen sie den Kopff nicht allzusehr drüber zerbrechen/ desto geschwinder der arbeit abkommen/ vnd den Beutel besser füllen.

Im Land zu Hessen ist in einem Kloster eine sonderliche Art von Posaunen funden worden/ do vff das Mundstück ein Messing bödemchen vffgelötet/ vnd in der mitten ein ziemlich lenglicht löchlein drinn/ darüber dann allererst das rechte zünglein oder blätlein gelegt/ vnd mit geglüeten Messings oder Stälenen Säiten druff gebunden wird/ daß es nicht also sehr schnarren vnd plarren kan. Vnd weil es dergestalt etwas mehr als sonsten gedempffet wird/ gibt es gleich einer Posaunen/ wenn die von einem guten Meister recht intonirt vnd geblasen wird/ einen pompenden/ dumpichten/ vnd nicht schnarrenden Resonantz.

Doch müssen sie gleichwol mit vff vnd niederziehung des obersten Corporis gestimmet werden/ vnd war bleiben/ Regalia mobilia: Sintemal das falsch werden nicht/ wie etliche meynen/ vom vff-vnd niederweichen der kröckel oder drötlin/ daran die Regal sonsten eingestimmet werden müssen/ herrühret; Sintemal vnmüglich/ daß die kröckel von sich selbsten hin vnd herwider/ auff vnd nieder steigen können: Sondern von wegen der subtilen Messingsblätlin/ welche sich im warmen Wetter von der hitze/ (daß denn auch am Papier oder dünnem holtze kan probiert werden) außwerts krümmen; Vnd weil dadurch das Loch am Mundstücke erweitert wird/ der Resonantz etwas tieffer vnter sich steiget. Im kalten Wetter aber das blätlein sich inwerts vnnd näher zu dem Mundstücke wendet/ dadurch das Loch kleiner/ vnd der Resonantz höher vber sich steiget: Wie dieselbige verenderung ein jeder so mit Orgeln vnd Regaln vmbgehet/ täglich erfähret: Daß/ so bald im Winter das kalte Wetter sich endert/ vnnd zum Dawwetter anlesset/ die Regal vnter sich steigen/ vnnd tieffer werden: So bald es aber hinwiederumb zu frieren beginnet/ werden

sie also

that the depth or height of the pitch stems not from the resonator (which nevertheless must be of the proper size), but from the shallot. Take note as well: if shallots are long and narrow, then they produce a much more pleasing tone than if they are short and wide. This holds true for the flue pipes as well: a wide scale never produces as pleasing a tone as a narrow one.

For that reason, every organbuilder ought diligently to pursue very narrow scales, since the narrower they are, the more gentle and charming they are. But because not every organbuilder is capable of making narrow-scale pipes speak properly (this requires much knowledge, great diligence, and considerable effort), most of them, being lazy fellows who find that further learning requires too much effort, continue to build with wide scales; then they need not rack their brains about the matter, they can finish the work all the quicker, and their purses can become all the fuller.

In a monastery in the Principality of Hesse I found an unusual sort of Posaune. Onto the shallot was soldered a brass plate, in the middle of which was a rather lengthy little hole. The actual tongue was then laid on top of it, and fastened with red-hot brass or steel wires, to keep the Posaune from rattling and crackling. And since this dampens the sound of the pipe more than usual, it gives the Posaune (when it is properly voiced and winded by a good builder) a pompous, muffled tone, without the rattling.

Such Posaunes, however, must be tuned by bending the top of the resonator up or down, and that indeed makes them unstable (Regalia mobilia[93]). Their going out of tune is not the result of the tuning wire (with which a regal must be tuned) shifting up or down, as some believe, since it is impossible for the tuning wire to shift up or down of its own accord. Rather it is due to the thin brass tongue that curves outward in warm weather, due to the heat (one can observe this with paper or thin wood, as well). This widens the distance between the tongue and shallot, and so the pitch drops. In cold weather, on the other hand, the tongue curves inward, moving nearer the shallot; thus the distance becomes smaller, and the pitch of all the pipes rises. Anyone who deals with organs and regals experiences this daily. In the winter, as soon as the cold weather gives way to a thaw, regals drop in pitch. As

---

93. i.e., reed stops that are constantly shifting their pitch. Perhaps the word "Regalia" is the impetus behind Praetorius's sudden leap to the ensuing discussion of regals.

sie also bald höher: Darumb denn auch das vffbinden der Kröckel nicht viel helffen kan.

Vnnd diß befindet sich auch gleicher gestalt nicht allein vff den Clavicymbeln vnd Symphonien an den Stälenen vmnd Messingssäitten/ sondern auch vff den Lauten vnd Geigen an den Säiten/ so von Schaffsdärmen gemacht seynd. Daß sie von der hitze nachlassen/ sich ausdehnen vnd erweitern/ vnd derowegen der Resonantz descendiret; von der kälte aber conrrahiret, vnd sich mehr in einander ziehen/ davon denn der Resonantz auch ascendiret, also/ daß im Winter die Instrumenta, wenn sie continuè etliche Wochen im kalten gestanden/ fast vmb einen halben Thon vnd mehr ascendiret vnd gestiegen seyn. Daher dann/ wann von einem verständigen Meister die Mensur vff Clavicymbeln vnnd Symphonien also/ daß ein jede Säite vmb ein halben Thon zur noth sich höher ziehen lassen kan/ nicht abgetheilet worden/ fast alle Säiten abgesprungen seyn. Welches ich nicht sonder schaden vnnd grossen Vnmuth zum offtern selbst erfahren.

Vnd aus diesem Fundamento, daß die Verenderung im Regall vnd Schnarrwercken von Messingsblätlein herrühre/ entstehet eine Proba, dadurch man erfahren kan/ Ob ein Regall mit den Zünglein oder blätlein durch vnd durch just vnd fleissig abgerichtet sey. Dann wann ein Schnarrwerck von einem guten Meister fleissig verfertiget ist/ so weichet es in wandelung des Wetters durchs gantze Clavier zugleich mit einander/ vnd tretten entweder in der wärm vnd hitz zugleich mit einander weiter ab: Oder begeben sich in der Kält vnd Frost näher zu dem Mundstücke/ also/ daß man vff einer Orgel/ oder sonsten/ dasselbige ohne mitzuziehung des Flötwercks vnd anderer Pfeiffen gar wol/ als wenn es noch gar just eingestimmet/ beständig blieben were/ gebrauchen kan.

Wann aber ein Flötwerck darzu gezogen wird/ so befindet sich der mangel/ daß sich entweder das Schnarrwerck vnter/ oder vber sich vom Flötwerck durch vnnd durch abgewendet habe: Vnd alsdenn ist dasselbe Schnarrwerck fleissig vnd just bereitet. Befindet sich aber/ daß das Schnarrwerck nicht zugleich mit einander durchs gantze Clavier abgetretten ist/ sondern der eine Clavis ist gegen dem Flötwerck zu tieff/ der andere zu hoch/ der dritte rein/ so ists ein gewiß Zeichen/ daß die Mundstücke nicht gleich beblettert/ sondern ein blätlein starck/ das andere schwach sey/ denn sich das starcke dicke nicht so bald von der hitze oder kälte zwingen lest/ als das dünne vnnd schwache.

Ob nun zwar sonsten auch allhier von allerley anderer Arten der Schnarrwercke außführliche meldung geschehen solte; So ist doch wegen der vielfältigen verenderung vnd mancherley Inventionen, solche alle zu beschreiben vnmüglich/ sonderlich

weil

soon as it begins to freeze, they rise again. Therefore it does little good to tie the tuning wire fast. The same thing happens not only to the steel and brass strings in a harpsichord, but also to lute and violin strings that are made of sheep-gut. They become slack with the heat, stretch longer, and thus the pitch drops. But in the cold, they contract and become shorter, and thus their pitch rises. Therefore, when [stringed] instruments stand for a number of weeks continuously in the cold, they will rise a half step or more in pitch. Thus, unless a knowledgeable builder designs harpsichords so that every string can stand the tension of occasionally rising a half step, almost all the strings will pop. I myself have all too often experienced this, with its accompanying damage and annoyance.

Because the instability in regals and reed stops originates from the brass tongue, there is a test by which one can ascertain whether the tongues in a regal are precisely and diligently adjusted throughout the entire instrument. For if a reed stop is diligently built by a fine builder, then when the weather changes, the pitch of the instrument shifts uniformly throughout the entire keyboard; when it gets warm, all the tongues bend uniformly outward, and when it gets cold, they move uniformly nearer the shallot. Therefore one can play on the reeds in an organ or other instrument[94] at all times, provided the flue stops are not drawn, just as well as if they were stable and precisely in tune.

When however a flue stop is drawn with the reeds, then the shortcoming becomes evident; the reed has moved uniformly either higher or lower than the flue, throughout the entire compass. This proves that the reed stop is diligently and precisely adjusted. If it turns out, though, that a reed stop does not shift uniformly in pitch throughout the entire compass of the keyboard, but that one note is flatter than the fluework, while another is sharper, and a third is right in tune, then it is a sure sign that the tongues on the shallots are not uniform, but that one tongue is too stiff while another is too weak, since a stiff, thick tongue is not affected as easily as a thin, weak one.

Although there ought actually to be a detailed report here about all the other kinds of reed stops, there are too many varieties and innovations to be able to de-

---

94. e.g., a Positive, or a Regal.

DE ORGANOGRAPHIA.

weil derselben noch täglich mehr/ vnd viel frembder erfunden werden; Vnd solch ein Schnarrwerck nach einem andern Instrument, welches mit dem Munde geblasen wird/ recht nach zu machen/ vnd dessen Art vnd Resonantz recht zu treffen/ sehr schwehr fellet; So wil ich nur etliche der fürnembsten Art zur nachrichtung allhier gedencken.

Schalmeyen seynd 8. Fuß Thon:

Aber besser nicht/ als mit rechten Schallmeyen Corporibus, jedoch etwas weiter/ nachzumachen; Wie sie denn auch dieselbige Art gar fein mit dem rechten Schallmeyenklange vereiniget.

Krumbhorn ist allein 8. Fuß Thon:

Vnd ob es auch wol müglich/ diß Stimmwerck vff 16. Fuß Thon/ darinnen es doch gar selten gefunden wird/ zu bringen: So ists doch/ weil es etwas starck lautet vnd so tieff gehet/ Manualiter nicht fast lieblich/ sondern besser Pedaliter allein in solcher tieffen zu gebrauchen.

Es ist aber derselben Invention mancherley: Denn ob wol etliche solchen Klang in einem rechten Regal Corpore (das oben mit eim deckel zugemacht/ vnd zwey/ drey oder mehr Löcherlein/ entweder oben im selbigen deckel/ oder vnten nebenst dem Mundstücke darein gebohret) oder sonsten durch andere Arten mehr zu wegen bringen wollen; Daher sie dann wol vnter die Gedacte Schnarrwercke auch könnten referirt werden: So ist doch diese Invention, daß die Corpora gleichaus weit/ oben offen/ vnd an der lenge 4. Fuß haben/ die beste vnd gleicheste Art der Krumbhörner.

Sie wollen aber gleich anderen solchen lieblichen Schnarrwercken durch guten vnd rechten Verstand gewiß/ vnd nicht leichtlich von einem jedem gemacht vnd gefertiget seyn.

Grob Regal seynd 8. Fuß Thon:

Werden in Orgeln meistlich von Messing/ vnd 5. oder 6. Zoll hoch an der Mensur gearbeitet: Wiewol man bißweilen/ sonderlich in den Regalliwercken/ so zu Augspurg vnd Nürnberg bißher gemacht worden/ gar kleine Corpora der Regalpfeifflin/ die kaum ein Zoll hoch seyn/ findet/ vnd doch 8. Fuß am Thon haben: Wie hiervon im vorhergehenden II. Theil/ Num. 43. weitläufftiger ist erinnert worden.

JungfrawenRegal oder Baß ist 4. Fuß Thon; An jhm selbsten ein klein offen Regal mit einem kleinen geringen Corpore, etwan ein/ oder vffs meiste zweene Zoll hoch; Wird aber darumb also geheissen/ weil es/ wenns zu andern Stimen vnd Flöltwercken im Pedal gebraucht wird/ gleich einer Jungfrawenstimme/ die einen Baß singen wolte/ gehöret wird.

T   Es

scribe them all, especially since new and more exotic ones are being invented every day. It is very difficult to model a reed stop accurately after another instrument that is blown by mouth, and to capture its unique tone. And therefore I will discuss here only some of the principal types.

Schalmey is at 8' pitch[95]

It is better to build this stop, not with true Schalmei[96] resonators, but somewhat wider. This sort blends admirably with the actual sound of the Schalmei.

Krummhorn[97] is only at 8' pitch

Although it is indeed possible to build this stop at 16' pitch, it is seldom encountered. Because it sounds rather loud and low, it is not very pleasant as a manual stop. Since it sounds at such a low pitch, it is better to put it only in the pedal.

This stop's resonators come in all varieties and sizes. Some builders attempt to achieve this timbre with a true regal resonator, covered on top by a cap, and with two, three, or more little holes, bored either into the cap itself or lower down near the shallot. There are other methods of achieving the timbre, as well. Therefore this stop can be counted among the reeds that are stopped. But the best kind, the one that sounds most like a krummhorn, is the one with half-length cylindrical resonators that are open at the top.

Just like other gentle reed stops, however, this one must be built by a fine and knowledgeable master; not just anyone is capable of building it.

Grob Regal is at 8' pitch[98]

In the organ this stop is for the most part built of brass, at a length of 5 or 6 inches. At times, though, the resonators are very small, hardly an inch long, yet producing an 8' pitch; this holds true especially in the [keyboard] instruments called regals, that have been built in Augsburg and Nuremberg. This is described in greater detail in Part II, No. 43 above.[99]

The Jungfrauenregal,[100] either in the manual or the pedal, is at 4' pitch. It is a small, open regal with a small, slight resonator, about one or at the most two inches in length. Its name is due to the fact that, when it is combined with flue stops in the pedal, it sounds as if a young woman's voice were singing in the bass register.

---

95. See *Theatrum Instrumentorum*, Plate XXXVIII, no. 10: "Schalmey 8 [or] 4 foot."
96. i.e., the wind instrument's.
97. See *Theatrum Instrumentorum*, Plate XXXVIII, no. 9: "Krumbhorn 8 foot"; nos. 16-18 illustrate other varieties of this stop.
98. See *Theatrum Instrumentorum*, Plate XXXVIII; nos. 14 and 15 illustrate two varieties of Regals: "Messing Regahl" (Brass Regal) and "Gedempfft Regal" (Muffled/Muted Regal).
99. Actually in Chapter 45, at the bottom of p. 73. See *Theatrum Instrumentorum*, Plate IV.2.
100. German "Maiden-regal."

Es wird auch solch klein Regal vff 4. Fuß Thon von etlichen Geigen- oder Giegends Regal genennet; Vnd solches darumb/ daß es/ wenn die Quintadehna vff 8. fuß Thon darzu gezogen/ etlicher massen (sonderlich wenns in der rechten Hand zum Discant allein gebraucht wird) einer Geigen gar ehnlich klinget.

Dieweil aber in jede Stimme für sich allein/ ohne anderer hülffe also klingen sol/ als sie wil/ vnd sol genennet werden/ so kan man diese Stimme nicht billicher/ als klein Regal nennen.

Zincken 8. Fuß Thon:

Werden allein durchs halbe Clavir im Discant gebraucht/ haben gleichaus weitte Corpora, vnten etwas zugespitzet/ oben offen; Darumb werden sie am klang etwas hol/ als ein Flöitwerck/ vnd nicht also schnarrend/ denn jhnen wegen der starcken bletzer/ vnd starcken windes das schnarren ziemlicher massen vergehet vnd verboten wird.

Cornett wird meistentheils im Baß allein gebraucht/ ist zwar RegalMensur, aber enger vnd lenger: Denn ob es gleich nur von 4. oder 2. fuß Thon/ so ist doch das Corpus 9. Zoll hoch/ vnd also höher/ als ein Regal Corpus 8. ß. Thon: Darumb es sich auch einer Menschenstimm gantz vnd gar vergleichen thut. Wiewol etliche die Corpora im Cornett kaum 4. oder 5. Zoll hoch machē: Denn hierinn von den Orgelmachern gar sehr variirt wird/vnd also nichts gewisses darvon kan geschrieben werdē.

VIII.
Gedäcte Schnarrwerck.
Sordunen sind 16. Fuß Thon:

Können auch wegen der Invention, daß sie gedäckt seyn müssen/ vnnd in sich noch ein verborgen Corpus mit ziemlichen langen Rohren haben/ nicht wol höher/ wenn sie jhre rechte Art behalten sollen/ intoniret werden: Jhr außwendiges Corpus ist zwar ohngefehr zwey fuß hoch/vnd seine weitte/ als ein Nachthorn Corpus von 4. Fuß Thon. Es ist aber sehr lieblich vnd stille/ wenn es seinen rechten Meister gehabt hat/ vnd also zu Saiten- oder Flöitwerck gar wol zu gebrauchen. Man muß aber dabey in guter acht haben/ daß es gleich wie ander grob Pfeiffwerck von oder vff 16. fuß/ mit den Concordantiis, als tertien oder Quinten in der lincken Hand zu greiffen verschonet/ vnd von solchem tieffem Thon nicht verderbet/ vnd vbel anzuhören gemacht werde; Vornemlich aber ist es zierlich im Pedal zu vielen enderungen zu gebrauchen.

Groß

Some also call such a small regal at 4' pitch "Geigen-"[101] or "Geigend-Regal," because, when a Quintadena at 8' pitch is drawn with it, it sounds in some ways much like a violin (especially when it is played by the right hand as a treble solo.

Since however each stop should be named according to the sound it produces in and of itself, the most appropriate name for this stop is "little Regal."

Zinck at 8' pitch[102]

This stop is found only in the treble range of the keyboard. It has conical resonators, somewhat tapered at the bottom and open at the top. And so its sound is somewhat hollow, like a flue stop, and without such a strong rattle. The rattling is largely prevented by its stiff tongues and ample wind.

The Cornett[103] is found for the most part in the pedal. Its dimensions are those of a Regal, though narrower and longer. For although it is only at 4' or 2' pitch, yet its resonator is 9 inches tall, that is, taller than the resonator of a Regal at 8' pitch. Therefore it may be quite credibly compared to the sound of the human voice. Some builders make their Cornet resonators barely 4 or 5 inches tall; in this matter there is much variety among organbuilders, and so nothing definitive can be written concerning it.

VIII.
Stopped Reeds.

Sordun is at 16' pitch.[104]

Because of the way it is constructed, with stopped pipes, and because it contains a concealed resonator, a rather long tube, this stop indeed cannot be built at a higher pitch, if it is to be true to its type. Its exterior resonator is, to be sure, approximately two feet high, and the width of a Nachthorn pipe-body of 4' pitch. If a true master builds it, then its sound is very gentle and quiet, and it sounds well in ensemble with stringed instruments and flutes. One must be mindful, however, just as with other low pipes sounding at 16', not to play intervals of thirds or fifths in the left hand, to avoid producing unpleasantly low sounds. It sounds best in the pedal, indeed quite elegant in all sorts of combinations.

---

101. German "Violin."
102. See *Theatrum Instrumentorum*, Plate XXXVIII, no. 12: "treble Zinck [or] Cornet."
103. In Part II, Chapter IX, p. 35, Praetorius has already explained that "Cornetti" is the Italian word for "Zinck."
104. See *Theatrum Instrumentorum*, Plate XXXVIII, no. 11: "Sorduen 16 foot."

DE ORGANOGRAPHIA.

Groß Rancket sind auch 16. Fuß Thon:
Rancket ist 8. Fuß Thon:

Sind auch außbündige liebliche zugedäckte Art von Schnarrwercken / gantz stille zu intoniren, vnd zu vielen variationibus vnd verenderungen gar bequem.

Es haben diese beyde Stimmen gleich kleine Corpora, jhr gröstes ist ohngefehr einer guten Spannen / oder neun Zoll lang / vnd haben in sich noch ein verborgen Corpus, gleich wie die Sordunen / derer vorher gedacht worden ist.

Baerpipen oder Baerpfeiffen sind auch 16. vnd 8. fuß Thon / vnd nicht kleiner zu arbeiten / oder sie verlieren jhren rechten namen vnd klang; Den sie vielleicht von eines Beeren stillen brummen haben: Wie sie denn auch gar in sich klingen / vnd mit einer brummenden intonation respondiren. Haben zwar nicht hohe Corpora, doch ziemlich weit / vnd als zweene zusammen gestülpte Tröchter / jedoch in der mitten einer gleichen weite / vnd fast gantz zugedäckt. Von holtze aber werden sie etwas anders gearbeitet / wie in der Sciagraphia zu sehen. Man kan sie vff mancherley Art formiren / allein ist diß jhr proprium, daß sie vnten eng / vnd alsobald gar in die weite außgestrecket werden müssen.

Zu Prag hab ich in der Jesuiterkirchen ein Schnarrwerck gesehen / so Pater Andreas erfunden / vnd gar eines lieblichen Resonantzes / do das Corpus vierecket neben einander hin vnd herwider geführt / vnd sich allezeit auch in die weite ergrösset hat: Wie in der Sciagraphia zu sehen.

Pombarda: Ist fast der Sordunen Invention gemeß / ohne daß die außlassung des Resonantzes durch die Löcherlein geendert wird / vnd grössere Mundstück vnd Zungen haben wil / daher sie denn auch sich lauterer vnd stärcker hören lessen; vnd ist vff 16. vnd 8. fuß Thon zu arbeiten. Die Pombarden gehören vnd schicken sich aber füglicher vnd besser zum Pedal / als zum Manual, denn sie einen anmutigen vnnd mittelmessigen Klang ein starcken Laut geben.

Fagott ist 8. Fuß Thon: Hat auch gleich auswerte vnd enge Corpora, das gröste von 4. fuß an der lenge / vnd wird Manualiter geschlagen.

Dulcian ist nur 8. Fuß Thon: Wird von etlichen oben zugedäckt / vnd durch etliche löcherlein sein Resonantz vnten an der einen seiten außgelassen / welche in denen Regalwercken / so zu Wien in Oesterreich gemacht werden / zu finden. Etliche aber lassen es oben gantz offen / darumb sie auch gleichwol so stille nicht seyn / vnd sich dem blasenden Instrumenten, welches mit diesem Namen genennet wird / gleich artet; gehöret auch billicher ins Pedal / dann zum Manual. Vnd weil derer Invention vff vnterschiedliche arten verendert wird / ist allhier mehr davon zu schreiben vnnötig.

DE ORGANOGRAPHIA.

Large Ranket is also at 16' pitch.[105]

Ranket is at 8' pitch.[106]

These are also exceedingly gentle stopped reed registers, very quietly voiced, and well suited to all sorts of combinations.

Both of these stops have small resonators of the same size, the largest being a good hand-span, about nine inches, tall. They both contain a concealed resonator, just like the abovementioned Sordun.

The Baerpipe or Baerpfeife is likewise found at 16' and 8' pitch; it cannot be built at any higher pitch, or it loses its proper tonal identity. It produces a muffled sound, rather like a growl, perhaps reminiscent of the quiet growling of a bear. Its resonators are not tall, to be sure, but quite wide, like two funnels of the same diameter, one inverted atop the other, and almost totally stopped. When it is made of wood, though, it is built somewhat differently; see the *Theatrum instrumentorum*.[107] The resonators may assume many shapes, but all of them are characteristically narrow at the bottom and broaden rapidly to become wide.

I saw a reed stop[108] in the Jesuit Church at Prague, invented by Father Andreas, which had a very gentle sound. Its resonators were mitered a number of times, and became gradually wider throughout their entire length, as depicted in the *Theatrum instrumentorum*.[109]

The Pombarda is almost the same as the Sordun, except that the holes through which the sound escapes are different and the shallots and reeds are larger. It therefore has a more powerful sound. It can be built at 16' and 8' pitch. Pombardes are better suited and belong more properly to the pedal, for they produce an agreeable, moderately loud sound.

The Fagott is at 8' pitch. It has narrow, cylindrical resonators, the tallest of which is 4' high. This stop appears in the manual.

The Dulcian is built only at 8' pitch. Some builders construct it as a stopped rank, with a number of small holes on one side at the bottom to let the sound escape, like the regals that are built in Vienna, Austria. Others, however, leave it entirely open at the top, and thus not as quiet. Then it sounds like the wind instrument that bears this name. It is more suited to the pedal than to the manual. And since this stop appears in a number of varieties, no more need be said about it here.

---

105. See *Theatrum Instrumentorum*, Plate XXXVIII, no. 13: "Rancket 8 [or] 16 foot."
106. Under this heading Praetorius groups a number of colorful reeds with fractional-length resonators, suggesting that he considers them essentially similar.
107. Plate XXXVIII, nos. 19-23
108. Presumably a type of Baerpfeiffe, since that is the stop Praetorius is describing.
109. Plate 38 depicts five varieties of Baerpfeiffen. None of them seems to correspond to Praetorius' description, unless one interprets the German freely to mean something like "all wound around itself." In that case, no. 21 may be a sketch of the resonator Praetorius is describing.

Apffel oder Knopff Regal ist 8. Fuß Thon;

Wird seiner Proportion halber / daß es / wie ein Apffel uffm Stiel stehet / also genennet; Das gröste Corpus ist etwa 4. Zoll hoch / hat eine kleine Röhr / an der grösse wie sein Mundstück / vnd uff derselben Röhren einen runden holen Knopff voller kleiner Löcher / gleich einem Bisemknopff gebohret / da der Sonus wieder außgehen muß: Ist auch nach Regal Art lieblicher vnd viel stiller / denn ein ander Regal anzuhören / dienet wol in Positiffen / so in Gemächern gebrauchet werden.

Köpfflin Regal sind 4. Fuß Thon / haben oben auch ein rund Knäufflein / als ein Knopff / vnd ist derselbige in der mitten von einander gethan / als ein offen Helm / also daß es den Resonantz gleich wieder ins vnter Corpus einwendet / ist gut vnnd lieblich.

Vnd diß sey also von den Stimmen in Orgeln vor dieses mal gnug.

Das III. Capitel.

Vnterricht / Wie man die Schnarrwercke in den Orgeln / so wol auch absonderlich die Regal Wercke vnd andere Instrumenta, als Clavicymbalen / Spinetten / vnd dergleichen vor sich selbsten recht vnd reine accordiren vnd einstimmen könne: Im gleichen welcher massen die andern Pfeiffen nachzustimmen / oder jhnen im Stimmen nach zuhelffen.

Es ist zwar gut / vnd keine sonderbahre Mühe / die Schnarrwercke in den Orgeln einzuziehen / vnd rein zu Stimmen / wenn die Fundament des andern Pfeiff- oder Flötwercks rein seyn. Dennoch aber ist dieses ein Vortheil / daß / wenn man ein Schnarrwerck / welches 16. Fuß am Thon ist / stimmen wil / eine andere Stimme vom Flötwerck / als Principal oder groß Octav von 8. Fuß darzu gezogen werde. Also / wenn ein Schnarrwerck / so 8. Fuß am Thon sol gestimmet werden / muß eine Stimme von 4. ff. als die Octava; Zum Schnarrwerck aber / so 4. Fuß Thon / eine Principal oder groß Octava, oder Quintadehn

Apfel- or Knopf-Regal[110] is at 8' pitch.

This stop gets its name from its shape, which looks like an apple sitting atop a stick. The tallest resonator is about 4 inches high, consisting of a little tube of the same size as its shallot, on top of which is a round, hollow little ball like a braided button, bored full of little holes, through which the sound escapes. Its sound is similar to that of a Regal, but quieter and more gentle. It is well suited to positives that are used in private chambers.

KöpflinRegal is a 4' pitch. At its top is a little round ball, like a button, slit across the middle like an open helmet, that immediately reflects the sound back into the lower part of the resonator. It is a fine and gentle stop.

This is enough for the present
about organ stops.

Chapter III.

Instruction concerning how to set a
temperament in reed stops within an organ, as well as in Regals (as separate instruments) and other instruments such as harpsichords, spinets, and such; also how to tune or touch up the remaining pipes.[111]

It is no particular problem to tune reed stops to the rest of the organ, once the flue pipes are in good tune. If the reed to be tuned is at 16', the best way to do this is to draw a flue stop such as a Principal or large Octave at 8' pitch. If the reed to be tuned is at 8', then draw a 4' stop such as an Octave. If the reed is at 4' pitch, then a Principal, large Octave, or Quintadena at 8' pitch, together with a 4' Octave, should be drawn; then the reed should be tuned against

---

110. German "Apple- or Button-Regal."
111. i.e., those higher and lower than the octave in which the temperament is set.

cadehn von 8. Fuß Thon / mit der Octav von 4. Fuß Thon darzu gezogen / vnd darnach gestimmet werden. Vnd das aus diesen Vrsachen / weil die Pfeiffwercks Stimmen / so mit den Schnarrwercken AEqual am Thon sind / betriegen vnd laviren.

Vnd ob es ja das Flöitwerck an Principalen, Octaven, oder Quintadecenen / darnach die Schnarrwercke gestimmet werden sollen / nicht gar just vnd rein wehre / vnd ein Organist köndte daß Regal vor sich alleine in sich selbst / nach der Art / wie ein Instrument reine accordiret wird / nicht durch concordanten Stimmen; So ist diß nach ein vortheil / daß man als dann zu einer jeden vnr einen Regalpfeiff / (jedoch das Flöit- vnnd Schnarrwercke nicht zugleich vff einem Clavir beysammen stehen) eine Concordant greiffe / vnd der schnarrenden Stimmen das jhrige darein oder darzwischen rein mache. Als zum Exempel: Wenn man das C oder c im Pedalschnarrwerck (es sey nun in der Posaun / Trummet / etc. vnd was mehr vnter die Schnarrwerck gerechnet wird) stimmen will / so greiff man vffm Manual also / c e g C / so muß das vnreine Pedal C oder c im Schnarrwerck zu derselben Concordant (weil darinnen eine tertia vnd sexta perfect, eine Quarta, Quinta vnd eine Octava begriffen) sich auffs reineste bringen lassen: Ob schon das andere zuvor enwehnete Pfeiffwerck auch nicht gar rein were.

Also auch / wenn im Rückpositiff ein Schnarrwerck nach einem Flöitwerck / welches vnrein / nicht just köndte eingezogen werden; So ist es besser / daß man im Oberwerck eine Flöitwercks Stimme zum Concordanten greiffen gebrauche / vnnd versuche / alsdenn die Regalpfeiffen im Rückpositiff / eine nach der andern gegen vorgedachte Concordanten im Oberwerck.

Hergegen kan man auch dergestalt ein Regal im Oberwerck nach einer Flöiten im Rückpositiff einziehen vnd accordiren. Jedoch muß man hierauff achtung geben / daß die Schnarewerck / weil derselben etliche gar stille klingen / nicht nach zu gar zu lautklingenden Stimmen eingezogen oder gestimmet werden können:

Gleich wie nun ein Regal oder Schnarrwercken bey dem Drath oder krucken / so durch die Pfeiffen gehet / hoch vnd niedrig gestimmet / vnd je mehr das Drath herausgezogen / oder mit einm Plectro geschlagen (davon denn dessen Labium erweitert) je tieffer die Pfeiffe klinget / vnd je tieffer das Drath hinein geschlagen / je enger vnnd höher dieselbe resonirend wird. Also werden auch die andern Pfeiffen in Orgeln vnd Positiffen / jedoch vff andere Art / hoch vnd niedrig gestimmet / als: Das öffen Flöitwerck wird höher / woferne die Pfeiffen oben erweitert / oder denselben etwas genommen wird; Niedriger aber wirds / so dieselben oben mit einm Stimmhorn enger gemachet / oder zugedruckt werden. Man muß sich aber wol fürsehen / damit man den Pfeiffen nicht leichtlich etwas nehme / denn es ist viel leichter eine Pfeiffe höher / denn niedriger

T iij

the flue. The reason for doing this is that tuning a reed to a flue of the same pitch is deceptive.

And if by chance the flue rank (be it Principal, Octave, or Quintadena) to which the reed is to be tuned is itself not perfectly in tune, or if an organist wants to tune a Regal within itself, without matching pitches to another instrument, the same way that a temperament is set in a [stringed keyboard] instrument, then the best way to do this is to play a chord on a flue stop (on another manual), and tune the reed against it. For example, if one wants to tune the C or c of a pedal reed (say, the Posaune, Trompet, or some other reed), then one should play the chord c e g c' on a manual [flue stop]; then the out-of-tune pedal C or c can be tuned perfectly to that chord (since the chord contains a pure third and sixth, a fourth, a fifth, and an octave). This procedure works even if the abovementioned [flue] pipes are not in perfect tune.

Likewise, if one has difficulty tuning a reed in the Rückpositiv to a flue stop in the same division, then it is best to draw a flue stop in the Oberwerk and play chords on it, against which the Regal[112] pipes can be tuned, one after the other.

Vice versa, one can tune an Oberwerk Regal in the same way against a Rückpositiv flue stop. But in that case, one must take care not to draw a very loud flue stop for purposes of tuning, since some of the reed stops[113] are very quiet.

If a Regal is tuned higher or lower by means of the wire or crook that comes out of the boot, then the further the wire is drawn out or driven upwards by a rod (thus making its tongue longer), the lower the pipe sounds; conversely, the further in the wire is driven, the shorter the tongue and the higher the pitch. In organs and positives, the other pipes are tuned differently: open flues get sharper when the top of the pipe is widened or cut down a bit. On the other hand, they get flatter when their tops are pressed inward or coned in with a tuning cone. One ought not to be too quick, though, to cut down the top of a pipe, since it is much easier to make a pipe shorter than longer. Where organ pipes are found to be pinched

---

112. At the beginning of the sentence Praetorius does not specify the reed stop to be tuned. Here he specifically mentions the Regal since, practically speaking, reeds with fractional-length resonators are the most unstable and in need of constant tuning.

113. i.e., Regals.

driger zustimmen/ vnd ist ein gewiß Merckzeichen/ wo die Pfeiffen in OrgelWercken oben sehr zugedruckt/ vnd gleich als ein hauffen zerkröckelte H. drey Königshüte gefunden werden/ daß ein fauler vnd vnfleissiger Orgelmacher/ welcher die Mensur nicht in acht genommen/ drüber gewesen sey.

Die Gedacten aber werden bey jhren decken oder stulpen/ so sie haben/ gestimmet; Denn in niedriger dieselben gedruckt/ oder mit eim drauffliegenden brätlein geschlagen werden/ je höher der Sonus, je höher sie aber gerückt/ je tieffer derselbe wird.

Es werden aber auch oben zugelöthe Gedacten funden/ dieselbe werden bey jhren habenden Bärten gestimmet/ je weiter solche vom Labio gethan/ je höher der Resonantz; je näher aber/ je nidriger er wird.

Zuweilen begibt sichs auch/ daß ein Flöit- oder Schnarrwerckspfeiffe gar erstummet/ welches denn leichtlich geschehen kan/ wenn sich ein stäublein oder Fliege ins Labial, oder zwischen das Blat vnd Röhre im Schnarrwerck setzet/ so mans aber subtil weg thut/ intonirt die Pfeiffe leichtlich wieder.

Ebener massen setzet sich auch zum offtern Salpeter/ Rost oder ander Vnflat in die Pfeiffen/ sonderlich aber an die Messingsblätlein vnd Röhren in Schnarrwercken/ welches jhnen gleichsfals kan benommen werden/ ehe denn man die blätter streichen wil. Man muß sich aber fürsehen/ daß man die blätter nicht zu hart/ noch zu gelinde streiche: Denn wo sie zu hart/ kan der wind dieselben nicht vberweltigen/ noch zum Resonantz bringen/ wo aber zu weich/ vberweltiget er gar zu sehr/ vnnd treibet die Blätter feste an die Röhren/ davon sie gleichsfalls erstummen.

Vnd ob wol zu förderst/ welcher gestalt eine Symphonia, Clavicymbel, oder dergleichen Instrument besäitet vnd bestödert werde/ meldung geschehen solte. Jedoch weil solches eigentlich die Instrumentmacher angehet/ vnd anderweit besser vnd mehr durch vbung/ dann schrifftlichen vnterricht kan erlernet werden/ sintemal die Rollen Säiten nach jhren Numeris numehr fast sehr vngleich/ sintemal einerley Numeri, theils grob/ theils klein; zun zeiten auch an den Tangenten, bald dieser/ bald jener defectus vorfellet/ als ist hievon weitläufftig zu schreiben vnvonnöten.

Wie man ein Regal, Clavicymbel, Symphonien vnd dergleichen Instrument vor sich selbst accordiren vnd rein stimmen könne.

Allhier muß vornemlich nachfolgends mit fleiß in acht genommen werden.

1. Daß man einen gewissen Clavem vor sich neme/ von welchem man zu stimen anhebe/ vnd nach welchem die andern/ doch allwege je einer nach dem andern einzuziehen.

2. Das alle Octaven vnd Tertiæ perfectæ seu majores gar rein gestimmet werden/ so wol der niedrigste Clavis nach dem höchstem/ als der höchste nach dem niedrigsten.

3. Daß alle Quinten nicht gerade vnd rein/ sondern gegen einander (doch vff gewisse maß) niedrig schwebend gelassen werden (zuverstehen/ der höchste Clavis muß gegen

drastically out of shape on top, like a pile of fanciful, twisted headgear, it is a sure sign that a lazy, careless organbuilder, who has paid no attention to their proper length, has been at them.[114]

Gedackt pipes, on the other hand, are tuned by the lids or caps they have [at their tops]. The further these are pressed down, or tapped with a little board, the more the pitch rises; the higher these are shifted, the lower the pitch becomes.

There are also Gedackts with soldered caps, and these are tuned by the ears they have [on both sides of their lips]. The further these are bent away from the lip, the higher the pitch; the more they are bent inward, the lower the pitch.

Sometimes one encounters a flue or reed pipe that has become entirely mute. This can easily happen when a fly or a bit of dust has become lodged in the lip or, in a reed, between the tongue and shallot. When this obstacle is removed, the pipe will speak without further ado.

Likewise, it is not uncommon for saltpeter, rust, or some other grime to attack pipes, especially the little brass tongues in reed pipes. This can be removed by scraping/filing the tongues. One must be careful, however, not to scrape/file the tongues until they are too stiff or too weak; if they are too stiff, the wind cannot force them into vibration,[115] and if they are too weak,[116] [the wind] presses against them too forcefully and drives them hard against the shallots, preventing them from speaking at all.

One ought to begin[117] by describing how a harpsichord (Symphonia, Clavicymbel) or other such [plucked string keyboard] instrument should be strung and quilled. Yet, because this is really the concern of the instrument-maker, and is furthermore better mastered by doing it than by reading about it, it is not essential here to write about it at length. This is especially the case, since there is considerable variety in string sizes, and the same number may signify thinner or thicker strings; also since a variety of defects can arise in the jacks.

How to temper and tune a Regal, Harpsichord, Spinet,
or similar instrument.

Following are the principal concerns that must be carefully considered:
1. One must choose the particular pitch from which to begin the tempering process; all subsequent pitches are determined by this first one.
2. All octaves and perfect or major thirds must be tuned pure, whether they are tuned from the lower pitch to the higher or vice versa.
3. All fifths must not be tuned pure, but they must beat flat (to a specific degree). Of

---

114. i.e., the builder has been careless about making the pipes at their proper lengths, and to compensate for this shortcoming and bring them into tune, he has had to pinch them out of shape.
115. Excessive pressure will harden the brass; then when it is set into vibration, the tongue will no longer function as previously.
116. Scraping the metal too thin will make the tongue flimsy.
117. In this paragraph Praetorius abruptly changes the subject and introduces the matter treated in the section following.

DE ORGANOGRAPHIA.

dem niedrigen etwas nachgelassen/ oder herunterwarts stehen: so man aber die Quinten von vntenwarts/ oder den vntersten Clavem gegen dem obern stimmen wil/ muß derselbe zu hoch stehen vnd schweben/ vnd also etwas mehr/ denn gar rein stehen.

Wenn nu diese dreyerley recht in acht genommen werden/ so kan man im stimmen nicht leichtlich jrren: doch ist das letzte die Quinten (vorbeschriebener art nach) recht einzuziehen das schwehrste/ oder in acht zu nemen das vornemiste. Denn nach Octaven vnd Quinten kan man ein gantz Instrument einstimmen/ nur allein/ daß die Tertiæ majores, als zu Richtern gebraucht werden/ davon weitläufftiger meldung geschicht.

Etliche geübte können auch nach Octaven vnd Quarten rein stimmen/ vnd werden dieselben den Quinten im schweben gleich/ aber contrariè, oder vice versa gestimmet: Dann der öberste Clavis sol nach dem vntern vmb etwas zu hoch/ der vnterste aber gegen dem oberstem zu niedrig schweben. Das wort Schweben aber ist ein Orgelmacherischer Terminus, vnd wird von jnen gebraucht/ wenn eine Concordantz nit reine stehet: Ist aber bey jnen/ vnd daher bey vielen Organisten so sehr vblich/ daß es schwerlich abzuschaffen. Dannenher ichs im künfftigen auch (wiewol gantz vngern) gebrauchen müssen/ nur das dabey gesagt/ hoch oder niedrig. Dann schweben sol so viel heissen/ wie vnrein/ das ist/ entweder zu hoch oder zu niedrig gestimmet/ sie derivirens aber daher; Wann man in den Orgeln/ sonderlich die Octaven, Quinten vnd Quarten einthen vnd stimmen wil/ so schwebt der Resonantz vnd klang in den Pfeiffen/ vnd schlägt gleich eim Tremulant etliche Schläge: Je näher man es aber mit dem einstimmen zur reinigkeit vnd accort bringt/ je mehr verleurt sich die schwebung allmehlich/ vnd werden der Schläge immer weniger/ biß so lang dz die Octava oder andere concordanten recht eintretē. Daher dan aus solcher schwebung die Dissonantiē in Orgeln viel leichter vn ehe/ als in dē Regaln/ Claviczymbel vn dergleichē Instrumentē observirt vn erkant werden könen. Demnach nu die Octava, welche eine Quintam vnd Quartam in sich begreifft/ gar rein seyn vnd bleiben muß/ der Quinten aber/ als dem ersten Theil etwas genommen wird/ so folgt nothwendig/ daß der Quarten, als den andern Theil/ so viel hinwiederum gegebē (als der Quinten abgebrochē) werde damit die Octava rein bleibe.

Die Quinta so eine Tertiam Majorem vnd Minorem in sich helt/ muß wie vor gemeldet/ nicht gar rein stehen: Die Tertia major aber ist rein/ so folget/ daß die Tertia minor (vmb so viel/ als die Quinta betrifft) vnrein sey.

Ex Tertia majore entspringet per Transpositionem sexta minor. Als wen der vnterste Clavis eine Octava höher/ oder der öberste eine Octava niedriger gesetzt oder genommē wird: gleich wie nu die tertia major rein/ so muß auch sexta minor rein werdē.

Also auch/ wo ein Clavis gegē dem audern rein stehet/ so müsse alle andere Claves (so desselben Namens sind) gegē demselben rein werdē. Als: der Clavis c ist gegē dē c rein/ so folgt/ daß alle Claves, so c heissen/ sie sein klein oder grob/ wie sie seynd/ gegen dem/

ober

course it is the higher pitch that must be slightly lowered in relation to the lower one; but on the other hand, if the lower note of the fifth is to be tuned against the upper one, then the lower note must beat sharp, must be somewhat larger than absolutely pure.[118]

If these three matters are carefully attended to, then one is quite unlikely to go astray when tempering. Drawing the final fifth into tune according to the method just described is, however, the most difficult task, and the one that needs the greatest attention. One can temper an entire instrument by octaves and fifths, except that more must be said about using the major thirds as guides/check-points.

Some persons with experience can also temper an instrument according to octaves and fourths. In that case, the fourths will beat just like fifths, but in reverse, or opposite. Thus the upper pitch needs to beat somewhat sharp against the lower, and the lower pitch should beat flat against the upper.[119] The word "beat" (Schweben) is the term that organbuilders use to describe intervals that are not tuned pure. It is in such common use among builders, and consequently among many organists, that it would be difficult to eradicate. Therefore in future I must also use it (though not at all happily), but always modified by "sharp" or "flat." For "beat," judging from its derivation, means the same thing as "impure," i.e., tuned either too sharp or too flat. When tuning an organ, especially the octaves, fifths, and fourths, the pitch beats a bit in the pipes, just like a tremulant. The closer to pure one tunes the interval, the less the beating gets; the beats gets slower and slower, until the octave or other concordant interval draws pure. It is much easier to perceive the out-of-tuneness in organs than in regals, harpsichords and other such instruments. The octave, which contains a fifth and a fourth within itself, must always be tuned exactly pure. When the fifth, one part of the whole octave, is made flat, then the fourth, the other part, must inevitably beat sharp to the same extent, so that the octave remains pure.

The fifth, which contains a major and a minor third, must, as noted above, not be tuned exactly pure. The major third, however, is pure, and so it follows that the minor third must beat to the same extent as does the entire fifth.

The minor sixth is the inversion of the major third; it is the result of the lower note [of the third] being taken up an octave, or the upper note being taken down an octave. Therefore, since the major third must be pure, so also must the minor sixth be pure.

Thus whenever one pitch is exactly in tune with another, then all the octaves of the former must be exactly in tune with the latter. For example, if the interval c/e is pure, it follows that all the octaves of the c, whether higher or lower, must be pure,

---

118. What Praetorius means by this statement becomes clear when he begins to treat specific tempering recipes, on pp. 153ff.
119. See the previous footnote.

oder andern T reln seyn müssen. Also ferner/ ein d ist gegen dem andern rein/ darumb folget das alle d/ eins gegen dem andern rein seyn müssen.

Ex Tertia minore kömpt vorbemeldter massen per Transpositionem, Sexta major. Gleich wie nun die Tertia minor vnrein vnd schwebend ist/ also muß auch die Sexta major schweben oder vnrein seyn; Doch solcher gestält: Die Tertia minor hat zu wenig/ ergo/ so muß sexta major zu viel haben/ damit die Octava just bleibe/ vnd also per inversionem; Sexta major schwebt zu viel/ ergo Tertia minor zu wenig/ denn wenn diese beyde zusammen gesetzt werden/ müssen sie eine reine Octavam geben. Weil man nun jedem Theil nicht gibt/ was jhm gebühret/ so folget daraus/ daß das eine Theil mehr/ dann das andere haben muß.

Also auch/ wo ein Clavis gegen den andern schwebet/ so ist gewiß/ daß alle andere (des Namens) Claves gegen demselben schweben/ vnd ist gleich damit/ wie jetzt gemelt/ da von den reinstehenden Clavibus meldung geschehen/ nur mit diesem vnterscheyd/ daß das eine Theil vmb so viel zu hoch/ als das ander zu niedrig wird.

Welcher massen aber ein Clavis gegen dem andern zu niedrig stehen müsse/ ist in folgender Tabel besser vnd vorständlicher zu ersehen. Als:

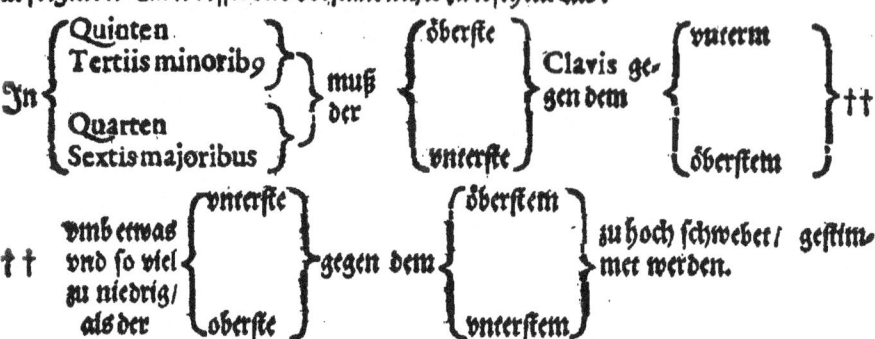

Die Octaven, Tertiæ majores vnnd Sextæ minores, (wie offt erwehnet) bleiben rein. Wann nun ein Intervallum, oder vielmehr eine Concordant sol just bleiben/ so müssen die Intermedia alle beyde gleich seyn/ entweder beyde rein/ oder beyde (eins zu hoch/ das andre zu niedrig) schweben.

Wenn aber das eine Intermedium falsch/ vnd das andere rein ist/ so muß das rechte Intervallum falsch seyn/ vnd kan nicht rein bleiben : Idq; ex principio Geometrico. Si enim ad certum numerum incertus addatur, tum totus ille fiet incertus : Vel si ad quantitatem definitam incerta addatur quantitas, tota illa quantitas fiet incerta, & dato uno inconvenienti, sequuntur plura.

Vnd

both against the corresponding e and all its octaves. Likewise, if the interval d/f♯ is pure, it follows that all d's must be pure against all f♯s.

In the same way, inverting a minor third produces a major sixth. If the minor third beats out-of-tune, then the minor sixth must also beat out-of-tune; but since the minor third beats flat, therefore the major sixth must beat sharp, so the the octave remains pure. And vice versa, since the major sixth beats sharp, therefore the minor third must beat flat, for when both are put together, they must produce a pure octave. When one part is narrower than its appropriate size, then what is lacking must be added to the other part.

Thus when one pitch beats against another, it must follow that all octaves of the former must beat against the latter. The same holds true in this case as with the pure intervals described above, the only difference being that the wider one part is, the narrower the other part must be.

This variance of intervals is depicted in the following table, to make it more comprehensible:

In { fifths, minor thirds, fourths, major sixths } the { upper, lower } note must be tuned flat against { the lower note, the upper note } ††

†† to the same extent that the { lower, upper } note beats sharp against { the upper note. the lower note. }

Octaves, major thirds, and minor sixths remain pure (as mentioned above). When an interval, or rather a consonant interval, is to remain pure, then the intermediate intervals lying within it must be treated in the same way, either both pure, or both beating (one sharp, the other flat).

If one intermediate interval beats and the other one is pure, then the interval proper [which is made up of these two intermediates] must beat; it can never be pure. Thus, according to the principles of geometry: if an indefinite number is added to a definite one, then the total of the two must be indefinite; or if an indefinite quantity is added to a definite quantity, the entire quantity will be indefinite.

DE ORGANOGRAPHIA.

Diß sey also einfältig geredt vnd deliniiret. Welcher gestalt aber die defectus vnd excessus der Quinten, Quarten, Tertiarum minorum, vnd sextarum majorum recht demonstriret werden können/ sol bald nach diesem auch in etwas angedeutet werden.

Vnd ob nun zwar nicht groß (sonderlich deme der des Stimmens läufftig) daran gelegen/ von welchem Clave man den anfang mache/ so ists doch bequemlich am f/ wenn dasselbe erstlich Chormässig intoniret wird/ anzufangen/ vnd folget demnach die richtige Ordnung der Concordanten, also:

1	f		Chormessiger oder rechter Thon/ nach deme sich das Instrument leiden wil/ darein wird f rein eingezogen.
2	f	c	
3	f	a	Proba.
4	c	c	Wenn die vorhergehende Concordanten vnnd Quinten,
5	c	g	nach vorschriebener Art recht eingezogen seyn/ so müssen diese fünff Proben auch recht seyn. Als wo in der 1. Proba die
6	c	e	
7	g	d	Quinta, d gegen dem gestimpten a nicht recht schwebet/ oder
8	g	h	etwas falsch stehet/ So muß den vorigen Concordanten allen (weil sie entweder in den Quinten zu rein oder zu falsch
9	d	d	
	d	a Prob.1	gemacht seyn) nachgeholffen werden/ biß das d vnd a auch
10	d	fi	seine rechte schwebung erlangt. Wann dañ diese Proba also
11	a	e	justificiret ist/ So ist kühnlich mit den folgenden fort zufahren/ vnd sich drauff zuverlassen.
	e	e Prob.2	
12	a	g	
13	g	g	Allhier aber/ wenn man zum 15. mal stimmen wil/ ist
14	g	h	in acht zu nehmen/ daß alsdenn die Quinten vom vntern
	e	h Prob.3	Clave gegen dem obersten/ vff andere weise rückwarts eingezogen werden. Als wenn der vnterste Clavis erstlich gar
15	f	b	
	b	b Prob.4	reine in die Quinten eintritt/ so muß er ferner hochschwebend
16	b	fi	gebracht oder gestimmet werden: Inmassen davon in voriger
	fi	g Prob.5	Tabell bericht geschehen.
17	fi	b	

Diese Claves vff diese Seiten werden reine/ vnd müssen die vff der andern Seiten gegen vber/ allezeit nach diesen gestimmet/ vnd eingezogen werden.

Nach diesem fengt man von dem gestimpten b an descendendo, vnd ziehet nach demselben die Octavam H gar rein ein/ Nach dem b das A/ nach dem a das X etc. vnd also vollends biß zum vntern Clave. Jedoch/ daß man fleissig drauff höre/ daß solche Octaven just/ vnd die vntersten Claves gegen dem allbereit rein gestimtem Clave ja nicht zu hoch gemacht werden/ denn wo das geschicht/ werden die Quinten

B so viel

DE ORGANOGRAPHIA. 153

That explains the matter simply. Below you will find an explanation as to what degree the fifths, fourths, minor thirds, and major sixths ought to beat either sharp or flat.

Although it is not especially important (particularly to one who is experienced in tuning) which key one begins with, it is convenient to begin by using the pitch f' as the fundamental pitch; then the proper sequence for tuning the concordant intervals is as follows:

	[step]			
(The notes in the left column are tuned first; the ones in the right column are tuned against them.)	1.	f		the basic, given pitch, [established] according to the capabilities of the instrument; f' is tuned pure against it.
	2.	f	c'	
	3.	f	a	
	4.	c'	c	
	5.	c	g	
	6.	c	e	
	7.	g	d'	
	8.	g	b	
	9.	d'	d	
		d	a	Test 1
	10.	d	f♯	
	11.	a	e'	
		c'	e'	Test 2
	12.	a	c♯'	
	13.	c♯'	c♯	
	14.	c♯	g♯	
		e	g♯	Test 3
	15.	f'	b♭	
		b♭	d	Test 4
	16.	b♭	d♯	
		d♯	g	Test 5
	17.	d♯	d♯'	

Regarding the tests:

If the above concordant intervals and fifths are tuned in the way described earlier, then the five tests must turn out satisfactorily. If in the first test the fifth d/a does not beat properly, then the previously tuned intervals must all be adjusted (either because the fifths are too pure or because they beat too rapidy) until the interval d/a reaches its proper rate of beat. If this test turns out to be accurate, then one may confidently proceed to the following steps without further ado.

From step 15 one must be careful to temper the fifths in the opposite way. That is, after the lowest note comes into perfect tune, it must then be tuned sharp, as reported in the above table.

When the above process has been completed, then one begins to tune down the scale from the b[120] that has already been tuned, drawing the lower octave, the B, into tune with it. Next comes b♭/B♭, then a/A, etc., all the way down to the lowest note. One must pay careful attention that these octaves are precisely in tune, and that the lower notes are not tuned sharp against the already-tuned notes. If that is

---

120. The original text reads "b" (i.e., b♭), but the context proves it to be an error.

soviel deren noch in der tieffen zu gebrauchen seyn/ gar zu vnrein/ vnd verderben das beste vnd reineste Gehör/ wenn volle Griffe gebraucht werden.

Wenn nun dieses descendendo also geschehen/ so procediret man alsdenn ascendendo, vnd zeucht das f̄ nach dem gestimpten f̄ auch gar rein ein/ daß ḡ nach dem g/ vnd so fort an/ biß gar hindurch so weit das Clavir disponiret ist.

Allhier aber in den obern Clavibus ist noch mehr vnd mit viel fleissigerm vnd schärfferm Gehör/ denn zuvor in den vntersten/ in acht zu haben/ daß man ebenmessig die Octaven gar rein ziehe/ also/ daß die beyden Claves in dem Octavenklange so gar gleich klingen/ als wenn es durchaus nur eine Pfeiffe oder Säite were; Vnnd denn/ daß man allezeit zur Proba die Tertien perfecten zum Iudice vnd Richter behalte; Als wenn das f̄ nach dem f̄ justificiret ist/ so probier solch f̄ mit dem d̄/ vnd höre ob diese Tertia perfecta gar reine sey. Item wenn das ḡ nach g gestimmet ist/ so probir das ḡ mit dem h̄/ wenn das ā mit dem a accordiret/ so probiere es mit dem f/ vnd wenn dieses alles also hindurch vollendet ist/ so gibt es ohne Betrug eine reine Harmoniam. Aber es wil aus vbung vnd vielem gebrauch erlernet werden.

Die 2. Art.

1	f	f̄
2	f	c̄
3	c̄	ḡ
4	ḡ	g
5	g	d̄
6	d̄	ā
	f	ā Prob. 1.
7	ā	a
8	a	ē
9	ē	h̄
	h̄ ḡ } Pr.-	
	ē c̄ } 3.2.	

Allhier muß mit den Quinten vnd Octaven eben diß/ was im vorigen erinnert allerdings auch in acht genommen werden.

Diese tertia major f ā (wie auch alle andere perfectæ tertiæ) oder Tertia majores muß gar rein seyn: Es kan aber die Tertia viel besser in der Decima, Als nemblich f ā gehöret vnd vnterschieden/ auch gar rein eingezogen werden; Aber doch also/ daß die Quinta ā d̄ nicht zu sehr falsch/ oder zu rein werde.

Diese beyde Proben müssen eben also/ wie jetzt vom f ā angedeutet worden/ vorgenommen werden.

Wann nun diese obgesetzte Claves(dann die Octaven, so wol die Tertiæ perfectæ müssen gar perfect vnd rein, vnd die Quarten noch mehr als rein eingezogen vnd gestimmet seyn; Die Quinten aber/ wie oben angedeutet/ etwas schweben/ Alsdann werden hernach nur die Octaven auff- vnd niederwerts im gantzen Clavir, ohne die Semitonia, gegen vnd nach einander rein fortgestimmet.

Was aber die Semitonia belangen thut/ muß man erstlich das b zu dem f/ (welches allbereit rein ist) schwebend/ wie alle andere Quinten einziehen/ vnd das b alsdenn gegen der Tertia majore d auch probieren vnd rein einziehen/ welches b/ wie hiebevor gesagt/ gegen der Decima f besser vernommen werden kan; Darauff die

Octav

allowed to happen, then when the fifths are played in the lower part of the compass, they will be far too out-of-tune, and will offend keen ears when full chords are played.

When all the lower notes are in tune, one should proceed up the scale, drawing the f♯' into perfect tune with the already-tuned f♯, then g/g', and so forth up to the keyboard's highest note.

The higher notes should be tuned with even greater diligence and with a more acute ear than the lower notes, in order to insure that the octaves are consistently drawn into perfect tune. Both notes of the octave must sound as perfectly in tune as if they were one pipe, or one string. One should always keep the major thirds as guides; e.g., after the f♯' is tuned to the f♯, then test the f♯' against the d' to be sure that the major third is pure. Likewise, after the g' has been tuned to the g, test the g' against the d♯; when the a' is in tune with the a, test it against the f'. After this entire process has been completed, one can be sure that the temperament will produce a proper harmony. It takes a great deal of practice, however, to learn how to do this.

The Second Method

[step]
1. f   f'
2. f   c'
3. c'   g'
4. g'   g
5. g   d'
6. d'   a'
   f'-a'- test 1
7. a'   a
8. a   e'
9. e'   b'
   b'-g' - test [2]
   e'- c' - [test] 3

Fifths and octaves must be treated here in the same way described in the previous temperament.

Just as all major thirds, the major third f'/a' must be perfectly in tune. It is much easier to hear and tune thirds, however, when they are played as tenths, i.e., f/a'. One must be careful, though, that the fifth a'/d' is neither too narrow nor too pure.

Tests 2 and 3 must be carried out in the same way as the first one, f'/a'.

In the procedure above, the octaves and perfect thirds must be pure, the fourths must beat sharp, and the fifths must beat somewhat flat. When it is completed, then the notes above and below it must be tuned by octaves, until all the notes of the keyboard (with the exception of the semitones) are tuned.

With regard to the semitones, the b♭ must first be tuned sharp against the f, like all other [descending] fifths, and then tested as a major third against the d' (as noted above, b♭ can be better perceived against the tenth above it, the d"). Next

DE ORGANOGRAPHIA.

Octav b vnd B b: Vnd die Quint ♄ b / doch schwebend. Alsdann muß das ♄ gegen der Decima g̃ probieret / vnd gar rein nachgezogen werden: Folgends die Octava g̃ vnd : Diese drey Claves aber q̃ ff̃ ♄ sollen gegen jhren Tertien als a d c gar rein einstimmen: Wiewol solches gegen jhren Decimis (wie jetzt offt gedacht) allezeit eigendlicher zu vernehmen: Vnd hernach jhre Octaven vollends auch einzuziehen seyn.

Die Quinten q ♄ / vnd ff̃ q̃ / müssen nicht so gar falsch / vnd nicht so gar reine seyn / sondern nur etzlicher massen / doch daß sie nicht so sehr wie andere Quinten schweben / damit es / wann aus frembden Clavibus, vnd durch die Semitonia etwas geschlagen wird / nicht gar zu sehr dissonire. Wiewol etliche meynen die Quinta q ♄ müsse gar rein seyn / welches aber meines erachtens nicht passiren kan.

Darumb dann auch die Alten das f ♄ den Wulff genennet haben / Dieweil diese beyde Claves (wenn zu zeiten Secundus Modus ein Thon niedriger auffm f / oder sonsten etwas ficktè vnd Chromaticè durch die Semitonia solle vnd müsse geschlagen oder getracirret werden) eine gar falsche Tertiam minorem geben: Vnd damit jhnen gleichwol in etwas geholffen würde / haben sie allen andern Clavibus ein gar geringes abgebrochen / vnd die Tertiam Majorem e ♄ nicht zu gar reines sondern etwas weiter von einander gezogen / damit das ♄ ein wenig in die höhe dem a näher / dem f aber weiter kemmen / vnd also fast / wiewol nicht gar pro Tertia Minore im Noth könne gebraucht werden.

Etliche wollen nicht / daß f vnd ♄ der Wulff sey / sondern der Wulff werde ins ♄ gebracht / dieweil vnd ♄ nicht kan rein seyn / welches denn die Proba gibt auff allen Orgeln: Etliche meinen der Wulff sey im ♄ sind b q: Ich aber lasse einem jeden seine Meynung / vnd ist zum besten / daß der Wulff mit seinem wiedrigen heulen im Walde bleibe / vnnd vnsere harmonicas Concordantias nicht interturbire.

Daß aber das ff̃ / ♄ vnd c̃ also stehen muß / geschicht vnter andern wegen der Clausulen, welche in diesen schwartzen Clavibus oder Semitoniis formiret werden / vnd gibt im f ff̃ / g ♄ / c q̃ kein la fa / oder mi fa; Wie es im a b vnd d ♄ thut. Hergegen so kan in diesen Semitoniis b vnd ♄ hinwiederumb nicht / wie in den andern vorigen clausuliret werden. Aber wenn die schwartze Claves duplirt werden / wie im 2. Theil Num. 39. zusehen / so kan mans haben / wie mans haben wil.

Aber hiervon sol ex consideratione Monochordi in einem andern Tractat ex regulis proportionum fundamentaliter hiernechst / ob Gott wil / mit mehrerm gesagt werden: Denn allhier hat sichs nicht anders schicken wollen / als daß auff gut Orgelmacherisch vnd Organistisch / damit es auch die einfältigen verstehen köndten / hiervon geschrieben vnd etwas auffgezeichnet würde.

come the octaves b♭/b♭' and b♭/B♭; then the fifth d♯/b♭, [the d♯] beating [sharp]. Then the d♯ must be tested against g', a tenth above it; it must be pure. Next come the octaves d♯' and d♯. The three notes c♯', f♯', and g♯' should then be tuned pure against their thirds,[121] keeping in mind, as mentioned above, that these pitches are more reliably perceived against their tenths. Finally, all the [higher and lower] octaves should be drawn into tune.

The fifths c♯/g♯ and f♯/c♯' must be neither too out-of-tune nor too pure, but rather somewhere in the middle. They must not beat as much as the other fifths, so that they do not cause such harsh dissonances when the semitones are played in distant keys. Some hold, however, that the fifth c♯/g♯ must be completely pure, which is inappropriate in my opinion.

Our forebears labeled the interval f/g♯ "the wolf," since these notes together produce a completely out-of-tune minor third (if perchance the second mode[122] must be played a step lower on f, or if some other chromatic passage needs to be played using the semitones). To improve this fault in some measure, they made all the other intervals a bit smaller. They set the major third e/g♯ not completely pure, but somewhat wide, pushing the g♯ a little sharp in the direction of the a, and [consequently] further from the f. Thus the interval f/g♯, though not actually a minor third, could be used in that way if necessary.

Some want to transfer the wolf from f/g♯ to d♯, since testing this interval on any organ will prove that the interval b/d♯ cannot be pure. Some want to put the wolf between d♯ and f♯, others between b♭ and c♯. I say, "Each to his own;" best that the wolf with his unpleasant howling stay in the forest, and not bother our harmonic consonances.

One reason, among others, that f♯, g♯, and c♯ must be as they are is because of the cadences that are formed using these black keys or semitones. The pitches f, g, and c are not leading tones to f♯, g♯, and c♯, as a is to b♭ and d is to e♭. On the other hand, the semitones b♭ and d♯ cannot function as leading tones, as a and d can. But if the black keys are divided,[123] as depicted in Part 2, Num. 39,[124] then these keys can function in both ways.

I intend, God willing, soon to publish a treatise on this matter (among others) from the standpoint of the monochord, *Tractat ex regulis proportionum fundamentaliter*.[125] For it is inappropriate here to describe this matter in any other way than in terms understandable to organbuilders and organists, so that the uneducated can also comprehend it.

---

121. i.e., against a, d', and e'.
122. i.e., transposed Dorian, beginning on g.
123. i.e., to create subsemitones.
124. This should read "Num. 40;" see pp. 64-65. Here Praetorius describes a "Clavicymbalum Universale" with 19 keys per octave. In 1606 the Italian harpsichord builder Vito Trasuntino built such an instrument, called "clavemusicum omnitonum," with 31 notes per octave; see *Groves Dictionary of Music and Musicians*, "Trasuntino." See also: http://www.instrument-und-kontext.de/ik/cembali/clavicymbalum.php
125. This treatise seems never to have been published.

Die 3. Art.

Etliche haben im Tanzustimmen/ vnd sagen diß sey Musicalisch/ vnd ex Fundamento. Dann gleich wie die Instrumenta vnd Orgeln vom C. (nach dessen Art süssen Thon sie denn genennet werden) mehrentheils anfangen/ vnnd denselben Clavem pro fundamento, nicht alleine vnten/ besondern auch oben haben/ also sey es auch am besten vnd füglichsten in der mitten von mehrgedachtem Clave den anfang zu machen/ deren Ordnung aber ist also:

Zu mercken:

Vom anfange biß vff Numero 14. werden die Quinten niedrig schwebend oder sinckend/ Nachmals aber müssen dieselben hochschwebend gestimmet werden/ denn alsdenn muß sich der vnterste Clavis nach dem obersten richten.

NB.
Hierbey habe ich auch des Calvisij Meynung de Temporatura Instrumentorum vffzusetzen nicht vnterlassen wollen.

Das ist gewiß (sagt er) wenn die Consonantix sollen recht klingen/ so müssen sie rein

The third method.

Some begin tuning from c', asserting that this is the most musical, since it begins with the basic pitch. For just as [stringed keyboard] instruments and organs mostly begin with C (and derive their name from this pitch's designation in feet), and this pitch is the fundamental one, not only on the bottom, but on the top as well,[126] it is best and most appropriate to begin in the middle, with c' as mentioned above. The tempering procedure then goes as follows:

[step]			
1.	c'	c	
2.	c	g	
3.	c	e	
4.	g	d'	
5.	g	b	
	e -	b -	test 1
6.	e	e'	
	c -	e'-	test 2
7.	d'	d	
8.	d	a	
	e' -	a -	test 3
9.	d'	f♯'	
	b -	f♯' -	test 4
10.	f♯'	f♯	
11.	f♯	c♯	
	a -	c♯' -	test 5
12.	c♯'	c♯	
13.	c♯	g♯	
	e -	g♯ -	test 6
14.	c'	f	
	a -	f-	test 7
15.	f	f'	
16.	f'	b♭	
	d' -	b♭ -	test 8
17.	b♭	d♯	
	g -	d♯ -	test 9

From step 1 through step 14 the fifths should be tuned to beat flat; thereafter the lower note must be tuned against the upper.[127]

N. B.

In this connection I have thought it important to include Mr. Calvisius's opinion about tempering instruments, *de Temp[e]ratura Instrumentorum.*[128]

He says: If consonances are to sound in proper tune, it is necessary that they

---

126. The standard organ manual compass until the 18th century was 4 octaves, C-c'''.
127. i.e., at that point the lower note must be tuned to beat sharp against the upper.
128. This treatise(?) appears not to have survived.

DE ORGANOGRAPHIA.

sie rein in jhren proportionibus stehen/ vnd weder vberheufft noch geringert werden; Vnd daßelbige befindet sich also in voce humana, auch in Posaunen vnd in andern/ welchen man mit menschlichem Athem etwas zugeben oder nemen kan. Denn vox humana lencket sich natürlich zu der rechten Proportion der Intervallorum, vnd legets jhnen zu/ wo etwas mangeln/ oder nimpt weg/ wo was vberley seyn solte.

Auff den Instrumenten aber vnd Orgeln hat es eine andere Meynung/ do seynd der Clavier gar zu wenig/ darumb muß man allda etlichen Consonantiis etwas nemen/ auff daß solches alles nicht auff einem Clave allein mangle.

Die Claves seynd also:

c vnd d distant tono majore $\frac{9}{8}$.

d vnd e Tono minore $\frac{10}{9}$.

e vnd f distant Semitonio Majore $\frac{16}{15}$.

f vnd g Tono majore $\frac{9}{8}$.

g vnd a distant Tono minoro $\frac{10}{9}$.

a vnd h tono majore $\frac{9}{8}$.

h vnd c Semitonio Majore $\frac{16}{15}$

Wenn nun die Instrumenta nach diesen proportionibus sollen gestimmet werden/ so würde alsobald aus dem d ins f Semiditonus imperfectus; Denn es ist Tonus minor cum semitonio, vnd fehlet ein gantz Comma; Item/ aus dem d ins a würde in der Quinta auch ein Comma mangeln/ welches dann gar zu viel/ vnd die Ohren können solchen mangel nicht erdulden. Darumb solte man billich mehr Clavier haben/ also/ daß man zwey d hette/die nur ein Comma von einander weren;

Aber weil solches auch in andern Clavibus geschicht / würden der Clavier, sonderlich wenn die geduppelte Semitonia auch noch darzu kemen/ gar zu viel werden; Darumb muß man die temperatur brauchen/ die ist also.

Dem Tono majori wird ein halb Comma genommen; Dem Tono minori hergegen wird ein halb Comma gegeben. Hinc manifestum, quod Tertiæ majori, quæ constat Tono majore & minore, nihil decedat, vnd bleibet rein; Vnd altera pars videlicet Sexta minor, (daß die Octava erfüllet werde) bleibet auch reut. Dem Semitonio majori aber wird ein vierthel eines commatis gegeben; Daher kompts/ daß nunmehr eine Quarta/ welche ein tonum majorem vnd minorem, vnd

be pure, i.e., in correct proportion one against the other. They must be neither too wide nor too narrow. The same holds true for the human voice, as well as trombones and other instruments whose pitch one can render either sharper or flatter by means of human breath. The human voice naturally tends to sing intervals pure, augmenting or diminishing them as the situation demands.

The matter is different, however, with [string keyboard] instruments and organs. These instruments have far too few keys, and thus some of their consonances must be contracted to prevent any single interval from bearing the entire discrepancy.

This is what the intervals are:[129]

c and d are separated by a large whole tone $9/8$

d and e are a small whole tone $10/9$

e and f are separated by a major semitone $16/15$

f and g are a large whole tone $9/8$

g and a are separated by a small whole tone $10/9$

a and b♮ are a large whole tone $9/8$

b♮ and c are a large semitone $16/15$

If [keyboard] instruments are tuned according to these proportions, then the interval d/f would immediately prove to be an imperfect minor third, since it is a minor whole tone plus a semitone, a whole comma too narrow. The fifth d/a will likewise be a comma too narrow, which is far too much; no one's ears could bear it. Therefore there simply ought to be more keys, so that there could be two d's, a comma apart.

But since the same thing happens with other intervals as well, there would end up being far too many keys, especially if the doubled semitones were to be included. This is why one must employ a temperament, which works as follows.[130]

The major whole tone is reduced by half a comma; the minor whole tone, on the other hand, is increased by half a comma. Thus it is clear that the major third, which consists of a major and minor whole tone, will lack nothing; it remains pure. The minor sixth, its counterpart in completing the octave, also remains pure. The major semitone, however, is increased by a quarter comma; this means that a fourth,

---

129. i.e., the pure intervals in the system of just intonation.
130. Praetorius now proceeds to explain the mean-tone system of temperament.

ein Semitonium majus hat/ zu grob ist/ weil dem Semitonio quarta pars commatis zugelegt ist.

Also die Quinta hat zween Tonos majores, einen minorem, vnd ein Semitonium; Weil allhier jederm tono majori ein halb comma, vnd also beyden/ ein gantz Comma genommen wird/ vnd hergegen nur drey viertheil commatis gegeben werden/ folget/ daß die Quinta in Instrumenten nicht vollkommen seyn kan.

Weil aber eine Quarta vnd eine Quinta, eine Octavam machen/ welche nicht kan geendert werden/ so folget nothwendig/ wenn ein theil grösser wird/ daß das ander kleiner werde/ vnd darff ferner keiner demonstration nicht. Divide grossum in duas partes, sunt utrobique sex nummi: Si jam alterutri parti dabis septem nummos, necesse est, altera pars habeat tantum quinque nummos, si grossus integritatem custodire debet, & non minui aut augeri.

Wenn aber die Orgelmacher sagen/ die Quarta d g schwebt: Die Tertia minor g b schwebt auch: Ergo so ist die Sexta minor d b rein/ etc. Das ist wol etwas nach jhrer Art/ aber nicht recht secundum artem & demonstrationem geredet/ sondern wenn ich demonstriren will/ daß die Sexta minor rein sey/ muß ich also sagen.

Tertia major & Sexta minor constituunt Octavam; Sed Tertia major in temperatura retinet suam veram proportionem; Ergo necesse est, ut & Sexta minor suam retineat, & legitima sit. Sic Quinta & Quarta constituunt duplam, sive octavam; & Quinta in temperatura per Quartam partem Commatis minuitur: Ergo necesse est, ut Quarta, quæ conjungitur, quartâ parte commatis augeatur: Et contra, sic de aliis. Necesse cuim est, ut de partibus judicetur ex integro.

Das IV. Capitel.

Alhier were zwar auch noch sehr hochnötig einen außführlichen Bericht zugleich mit einzubringen/ wie vnd welcher gestalt eine Newe Orgel könne/ müsse vnd solle/ geliefert/ auch durch vnd durch im Augenschein vnd Gehör (visu & auditu) 1. An dem Geheimnisse des Windes / so aus der wilden Lufft durch die Blasebälge vnnd alle Windführungen/ biß oben zur Pfeiffen hinaus wiederumb in die Lufft/ observiret; 2. Der Laden Fundamenta an allen verborgenen Gebrechligkeiten/ so allbereit verhanden vnd künfftig erfolgen/ examiniret; 3. Die Pfeiffen an Flöt- vnd Schnarr-Wercken in jhren justen mensuren vnd intonationen

mit

which contains a major and minor whole tone and a major semitone, is too wide, because the major semitone is increased by a quarter comma.

The fifth consists of two major whole tones, a minor [whole tone], and a semitone. Since a half comma is removed from each major whole tone, totaling a whole comma, and on the other hand only ¾ of a comma is added to it, it follows that fifths in [keyboard] instruments cannot be pure.

Because a fourth and a fifth form an octave, which must remain pure, it inevitably follows that, if one part becomes greater, the other must become smaller; this requires no further demonstration: divide a whole into two parts, each of which has six equal units; given that the whole is to retain its integrity, and be neither increased or diminished, if one of the parts is increased to seven units, it is necessary that the other part have only five units.

When organbuilders say that the fourth d/g beats and the minor third g/b♭ beats as well, and thus the minor sixth d/b♭ is pure, that is their own way of expressing the matter, but not properly formulated according to scientific demonstration. If I want to demonstrate that the minor sixth is pure, I must state it this way:

A major third and a minor sixth form an octave. When tempering, however, the major third retains its proper proportion; thus it is necessary that the minor sixth retain its proper proportion as well, and be pure. If a fifth and a fourth form a duple, or octave, and tempering the quint reduces it by a quarter comma, then it is necessary that the fourth to which it is linked be increased by a quarter comma. The entire tempering process works in this same way. Every part must be determined according to the whole.

Chapter IV.

t would fill a great need to include here a detailed report as to how a new organ ought to look and sound: 1.) to note the difficult art of mastering the wind, that proceeds from the open air through the bellows and all the wind ducts, until it passes up through the pipes and out again into the air; 2.) to examine all the hidden faults of the wind chest, both ones that are already present and ones that may arise in the future; 3.) to describe with particular care the proper scales and voicing of flue and reed

mit sonderlichen fleiß probieret werden: 4. Item/ Was vom Bestande vnnd Verstande der Inventionen des Eingebewdes/ vnd andern geheimbten defecten, (so billich zuverwerffen/ vnd vielleicht auch denen/ die sich/ es nicht düncken lassen/ vnbekant seyn möchten) zu eröffnen vnd zu demonstriren nöthig seyn möchte. 5. Vnd dann wie ein OrgelWerck/ zusampt den SchnarrWercken/ vnd in allen fürfallen den mangeln/ so nicht fundamentaliter oder im Fundament entstehen/ von einem Organisten in gebewlichen wesen erhalten werden könne.

In billicher Betrachtung/ daß jetzo auch in den kleinen/ so wol als grössern Städten/ die Gemeinten zu Ehren/ Lob vnd Preiß dem Namen Gottes des Allerhöchsten ein OrgelWerck zuverfertigen vnd setzen zu lassen/ keine Vnkosten sparen/ vnd doch vnterschiedlichen sehr vbel angeführet werden; Also/ daß hernacher an solchen Wercken offte mehr nachzubessern/ vnd von einem Jahr zum andern zu flicken vnd zu sticken fürfelt/ dahero dann vngleich höhere Vnkosten vervrsacht werden/ als es anfänglichen nicht hette gekostet/ wenn man es einem rechtschaffenen Meister verdinget hette.

Denn wenn etliche deroselben Orgeln von jhren Meistern (es geschehe denn auß Geitz/ Vnwissendheit der Kunst/ oder aus laßfertigem zuschen auffs Gesinde/ vnd vnbestendigkeit allerhand materialien) also obiter vnd nicht fundamentaliter hingemacht/ vnd auch wol der zeit halber (damit mancher den Namen haben wil/ daß er vor andern bald fertig werden könne) von der Hand hinweg geschlagen werden; da erhebt vnd findet sich den alsobald ein heule/ so außm bösem Fundament gebrechen der Laden/ oder sticken vnd hemmen im angehenge der Ventilen vnnd Claviren, oder aus dem außeinander quellen/ vnd zusammen trucknen des Holtzes/ an vnterschiedlichen örthern herfleust: Bald zeucht ein Register linde/ das andere hart; Eins halb/ das andere gantz abe; Bald bleiben sie gar behalten/ zerbrechen vnd zerreissen/ daraus grosse Vngelegenheit erfolget: Bald setzen sich die Pfeiffen/ wegen jhrer Schwachheit/ vnd allzu geringen Metalls/ bald fallen dieselb jhrer Oberlast vnd vbeln fassung halber gar vberhauffen/ oder stehen vnd hengen durch vnd vber einander/ als wenn volle Bauren eine Kirchmeßtantz darunter gehalten; Daher die Intonation verhindert/ das accort Stimmen zergehet/ vnd ein abscheulich Gehör daraus vervrsachet wird. Bald gehet der Wind hier vnd dar aus/ vnd verschwindet/ bleibt auch noch wol gar ausser seiner Macht: Bald ist er im Winter zu starck/ im Sommer zu schwach; Bald muß man zweene/ bald drey Calcanten, offt vmb des schweren trettens/ offt vmb des geschwinden lauffens willen/ zulegen/ etc. Vnnd was der vielen Mängel vnnd defecten, die sich von einer zeit

ranks; 4.) also to reveal what should be known about how the interior parts of the organ work, as well as hidden faults that ought rightly to be criticized, and that may perhaps be unknown to those who have never thought about them; 5.) and then [to explain] how an organ's mechanical aspects, together with its reed stops, can be preserved from all the various faults that do not arise from fundamental defects.

It is a fact that churches nowadays, both in small as well as larger cities, are having organs built to the glory, honor, and praise of the exalted Name of God. These congregations spare no expense, and yet are deceived in all sorts of ways. The resulting instruments need so many repairs and so much patching up as the years go by, that they end up costing far more than they would have, had a reputable organ-builder been given the contract in the first place.

Whether out of greed, technical ignorance, lax oversight of apprentices, or poor quality of materials, some builders do not build substantially, but throw their organs together in a slapdash manner. In order to save time (and gain a reputation for finishing organs faster than anyone else), these builders cut corners. Then ciphers immediately appear in various places, due to faulty basic construction of the chest, or the linkage between pallets and keys rubbing or sticking, or wood swelling and shrinking. One stop draws too easily, another too stiffly; one pulls out half-way, another all the way. Sometimes the stops stick fast, break, and tear apart, causing great inconvenience. Sometimes pipes sag, due to weak construction and metal that is too thin and of poor quality. Sometimes they topple all over each other in a heap, because they are top-heavy and poorly anchored. Sometimes they stand lopsided and lean on each other, as if drunken peasants had done a carnival dance on the chest. Then they speak poorly, their tuning is ruined, and they sound dreadful. The wind escapes first at one place, then at another, getting weaker and weaker until it becomes completely insufficient; sometimes it is too strong in summer, or too weak in winter. Sometimes two or even three bellows-treaders are needed, either because the bellows are so difficult to tread, or because they must be trod so fast. There are all sorts of other faults that manifest themselves from time to time. Sometimes

zur andern vernemen laſſen/ mehr ſeynd. Daß demnach aus oberzehlten fürfallenden defecten offtmals einem rechtſchaffenen Organiſten ſo bange dabey wird/ daß er viel lieber in eine Scheuren zu treſchen/ als auff eine ſolche Orgel zu ſchlagen gehen ſolte.

Vnnd ob zwar wir Menſchen nicht ewigwerende dinge/ daran ſich gantz kein mangel ereugen ſolte/ machen können: So bezeugt doch die Erfahrung/ daß etliche Orgelwercke/ wenn ſie von erfahrnen vnd fleiſſigen obſervanten gefertiget worden/ zu 50. 60. 70. 80. Jahren ohne ſonderbare Revidirung dahin ſtehen/ vnd ohne einigen Fundament defect an Laden/ Pfeiffen/ Bälgen/ Eingebäwde vnd aller anderer Bewegligkeit ſich ſo juſt befinden laſſen/ daß ſolche zum offtern die newen Orgeln weit vbertreffen/ vnd daher billich ſolch herrlich Geſchöpff Gottes/ an deſſen Invention vnſere liebe Vorfahren ſo groſſen fleiß gewendet/ höchlich gerühmet/ gelobt/ vnd davon geſchrieben wird.

Damit aber nun dieſem allen auffs beſte vnd müglichſte fürzukommen/ die Kirchen nicht alſo bößlich in Vnkoſten gebracht/ vnd mancher guter Organiſt ſolcher ſchweren perturbirung an den Orgeln geübriget ſeyn möge; So iſt nicht alleine hoch von nöten / daß die Inſpectores vnnd Kirchväter zuvor/ ehe ſie bawen laſſen wollen/ mit erfahrnen Organiſten/ die mit den Orgelmachers nicht laviren oder heucheln möchten/ ſich bereden/ vnd in jhrem beyſein die diſpoſition der ſtimmen vnnd des gantzen Wercks vordingnüſſe/ dem Orgelmacher antragen vnnd contrahiren helffen; Sondern es wil auch allhier die noth erfodern/ daß/ wie oben erwehnet/ ein gewiß Tractetlein von dieſem allen richtig verfaſſet/ vnd in druck publiciret werde.

Derowegen ich dann bey vorgedachtem meines gnädigen Fürſten vnd Herrn beſtaltem Orgel- vnd Inſtrumentmacher/ Eſaia Compenio, (welcher mir in vorgeſetztem Bericht vnd Vnterricht von alten vnd newen Orgeln ſehr beyräthig geweſen) mit allem fleiß angehalten/ daß er ein ſolch Tractätlin faſſen/ vnd den Kirchen/ Organiſten vnd Orgelmachern zum beſten in öffentlichen druck kommen laſſen wolte:

Worzu ich jhme dann meines Theils nicht allein beförderlich / ſondern auch nach meinem geringen verſtande vnd vermügen/ beyräthig vnd behülfflich zu ſeyn/ dem gemeinen Nutzen zum beſten/ mich ſchuldig erachte.

Vnd ſol ein ſolch Opuſculum vnd Tractätlin/ weil es ſich hier hinten an zu ſetzen nicht allerdings ſchicken wollen/ ob Gott
wil/ bald folgen.

ENDE.

Fünffter

all the ills enumerated above cause decent organists so much frustration that they would rather go threshing in a barn that play such an organ.

Although humans are not capable of making things that last forever without repairs, experience confirms that some organs, if they are constructed by experienced and diligent practitioners of the art, can last up to 60, 70, or 80 years without any special attention. They turn out to be so well-built, without any basic faults in their chests, pipes, bellows, inner workings, and moving parts, that they are far superior to newly-built organs. Thus they are worthy to be praised, honored, and recorded as splendid divine creations, upon whose invention our forebears expended so much diligence.

To insure the greatest possible success in the undertaking, to keep churches from incurring exorbitant expense, and to spare many a good organist severe vexation, it is highly necessary that church officials, before they sign a contract to build an organ, seek the counsel of experienced organists who are above collusion with organbuilders, and in their presence to specify and agree with the organ builder on the stoplist and other matters concerning the instrument. Beyond that, it would fill a great need, as mentioned above,[131] to write and publish a specific little treatise about all these matters.

I have therefore prevailed upon the abovementioned Esaias Compenius, the official organbuilder for My Gracious Prince and Lord[132] (who has afforded me much good counsel in writing the above report and instruction), to author such a little treatise,[133] to be made available to the public in print, for the benefit of organists and organbuilders.

I for my part consider it not only necessary, but also my duty, within my limited ability and understanding, to help and counsel him in any way possible.

Since it is not convenient to append such a little treatise here,
it will soon be published [separately],
God willing.

THE END.

---

131. p. 158.

132. Duke Heinrich Julius of Brunswick-Wolfenbüttel?; see p. 139 above. The Duke died in 1613; however, this reference may have remained unaltered when *Syntagma musicum II* was finally published in 1619.

133. This treatise survives as a manuscript, entitled *Kurtzer Bericht, waß beÿ überlieferung einer Klein und grosverfertigten Orgell zu observiren*, now in the Herzog August Bibliothek, Wolfenbüttel, Germany. For an English translation of the treatise, see: Vincent Panetta, "An Early Handbook for Organ Inspection: the 'Kurtzer Bericht' of Michael Praetorius and Esaias Compenius," in: *The Organ Yearbook*, 1990, pp. 5-33. See also: Vincent J. Panetta, Jr., "Praetorius, Compenius, and Werckmeister: A Tale of Two Treatises," in: *Church, Stage, and Studio: Music and Its Contexts in Seventeenth-Century Germany* (Ann Arbor: Research Press [c.1990]), pp. 67-85.

DE ORGANOGRAPHIA.

Fünffter Theil
TOMI SECUNDI:

Darinnen
Dispositiones etlicher
Vornehmen OrgelnWerck in
Deutschland/
Als

I. Costnitz.
II. Ulm.
III. Dantzig.
IV. Rostock.
V. Lübeck. { S. Peter. / vnser lieben Frawen. / im Thumb.
VI. Stralsund.
VII. Hamburg. { S. Jacob. / S. Peter.
VIII. Lünenburg/ S. Johannis.
IX. Breßlaw.
X. Magdeburg. { Thumb. / S. Johannis. / S. Ulrich. / S. Peter. / S. Catharinen.
XI. Bernaw.

XII. Halla vnser lieben Frawen.
XIII. Braunschweig im Thumb.
XIV. Leipzig { S. Niclas. / S. Thomas.
XV. Torgaw.
XVI. Halberstadt. { S. Merten. / zun Barfüssern.
XVII. Cassel. { Freyheiter Kirchen. / Brüderkirchen. / Schloßkirchen.
XVIII. Bückeburg.
XIX. Dreßden Schloßkirchen.
XX. Grüningen Schloßkirchen.
XXI. Hessen die hölzerne Orgel.
XXII. Schöningen SchloßCapell.
XXIII. Noch andere sechs Dispositiones.

M. P. C.

I.
Costnitzer Orgel.

Der Costnitzer vnd Ulmer Orgel Disposition, hat mir/ wie sehr ich mich auch darnach

Part Five of
VOLUME TWO:
Containing
Stoplists of various
Distinguished Organs in Germany,[1]
i.e.

I. Constance [Switzerland]	XII. Halle, Marktkirche
II. Ulm	XIII. Braunschweig Cathedral
III. Danzig	XIV. Leipzig: { Nicolaikirche / Thomaskirche
IV. Rostock	
V. Lübeck: { Petrikirche / Marienkirche / Cathedral	XV. Torgau
	XVI. Halberstadt: { Martinikirche / Franziskanerkirche
VI: Stralsund	
VII. Hamburg: { Jacobikirche / Petrikirche	XVII. Kassel: { Freiheiterkirche (=Martinskirche) / Brüderkirche / Castle Church
VIII. Lüneburg: Johanniskirche	
IX. Breslau	XVIII. Bückeburg
X. Magdeburg: { Cathedral / Johanniskirche / Ulrichskirche / Petrikirche / Katharinenkirche	XIX. Dresden, Castle Church
	XX. Gröningen, Castle Church
	XXI. Hessen: the wooden organ
	XXII: Schöningen: Castle Chapel
	XXIII: Six other stoplists[2]
XI. Bernau	M[ichael] P[raetorius from] C[reuzburg]

[*Six additional stoplists are found on pp. 197-203:*
I. Sondershausen; II. Sondershausen: a cabinet-organ; III. Hildesheim: St. Godehard; IV. Riddagshausen: Monastery; V. Another hypothetical stoplist for an organ of 34 or 35 stops, of the sort found in Dresden and Schöningen; VI. Yet another stoplist for a small instrument with a very gentle sound.
Finally, a stoplist of the organ at St. Lambrecht in Lüneburg is found on pp. 233-4.]

I.

The Organ in Constance
In spite of my diligent efforts, at this time I have not been able to procure

---

1. In the errata on p. 235, Praetorius states that the stoplist of the organ at St. Lambrecht should have been included among these stoplists. It is found on pp. 233-4.
2. Praetorius in fact gives seven additional stoplists.

darnach bemühet/ biß anher nicht werden können: Allein daß mir es also/ wie allhier gemeldet wird/ zugeschickt worden.

Die Orgel zu Edstniz sol ein groß gantz Werck seyn: Der erste Organist hat Hans Bucher geheissen/ der jetzige Johann Deutlein.

Hat vber 3000. Pfeiffen/ vnd 70. Register. Die gröste Pfeiffe wigt mehr denn 3. Centner/ vnd ist 24. Schuh lang.

Auff der Lehnen vmbher stehen 14. Engel/ haben rechte Pfeiffen/ so mit eingehen.

Der Blaßbälge sind 22. ein jeder 10. Schuch lang/ vnd 4. Schuch breit: Das Leder kostet mehr als 200. gute gülden.

II.
Ulmer Orgel.

Diese Orgel ist vor 30. Jahren erbawet/ vor 12. Jahren aber wiederumb renoviret: Die Renovation ist bey 7000. gute gülden zu stehen kommen.

Die gröste Pfeiff helt 315. Ulmer Maß Wein/ das sind 157½. Stübichen/ oder bald 8. Emmer oder vier Ahmen.

III.
Die grosse Orgel zu
Dantzig

In S. Marienkirche/ So Anno 1585. von Iulio Antonio erbawet worden/ helt 55. Stimmen.

Im OberWerck seynd 13. Stimmen.

Dieser Stimm ein jede hat 48. Pfeiffen.
1. Principal — 16. fuß
2. Holflöite — 16. fuß
3. Quintadehna — 16. fuß
4. Spillpfeiffe — 8. fuß
5. Octava — 8. fuß
6. Quintadehna — 8. fuß
7. Offenflöite oder Viol 3. fuß
8. Spillpfeiffe ⎫ 4. fuß
9. Viol ⎬
10. Sedecima ⎪
11. Rauschquinte ⎭

12. Zimbel hat 144. Pfeiffen. Ist derwegen drey Chöricht.
13. Mixtur hat in alles 1152. vnd auff jeder Clavem 24. Pfeiffen.

In der Brust- oder VorPositiff 8. Stimmen.

1. Gedacte Stimm — 8. fuß
2. Gedact — 4. fuß
3. Principal — 4. fuß
4. Quintadehna — 4. fuß
5. Zimbel
6. Duneeken — 2. fuß
7. Regal singend — 8.
8. Zin-

stoplists of the organs in Constance and Ulm. Only the following information has been reported to me.

The organ at Constance is said to be a large and complete instrument. The name of the first organist was Hans Bucher;[3] the present organist is Johann Deutlein.

It has over 3000 pipes, and seventy stops. The largest pipe weighs more than 3 Centner, and is 24 feet long. On the railing surrounding it stand 14 angels holding real trumpets that sound.

There are 22 bellows, each 10 feet long and 4 feet wide; their leather cost more than 200 Gulden.

II.
The Organ at Ulm

This organ was built 30 years ago, and then renovated twelve years ago. The renovation cost 7000 Gulden.

The largest pipe holds 315 Ulmer Mass of wine; that is 157½ Stübchen, or almost 8 Eimer or 4 Ohms.[4]

III.
The large organ at
Danzig

Built in St. Mary's Church in the year 1585 by Julius Antonius, contains 55 stops.

In the OberWerck there are

13 stops

Each of the stops has 48 pipes.

1. Principal — 16'
2. Holflöite — 16'
3. Quintadehna — 16'
4. Octava — 8'
5. Spillpfeiffe — 8'
6. Quintadehna — 8'
7. Spillpfeiffe — 4'
8. Viol — 4'
9. Offenflöite or Viol — 3'
10. Sedecima — [2']
11. Rauschquint
12. Zimbel with 144 pipes; therefore it has three ranks.
13. Mixtur with a total of 1,152 pipes, 24 pipes per note.

In the Brust- or VorPositiff there are

8 stops

1. Gedacte Stimm[5] — 8'
2. Principal — 4'
3. Gedact — 4'
4. Quintadehna — 4'
5. Dunecken — 2'
6. Zimbel
7. Regal singend — 8'
8. Zincken — 4'

---

3. Hans Buchner (1483-1538); Buchner became organist there in 1506, but he was certainly not the first organist at the Constance Münster.
4. An *Ohm* is about 35 modern gallons or 168 liters; thus the pipe would have held about 140 gallons or 672 liters.
5. "Gedeckt stop"?

DE ORGANOGRAPHIA.

8. Zincken   4

Im Rückpositiff.
18. Stimmen.

1. Principal
2. Holflöit oder Holpfeiff ⎫ 8. fuß
3. Spillpfeiff oder Blockfl. ⎭
4. Octav
5. Offenflöit oder Viol ⎫ 4. fuß
6. Kleine Blockflöit ⎭
7. Gemßhorn
8. Sedecima
9. Flöit
10. Waldflöit
11. Rauschquint
12. Nasatt
13. Zimbel von 144. Pfeiffen
14. Mixtur von 220. Pfeiffen
15. Trommet ⎫ 8. fuß
16. Krumbhorn ⎭
17. Zincken ⎫ 4. fuß
18. Schallmeyen ⎭

Im Pedal zum OberWercke
4. Stimmen/ein jede von
43. Pfeiffen.

1. Groß UnterBaß von   32. fuß
2. UnterBaß   16
3. PosaunenBaß   16
4. Trommete   8. fuß

Im Pedal auff beyden
Seitten.
12. Stimmen.

1. Flöiten oder Octava   8. fuß
2. Gedact   8. fuß
3. Quintadehna   4. fuß
4. Superoctav   2.
5. Nachthorn
6. Rauschquint
7. Bawerpfeiff
8. Zimbel von 144. Pfeiffen
9. Mixtur von 220. Pfeiffen
10. Spitz oder Cornett
11. Trommeten oder Schallmeyen.
12. Krumbhörner.

Uber das seynd noch in der gantzen Orgel 3. Tremulanten, vnd 1. Trummel im Baß.

Daß also 60. Register in alles verhanden seyn.

IV.
Das Werck zu
Rostock/

Welches von Heinrich Glovatz Bürger daselbsten gebawet/ vnnd Anno 93. absolvirt worden/ Auch zu bawen 5000. gülden gekostet/ hat 39. Stimmen.

      14. Blaßbälge.

      3. Clavir, deren das oberste zum OberWerck/ das mittelste zur Brust/ vnnd das vnterste zum Rückpositiff gehört vnd gebrauchet wird.

In the Rückpositiff.
18 stops.

1. Principal — 8′
2. Holflöit or Holpfeiff — 8′
3. Spillpfeiff or Blockfl. — 8′
4. Octav — 4′
5. Offenflöit or Viol — 4′
6. Kleine Blockflöit — 4′
7. Gemsshorn
8. Sedecima
9. Flöit
10. Waldflöit
11. Rauschquint
12. Nasatt
13. Zimbel with 144 pipes
14. Mixtur with 220 pipes
15. Trommet — 8′
16. Krumbhorn — 8′
17. Zincken — 4′
18. Schallmeyen — 4′

In the Pedal
[located] with the OberWerck
4 stops, each with 43 [?] pipes.

1. Gross UnterBass at — 32′
2. UnterBass — 16′
3. PosaunenBass — 16′
4. Trommete — 8′

In the Pedal
[located] at both sides
12 stops

1. Flöiten or Octava — 8′
2. Gedact — 8′
3. Quintadehna — 4′
4. Superoctav — 2′
5. Nachthorn
6. Rauschquint
7. Bawerpfeiff
8. Zimbel with 144 pipes[6]
9. Mixtur with 220 pipes
10. Spitz or Cornett
11. Trommeten or Schallmeyen
12. Krumbhörner

Moreover there are three tremulants in the organ (in der gantzen Orgel[7]), and one drum [operated by] the pedal.

Thus there is a total of 60 stops to be found [in this organ].

IV.
The instrument at
Rostock,

that was built by Heinrich Glovatz, a citizen of that city, and completed in the year [15]93, has 39 stops. It cost 5000 Gulden to build. [It has]

39 stops,
14 bellows and
3 manuals, of which the top one belongs to the Oberwerk, the middle to the Brust, and the bottom to the Rückpositiv.

---

6. Both this stop and the one below it seem to be drawn from the Rückpositiv. If this is true, the number of pipes is misleading; the Zimbel seems to have 3 ranks, while the Mixtur has up to five.

7. This might also mean "for various divisions throughout the organ."

Im OberWerck
6. Stimmen.

1. Weit Principal.   16. Fuß
2. Mixtur.
3. Zimbel.
4. Gedact.   16. Fuß
5. Octav.   8
6. Superoctav.   4

Im BrustWerck
12. Stimmen.

1. GeigenRegal.   4
2. Krumbhorn.   8
3. Sedetz.   1
4. Suißlöit.   1
5. Superoctav.   2
6. Blockflöit.
7. Regal.   8
8. Zimbel.
9. Waltflöit.   1
10. Spilpfeiffe.
11. Naßpfeiffe.   1
12. Gedact.   8

Im Rückpositiff.
12. Stimmen.

1. Principal.   8
2. Quintadehna.   8
3. Octav.
4. Waldflöit.
5. Mixtur.
6. Trommet.
7. Gedact.
8. Offenflöit.
9. Gemßhorn.

10. Superoctav.
11. Zimbel.
12. Pommert.

In den SäittenBässen zur lincken Hand:
9. Stimmen.

1. Posaunen.
2. Schallmey.
3. Cornett.
4. Barem.   (Barem ist ein Ae-
5. Gedact.   qualgedact gar still
6. Octav.   vñ linde intoniret)
7. Superoctav.
8. Bawerflöiten.   } Baß.
9. Regal.

V.
In Lübeck.

I.

Die Orgel zu S. Peters Kirchen/ so M. Gottschaldt Burckart ein Niederländer gemacht/ hat 45. Stimmen. 3. ManualClavir von C biß ā Coppel zum Oberwerck vnnd Rückpositiff vnnd Coppel zum Pedal vnd Rückpositiff. Das Pedal aber gehet vom C mit dem G vnd A biß oben ins E.

Im OberWerck seynd
13. Stimmen.

1. Principal von   16. Füssen
2. Spilpipe   8. fi.
3. Klein Spilpipe.   4
                              4. Super-

In the OberWerck
are 6 stops.
1. Weit[8] Principal   16′
2. Gedact   16′
3. Octav   8′
4. Superoctav   4′
5. Mixtur
6. Zimbel

In the Rückpositiff
are 12 stops.
1. Principal   8′
2. Quintadehna   8′
3. Octav
4. Waldflöit
5. Gedact
6. Offenflöit
7. Gemshorn
8. Superoctav
9. Mixtur
10. Zimbel
11. Pommert
12. Trommet

In the BrustWerck
are 12 stops.
1. Gedact   8′
2. Superoctav   2′
3. Sedetz   1′
4. Suiflöit   1′
5. Waldflöit   1′
6. Nasspfeiffe [?]   1′
7. Blockflöit
8. Spillfpfeiffe
9. Zimbel
10. Krumbhorn   8′
11. Regal   8′
12. Geigen Regal   4′

In the Side-Pedal on the left side[9]
there are 9 pedal stops.
1. Gedact
2. Barem
3. Octav
4. Superoctav
5. Bawerflöiten
6. Posaunen
7. Schallmey
8. Regal
9. Cornett

} Barem is an 8′ Gedact, very quietly and gently voiced.

V.
In Lübeck
I.

The organ at St. Peter's Church in Lübeck, built by Mr. Gottschaldt Burckart, a Netherlander, has 45 stops, 3 manuals from C to a″, a Rückpositiff/Oberwerck coupler and a Rückpositiff/Pedal coupler. The pedal extends from C with the C♯ and D up to d′.

In the Ober-Werck
there are 13 stops.
1. Borduna   24′ [10]
2. Principal   16′
3. Gross Octava   4′ [8′?]

---

8. Wide-scale
9. "zur lincken Hand"; this might also be translated "at the [organist's] left hand," referring to the position of the stopknobs instead of the case.
10. i.e., a 32′ from low F.

4. Superoctava. 4
5. Rauschquinta 4
6. Kleinoctava 4
7. GroßOctava 4
8. Borduna 24. ff.
9. Dulcian 16
10. Feld Trommeten 16
11. Scharff Zimbel
12. Mixtura
13. Gedact 8. ff.

In der Brust 8 Stimmen.

1. Gedact vff 8. ff.
2. Offenflöit 4. ff.
3. Scharff Regal
4. Harffen Regal
5. Geigen Regal
6. Sifflitt.
7. klein Quintadehna
8. Sedecima

Im Rückpositiff 14. Stimmen.

1. Principal von 8. Fuß
2. Octava 4
3. Quintadehna.
4. Gemßhorn
5. Krumbhörner
6. Gedact vff 8. ff.
7. Querpipe
8. Feldpipe
9. Superoctava 8. ff.
10. Trommeten
11. Baerpipen
12. Blockflöiten 4. ff.

13. Zimbel 4
14. Mixtur.

Im Pedal 10 Stimmen.

1. PrincipalBaß 32. ff.
2. GedactBaß 16. ff.
3. Blockflöiten B. 16
4. Decem Baß
5. Super octaven B. 8
6. Mixtur B. 8
7. Dusan B. 16
8. Passunen Baß 16
9. Schallmeyen B.
10. Cornett Baß 8

Die 2. Orgel.

Bey vnser lieben Frawen/ welche M. Bartold N. verfertiget/ begreifft 46. Stimmen/ 3. ManualClavir, deren die beyde obersten vom D. biß ins T. Das vnterste vom C biß ins T. Das Pedal aber vom C biß ins h hinauff steiget.

Item Coppel zum Pedal vnnd Manual.

Oben in der Orgel sind 7. Stimmen.

1. Principal vnd Ventile
2. Großoctava
3. Kleinoctava
4. Ruschquint
5. Scharff Zimbel 8. ff.
6. Superoctava
7. Mixtur 4. ff.

4. Spilpipe	8'
5. Gedact	8'
6. Kleinoctava	4'
7. Klein Spillpipe	4'
8. Superoctava	4' [2'?]
9. Rauschquinta	4' [?]
10. Mixtura	
11. Scharff Zimbel	
12. Feld Trommeten	16'
13. Dulcian	16'

In the Brust
8 stops.

1. Gedact at	8'
2. Offenflöit	4'
3. klein Quintadehna	
4. Sedecima	
5. Sifelitt	
6. Scharff Regal	
7. Harffen Regal	
8. Geigen Regal	

In the Rückpositiff
14 stops

1. Principal	8'
2. Gedact	8'
3. Octava	4'
4. Blockflöiten	4'
5. Quintadehna	
6. Gemsshorn	
7. Querpipe	
8. Feldpipe	
9. Superoctava	
10. Mixtur	
11. Zimbel	
12. Trommeten	8'

13. Krumbhörner	
14. Baerpipen	

In the Pedal
10 stops.

1. Principal Bass	32'
2. Gedact Bass	16'
3. Blockflöiten B[ass]	16'
4. Decem Bass[11]	
5. Super octaven B[ass]	8'
6. Mixtur B[ass]	8'[?]
7. Passunen Bass	16'
8. Dusan B[ass][12]	16'
9. Cornett Bass	8'
10. Schallmeyen B[ass]	

The 2nd Organ
[in Lübeck]

In the [Church of] Our Dear Lady[13], built by M[aster] Bartold N.[14], comprises 46 stops [on] 3 manuals, of which the two upper ones [extend] from D up to a". The lowest [extends] from C up to a". The Pedal extends from C up to d'.

There is also a Manual/Pedal coupler.

Above in the organ[15] are
7 stops.

1. Principal with ventil
2. Grossoctava
3. Kleinoctava
4. Superoctava
5. Ruschquint
6. Mixtur
7. SchaarffZimbel

---

11. In his *Musica mechanica organœdi* (Berlin, 1768), Vol. I, p. 87-8 (§.135) and p. 147 (§.197), Jacob Adlung suggests this stop may be a 1 3/5'.
12. See Adlung, op. cit., p. 92 (§.140). Because of its position in the stoplist as given by Praetorius, this stop is listed here among the reeds; no other circumstance, however, marks it either as a reed or flue stop.
13. i.e., the Marienkirche (Church of St. Mary).
14. Barthold Hering, who built the organ 1516-1518.
15. i.e., the Hauptwerk, the division in the upper part of the main case.

Im Rückpositiff
20. Stimmen.

1. Gemßhörner
2. Blockpfeiff — 4. fuß
3. Principal
4. Zimbel
5. Mixtur
6. Superoctava
7. Principale
8. Feldpfeiffe
9. Octava
10. Borduna
11. Offenflöit — von 8. fuß
12. Gedact — von 8. fuß
13. Dulcian oder Fagott — 8. fi.
14. Querpfeiffe — 4
15. Offenflöit — 4
16. Octava — 4
17. Superoctav
18. Mixtur
19. Dulcian oder Fagott — 16
20. Trommeten

In der Brust
5. Stimmen.

1. Regal
2. Zinck oder Cornett
3. Krumbhorn
4. Baarpfeiffe
5. Gedact.

Im Pedal 14. Stimmen.

1. GroßPrincipal UnterBaß.
2. Duppelt UnterBaß.
   Ventile zu allen Röhren Bässen oben in der Orgel/ als Dulcian B. Schallmeyen B. und Cornet B.
3. UnterBaß.
   Ventile zu allen Pfeiffen und Bässen im Stuel.
4. MixturBaß im Stuel.
5. Trommeten Baß.
6. Bassunen B.
7. Schallmeyen B.
8. Feldpfeiffen B. im Stuel.
9. Klein Octaven B.
   Ventile zum Bassunen- und Trommeten B. im Stuele.
10. Dulcian Baß
11. Cornett B.
12. Groß Octaven Baß im Stuel.
13. Dezehm Baß im Stuel.
14. Quintadehnen B. im Stuel.

Die 3. Orgel.

In der Thumbkirchen hat M. Jacob N. Anno 1606. zu ende gebracht/ darinn 30. Stimmen. 2. ManualClavir von F biß ins a.

Und Pedal vom G biß ins c zu finden.

Im OberWerck
sind 7. Stimmen.

1. Principal von — 8. fi.
2. Bordun oder Gedact — 16. fi
3. Octava — 4
4. Superoctava — 4
5. Quint.

In the Brustwerk
5 stops.
1. Gedact
2. Regal
3. Zinck or Cornett
4. Krumbhorn
5. Baarpfeiffe

In the Rückpositiff
20 stops
1. Principal
2. Principale
3. Borduna
4. Gedact — 8'
5. Offenflöit — 8'
6. Octava — 4'
7. Blockpfeiff — 4'
8. Querpfeiffe — 4'
9. Offenflöit — 4'
10. Octava
11. Superoctav
12. Superoctava
13. Gemshörner
14. Feldpfeiffe
15. Mixtur
16. Mixtur [sic]
17. Zimbel
18. Dulcian or Fagott — 16'
19. Trommeten
20. Dulcian or Fagott — 8'

In the Pedal
14 stops
1. Gross Principal UnterBass
2. UnterBass, doubled[16]
3. UnterBass
4. Gross OctavenBass in the Stuel[17]
5. QuintadehnenBass in the "Stuel"
6. Detzehm Bass[18] in the "Stuel"
7. Klein OctavenBass
8. FeldpfeiffenBass in the "Stuel"
9. MixturBass in the "Stuel"
10. BassunenBass
11. Dulcianbass
12. TrommetenBass
13. SchallmeyenBass
14. CornettBass

A ventil for all the pedal reeds [placed] above in the organ, i.e. DulcianBass, SchallmeyenBass and CornetBass

A ventil for all manual and pedal stops in the "Stuel."

A ventil for the Bassunen- and Trommeten Bass in the "Stuel."

The 3rd Organ [in Lübeck],

in the Cathedral, was completed by by Master Jacob N. in the year 1606. In it are found 30 stops [with] two manuals [extending] from [F?] up to a" and Pedal from C up to c'.

In the Oberwerck
are 7 stops.
1. Bordun or Gedact — 16'
2. Principal — 8'
3. Octava — [4']
4. Quint — 3'

---

16. i.e., two pipes per note.
17. The meaning of this word is uncertain. The most frequent interpretation of the word is "Rückpositiv" (i.e., "Stuhl" ("chair"), in the same sense that the corresponding division in England was sometimes called the "Chair organ". But in his *Orgelwörterbuch* (3. Auflage. Mainz: Rheingold-Verlag [1949], p. 60) Carl Elis defines the word "Orgelstuhl" as follows: "The old term for the lower case (das untere Stockwerk) of the organ in which is located the mechanism, and where pipes, especially pedal pipes, may occasionally be placed." This description suggests that "im Stuhl" (or "Stuel") may also mean "in Brustwerk position" (cf.: J. F. van Os, "A 15th-century Organ reconstructed in Switzerland...," trans. James L. Wallmann. *The American Organist*, Vol. 24, No. 3 (March 1990), p. 62, note 13).
18. In his *Musica mechanica organœdi* (Berlin, 1768), Vol. I, p. 87-8 (§.135), Jacob Adlung interprets the word "Detzehm" to mean "compound third."

DE ORGANOGRAPHIA.

5. Quint 3
6. Zimbel
7. Mixtur.

Im RückPositiff
14. Stimmen.

1. Principal	8. fl.
2. Gedact	8. fl.
3. Octava	4. fl.
4. Superoctava	2. fl.
5. Querflöiten	4. fl.
6. Blockflöiten	
7. Gemßhorn	
8. Offenflöit	
9. Nasatt	
10. Sifflitt	
11. Mixtur	
12. Zimbel	
13. Trommet	8. fl.
14. Regal.	

Im Pedal 9 Stimmen.

1. Untersatz	von 16. fl.
2. DulcianBaß	16
3. DecemB.	
4. FeldpipenB.	
5. OctavenBaß	
6. CornettenB.	
7. TrommetenB.	8. fl.
8. QuintadehnenB.	
9. GedactBaß.	

VI.
Das Werck zu

Stralsund /

Dessen Meister Nicolaus Maaß gewesen/ der sich hernach bey Kön. Majest. In Dennemarck uffgehalten/ hat 43. Stimmen.

Im OberWerck
sind 10. Stimmen.

1. Principal	16. fuß
2. Quintadehna	16. fuß
3. Spillpfeiff	8. fuß
4. Octava	8. fuß
5. Octava	4
6. Dolcian	8
7. Quint	3
8. GroßGedact	8
9. Mixtur	12. fach
10. Zimbel	3. fach

Im Pedal 11. Stimmen.

1. Untersatz	16. fuß
2. Principal	8
3. OctavenBaß	4
4. Bawrflöit	2
5. Nachthorn	2
6. Zimbel	2. fach
7. PosaunenBaß	16
TrommetBaß	8
CornettBaß	4
GedactBaß	8
QuintadeenBaß	4

Im

5. Superoctava [2']
6. Mixtur
7. Zimbel

In the Rückpositiff
14 stops.

1. Principal   8'
2. Gedact   8'
3. Octava   4'
4. Querflöiten   4'
5. Superoctava   2'
6. Blockflöiten
7. Gemsshorn
8. Offenflöit
9. Nasatt
10. Siflitt
11. Mixtur
12. Zimbel
13. Trommet   8'
14. Regal

In the Pedal
9 stops.

1. Untersatz   16'
2. OctavenBass
3. GedactBass
4. QuintadehnenB[ass]
5. FeldpipenB[ass]
6. DetzemB[ass][19]
7. DulcianBass   16'
8. TrommetenB[ass]   8'
9. CornettenBass

IV.
The instrument at
[St. Nicholas Church,]

Stralsund,

Built by master Nicolaus Maass,[20] who later took up residence at the Danish royal court, has 43 stops.

In the OberWerck
are 10 stops.

1. Principal   16'
2. Quintadehna   16'
3. Octava   8'
4. Spillpfeiff   8'
5. Gross Gedact   8'
6. Octava   4'
7. Quint   3'
8. Mixtur   XII
9. Zimbel   III
10. Dolcian   8'

In the Pedal
there are 11 stops.

1. Untersatz   16'
2. Principal   8'
3. GedactBass   8'
4. OctavenBass   4'
5. QuintadeenBass   4'
6. Bawrflöit   1'[?]
7. Nachthorn   1'[?]
8. Zimbel   II
9. PosaunenBass   16'
10. TrommetBass   8'
11. CornettBass   4'

---

19. See note 18 above.
20. In 1599.

Im Rückpositiff
11. Stimmen

1. Principal
2. Gedact
3. Quintadehn
4. Octava
5. Holflöite
6. Spillpfeiffe.
7. Mixtur
8. Zimbel
9. Trommeten
10. Fagott
11. Ein Schnarrwerck mit engen Cörperen gleich aus: L B böße.

In der Brust 11
Stimmen.

1. Principal   4. fi.
2. Gedact   4
3. Nasatt   2
4. Suiflöit   2
5. Schweitzerflöit   1
6. Krumbhorn   8
7. Regal   8
8. GeigendRegal   4
9. Querpfeiffe im Discant
10. Zimbel
11. Mixtur.

VII.
In Hamburg
I.

Die zu S. Jacob hat 53. Stimmen neben den Trebulanten, vnd 18. kleinen Blaßbälgen/ auch 3. Clavir.

Im OberWerck 9
Stimmen.

1. Principal   12. Fuß Thon
   im F angehende.
2. Octava   6. Fuß
3. Quintadeen   12. Fuß
4. Holpipe   6. Fuß
5. Holflöit   3. Fuß
6. Querpipe   6. fuß Thon
   12. Schue lang/vnd ist offen.
7. Rußpipe
8. Scharp.
9. Mixtur.

Oben in der Brust 11
Stimmen.

1. Principal   8. fuß/ angehende im C
2. Holpipe   8. fuß
3. Flöite   4. fuß
4. Offen Querflöite 4. fuß Thon / 8. füsse lang.
5. Nasatt vff die Quint   3. fuß
6. Gemßhorn   2. fuß
7. Kleinflöit   2. fuß
8. Klingende Zimbel   3. Pfeiffen starck
9. Trompette   8. Fuß
10. Regal   8. fuß
11. Zincke   8. fuß
    vom f biß ins ā / wie gebräuchlich.

Vnten in der Brust 4
Stimmen.

1. Krumbhorn   8. fuß
2. Quint.

In the Rückpositiff
are 11 stops.
1. Principal
2. Gedact
3. Quintadehn
4. Octava
5. Holflöite
6. Spillpfeiffe
7. Mixtur
8. Zimbel
9. Fagott
10. Trommeten
11. A reed with narrow resonators throughout [its compass]: L B bötze[?]

In the Brust
11 stops.
1. Principal — 4'
2. Gedact — 4'
3. Querpfeiffe in the treble — [4'?]
4. Nasatt — 2' [3'?]
5. Suiflöit — 2'
6. Schweitzerflöit — 1'
7. Mixtur
8. Zimbel
9. Krumbhorn — 8'
10. Regal — 8'
11. Geigend Regal — 4'

VII.
In Hamburg
I.
The organ at St. Jacob has 53 stops on three manuals, together with the tremulants and 18 small bellows.

In the OberWerck
9 stops.
1. Principal, commencing at F — 12'
2. Quintadeen — 12'
3. Octava — 6'
4. Holpipe — 6'
5. Querpipe open, 12' long[21] — 6'
6. Holflöit — 3'
7. Russpipe [i.e., Rauschpfeife]
8. Mixtur
9. Scharp

Above in the Brust
11 stops.
1. Principal, commencing at C — 8'
2. Holpipe — 8'
3. Flöite — 4'
4. Open Querflöite, 8 feet long[22] — 4'
5. Nasatt, sounding the fifth — 3'
6. Gemsshorn — 2'
7. Kleinflöit — 2'
8. Klingende Zimbel — III
9. Trompete — 8'
10. Regal — 8'
11. Zincke — 8'
    from f to a", as usual

Beneath in the Brust,
4 stops.
1. Spitzflöit in the treble, at — 4'
2. Quintflöit — 3'
3. Waltflöit — 2'
4. Krumbhorn — 8'

---

21. See p. 138.
22. Ibid.

2. Quintflöit	3. Fuß	12. Bassaune	16. fuß
3. Waltflöit	2. Fuß	13. Trommete	8. fuß
4. Spitzflöite uff	4. Fuß	14. Cornett	2. fuß
im Discant.			

Im Rückpositiff.
15. Stimmen.

1. Principal	8. Fuß im C
2. Octava	4 Fuß
3. Scharp. ⎫	
4. Mixtur. ⎭	
5. Gedact	8. ff.
6. Quintadeen.	8. Fuß
7. Holflöit	4. fuß
8. Blockflöit	4. fuß
9. Gemßhorn	2. fuß
10. Zisflöit	
11. Klingende Zimbel	
12. Schalmeyen	4. fuß
13. Baapfeiffe	8. fuß
14. Regal	8. fuß
15. Krumbhorn.	8. fuß

Im Pedal 14.
Stimmen.

1. Principal aus dem F 24. fuß	
2. Mixtur, wobey 1. Baß von 12. fuß	
3. Principal C	16. fuß
4. Groß Baß	16. fuß
5. Octava	4. fuß
6. Gemßhorn Baß	
7. Spitzquinte	
8. Zimbel ⎫	
9. Mixtur ⎭	
10. Spillpipe	4. fuß
11. Krumbhorn	16. fuß

II.

Die bey S. Peter helt in sich gleicher gestalt 3. Clavir 42. Stimmen/ 9. Bälge vnd Tremulanten.

Das OberWerck im mittelsten Clavier hat 9. Stimmen.

1. Principal 12. Fuß angehende im F.	
2. Quintadehna	12. fuß F
3. Octava	6. fuß F
4. Gedact	8. fuß C
5. Holflöite	3. fuß F
6. Rußpipe	
7. Scharp	
8. Mixtur	
9. Zimbel	

Das Brustpositiff oben in der Orgel/ gehört zum obersten Clavir, vnd hat 10. Stimmen.

1. Principal	8. fuß G
2. Holpipe	8. fuß
3. Holflöite	4. fuß
4. Nasart auff die Quinta	3. fuß
5. Gemßhorn	2. fuß
6. Kleinflöit	2. fuß
7. Zimbel	3. Pfeiffen starck
8. Trompette	8. fuß
9. Regal	8. fuß
10. Zincke	8. fuß

In the Rückpositiff,
15 stops.
1. Principal (beginning) at C — 8'
2. Gedact — 8'
3. Quintadeen — 8'
4. Octava — 4'
5. Holflöit — 4'
6. Blockflöit — 4'
7. Gemsshorn — 2'
8.Ziflöit
9. Mixtur
10. Scharp
11. Klingende Zimbel
12. Baa[r]pfeiffe — 8'
13. Regal — 8'
14. Krumbhorn — 8'
15. Schalmeyen — 4'

in the Pedal
14 stops.
1. Principal, from F — 24'
2. Mixtur, lowest pipe at — 12'
3. Principal [from] C — 16'
4. GrossBass — 16'
5. Octava — 4'
6. Spillpipe — 4'
7. GemsshornBass
8. Spitzquinte
9. Mixtur
10. Zimbel
11. Bassaune — 16'
12. Krumbhorn — 16'
13. Trommete — 8'
14. Cornett — 2'

II.
The [organ] at St. Peter likewise consists of 3 manuals [with] 42 stops, nine bellows and tremulants.

The OberWerck on the middle keyboard
has 9 stops.
1. Principal, beginning at F — 12'
2. Quintadehna [from] F — 12'
3. Octava [from] F — 6'
4. Gedact [from] C — 8'
5. Holflöite [from] F — 3'
6. Russpipe [Rauschpfeife]
7. Mixtur
8. Scharp
9. Zimbel

The Brustpositiff above in the organ is played from the upper keyboard, and has 10 stops.
1. Principal [from] C — 8'
2. Holpipe — 8'
3. Holflöite — 4'
4. Nasatt sounding the fifth — 3'
5. Gemsshorn — 2'
6. Kleinflöit — 2'
7. Zimbel — III
8. Trompete — 8'
9. Regal — 8'
10. Zincke — 8'

Das vnterste BrustPositiff ist an das OberBrustPositiff angehenget: Vnnd hat nur.

1. Krumbhorn — 8.fuß

Das RückPositiff gehöret zum vntersten Clavir.
Vnd hat 11. Stimmen.

1. Principal. — 8.fuß E.
2. Quintadehna. — 8.fuß.
3. Gedact. — 8.fuß.
4. Hollflötte. — 4.fuß.
5. Octava. — 4.fuß
6. Sifflöit.
7. Scharp.
8. Mixtur.
9. Baarpfeiffe. — 8.fuß.
10. Regall. — 8.fuß.
11. Krumbhorn. — 8.fuß.

Im Pedal seynd 11 Stimmen.

1. Principal. — 24. f. ex F
2. Groß Baß oder Vntersatz von 16. fuß ins C.
3. Octava — 8. fi.
4. Gedact — 8. fi.
5. Gemßhorn Baß
6. Zimbel
7. Mixtur
8. Bassaune — 16. fuß
9. Trompette — 8. fuß
10. Krumbhorn — 16. fuß
11. Cornett. — 2. fuß

VIII.
Die Orgel zu S. Johannes in
Lüneburgk.

Welches ein trefflich Werck von 27. Stimmen/gar hell vnd scharff/vnnd mit Springladen gezieret/sol im Niederlande/vnnd wie man saget/zum Hertzogen Busch/ohn gefehr vor siebentzig Jahren verfertigt/vnd zu Schiff herausser gebracht seyn/hat 1. Tremulant. 2. Ventil, vnter welchem eines zum obersten Clavir/das andere zum Rückpositiff gehöret.

3. Clavir, das mittelste/als das gröste Werck hat vnten ein gantz Octava mehr/als sonsten andere Clavir in gemein: Nemblich noch eine andere Octaven vnter das grosse C/welche Octava dem Pedal angehenget ist/vnd darzu gebrauchet wird. Sonsten seynd diese 3. Præstanten oder Principale in den dreyen Claviren alle gleich/vnd nicht tieffer als 4. fi. th on.

Das mittelste Clavir/welches das gröbste Werck seyn sol:
Hat 8. Stimmen.

1. Mixtur
2. Præstant
3. Octava
4. Nachthorn Baß } stehen alle vff der
5. Scharp   } Laden.
6. Trommeten B.
7. Buerflöiten B.
8. Vntersatz. Diese Stimme stehet an der halbe/

The Brustpositiff beneath is connected to the upper Brust-positiff, and has only a

    1. Krumbhorn   8'

The RückPositiff is played from the bottom keyboard and has 11 stops

1. Principal from E   8'
2. Quintadehna   8'
3. Gedact   8'
4. Octava   4'
5. Hollfloitte   4'
6. Siflöit
7. Mixtur
8. Scharp
9. Baarpfeiffe   8'
10. Regall   8'
11. Krumbhorn   8'

In the Pedal there are 11 stops.

1. Principal from F   24'
2. Gross Bass or Untersatz from C 16'
3. Octava   8'
4. Gedact   8'
5. GemsshornBass
6. Mixtur
7. Zimbel
8. Bassaune   16'
9. Krumbhorn   16'
10. Trompette   8'
11. Cornett   2'

[*The stoplist of the organ at St. Lambrecht in Lüneburg should be inserted here; see pp. 233-4.*]

VIII.
The Organ at St. Johannes in
Lüneburg.

[http://de.wikipedia.org/wiki/Orgeln_von_St._Johannis_(Lüneburg)]

The organ at St. Johannes in Lüneburg, an admirable instrument of 27 stops, quite brilliant and incisive and graced with spring chests, is reported to have been constructed about seventy years ago in the Netherlands[23] (at 's Hertogenbosch, it is said), and brought over by ship. It has 1 tremulant, 2 ventils (one of which operates the top manual, the other the Rückpositiv, and 3 manuals.

The middle manual, the primary division, extends an entire octave lower in the bass than the other manuals do; that is, an octave lower than great C. The pedal is suspended from this [extra] octave, which provides the pedal [for this instrument.] Moreover the 3 Præstants or Principals on the three manuals are all identical, none extending lower than 4' pitch.

The middle manual, the loudest/deepest division, has 8 stops.

1. Præstant   ⎫
2. Octava   ⎪
3. Mixtur   ⎬ [All these]
4. Scharp   ⎪ stand on [the
5. NachthornBass ⎪ same] chest.
6. B[a]uerflöitenBass ⎪
7. TrommetenBass ⎭
8. Untersatz: this stop extends over

---

23. The church signed the contract for the organ in 1551 with Hendrik Niehoff and Jasper Johansen; it was completed in 1553.

halbe/ vnnd ist von eim Orgelmacher zu Hamburg/ mit Namen M. Dirich/ ohngefehr vor 40. Jahren daran gesetzt worden.

Das oberste Positiff vnnd Clavir hat 8. Stimmen.

1. Superoctava
2. Nasatt
3. Flöite
4. Gemßhorn
5. Præstant
6. Zimbel
7. Holpipe
8. Tormmete

Das RückPositiff oder vnterste Clavir: 11. Stimmen.

1. Præstant
2. Scharp
3. Klein Holpipe
4. Quintadehna
5. Baarpipe
6. Mixtur
7. Schallmey
8. Regal
9. Sifflöit
10. Koppeldone oder Octava
11. Rußpipe

IX.
Die newe Orgel zu
Breßlaw

Ist von Michael Hirschfeldern zwar angefangen/ hat aber wegen seines zeittigen absterbens nicht verfertiget können werden/ vnd wenn dieses Werck dergestalt/ als hier nachfolgende Verzeichniß lautet/ absolvirt were worden/ hette ich mir dasselbe zu sehen vnd zu hören wol wüntschen mögen.

1. { Groß Principal / Chormaß Principal / Doppelt Principal } { Mit eim Register 8. fuß }
2. { Gedactfl. vnter Chor. / Gedactflöite Chormaß / Doppeltflöite } { Mit einem Register. }
3. { Offen Chormaß besondere Art / Octava / Duplicat dieses }
4. { Offen Octava / Sedecima offen / Duplicat dieses. }
5. { Sedecima offen / SuperSedecima offen / Duplicat dieses. }
6. { Gedactflöite / Sedecima / Duplicat dieses. }
7. { Thubalflöite Chormaß / Thubalflöite Octav / Duplicat dieses. }
8. { Dulcian vnter Chormaß / Krumbhörner Chormaß / Duplicat dieses. }
9. { Quinta ex Octava / Quinta ex Sedecima / Duplicat dieses. }
10. { Zimbel grob / Zimbel klein / Duplicat dieses. }

half the manual,[24] and was added about 40 years ago[25] by an organbuilder from Hamburg by the name of Master Dirich.[26]

The Positiv manual, on top, has 8 stops.

1. Superoctava
2. Nasatt
3. Flöite
4. Gemsshorn
5. Præstant
6. Holpipe
7. Zimbel
8. Trommete

The RückPositiff, the lowest manual, [has] 11 stops.

1. Præstant
2. Small Holpipe
3. Quintadehna
4. Koppeldone or Octava
5. Siflöit
6. Russpipe [Rauschpfeife]
7. Mixtur
8. Scharp
9. Schallmey
10. Baarpipe
11. Regal

IX.
The new Organ at
Breslau[27]

Michael Hirschfelder did indeed begin [to build] the new organ in Breslau,[28] but was unable to complete it due to his untimely death. If the instrument should ever be completed in the form recorded in the following stoplist, I certainly would like to see and hear it.

1. { Gross Principal / Chormass Principal / Doppelt Principal } on one stop, 8'
2. { Gedactfl. unterChor[mass] / Gedactflöite Chormass / Doppeltflöite } on one stop
3. { Open Chormass of a special type / Octava / Duplicat dieses [i.e., doubled] }
4. { Open Octava / Sedecima, open / Duplicat dieses }
5. { Sedecima open / SuperSedecima, open / Duplicat dieses }
6. { Gedactflöite / Sedecima / Duplicat dieses }
7. { Thubalflöite Chormass / Thubalflöite Octav / Duplicat dieses }
8. { Dulcian unter Chormass / Krumbhörner Chormass / Duplicat dieses }
9. { Quinta from the Octav / Quinta from Sedecima / Duplicat dieses }
10. { Zimbel grob [i.e., low] / Zimbel klein [i.e., high] / Duplicat dieses }

---

24. presumably the lower half.
25. In 1576.
26. Dirck Hoyer (active c.1556-1582).
27. Now Wroclaw, Poland.
28. In St. Maria Magdalena.

⎧ Grobe Mixtur vnter Chormaß.
11 ⎨ Kleine Mixtur Chormaß.
⎩ Duplicat dieses

NB. Vnter Chormaß ist   16. fuß
     Chormaß   8. fuß
     Octava   4. fuß

Summa 33. Stimmen vnd 11. Register.

1. Sedecima offen/ Principal Art.
2. SuperSedecima offen scharff
3. Zimbel scharff
4. Spitzflöite oder Gemßhorn
5. Querpfeiffe
6. Gar klein Flöiten
7. Sedecima offen ander Art
8. SuperSedecima vffn andere art.
9. Quint de tono Chormaß.
10. Gedacktflöite Octava
11. Quint ex Sedecima
12. Zimbel scharff
13. Gedacktflöite Chormaß laut
14. Mixtur Chormaß
15. Schallmeyen Baß/ welcher Geigen art Chormaß
16. HarffenPrincipal.

Aus diesen Stimmen werden nun zum vnter Clavir einzelne Stimmen genommen.

Als

1. Gedacktflöite Octava.
2. Gedacktflöite Sedecima.
3. Quint de tono Chormaß.
4. Quint ex sedecima
5. Sedecima offen
6. Zimbel
7. Querpfeiffe
8. SchallmeyenChor
9. MixturChor.

Bässe im Pedal.

1. Groß Baß
2. Vnter ChorBaß
3. ChorBaß
4. OctavBaß
5. FlöitenBaß vnter Chor
6. DulcianBaß
7. Vnter ChormaßBaß
8. MixturBaß
9. Posaunen vnter ChorBaß
10. Posaunen ChormaßBaß
11. TrommetenBaß Chormaß.

X.
Verzeichniß der Stimmen vnd Registern in den Orgeln zu Magdeburg.

Die 1. im Thumb.

Von M. Heinrico Compenio vffgerichtet/ vermag 42. Stimmen. 2. Tremulant. Vogelgesang/ Trummel. 2. Clavir vom C biß c̄. Pedal von g biß ins d̄. 12. Lederne Blasbälge.

Im OberWerck

1. Principal   16. fuß
2. PrincipalBaß abgesondert   16. fuß
3. Principal grosser Vntersatz.

biß.

	Grobe Mixtur unter Chormass	
11.	Kleine Mixtur Chormass	
	Duplicat dieses	
	N.B. Unter Chormass is	16'
	Chormass [is]	8'
	Octava [is]	4'

A total of 33 ranks and 11 stops.

1. Sedecima, open, of Principal scale
2. Super Sedecima, open, penetrating
3. Zimbel, penetrating
4. Spitzflöite or Gemsshorn
5. Querpfeiffe
6. Very small Flöiten
7. Sedecima, open, of another type
8. Super Sedecima, open, of another type
9. Quint de tono Chormass
10. Gedacktflöite Octava
11. Quint ex Sedecima
12. Zimbel, penetrating
13. Gedactflöite Chormass, loud
14. Mixtur Chormass
15. Schallmey, violin-like, Chormass
16. Harffen Principal

From these stops [above], single stops are brought to the lower keyboard, [those being:]

1. Gedactflöite Octava
2. Gedactflöite Sedecima
3. Quint de tono Chormass
4. Quint ex sedecima
5. Sedecima (open)

6. Zimbel
7. Querpfeiffe
8. Schallmey Chor[mass]
9. Mixtur Chor[mass]

Stops in the Pedal

1. GrossBass
2. Unter Chorbass
3. ChorBass
4. OctavBass
5. FlöitenBass unter Chor[mass]
6. DulcianBass
7. Unter ChormassBass
8. MixturBass
9. Posaunen unter Chor[mass]Bass
10. Posaunen ChormassBass
11. Trommeten Bass Chormass

X.
A List of the Stops
and Registers in the Organs at Magdeburg.

The first, in the Cathedral, erected by Mr. Heinrich Compenius, possesses 42 stops, 2 tremulants, birdsong, drum, 2 manuals from C - c"[?], a pedal from g to d, and 12 leather bellows.

In the OberWerck

1. Principal great Untersatz down to F	24'
2. Principal	16'
3. Quintadehn Untersatz	16'

DE ORGANOGRAPHIA.

     biß ins F. von 24. fuß
4. Zimbel mit 3. Pfeiffen
5. Mixtur mit 12. vnd 15. Pfeiffen
6. ⎫ Quintadehn Vntersatz mit ein ab-
7. ⎭   gesonderten Baß. 16. fuß
8. ⎫ Grosse Octava 8. fuß mit ein abge-
9. ⎭   sondertem Baß.
10. Grosse Quinta   6. fl.
11. Klein Octava   4. fl.
12. Grob Gedact   8. fl.
13. Klein Gedact   4. fl.
14. Klein Quint   3. fl.
15. Nasatt   1. oder 3. fl.
16. Nachthorn.   4. fl.

In der Brust 6 Stimmen.

1. Principal.   2. fl.
2. Zimbel doppelt.
3. Mixtur 6. fach
4. Flachflöite.   4. fl.
5. Grob Messing Regal.   8. fl.
6. Messing Regal singend   4. fuß

Zum Pedal auff beyden Seitten.
     9. Stimmen.

1. Posaun Baß   16. fuß
2. Klein Posaun Baß   8. fuß
3. Schalmey oder Cornet   4. fuß
4. Singend Cornett von Messing 2. fuß
5. Bawrflöit Baß   1. fuß
6. Nachthorn Baß   4. fuß
7. Zimbel Baß 3. Pfeiffen starck

Hinderm Wercke stehet auff einer sonderlichen Lade.

8. Gedacter VnterBaß   16. fuß
9. Grosz Gemßhorn Baß   8. fuß

Im Rückpositiff.

1. Principal   8. fuß
2. Zimbel doppelt
3. Mixtur   3. fach
4. Rohrflöite   4. fuß
5. Quintadehn   8. fuß
6. Schwiegel   4. fuß
7. Octava   4. fuß
8. Gemßhorn   4. fuß
9. Quinta   3. fuß
10. Suiflöit   2. fuß
11. Gedact Quinta   3. fuß
12. Kleine Gedact   2. fuß
13. Trommeten   8. fuß
14. Dulcian von Holtz   16. fuß

Die 2. Orgel zu S. Johannis hat 32. Stimmen.

Im OberWerck seynd 14. Stimmen.

1. Præstantem   16. fuß
2. Quintadena   ⎫ mit einem Regi-
3. Quintadeen Baß   ⎭ ster   16. fuß
4. VntersatzBaß   16. fuß
5. Octava   8. fuß
6. Gedact   8. fuß
7. Gemshorn   8. fuß
         8. Super-

DE ORGANOGRAPHIA.

4. Large Octava	8'
5. Grob Gedact	8'
6. Large Quinta	6'
7. Small Octava	4'
8. Small Gedact	4'
9. Nachthorn	4'
10. Small Quint	3'
11. Nasatt	1 or 3' [?]
12. Mixtur	XIII–XV
13. Zimbel	III
[PrincipalBass from the Oberwerk	16']
[QuintadehnBass " " "	16']
[Grosse OctavaBass " " "	16']

In the Brust,
6 stops.

1. Flachflöite	4'
2. Principal	2'
3. Mixtur	VI
4. Zimbel	II
5. Grobregal of brass	8'
6. Singendregal of brass	4'

In the Rückpositiff

1. Principal	8'
2. Quintadehn	8'
3. Octava	4'
4. Rohrflöte	4'
5. Schwiegel	4'
6. Gemsshorn	4'
7. Quinta	3'
8. Gedact Quinta	3'
9. Suiflöit	2'
10. Small Gedact	2'

11. Mixtur	III
12. Zimbel	II
13. Dulzian of wood	16'
14. Trommeten	8'

In the Pedal on both sides,
9 stops.

1. NachthornBass	4'
2. BawrflöitBass	1'
3. ZimbelBass	III
4. PosaunBass	16'
5. Small PosaunBass	8'
6. Schalmey or Cornet	4'
7. Singend Cornett of brass	2'

The rear [Pedal] division stands on a separate chest.

8. Stopped UnterBass	16'
9. Large GemsshornBass	8'

The 2nd Organ, at St. Johannis,
has 32 stops.
In the OberWerk
are 14 stops.

1. Præstanten	16'
2. Quintadena	⎰on one [16']
3. QuintadeenBass [pedal]	⎱stop 16'
4. UntersatzBass [pedal]	16'
5. Octava	8'
6. Gedact	8'
7. Gemshorn	8'

8. Superoctava 4.fuß
9. Quintflöiten 4.fuß
10. Quinta 3.fuß
11. Mixtur
12. Zimbeln
13. QuintBaß } Mit einem Regi-
14. ZimbelBaß. } ster.

In der Brust
6. Stimmen.

15. Nachthörnichen.
16. Zimbelchen.
17. Quintadeen.
18. BassunenBaß.
19. CornettenBaß.
20. BawrflöitenBaß.

Im Rückpositiff.
12. Stimmen.

21. Præstanten 8.fuß
22. Quintadeena 8.fuß
23. Spitzflöiten
24. Octava 4.fuß
25. Gedact klein
26. Quinta
27. Superoctav
28. Sifflitt
29. Mixtur
30. Zimbeln
31. Trommeten
32. Sordunen.

Die 3. Orgel zu S. Ulrichs Kirchen ist von 41. Stimmen/ deren etliche halbieret/ die aber nicht halbieret/ haben 43. Pfeiffen. 2. Tremulanten, Ventil zum Werck- Brust- vnd Positiff. Item/ Alteration, Trummel.

Im OberWerck
sind 12. Stimmen.

1. Præstanten 16.fuß
2. Principal 8.fuß
3. GroßGedact. 8.fuß
4. Quinta 6.fuß
5. Quintadeen 4.fuß
6. Holschell 4
7. Sedez 4
8. Octav 4
9. Schwiegel 4
10. Mixtur Graphicalis 10 Pfeiffen pro Choro, in der Summ. 864.
11. Mixtur Minoralis 8. pro Choro
12. VntersatzBaß 16.fuß

Im BrustPositiff.

1. Siffloit
2. Quindez
3. Regal
4. Vogelgesang oder Nachtigall.
5. Coppel
6. 7. PosaunBaß } Jeden 2. Register
8. 9. RegalBaß. } zertheilt.
10. FlöitenBaß
11. 12. Kleinen Schreyer. 2. Register.

Im RückPositiff.

1. Principal oder Præstanten. 8.fuß
2. Octavagiol
3. Quint
4. GroßGedact
5. Superoctav
6. Klein-

8. Superoctava	4'
9. Quintflöiten	4'
10. Quinta	3'
11. Mixtur	
12. Zimbeln	
13. QuintBass [pedal]	} on one stop
14. ZimbelBass [pedal]	

In the Brust[werk]
6 stops.

1. Quintadeen
2. Little Nachthorn
3. Little Zimbel
4. BawrflöitenBass [pedal]
5. BassunenBass [pedal]
6. CornettenBass [pedal]

In the Rückpositiff
12 stops.

1. Præstanten	8'
2. Quintadeen	8'
3. Spitzflöiten	
4. Octava	4'
5. Gedact, little	
6. Quinta	
7. Superoctav	
8. Sifflitt	
9. Mixtur	
10. Zimbeln	
11. Trommeten	
12. Sordunen	

The third organ, at St. Ulrich's Church, has 41 stops, of which some are halved[?]; those that are not halved have 43 pipes. There are 2 Tremulants and ventils for the [Ober]werck, Brust[Positiff], and [Rück]Positiff, as well as *Alteration*[?] and Drum.

In the OberWerck
are 12 stops.

1. Præstanten	16'
2. Principal	8'
3. GrossGedact	8'
4. Quinta	6'
5. Octav	4'
6. Quintadeen	4'
7. Holschell	4'
8. Sedetz	4'
9. Schwiegel	4'
10. Mixtur Graphicalis[?] 10 pipes per note, 864 in total.	
11. UntersatzBass	16'

In the BrustPositiff

1. Siffloit
2. Quindetz
3. Coppel
4-5. Kleinen Schreyer[?], two stops
6. Regal
7. Birdsong or Nightingale
8. FlöitenBass[29]
9-10. PosaunBass } each divided
11-12. RegalBass } into two stops.

In the RückPositiff

1. Principal or Præstanten	8'
2. Octavagiol	
3. Quint	
4. Gross Gedact	
5. Superoctav	
6. Klein Gedact	
7. Sifflitt	

---

29. A number of stops scattered throughout the various divisions of this organ are designated as "Bass," the common designation for a pedal rank. Since this stoplist does not specify an independent pedal division, it seems that the stops ending in "Bass" are pedal ranks housed in some way in the manual divisions.

6. Klein Gedact
7. Siffiitt
8. Zimbel
9. SingendRegal
10. Gemßhorn
11. QuintSpitz
12. GedactBaß
13. Superoctav
14. Klein GedactBaß
15. Sedetz
16. Cornett oder Zincken.
17. Krumbhörner.

IV.

In der Orgel zu S. Peter/ sind alles in allen 33. Stimmen.

1. Principal	8. füssen
2. Zimbeln	
3. Quint	3. fuß
4. Mixtur	
5. Octav	4. fuß
6. Querflöiten	4. fuß
7. GrobgedactManualiter	8. fuß
8. Grob Gemßhorn	8. fuß
9. Groß Quintadeen/manualiter	8. fuß

Bässe im Pedal.

1. Groß QuintadeenBaß.	16. fuß
2. Gedacter Untersatz	16. fuß
3. ZimbelnBaß	
4. BawrflöitenBaß	1. fuß
5. HolflöitenBaß	2. fuß
6. QuintflöitenBaß.	

In der Brust zum Manual
4. Stimmen.

1. Nachthorn	4. fuß
2. Quinteflött oder klein Gedact	2. fuß
3. Zimbeln zweyfach	
4. Regal.	

In der Brust auff beyden seiten zum Pedal.
3. Stimmen.

1. PosaunenBaß
2. TrommetenBaß
3. SchallmeyenBaß.

Im Rückpositiff
12. Stimmen.

1. Principal	4. fuß
2. Trommeten	8. fuß
3. Quintadehna	8. fuß
4. Gemßhorn	4. fuß
5. Mittelgedact	4. fuß
6. KleinRegal	
7. Octava	
8. Quinta	
9. Kleingedact	
10. Sifflit	
11. Mixtur	
12. Zimbeln.	

V.

Die newe Orgel bey S. Catharinen ist gesetzt mit 33. Stimmen. 3. Claviern/ zum OberWerck Brust- vnnd RückPositiff. Auch 2. Tremulanten. 8. Spleenbälge. Vogelgeschrey. Kuckuck.

Im

8. Gemsshorn
9. Tapered Quint
10. Superoctav
11. Sedetz
12. Zimbel
13. Singend Regal
14. Cornett or Zincken
15. Krumbhörner
16. GedactBass
17. Klein GedactBass

IV.
In the Organ at St. Peter there is a total of 33 stops.

[Werck]

1. Principal   8'
2. Grobgedact, manual   8'
3. Grob Gemsshorn   8'
4. Gross Quintadeen, manual 8'
5. Octav   4'
6. Querflöiten   4'
7. Quint   3'
8. Mixtur
9. Zimbeln

In the Manual Brust
4 stops.

1. Nachthorn   4'
2. Quintflöit or small Gedact 2'[sic]
3. Zimbel   II
4. Regal   [8'?]

In the Pedal Brust on
either side.
3 stops.

1. PosaunenBass
2. TrommetenBass
3. SchallmeyenBass

Bass [stops] in the Pedal

1. Stopped Untersatz   16'
2. Gross QuintadeenBass   16'
3. QuintflöitenBass
4. HolflöitenBass   2'
5. BawrflöitenBass   1'
6. ZimbelnBass

In the Rückpositiff
12 stops.

1. Quintadehna   8'
2. Principal   4'
3. Gemsshorn   4'
4. Mittelgedact   4'
5. Octava   [2'?]
6. Kleingedact   [2'?]
7. Quinta
8. Sifflit
9. Mixtur
10. Zimbeln
11. Trommeten   8'
12. Klein Regal   [4'?]

V.
The New Organ at St. Catharinen

is furnished with 33 stops and 3 manuals: Oberwerck, Brust- and RuckPositiff. [There are] also 2 Tremulants, 8 wedge bellows, Birdcall and Cuckoo.

Im OberWerck.

1. Quintadehna — 16. fuß
2. Gemshorn — 8. fuß
3. Grobgedact — 8. fuß
4. Octava — 4. fuß
5. Rohrflöite — 4. fuß
6. Schweitzerpfeiffe — 8. fuß
7. Superoctava — 2. fuß
8. Mixtur
9. Quinta — 6. fuß
10. Principal — 8. fuß

BrustPositiff.

1. Nachthorn — 4. fuß
2. Blockflöite — 4. fuß
3. Kleingedact — 2. fuß
4. Krumbhorn
5. Zincken
6. Principal — 2. fuß

RückPositiff.

1. Principal — 4. fuß
2. Quintadeen — 4. fuß
3. Gemshorn — 4. fuß
4. Mittelgedact — 4. fuß
5. Octava — 2. fuß
6. Kleingedact — 2. fuß
7. Rauschflöite — 1. fuß
8. Zimbel
9. Trommete — 8. fuß
10. Klein Regal — 4. fuß

In beyden SeitTörmen neben dem RückPositiff.

1. Præstanten — 16. fuß
2. Gedacten Untersatz — 16. fuß
3. Schweitzer Baß — 2. fuß
4. Nachthorn Baß — 2. fuß
5. Bawrflöiten Baß — 1. fuß
6. Mixtur Baß
7. Posaunen Baß — 16. fuß
8. Sordunen Baß — 16. fuß
9. Dulcian — 8. fuß
10. Cornett — 1. fuß

XI.

Zu Bernaw in der Marck Anno 1576. Wie auch zu Stendahl bey unser lieben Frawen im Jahr 1580. ist von M. Hans Scherern uff nachbeschriebene Art eine Orgel gesetzt worden / welche 29. Stimmen. 1. Tremulant, Coppel in beyden Manualen, Coppel des Pedals im Rückpositiff. Das Clavir im Manual, hat 4. volle Octav, von C biß ins c̄ machen 48. Claves. Im Pedal aber so gehet vom C biß ins d̄ mit allen Semitoniis, seynd 26. Claves.

Im Wercke zum Manual und Pedal.

1. Untersatz durch das gantze Clavir 16. Schuch die lenge.
2. Untersatzter Baß
3. Principal 8. Schuch lang.
4. Grobgedact
5. Quintadehna
6. Zimbel
7. Mixtur 12. Pfeiffen starck in zehen Claves.
8. Jule

In the Oberwerck

1. Quintadehna 16′
2. Principal 8′
3. Grobgedact 8′
4. Gemshorn 8′
5. Schweitzerpfeiffe 8′
6. Quinta 6′
7. Octava 4′
8. Rohrflöite 4′
9. Superoctava 2′
10. Mixtur

BrustPositiff

1. Nachthorn 4′
2. Blockflöite 4′
3. Principal 2′
4. Kleingedact 2′
5. Krumbhorn
6. Zincken

Rückpositiff

1. Principal 4′
2. Mittelgedact 4′
3. Quintadeen 4′
4. Gemshorn 4′
5. Octava 2′
6. Kleingedact 2′
7. Rauschflöite 1′
8. Zimbel
9. Trommete 8′
10. Little Regal 4′

[Pedal] in both Side Towers
on either side of the Rückpositiff.

1. Præstanten 16′
2. Stopped Untersatz 16′
3. SchweitzerBass 2′
4. NachthornBass 2′
5. BawrflöitenBass 1′
6. MixturBass
7. PosaunenBass 16′
8. SordunenBass 16′
9. Dulcian 8′
10. Cornett 1′

XI.

Mr. Hans Scherer [the Elder] erected an organ at Bernau in the Mark [Brandenburg] in the year 1576 (as also in St. Mary's Church at Stendahl in the year 1580) that has 29 stops, as described below.

In the Werck,
for both manual and pedal

1. Untersatz throughout the entire keyboard 16′
2. Untersatz [in the] pedal 16′
3. Principal 8′
4. Grobgedact
5. Quintadehna
6. Zimbel
7. Mixtur "in zehen Claves"[30]   XII
8. Jule, the Quint of the large Principal

---

30. Literally "in ten keys"; the meaning is obscure.

DE ORGANOGRAPHIA.

8. Jule/ ist die Quint von dem groben Principal.
9. Starck Regal fornen in der Brust.
10. Bawrpfeiffe oder Blockflöite.
11. Halb Principal oder Octav 4. fuß
12. Eine Holflöite 4. fl. oder Octav vom groben Gedacten.
13. Nachthorn 4. fl. oder die Octav von der Quintadeena.
14. Quinta gibt mit dem Principal oder Gedact eine Rauschpfeiffe.
15. Superoctav
16. Nasatt/ oder klein offene Quint von der Superoctav.
17. Groß Posaunen Baß.
18. Bawrpfeiffen Baß.

Im Rückpositiff.

1. Principal
2. Holpfeiffe
3. Spillpfeiffe
4. Klingend Zimbel 3. Pfeiffen starck in 10. Claviren.
5. Quinta
6. Superoctav
7. Sisflöit
8. Singend- oder Geigend Regal.
9. Trommet
10. Gemßhorn
11. Principal im Discant.

XII.
Das Werck zu
Hall

Bey vnser lieben Frawen Kirchen. Hat 31. Stimmen.

Im OberWerck
6. Stimmen.

1. Principal im Pedal 16. Im Manual 8. fuß Thon.
2. Octava, 4. fl. Thon im Manual allein.
3. Mixtur
4. Zimbel
5. Nachthorn 4. fuß thon ⎫ im Manual
6. Querpfeiff 8. fuß thon ⎭ allein.

In der Brust
6. Stimmen.

1. Principal   2. fuß Thon
2. Mixtur
3. Zimbel
4. Regal   8. fuß
5. Walefflötgen   1. fuß
6. Flachflötgen   4. fuß

Neben der Brust
4. Stimmen.

1. Trommeten Baß   8. fuß
2. Schallmeyen Baß   4. fuß
3. Zimbel Baß
4. Quintflöit Baß   3. fuß

Auff der Seitten sind newlich hinan gesetzet.
3. Stimmen.

1. Grober Posaunen Untersatz   16 fuß
2. Quintadehn Baß   8. fuß
3. Nachthorn.   4. fuß

9. a loud Regal at the front of the Brust
10. Bawrpfeiffe or Blockflöit
11. Half-Principal or Octave   4'
12. A Holflöite, the octave of the Grobgedact   4'
13. Nachthorn, the octave of the Quintadeena   4'
14. Quinta, producing a Rauschpfeiff with the Principal or Gedact
15. Superoctav
16. Nasat, or little open Quint of the Superoctav
17. Gross Posaune [in the] pedal
18. Bawrpfeiffe [in the] pedal

In the Rückpositiff

1. Principal
2. Holpfeiffe
3. Spillpfeiffe
4. Klingend Zimbel   III
   "in 10. Claviren"[31]
5. Quinta
6. Superoctav
7. Siflöit
8. Singend- or GeigendRegal
9. Trommet
10. Gemsshorn
11. Principal in the treble

1 Tremulant
Coupler between the manuals
Rückpositiff to pedal coupler
Manual compass: 4 octaves C to c["], with a total of 48 keys.
Pedal compass: C-d', with all semitones [except C#], 26 keys.

XII.
The Instrument at
Hall[e]
in the church of Our Dear Lady [Marktkirche], has 31 stops.

In the Ober-Werck
6 stops.

1. Principal at 16' pitch in the pedal and 8' in the manual.
2. Querpfeiff 8' only in the manual.
3. Octava 4' only in the manual.
4. Nachthorn 4' only in the manual.
5. Mixtur
6. Zimbel

In the Brust
6 stops.

1. Flachflötgen   4'
2. Principal   2'
3. Waltflötgen   1'
4. Mixtur
5. Zimbel
6. Regal   8'

Beside the Brust
4 [pedal] stops

1. QuintflöitBass   3'
2. ZimbelBass
3. TrommetenBass   8'
4. SchallmeyenBass   4'

At the side there have
recently been added 3 [pedal] stops.

1. QuintadehnBass   8'
2. Nachthorn   4'
3. Heavy Posaunen Untersatz   16'

---

31. Literally "in 10 keyboards"; the meaning is obscure.

Im RückPositiff.

1. Principal	4. fuß Thon
2. Mixtur	
3. Zimbel	
4. Octava	2. fuß
5. Quinta	9. fuß
6. Quintadeen	8. fuß
7. Gedactes	4. fuß
8. Kleingedactes	2. fuß
9. Spitzflöit	2. fuß
10. Sifflöit	2. fuß
11. Trommeten	8. fuß
12. Singend Regal	4. fuß

XIII.
Die Orgel zu
Braunschweig

Im Stifft S. Blasij. Welche M. Hennig aus Hildesheimb gemacht/ hat 35. Stimmen.

Im OberWerck seynd 13. Stimmen.

1. Principal	16. fuß
2. Principal	8. fuß
3. Octava	8. fuß
4. Quintadeena	16
5. Quinta	3
6. Mixtur	2. fuß
oben im Discant 12. Pfeiffen. im Baß	7. starck.
7. Zimbel	3. Pfeiffen starck.
8. Holflöite	16
9. Holflöite	8
10. Coppelflöite	4
11. Gemßhorn	2
12. Trommeten	8
13. Dulcian	8

Diese Stimmen / wie auch im Rückpositiff gehen durchaus ins C sampt ♊ ♭ F♯. vnd oben ins C sampt F̄ vnd ♮.

Im Rückpositiff 11. Stimmen.

1. Holflöite	8. fuß
2. Quintadehna	8
3. Principal	4
4. Octava	4
5. Zimbel	2. Pfeiffen starck
6. Querflöiten	8
7. Schallmeyen	4
8. Krumbhörner	8
9. BlockPfeiffe	4
10. Sifflöit	2
11. Zincken vom ♮ biß oben hinaus.	

Im Pedal 14. Stimmen.

1. Gar grosser Untersatz Gedact.	32. fuß
2. Principal	16
3. Octava	8
4. Gedact	16
5. Holflöiten	8
6. Posaunen	16
7. Trommeten	8
8. Krumbhorn	16
9. Gemßhorn	4

10. Zim-

In the RückPositiff

1. Quintadeen 8'
2. Principal 4'
3. Gedactes 4'
4. Quinta 9' [3'?]
5. Octava 2'
6. Kleingedactes 2'
7. Spissflöit 2'
8. Sifflöit 2'
9. Mixtur
10. Zimbel
11. Trommeten 8'
12. SingendRegal 4'

XIII.
The organ at
Braunschweig

in the Collegiate Church of St. Blasius[32] in Braunschweig, which Master Henni[n]g[33] from Hildesheim built, has 35 stops.

In the OberWerck
Are 13 stops.

1. Principal 16'
2. Quintadeena 16'
3. Holflöite 16'
4. Principal 8'
5. Holflöite 8'
6. Octava 8' [4'?]
7. Coppelflöite 4'
8. Quinta 3'
9. Gemsshorn 2'
10. Mixtur 2' VII-XII
11. Zimbel III
12. Trommeten 8'
13. Dulcian 8'

These stops, just as those in the Rückpositiv, run complete from C, with D♯, F♯ and G♯, up to c''' with g'' and b♭['].

In the Rückpositiff
11 stops.

1. Holflöite 8'
2. Quintadehna 8'
3. Querflöiten 8'
4. Principal 4'
5. Octava 4' [2'?]
6. BlockPfeiffe 4'
7. Sifflöit 2'
8. Zimbel II
9. Krumbhörner 8'
10. Schallmeyen 4'
11. Zincken from b on up

In the Pedal
14 stops.

1. Great Untersatz stopped 32'
2. Principal 16'
3. Gedact 16'
4. Octava 8'
5. Holflöiten 8'
6. Gemsshorn 4'
7. Bawrflöiten 2'
Mixtur { 8. Superoctav 4'
9. Rauschpfeiffen
10. Zimbel II }

---

32. This church is the cathedral at Braunschweig.
33. Master Henning Hencke (c. 1550-c. 1620).

Mixtur { 10. Zimbel   2. Pfeiffen starck
        { 11. Rauschpfeiffen
        { 12. SuperOctav   4. fi.
13. Bawrflöiten   2
14. Trummel   2. Pfeiffen starck
    Tremulant
    Coppel zu beyden Clavirn.

Fünff Ventile,
1. Zum OberWerck.
2. Zun Bässen.
3. Zun RückPositiff.
4. Zur Sonnen
5. Zun Sternen.

Diese Bässe im Pedal sind also gemacht/ daß man einen jeglichen besonders gebrauchen kan: Vnd haben jhre eigne Laden/ gehen alle vnten ins grosse C sampt D♯. F♯. G♯. vnnd oben ins d sampt c♯.

Die Laden seynd nicht vff die gemeine/ sondern eine andere Art gerichtet/ vnd werden Springladen genennet/ davon im dritten Theil dieses Tomi Secundi etwas angedeutet werden.

Es sind auch die SpanBälge/ deren achte vorhanden/ vff eine sondere Art gemacht/ also daß ein jeglicher 9. guter Schuch lang/ mit einer eintzigen Falten; Die Spuene sind 2. starcke Eichene Bretter gantz beständig/ vnd gehen dichte zusammen/ daß keine Mauß darbey kommen kan.

Das oberste Werck hat fünff Felder/ in der mitten einen raum/ die spitzen vnd ein flachfeld/ auff beyden seitten die Baßthürmer.

Das Rückpositiff hat mitten eine spitzen/ vnd den raum/ flachfeld/ vnd so vor dann hat 7. felder.

XIV.
Disposition derer Orgel in
Leipzig.

Die 1. bey S. Niclas hat 29. Stimmen. Coppel zum Rückpositiff/ vnd Pedal. Coppel zu beyden Manualn. Vogelgesang. 10. Spänbälge.

1. Principal   8. fuß
2. Gedact   8. fuß
3. Quintadeena   8. fuß
4. Dreyfache Zimbel.
5. Eine Mixtur im Baß von 4. Pfeiffn/ im T. 6. vnd im Disc. 8. Pfeiffen starck.
6. SuperOctava   2. fuß
7. RauschQuinta
8. Octava   4. fuß
9. Gemßhorn
10. NasattQuinta
11. Grobgedact/ von 16. fuß Manualiter.
12. Vnd Pedaliter abgesondertet Baß.

In der Brust
13. Grob SordvenRegal vff   16. fuß
14. Regal von   8. fuß
15. Regal   4. fuß
16. Tremulant zum SchnarrWercke gut.

11. Posaunen	16'
12. Krumbhorn	16'
13. Trommeten	8'
14. Trummel	II
Tremulant	

A coupler to both keyboards.

Five Ventils:
1. For the OberWerck.
2. For the Pedal.
3. For the Rückpositiff.
4. For the Suns.
5. For the [Cymbel]sterns.

The pedal stops are built so that each one of them can be used separately. They have their own chest, and all go down to low C, complete with D♯, F♯ and G♯, and up to d', complete with c♯'.

The chests are not of the usual sort, but are built in a different way, and are called spring chests, as alluded to in the third part of this Vol. II.[34]

Also to be found here are wedge bellows, eight in number, made in a special way, so that each of them is fully 9 feet long, with only a single fold. The bellows-boards are 2 strong, very durable oak boards, that fit tightly together so that not even a mouse can get between them.[35]

The uppermost division has five flats: in the middle a space with pointed towers and a flat tower, and on both sides the pedal towers.

The Rückpositiff has a pointed tower in the middle, a space, a flat tower, and thus has 7 flats.

XIV.
Stoplist[s] of the organs in

Leipzig.

The first, at St. Nicholas, has 29 stops, a Rückpositiff/Pedal coupler, a coupler between manuals, Birdsong, and 10 wedge bellows.

[Werck]

1. Grobgedact, manual only	16'
2. Principal	8'
3. Gedact	8'
4. Quintadeena	8'
5. Octava	4'
6. Gemshorn	[4'?]
7. NasattQuinta	[3'?]
8. SuperOctava	2'
9. RauschQuinta	
10. Mixtur	IV-VI-VIII
11. Zimbel	III

In the Brust

1. Grob Sorduen Regal	16'
2. Regal	8'
3. Regal	4'
Tremulant for the reeds	

---

34. pp. 107f.
35. cf. the comments accompanying Praetorius's stoplist for St. Gotthart, Hildesheim, on p. 199.

Im RückPositiff.

17. Principal	4.fuß
18. Gröbflöite	8.fuß
19. Holflöite	4.fuß
20. Spillpfeiff	4.fuß
21. Nachthorn.	4.fuß
22. Quintflöit	
23. Sufflöit	
24. Klingend Zimbel mit 3. Pfeiffen.	
25. Trommet.	8.fuß
26. Krumbhorn.	8.fuß

Im Pedal.

27. Offenflöit	4.fuß
28. PosaunenBaß	16.fuß
29. Schallmeyen Baß	4.fuß

Die 2. zu S. Thomas.
Ist starck von 25. Stimmen.

1. Coppeln der beyden ManualClavirn.
2. Coppeln des Pedals zum RückPositiff.

Im OberWerck
9. Stimmen.

1. Principal	16.fuß
Pedaliter vnd Manualiter.	
2. Octava	8.fuß
3. Superoctava	4.fuß
4. Sedez	2.fuß
5. Gedact	8.fuß
6. Offenflöit	4.fuß
7. Zimbeln	3.fach
8. Mixtur	6.fach
9. Quinta	

In der Brust
2. Stimmen.

10. Regal	8.fuß Thon
11. Regal.	4.fuß

Im Rückpositiff
12. Stimmen.

12. Principal	8.fuß
13. Quintadeena	8.fuß
14. Ein linde Gedact	8.fuß
15. Holflöite	4.fuß
16. Spillpfeiff	4.fuß
17 Trommet	8.fuß
18. Krumbhörner	8.fuß
19. Nachthorn	4.fuß
20. Sedez	
21. Quintflötgen.	
22. Gemßhorn	2.fuß
23. Klingend Zimbel.	

Noch im Pedal.

24. PosaunenBaß	16.fuß
25. Schallmey	4.fuß

XV.
Disposition der Orgel zu
Torgaw
Hat 26. Stimmen.

Im OberWerck seynd
11. Stimmen.

1. Prin-

In the RückPositiff

1. Grobflöite — 8'
2. Principal — 4'
3. Holflöite — 4'
4. Spillpfeiff — 4'
5. Nachthorn — 4'
6. Quintflöit
7. Sufflöit
8. Klingend Zimbel — III
9. Trommet — 8'
10. Krumbhorn — 8'

In the Pedal

1. GrobgedactBass — 16'
   from the manual, on a separate stopknob.
2. Offenflöit — 4'
3. PosaunenBass — 16'
4. SchallmeyenBass — 4'

The second, at St. Thomas,
has 25 stops,
a coupler between both manuals, and a Rückpositiff/Pedal coupler.

In the OberWerck
9 stops.

1. Principal — 16'
2. Octava — 8'
3. Gedact — 8'
4. Superoctava — 4'
5. Offenflöit — 4'
6. Quinta — [3'?]
7. Sedetz — 2'
8. Mixtur — VI
9. Zimbeln — III

In the Brust
2 stops.

1. Regal — 8' pitch
2. Regal — 4'

In the Rückpositiff
12 stops

1. Principal — 8'
2. Quintadeena — 8'
3. A gentle Gedact — 8'
4. Holflöite — 4'
5. Spillpfeiff — 4'
6. Nachthorn — 4'
7. Sedetz — [2'?]
8. Gemshorn — 2'
9. Quintflötgen — [1 1/3'?]
10. Klingend Zimbel
11. Trommet — 8'
12. Krumbhörner — 8'

In the Pedal

1. Principal (Oberwerck) — 16'
2. PosaunenBass — 16'
3. Schallmey — 4'

XV.
Stoplist of the organ at
Torgau
having 26 stops.

In the OberWerck are
11 stops.

1. Principal	von 8. fuß
2. Octava	4
3. Superoctava	2
4. Quinta	
5. Zimbeln	
6. Mixtur	6. Pfeiffenstarck.
7. Grobgedact	16. fuß
8. Gedactes	8
9. Quintadeena.	8
10. Gemßhorn	4. fuß
11. Nasatt	

In der Brust
2. Stimmen.

12. Regal	vff 8. fuß
13. Klein Regal	4

Im RückPositiff
10. Stimmen.

14. Principal	4. fuß
15. Gedactes	8. fuß
16. Holflöiten	4
17. Gemßhorn	2
18. Sufflöite	
19. Quintflöite	
20. Sedecima	
21. Zimbeln	
22. GrobgedactRegal	16. fuß
23. Trommeten.	8

Im Pedal 3. Stim-
men.

24. Gedacter vnterBaß	16. fuß
25. Posaunen	16
26. Schallmeyen	4

Vber diese noch:

1. Trummel
2. Vogelgesang.
3. Coppel ins Mannal.
4. Coppel zum Pedal
5. Ventiel zum RückPositiff.
6. Tremulant.

XVI.

Verzeichnüß derer Register vnd Stimmen / so in den Orgeln zu

Halberstadt
zu finden.

Das 1. Werck in S. Martini Kirchen hat M. David Becke mit 39. Stimmen vnd einem Tremulant gesetzet. Der Tremulant, ob er wol keinen laut von sich gibt / so wird er doch von etlichen / Auch vor eine Stimme: (weil man viel verenderung damit haben kan) gerechnet.

Im OberWercke
8. Stimmen.

1. Quintadehna.	16. fuß
2. Principal	
3. Grobgedact.	
4. GrobGemßhorn	
5. Octava	
6. Quinta	
7. Mixtur	
8. Zimbel	

In der Brust
6. Stimmen.

1. Grobgedackt   16'
2. Principal   8'
3. Gedactes   8'
4. Quintadeena   8'
5. Octava   4'
6. Gemsshorn   4'
7. Quinta   [3'?]
8. Nasatt   [3'?]
9. Superoctava   2'
10. Mixtur   VI
11. Zimbeln

In the Brust
2 stops.

1. Regal   at 8'
2. Klein Regal   4'

In the Rückpositiff
10 stops.

1. Gedactes   8'
2. Principal   4'
3. Holflöiten   4'
4. Gemshorn   2'
5. Sufflöite   [2'?]
6. Quintflöite   [1 1/3'?]
7. Sedecima   [1'?]
8. Zimbeln
9. GrobgedactRegal   16'
10. Trommeten   8'

In the Pedal
3 stops.

1. Gedacter UnterBass   16'
2. Posaunen   16'
3. Schallmeyen   4'

In addition there are:
1. Drum
2. Birdsong
3. Manual coupler
4. Pedal coupler
5. Ventil for the Rückpositiv
6. Tremulant

XVI.

A list of the registers and stops to be found in the organs at

Halberstadt.

Mr. David Beck put the first instrument, with 39 stops and a tremulant in St. Martini Church. Although the tremulant produces no actual sound of its own, yet some still consider it a stop (since it can produce so much variety).

In the OberWerck
8 stops.

1. Quintadehna   16'
2. Principal   [8'?]
3. Grobgedact   [8'?]
4. GrobGemsshorn   [8'?]
5. Octava   [4'?]
6. Quinta   [3'?]
7. Mixtur
8. Zimbel

In the Brust
6 stops.

1. Principal
2. Gedact
3. Nachthorn
4. Zimbel
5. Mixtur
6. Regal.

Im Pedal
12. Stimmen.

1. Untersatz
2. Principal
3. GedactBaß
4. OctavenBaß
5. ZimbelBaß
6. FlöitenB.
7. HolQuintenB.
8. QuintflöitenB.
9. PosaunenB.
10. TrommetenB.
11. SchallmeyenB.
12. CornettenB.

Im RückPositiff
12. Stimmen.

1. Principal
2. Quinta
3. Octava
4. Quintadeena
5. Mixtur
6. Zimbel
7. Spitzflöite
8. Gemßhorn
9. Gedact
10. Suifflöit
11. Krumbhorn.

12. GeigendRegal.

Das 2. zun Baarfüssern/ dessen M. Elias Winnigsteten gewesen/ vnd zu stehen 700. Thaler/ ohne das Mahlwerck gekostet/ hat 27. Stimmen. 1. Tremulant. 8 Blaßbälge.

Im Werck.
8. Stimmen.

1. Principal	8. fuß
2. Grobgedact	8. fuß
3. Groß Gemßhorn	8. fuß
4. Octava	4. fuß
5. Querflöit	4
6. Superoctävlin	2
7. Quinta	
8. Zimbel	2. fach
9. Mixtur 6. fach vnten/ c̄ 7. fach/ c̄ 8. fach. c̄ 9. fach).	

Im Pedal oben
8. Stimmen.

1. QuintadeenB.	8. fuß
2. GedactB.	8. fuß
3. HolflöitenB.	2. fuß
4. QuinB.	
5. Bawrflöiten	
6. ZimbelBaß	
7. Groß Quintadeen	16. fuß
8. Vntersatz	16. fuß

In der Brust zum Manual
5. Stimmen.

1. Prin.

1. Principal
2. Gedact
3. Nachthorn
4. Mixtur
5. Zimbel
6. Regal

In the Rückpositiff
12 stops.
1. Principal
2. Quinta
3. Octava
4. Quintadeena
5. Mixtur
6. Zimbel
7. Spitzflöte
8. Gemsshorn
9. Gedact
10. Suifflöit
11. Krumbhorn
12. GeigendRegal

In the Pedal
12 stops.
1. Untersatz
2. Principal
3. GedactBass
4. OctavenBass
5. FlöitenB[ass]
6. HolQuinten B[ass]
7. QuintflöitenB[ass]
8. ZimbelBass
9. PosaunenB[ass]
10. TrommetenB[ass]
11. SchallmeyenB[ass]
12. CornettenB[ass]

The second [instrument] at the Barfüsserkirche, which is Mr. Elias Winnigstädt's [instrument], cost 700 Thaler without the painting. It has 27 stops, 1 tremulant and 8 bellows.

In the Werck
8 stops.
1. Principal	8'
2. Grobgedact	8'
3. Gross Gemsshorn	8'
4. Octava	4'
5. Querflöit	4'
6. Superoctävlin	2'
7. Quinta	
8. Mixtur VI in the bass, VII at c', VIII at c", XI at c'''	
9. Zimbel	II

In the Brust,
5 manual stops.
1. Principal	2'
2. Nachthorn	2'
3. Querflöit	
4. Mixtur	III
5. Zimbel	II

In the Brust,
3 pedal stops.
1. Posaun	[16'?]
2. Trommetten	[8'?]
3. Cornett	[4'? 2'?]

1. Principal   2. fuß
2. Nachthorn   2. fuß
3. Querflöit
4. Zimbel 2. Chöricht.
5. Mixtur 3. Chöricht.

In der Brust zum
Pedal
3. Stimmen.

1. Posaun
2. Trommetten
3. Cornett.

Im Rückpositiff
13. Stimmen.

1. Quintadeena   8. fuß
2. Principal   4. fuß
3. Octava   2. fuß
4. Quinta
5. Gemßhorn   4
6. Gedact   4
7. Klein Gedact
8. Sifflöit
9. Zimbel   3. fach
10. Mixtur   4. fach
11. Trommet   8. fuß
12. Regal   8. fuß
13. Geigend Regal   4. fuß

XVII.
Zu Cassel

In Hessen seynd vff des Herrn Landgrafen daselbst auffgewandte Vnkosten drey vornehme Orgeln von den Hamburgern (wie sie bey vns genennet werden) innerhalb fünff Jahren erbawet vnd vffgerichtet worden.

Derer die 1.

In der Freyheiter Kirchen/ ohne die Coppel vnd Tremulant von 33. Stimmen.

Im OberWercke
8. Stimmen.

1. Principal   16. fuß
2. Octava
3. RauschPfeiffe
4. Scharff
5. Mixtur
6. Quintadeena.
7. Holpfeiffe
8. Flöiten

Im Obern Positiff
8. Stimmen.

1. Principal   8. fuß
2. Holpfeiffe
3. Gemßhorn
4. Waltflöite
5. Nasatt
6. Trommette
7. Zincken
8. Zimbel.

Im Rück Positiff
9. Stimmen.

1. Prin-

In the Rückpositiff
13 stops.

1. Quintadeena — 8'
2. Principal — 4'
3. Gedact — 4'
4. Gemsshorn — 4'
5. Quinta — [2 2/3'? 1 1/3'?]
6. Octava — 2'
7. Klein Gedact — [2'?]
8. Siffloit — [1'?]
9. Mixtur — IV
10. Zimbel — III
11. Trommet — 8'
12. Regal — 8'
13. GeigendRegal — 4'

In the upper Pedal[36]
8 stops.

1. Untersatz — 16'
2. Gross Quintadeen — 16'
3. GedactB[ass] — 8'
4. QuintadeenB[ass] — 8'
5. QuintB[ass] — [5 1/3'? 2 2/3'?]
6. HolflöitenB[ass] — 2'
7. Bawrflöiten — [1'?]
8. ZimbelBass

XVII.
at Cassel

At Cassel in Hesse three distinguished organs were built and erected within five years, [underwritten] by the Landgrave at great expense, by the "Hamburgers",[37] as we call them.

Of these, the first is at the Freiheiterkirche[38]; it has 33 stops, not counting the coupler and the tremulant.

In the OberWerck
8 stops.

1. Principal — 16'
2. Octava
3. Holpfeiffe[39]
4. Flöiten
5. Quintadeena
6. RauschPfeiffe
7. Mixtur
8. Scharff

In the OberPositiff
8 stops.

1. Principal — 8'
2. Holpfeiffe
3. Gemsshorn
4. Waltflöite
5. Nasatt
6. Zimbel
7. Trommete
8. Zincken

In the Rückpositiff
9 stops.

1. Principal — 8'
2. Gedact — 8'

---

36. "im Pedal oben," perhaps signifying that these pedal stops are in the upper part of the case, with the stops of the Werck.

37. Hans Scherer the Younger and his helpers (fl. 1611-ca. 1631); see: Gustav Fock, *Arp Schnitger und seine Schule* (Kassel et al.: Bärenreiter, 1974), p. 43; see also: Gustav Fock, trans. & ed. Lynn Edwards & Edward C. Pepe, *Hamburg's Role in Northern European Organ Building* (Easthampton, Mass.: Westfield Center [1997]), pp. 49-54.

38. i.e., Martinskirche.

39. This is Prætorius' error; it should read "Gedackt." See: Gerhard Aumüller, "Orgeln, Orgelbauer und Organisten der Schütz-Zeit in Hessen." in: *Schütz-Jahrbuch* 2012 (Kassel: Bärenreiter, 2013), p. 126).

1. Principal   8. fuß
2. Gedact   8
3. Quintadeena   8
4. Querpfeiffe   4
5. Octava   4
6. Scharff
7. Mixtur
8. Krumbhorn
9. MessingRegal

Im Pedal.

1. Principal   32. fuß
2. Octava
3. Untersatz
4. Gedact
5. Rauschpfeiffe
6. PosaunenBaß
7. TrommetenBaß
8. CornettBaß
   Coppel
   Tremulant.

Die 2. in der Brüder Kirchen von 25. Stimmen. Coppel vnd Tremulant.

Im Werck.

1. Principal   8. fuß
2. Octava   4
3. Octava   2
4. Kleingedact
5. Nasatt
6. Mixtur
7. Scharff
8. Zimbel
9. Trommette
10. Zinck.

Im RückPositiff
8. Stimmen.

1. Principal   4. fuß
2. Grobgedact   8
3. Octävlin
4. Mixtur
5. Flötgen
6. Waltflöite
7. Querpfeiffe
8. Klein Regal.

Im Pedal in beyden Thörmen. 7. Stimmen.

1. Offenes Principal   16. fuß
2. Untersatz   16
3. Octava
4. PosaunenBaß   16
5. DulcianBaß   16
6. TrommetenBaß   8. fuß
7. Cornett   3
   Coppel
   Tremulant.

Die 3. in der Schloß Kirchen. Von 20. Stimmen/ auch Coppel vnnd Tremulant gesetzet vnd gestellet ist.

Im Werck 8. Stimmen.

1. Principal halb hinaus doppelt   8. fuß
2. Quint Tenor   8
3. Gedact   8
4. Octava   4
5. Flöite   4
6. Krumbhorn

7. Mix-

3. Quintadeena	8'
4. Octava	4'
5. Querpfeiffe	4'
6. Mixtur	
7. Scharff	
8. Krumbhorn	
9. MessingRegal	

In the Pedal

1. Principal	32'
2. Untersatz	
3. Octava	
4. Gedact	
5. Rauschpfeiffe	
6. PosaunenBass	
7. TrommetenBass	
8. CornettBass	
Coupler	
Tremulant	

The second, in the Brüderkirche, has 25 stops, coupler and tremulant.

In the Werck

1. Principal	8'
2. Octava	4'
3. Octava	2'
4. Kleingedact	
5. Nasatt	
6. Mixtur	
7. Scharff	
8. Zimbel	
9. Trommette	
10. Zincke	

In the RückPositiff
8 stops.

1. Grobgedact	8'
2. Principal	4'
3. Querpfeiffe	
4. Waltflöite	
5. Octävlin	
6. Flötgen	
7. Mixtur	
8. KleinRegal	

In the two Pedal towers
7 stops.

1. Open Principal	16'
2. Untersatz	16'
3. Octava	
4. PosaunenBass	16'
5. DulcianBass	16'
6. TrommetenBass	8'
7. Cornett	3' [2'?]
Coppel	
Tremulant	

The Third, in the Castle Church, has 20 stops, as well as a coupler and tremulant.

In the Werck
8 stops.

1. Principal with doubled trebles	8'
2. Quint Tenor [40]	8'
3. Gedact	8'
4. Octava	4'
5. Flöite	
6. Rauschpfeiffe	

---

40. Quintadena?

7. Mixtur
8. Rauschpfeiffe

Im ober Positiff
6. Stimmen.

1. Principal von Bley   8. fuß
2. Gemßhorn
3. Holpfeiffe
4. Trommette
5. Zimbel.
6. NasattQuinta.

Im Pedal 6. Stimmen.

1. Untersatz
2. Gedact
3. Klein Gemßhorn
4. PosaunenBaß
5. TrommetenBaß
6. Cornett B.

XVIII.
Das grosse Werck zu
Bückeburgk

So der Hochgeborne Graff vnd Herr/ Herr Ernst/ Graff zu Holstein/ Schaumburgk vnd Sternberg/ Herren zu Gehmen/ durch M. Esaiam Compenium, Fürstl. Braunsch. Orgel- vnnd Instrumentmacher/ auch Organisten, An. 1615. verfertigen lassen. Hat 48. Stimmen. 3. Clavir im Manual.

Coppel zum OberWerck vnd BrustClavir.

Drey Tremulanten
1. Im OberWerck/ 2. Rückpositiff/ vnd 3. im Pedal.

9. Spänbälge/ oben vffn Kirchgewelbe/ gleich vber der Orgel.

Ein Register/ daß die Blaßbälge allzuglich loß lest/ vnd zugleich einschleust/ daß sie der Calcant nicht mehr tretten kan.

Im OberWerck seynd
12. Stimmen.

1. Groß Principal   16. fl.
2. Groß Quintadehn   16.
3. Groß Octava   8
4. Gemßhorn   8
5. Gedacte Blockpfeiffe   8
6. Viol de Gamba   8
7. Querpfeiffe   4
8. Octava   4
9. Klein Gedact Blockpfeiff   4
10. Gemßhorn Quinta   3
11. Klein Flachflöit.   2
12. Mixtur   8. 10. 12. 14. Chor.

In der Brust
8. Stimmen.

1. Rohrflöiten   8
2. Nachthorn   4
3. Offenflöit/ sol fornen an zu stehen kommen von Elffenbein   4. fl.
4. Klein Gemßhorn   2
5. Holquintlein.   anderthalb
6. Zimbeln kleine   2. Chor
7. Regal   8
8. Geigend Regal von holtz.   4

7. Mixtur
8. Krumbhorn

In the OberPositiff
6 stops.
1. Principal of lead   8'
2. Gemsshorn
3. Holpfeiffe
4. NasattQuinta
5. Zimbel
6. Trommette
[Coupler]
[Tremulant]

In the Pedal
6 stops.
1. Untersatz
3. Klein Gemsshorn
2. Gedact
4. PosaunenBass
5. TrommetenBass
6. CornettBass

XVIII.
The large instrument at
Bückeburg

As the noble count and Lord, Ernst, Count of Holstein, Schaumburgk and Sternberg, Lord at Gehmen, had it built in the year 1615 by Esaias Compenius, M.A., organ and instrument builder to the ducal court at Braunschweig, as well as an organist. It has 48 stops and 3 manuals.

In the OberWerck
are 12 stops.
1. GrossPrincipal   16'
2. GrossQuintadehn   16'
3. GrossOctava   8'
4. Gemsshorn   8'
5. Stopped Blockpfeiffe   8'
6. Viol deGamba   8'
7. Octava   4'
8. Querpfeiffe   4'
9. Little stopped Blockpfeiff   4'
10. Gemsshorn/Quinta   3'
11. Little Flachflöit   2'
12. Mixtur   VIII-X-XII-XIV

In the Brust
8 stops.
1. Rohrflöiten   8'
2. Nachthorn   4'
3. Offenflöit   4'
   reported to stand in front; of ivory
4. Little Gemsshorn   2'
5. Holquintlein   1½'
6. Little Zimbel   II
7. Regal   8'
8. Geigend Regal of wood   4'

In the RückPositiff
12 stops.
1. Principal   8'
2. GrossNachthorn   8'
3. Gedactflöite of wood   8'
4. NasattPfeiffe of wood   4'
5. SpillPfeiff   4'
6. Klein Rohrflöit   4'

Im RückPositiff
12. Stimmen.

1. Principal — 8. fuß
2. Groß Nachthorn — 8
3. Gedactflöite von Holtz — 8
4. Nasati Pfeiffe von Holtz — 4
5. Spill Pfeiff — 4
6. Klein Rohrflöit — 4
7. Klein Octava — 2
8. Klein Gedact — 2
9. Suiflöit — 1
10. Klingend Zimbel — 3. Chor
11. Rancket von Holtz — 16
12. Krumbhorn. — 8

Im Pedal sind
13. Stimmen.

1. SubPrincipalBaß — 32
2. Groß RohrflöitB. — 16
3. Groß GemßhornB. — 16
4. HolpfeiffenB. — 8
5. Groß NachthornB. — 8
6. Querflöiten Baß von Holtz — 8
7. OctavenB. — 4
8. Klein GemßhornB. — 4
9. TrommetenB. — 8
10. Posaun oder BombardB. — 16

Bruſt Pedalia.

11. Hornbäßlein — 2
12. Bawrpfeifflein — 1
13. ZimbelBaß — 3. Chöricht
14. Sordunbaß von Holtz — 16. fl.
15. Dolcianbaß von Holtz — 8. fl.
16. Cornett Baß — 2. fl.

Manual Clavirs Diſpoſition.
C D E F G A B ♮ c d ef g a cc. biß ins c̄

Pedal Clavier.
C F G A ♮ c d ef g a b c̄ d̄ ē f̄

XIX.
Zu Dreßden

In der Schloßkirchen ist ein Werck/ so M. Gottfried Fritzsche An. 1614. von 33. Stimmen. Coppel zu beyden Manualen, Coppel zum Pedal vnd Rückpositiff/

Herr-

7. Klein Octava — 2'
8. Klein Gedact — 2'
9. Suiflöit — 1'
10. Klingend Zimbel — III
11. Rancket of wood — 16'
12. Krumbhorn — 8'

In the Pedal are
13[sic] stops.

1. SubPrincipalBass — 32'
2. GrossRohrflöitB[ass] — 16'
3. Gross GemshornB[ass] — 16'
4. HolpfeiffenB[ass] — 8'
5. GrossNachthornB[ass] — 8'
6. QuerflöitenBass of wood — 8'
7. OctavenB[ass] — 4'
8. Klein GemsshornB[ass] — 4'
9. Posaun or BombardB[ass] — 16'
10. TrommetenB[ass] — 8'

Pedal Stops in the Brust

11. Little Hornbass — 2'
12. Little Bawrpfeiff — 1'
13. ZimbelBass — III
14. Sordunbass of wood — 16'
15. Dolcianbass of wood — 8'
16. CornettBass — 2'

A coupler between the OberWerck and Brust keyboard.

Three tremulants: 1. OberWerck, 2. Rückpositiff, and 3. Pedal.

9 wedge bellows, on top of the church vaulting, directly above the organ.

A stop that releases [the air from] the bellows simultaneously, while at the same time locking them so that the pumper can no longer pump them.

The Lay-out of the Manual Keyboards[41]: C D D♯ E F F♯ G G♯ A A♯ B♭ B c c♯ d d♯ e♭ e f f♯ g g♯ a♭ a etc., up to e''' f'''

The Pedalboard: C D F♯ G♯ D♯ E F F♯ G G♯ A A♯ B♭ B c c♯ d d♯ e♭ e

XIX.
At Dresden

In the Palace Church[42] there is an instrument by Master Gottfried Fritzsche from the year 1614, with 33 stops. There is a coupler between the two manuals and a coupler from the Rückpositiv to the Pedal; also kettle drums [sounding] E [C?] and F, and little tinkling bell[s] set upon a [revolving] star.

---

41. The meaning of this statement is unclear; this seems to be what Praetorius intends to say.
42. The "Palace Church" referred to here is the old court chapel in the palace, not to be confused with the Catholic Court Church, build from 1739-54. The title page of Christoph Bernhard's *Geistreiches Gesang-Buch* (1676) has a copper engraving of the church, showing the organ as well as Heinrich Schütz in the company of his singers.

Heer Trummeln E vnd F.
Zimbelglöcklin am Stern/ gesetzet vnnd
verfertiget hat.

Das ManualClavir gehet vom C biß
ins f̄ vnd ist also gesetzt.

```
        h   a
    D E B ♭ ☉ h ♯ ♭
C F  G A H c d e f g a ♮
biß ins c̄ ♯ ☉ sind 53. Claves.
```

Das Pedal aber vom C biß ins f̄.

```
     D E
C F  G  A etc. biß ins f̄.
```

Im OberWerck seynd 13. Stimmen.

1. Gantz vbergüldete Trom. 8.fi. ⎫ drey
2. Schön zinnern Octava.   ⎬ Prin-
3. Schön zinnern Principal   ⎭ cipal.
4. Groß Quintadeena   16
5. Quintadeena   8
6. Hölzern Principal   8
7. Coppel Octava.   4
8. Quinta vber Octava.
9. Gedact Nasatt   3
10. Gemßhorn   6
11. Super Quinta   anderthalb
12. Zimbel gedoppelt
13. Mixtur 4. fach.

Tremulant.

BrustPositiff
5. Stimmen.

1. Regal gantz vergüldet 4. fuß ⎫ 3.
2. schön zinern Schwigelpf. 1.   ⎬ Prin-
3. schön zinern Quintadeena. 4. ⎭ cipalia
4. Gedactflöitlin.   2
5. Scharff Octav   2

Tremulant.

Das Positiff vff beyden seiten/ an statt des RückPositiffs
7. Stimmen.

1. Kruthorn gantz vergüld 8.fi. ⎫ 3.
2. Schön zinnern Superoctav. 2. ⎬ Prin-
3. Schön zinnern Principal. 4.   ⎭ cipal.
4. Liebliche Flöiten oder Flauten. 8
5. Octav Quint
6. Spitz Pfeiffen oder QuerFlöten von Holtz 4. fuß
7. Gedoppelt Zimbel.

Tremulant.

Im Pedal
8. Stimmen.

1. Grosser SubBaß offen von Holtz. 16. fuß
2. Gedacter SubBaß   16
3. Groß Quintadeena   16
4. SubBaß Posaunen   16
5. Offen Principa   8
6. Cornett   2
7. Spitzflöitlein   1

The manual[s] extend from C to d''', constructed like this:

     e♭ a♭
  D E♭ c♯ d♯ f♯ g♯ b♭
C F G A B c d e f g a b
up to c'' c♯''' d''', [a total of] 53 keys.

The pedal extends from C to d':
   D E
C F G A etc. up to d'.

In the OberWerck
there are 13 stops.

1. Completely gilded Trom[meten] 8' ⎫
2. Beautiful tin Octava [4'] ⎬ three Principalia[43]
3. Beautiful tin Principal [8'] ⎭
4. Gross Quintadeena 16'
5. Quintadeena 8'
6. Wooden Principal 8'
7. CoppelOctava 4'
8. Quinta above the Octava [3']
9. Stopped Nasatt 3'
10. Gemsshorn 6' [2'?]
11. SuperQuinta 1½'
12. Zimbel II
13. Mixtur IV
  Tremulant

Brustpositiff
5 stops.[44]

1. Regal, completely gilded 4' ⎫
2. Beautiful tin Schwigel-pf[eife] 1' ⎬ three Principalia
3. Beautiful tin Quintadeena 4' ⎭
4. Gedactflöitlin 2'
5. Scharff [i.e., narrow-scale] Octav 2'
  Tremulant

The Positiff on both sides,
in place of a Rückpositiff
7 stops

1. Krummhorn, completely gilded 8' ⎫
2. Beautiful tin Superoctav 2' ⎬ three Principalia
3. Beautiful tin Principal 4' ⎭
4. Gentle Flöiten or Flauten 8'
5. OctavQuint [3'? 1½'?]
6. SpitzPfeiffen or QuerFlöiten of wood 4'
7. Zimbel II
  Tremulant

In the Pedal
8 stops.

1. Large open SubBass of wood, open 16'
2. Stopped SubBaß 16'
3. Large Quintadeena 16'
4. Open Principa[l] 8'
5. Spitzflöitlein 1'
6. SubBass Posaunen 16'
7. Cornett 2'
8. Birdsong through the entire pedal.

---

43. The term "Principalia" signifies ranks standing in the front of the case of each of the manual divisions. This is perhaps the most striking visual characteristic of Fritzsche's earlier work in middle Germany.

44. In his Appendix to F.E. Niedt's *Musicalische Handleitung* (Hamburg: Benjamin Schiller, 1710), p. 171, Johann Mattheson indicates that this division was played from the Oberwerck keyboard.

8. Vogelgesang durchs gantze Pedal.

XX.

In der Schloßkirchen zu
Grüningen
Ward Anno 1596. ein Werck von M. David Becken/ Bürgern vnd Orgelmachern in Halberstadt uffgerichtet/ welches 59. Stimmen / Tremulant vnnd Coppel zu beyden Manualen vermag.

Im OberWerck Manual
12. Stimmen.

1 Principal	8. fuß
2. Zimbeldoppelt	
3. Groß Querflöit	8
4. Mixtur	8
5. Nachthorn	4
6. Holflöiten	8
7. Klein Querflöite	4
8. Quinta	6
9. Octava	4
10. Grobgedact	8
11. Gemßhorn	8
12. GroßQuintadehna	16

Im Pedal auff der OberLade
10. Stimmen.

1. Untersatz	16
2. OctavenBaß	8
3. QuintadeenB.	16
4. Klein OctavenB.	4
5. Klein QuintadeenB.	4
6. RauschQuintenB.	
7. HolflöitenB.	2
8. HolQuintenB.	
9. NachthornB.	4
10. Mixtur	

Im Rückpositiff 14. Stimmen.

1. Principal	4
2. Gemßhorn	4
3. Quintadehn	8
4. Spitzflöite	2
5. Gedact	4
6. Octava	2
7. Quinta	anderthalb
8. Subflöite	1
9. Mixtur	4
10. Zimbel	3
11. Sordunen	16
12. Trommet	8
13. Krumbhorn	8
14. Klein Regal	4

In den beyden SeitThörmen zum Pedal 10. Stimmen.

1. Groß PrincipalBaß	16
2. Groß GemßhornB.	16
3. Groß QuerflöitenB.	8
4. GemßbornB.	8
5. KleingedactB	4
6. QuinsflöitenB.	6
7. SordunenB.	16
8. PosaunenB.	16
9. TrommetenB.	8
10. SchallmeyenB.	4

Fornen in der Brust
zum Manual 7. Stimmen.

1. Klein Gedact	2
2. Klein Octava	1
3. Klein Mixtur	2
4. Zimbel doppelt	

XX.
In the Palace Church at
Gröningen[45]

In the year 1596 Master David Beck, citizen and organbuilder of Halberstadt, erected an instrument that possesses 59 stops, a tremulant and a coupler between both manuals.

In the OberWerck Manual
12 stops.

1. Large Quintadehna — 16'
2. Principal — 8'
3. Large Querflöit — 8'
4. Holflöiten — 8'
5. Grobgedact — 8'
6. Gemshorn — 8'
7. Quinta — 6'
8. Octava — 4'
9. Nachthorn — 4'
10. Small Querflöite — 4'
11. Mixtur — 8 [VIII]
12. Zimbel doppelt — [II]

In the Pedal on the Upper Chest
10 stops.

1. Untersatz — 16'
2. QuintadeenB[ass] — 16'
3. OctavenBass — 8'
4. Small OctavenB[ass] — 4'
5. Small QuintadeenB[ass] — 4'
6. NachthornB[ass] — 4'
7. HolQuintenB[ass] — [3'?]
8. HolflöitenB[ass] — 2'
9. RauschQuintenB[ass]
10. Mixtur

In the Rückpositiff,
14 stops.

1. Quintadehn — 8'
2. Principal — 4'
3. Gedact — 4'
4. Gemshorn — 4'
5. Octava — 2'
6. Spitzflöite — 2'
7. Quinta — 1½'
8. Subflöite [sic: Suiflöite?] — 1'
9. Mixtur — 4 [IV]
10. Zimbel — 3 [III]
11. Sordunen — 16'
12. Trommet — 8'
13. Krumbhorn — 8'
14. Small Regal — 4'

In the two side towers
for the Pedal: 10 stops.

1. Large PrincipalBass — 16'
2. Large GemshornB[ass] — 16'
3. Large QuerflöitenB[ass] — 8'
4. GemshornB[ass] — 8'
5. QuintflöitenB[ass] — 6'
6. Kleingedact B[ass] — 4'
7. PosaunenB[ass] — 16'
8. SordunenB[ass] — 16'
9. TrommetenB[ass] — 8'
10. SchallmeyenB[ass] — 4'

In the Brust, on both sides,
for the Pedal: 6 stops.

1. QuintflöitenB[ass] — 12'
2. BawrflöitenB[ass] — 4'
3. ZimbelB[ass] — 3 [III]
4. RancketB[ass] — 8'
5. KrumbhornB[ass] — 8'
6. KleinRegalB[ass] — 4'

---

45. A village northeast of Halberstadt; not to be confused with the city in Holland.

5. Rancket 8
6. Regal 8
7. Zimbel Regal. 2

In der Brust auff beyden
Seiten zum Pedal.
6. Stimmen.

1. Quintflöiten Baß 12
2. Bawrflöiten B. 4
3. Zimbel B. 8
4. Rancket B. 8
5. Krumbhorn B. 8
6. Klein Regal B. 84

XXI.
Zu Hessen vffm Schlosse.

Das hölzern/ Aber doch sehr herrliche Orgelwerck so von M. Esaia Compenio An. 1612. gemacht. Jetzo aber dē König in Dennemarck verehret/ vnd Annn 1616. doselbsten zu Friedrichsburg in der Kirchen gesetzet worden/ ist starck von 27. Stimmen/ Coppel zu beyden Manualn. Tremulant. Grosser Bock. Sackpfeiffe. Kleinhümlichen.

Im obern Manual
9. Stimmen.

1. Principal 8. fuß
2. Klein Principal von Elffenbein vnd Ebenholtz. 4
3. Gedacktflöte 8
4. Gemßhorn oder klein Violn 4
5. Nachthorn 4
6. Blockpfeiffen 4
7. Gedact Quint 3
8. Supergedacktflöitlin 2
9. Rancket. 16

Im Vnter Manual / vnten
an statt des Positiffs
9. Stimmen.

1. Quintadehna 8. ft.
2. Klein Gedacktflöte 4
3. Super Gemßhörnlein 2
4. Nasatt anderthalb
5. Klein repetirt Zimbel einfach.
6. Principal Discant 4
7. Blockpfeiffen Discant 4
8. Krumbhorn 8
9. Geigend Regal. 4

Im Pedal
9. Stimmen.

1. Grosser Gedacktflötten Baß 16. fuß
2. Gemßhorn B. 8
3. Quintadeen B. 8
4. Querflötzen B. 4
5. Nachthorn B. 2
6. Bawrflöiten Bäßlein 1
7. Sordunen B. 6
8. Dolzian B. 8
9. Jungfrawen Regal Baß. 4

XXIII.

Die Fürstliche Widwe zu Braunschweig vnnd Lüneburg lest jetzo in ihrer F. G. Schloß Capell durch den Churf. Sächsischen Orgelmacher M. Gotfried Fritz

In front, in the Brust
7 stops [played from the Oberwerck] Manual

1. Small Gedact	2'
2. Small Octava	1'
3. Small Mixtur	2 [II]
4. Zimbel doppelt	II
5. Rancket	8'
6. Regal	8'
7. ZimbelRegal	2'

XXI.
At Hessen in the Palace.

The wooden, yet very magnificent organ[46] built by Mr. Esaias Compenius in the year 1612; now presented to the King of Denmark, however, and placed in the church at Frederiksborg in that country in the year 1616. Its stops are 27 in number, [together with] a coupler between manuals, a tremulant,[47] a Grosser Bock,[48] Sackpfeiffe[49] and Kleinhümlichen.[50]

On the Upper Manual
9 stops.

1. Principal	8'
2. Gedacteflöite	8'
3. Small Principal of ivory and ebony	4'
4. Gemsshorn or small Violn	4'
5. Nachthorn	4'
6. Blockpfeiffen	4'
7. GedactQuint	3'
8. Superfedactflöitlin	2'
9. Rancket	16'

On the Lower Manual below
[in the case,] in place of the Positiff
9 stops.

1. Quintadehna	8'
2. Principal treble	4'
3. Blockpfeiffen treble	4'
4. Small Gedactflöite	4'
5. Supergedactflöitlin	2'
6. Nasatt	1½'
7. Small repeating Zimbel	I
8. Krumbhorn	8'
9. GeigendRegal	4'

In the Pedal
9 stops.

1. Large GedactflöitenBass	16'
2. GemsshornB[ass]	8'
3. QuintadeenB[ass]	8'
4. QuerflöitenB[ass]	4'
5. NachthornB[ass]	2'
6. BawrflöitenBässlein	1'
7. SordunenB[ass]	[1]6'
8. DolzianB[ass]	8'
9. Jungfrawen RegalBass.	4'

XXII.[51]
[Schöningen][52]

At the present time[53] the widow of the Prince of Braunschweig and Lüneburg is having an organ of veneered wood

---

46. Esaias Compenius built this organ in 1610 for the Duke of Braunschweig, at the Hessen Palace (near Wolfenbüttel). In the year 1617 it was presented as a gift to King Christian IV of Denmark; Compenius re-erected it in the Frederiksborg Palace Church in Hillerød. The instrument still exists, minimally altered from its original state.
47. Tremblant doux.
48. Tremblant fort.
49. Bagpipe (drone): three octaves of reed pipes sounding C & F.
50. small bagpipe (drone): regal pipes.
51. incorrectly numbered "XXIII."
52. See p. 161 above.
53. i.e., 1619.

Fritzschen eine Orgel von schwartzgebeitztem formirtem Holtz mit Golde gestaffiret/fertigen:

Welche nachfolgende 20. Stimmen in sich begreifft.

Im OberWercke
10. Stimmen.

1. Gantz vergüldete Posaunen dem eusserlichem ansehen nach/ sonsten sol es Krumbhörner Art seyn/ vnd also das erste vnd förderste Principal vff 8. fuß
2. Schön zinnern SuperOctav von 2. fl. vnd ist das ander Principal.
3. Schön zinnern Octav von 4. fuß vnd ist das dritte Principal.
4. Gedacter Subbaß vff 16. fuß Durchs gantze Clavir/ aber doch mit zwey Registern/ also/ das ein jedes absonderlich/ eins zum Manual/ das ander zum Pedal zu gebrauchen.
5. Vnd dahero seynd es zwo Stimmen.
6. Höltzern Principal gar enger Mensur, lieblich/ vnd rechter Flöiten Art von 8. fuß
7. Quintadeena von 8. fuß
8. Spitzflöit/ ist fast wie ein Gemßhorn/ doch lieblicher. 4. fuß
9. Mixtur 3. fach
10. Posaunen/ doch nicht so gar starck/ sondern vff Dolcianen art vff 16. fuß

Welche auch mit zwey Registern/ gleich wie der Subbaß sol gemacht werden/ Wofern es wegen des engen vnd kleinen raums die Lade ertragen vnnd leyden wil.

In der Brust
5. Stimmen.

11. Blockflötelin 2. fuß
12. Nasatt Quinta anderthalb fuß
13. Steffflötlin oder Schwiegelpfeiff 1. fl.
14. Zimbeln 2. Chöricht
15. Geigend Regal. 4. fuß

Im Rückpositiff
5. Stimmen.

16. Kleine Trommeten/ oder Posaunen zum södderften Principal, allein zum Augenschein/ vnnd daß es mit dem Oberwercklin dem ansehen nach correspondiret; Seind aber blind: vnd an deren statt eine Baerpfeiffe von 8. fuß
17. Octävlin das ander Principal Querpfeiffen Art. 2. fuß
18. Querflöiten/ das dritte vnnd rechte Principal von 4. fuß
19. Nachthorn von 4. fuß
20. Quintlein scharff offen anderhalb fl.

1. Coppel zu beyden Clavieren.
2. Tremulant zum gantzen Werck durch vnd durch.
3. Bock zum Rückpositiff absonderlich.
4. Zimbelglöcklin.
5. Vogelgesang.

D E
Die Clav. im Mä. C F G A biß ins c̄ d̄
vnd die dis gedoppelt.
D E
Claves im Pedal C F G A biß ins c̄ d̄

Hier-

stained black and trimmed with gold constructed in Her Noble Grace's Palace Church at Schöningen by the electoral-Saxon organbuilder Mr. Gottfried Fritzsche. It is comprised of the following 20 stops.

In the Ober-Werck
10 stops.

1. [A rank that] looks like a Posaune, entirely gilt, but will actually sound like a Krummhorn; it is the first and furthest forward of the *Principalia*, at 8'
2. A beautiful tin SuperOctav at   2' that is the second of the *Principalia*.
3. A beautiful tin Octav at   4' that is the third of the *Principalia*.
4. A stopped Subbass at   16' Full-compass, but having two independent stop-knobs, one that allows it to be used in the manual, the other in the pedal.
5. And thus it [i.e., the Subbass] is two stops.
6. A wooden Principal of a very narrow scale, gentle and much like a flute, at   8'
7. Quintadeena at   8'
8. A Spitzflöit, almost like a Gemshorn, but gentler   4'
9. Mixtur   III
10. A Posaune, yet not so very loud, but rather like a Dolcian, at   16'

[This stop] is also to be built with two stop-knobs, just like the Subbass, insofar as the narrow and small space on the windchest will allow it.

In the Brust
5 stops.

11. Blockflöitlin   2'
12. NasattQuinta   1½'
13. Siefflöitlin or Schwiegelpfeiff   1'
14. Zimbeln   II
15. GeigendRegal   4'

In the Rückpositiff
5 stops.

16. A little Trommete or Posaune, the furthest forward of the *Principalia*, but only for the sake of appearance, so that it corresponds visually to the Oberwerk. It is however, a false stop, and in its place [there sounds] a Bärpfeiffe at   8'
17. Octävlin, the second of the *Principalia*, resembling a Quer-Pfeiffe   2'
18. Querflöite, the third and primary member of the *Principalia*, at   4'
19. Nachthorn at   4'
20. A little Quint, keen and open   1½'

[Auxiliary stops]

1. A Coupler between the manuals.
2. A Tremulant for the entire instrument.[54]
3. A Tremulant (Bock[55]) especially for the Rückpositiff.
4. Zimbelglöcklin [i.e., Zimbelstern].
5. Birdsong.

The manual keyboards: C F $\overset{D}{G}$ $\overset{E}{A}$ up to c♯''' d''', with doubled d♯s[56]

The pedal keyboard: C F $\overset{D}{G}$ $\overset{E}{A}$ up to c♯' d'

---

54. Tremblant doux.
55. Tremblant fort.
56. i.e., with subsemitones?

XXIII.

Hierauff folget nun eine Verzeichniß etlicher Orgeln/ derer Dispositiones von mir selber nach meiner wenigkeit uffgesetzet sind.

1.

Eine Orgel sampt jhren Registern zu setzen.

Von 27. Stimmen.

1. Zinnern Principal	8. fuß
2. Grob Gedacktflöte	8
3. Octava	4
4. Gemßhorn	4
5. Gedact Holflöit von Holtz.	4
6. Nasatt	3
7. Scharff Quinta	4
8. Superoctava	2
9. Mixtur 3. fach	2

BrustPositiff.

10. Krumbhorn hölzern	8
11. Quintetz	anderthalb
12. Doppelt Zimbel.	
13. Sufflöit	1

RückPositiff oder unter Clavir.

14. Schön zinnern Principal	4
15. Quintadeena	8
16. Holflöit	4
17. Nachthorn von Holtz	4
18. Klein Blockflöitlein	2
19. Octav	2
20. Quinta	anderthalb
21. Kleiner Zimbel.	
22. Schallmey	8

Zum Pedal.

23. Offener untersatz von Holtz	16. fuß
24. Posaunen Sordunen Art	16. fuß
25. Starcker Dulcian	8
26. Bawrflöitlein	1
27. Singend Cornett.	2

Hierzu werden erfodert.

2. Tremulanten im OberWercke unnd RückPositiff ein jeden sonderlichen zu gebrauchen.
Coppel zu beyden Claviren.
Coppel des Pedals zum Positiff.
8. gute beständige Blaßbälge.

2.

Designatio einer andern/ von 19. Stimmen / Coppel zu beyden Manualn. Coppel des Pedals zum RückPositiff.
Stern zum Zimbelglöcklin.
Vogelgesang. Trummel.

OberWerck.

1. Principal	8. fuß
2. Octava	4. fuß
3. Mixtur 4. fach/ dorinnen Octav, 2. fuß. Quint anderthalb fuß	
4. Grob Gedact/Rohrflöit	8. fuß
5. Nachthorn	4. fuß
6. Schwiegelpfeiff.	1. fuß
7. Rancket oder stille Posaun	16. fuß

XXIII.
There follows here a list of a number of organs whose stoplists I myself have drafted according to my modest abilities.

1.
An organ to be built with 27 stops.

[Oberwerk]
1. Tin Principal — 8'
2. Grob Gedactflöite — 8'
3. Octava — 4'
4. Gemsshorn — 4'
5. Stopped Holflöit of wood — 4'
6. Nasatt — 3'
7. ScharffQuinta — 4' [3'?]
8. Superoctava — 2'
9. Mixtur III [beginning at] 2'

BrustPositiff
10. Wooden Krumbhorn — 8'
11. Quintetz — 1½'
12. Zimbel — II
13. Sufflöit — 1'

RückPositiff or lower Manual
14. Quintadeena — 8'
15. Beautiful tin Principal — 4'
16. Holflöit — 4'
17. Nachthorn of wood — 4'
18. Little Blockflöitlein — 2'
19. Octav — 2'
20. Quinta — 1½'
21. Little Zimbel
22. Schallmey — 8'

In the Pedal
23. Open Untersatz of wood — 16'
24. Bawrflöitlein — 1'
25. Posaune, like a Sordun — 16'
26. Loud Dulcian — 8'
27. SingendCornett — 2'

In addition are provided:
Two tremulants, one for the Oberwerck only, one for the RückPositiff only.
A coupler between the two manuals.[57]
A Positiff/Pedal coupler.
8 good, durable bellows.

2.
A design for a second [organ], of 19 stops, a coupler between the two manuals, [and a] Rückpositiff/Pedal coupler, [as well as Zimbel]stern with little bells, Birdsong, [and] drum.

OberWerck
1. Principal — 8'
2. Loud stopped Rohrflöte — 8'
3. Octava — 4'
4. Nachthorn — 4'
5. Schwiegelpfeiff — 1'
6. Mixtur with Octave 2' and Quint 1½' — IV
7. Rancket or quiet Posaun — 16'

---

57. This indicates that the stops of the BrustPositiff were played on the Oberwerck manual.

Rück Positiff.

8. Quintadeena   8. fuß
9. Blockflöit   4. fuß
10. Gemßhörnlein   2. fuß
11. Zimbel doppelt/ gar klein vnd scharff.
12. Spitzflöit oder Spitzflöit   4. fuß
13. Krumbhorn.   8. fuß

In die Brust.

14. Klein lieblich Gedactflöit.
    Rohrflöit   2. fuß
15. Baerpfeiff   8
16. Geigend Regal.   4. fuß

Zum Pedal.

17. Vntersatz starck   16. fuß
18. Posaunen Baß   16. fuß
19. Cornett   2. fuß

---

8. Sordun oder Rancket.   16. fuß

Seiten Positifflin.

9. Krumbhorn   8. fuß
10. Nachthorn   4. fuß
11. Spitzflöit   2. fuß
12. Nasatt   anderthalb fuß
13. Zimbel   2. fach

Pedal.

14. Vntersatz von Holtz   16. fuß
15. Posaun Baß   16. oder 8. fuß
Coppel des Pedals zum Rückpositiff.
Coppel zu beyden Manualn.
Trummel.
Tremulant zum gantzen Werck.
Bock zum Rückpositiff.
Vogelgeschrey.

3.
Ein Werck von 15. Stimmen zu setzen.

1. Principal   4. fuß
2. Gedact lieblich   8. fuß
3. Spitzflöit   4. fuß
4. Octaven lieblich   2. fuß
5. Schwiegel oder Schweitzerpfeiff/ lieblich   1. fuß
6. Zimbel/ darinnen eine kleine Quint 3. fach/ gar klein.

In die Brust.

7. Geigend Regal   4. fuß

4.
Disposition einer gar kleinen Orgel: von 10. oder 11. Stimmen.

1. Principal   4. fuß
2. Rohrflöit oder Gedact mit einem abgesondertem Baß   8. fuß
3. Octava   2. fuß
4. Sciflöit   1. fuß
5. Nasatt Quinta   anderthalb fuß
6. Zimbel gar klein. 2. oder 3. Chöricht/ anstatt der Mixtur.
7. Blockflöit   4. fuß
8. Nachthorn   4. fuß
9. Krumbhorn   8. fuß
10. Pedal Vntersatz von Holtz   16. fuß

Köndte

Rückpositiff

8. Quintadeena	8'
9. Blockflöit	4'
10. Spitz- or Spillflöit	4'
11. Little Gemsshorn	2'
12. Zimbel, very small and penetrating	II
13. Krumbhorn	8'

In the Brust

14. Baerpfeiff	8'
15. GeigendRegal	4'
16. Little gentle stopped Rohrflöit	2'

For the Pedal

17. Powerful Untersatz	16'
18. PosaunenBass	16'
19. Cornett	2'

Little Side-Positiff

9. Krumbhorn	8'
10. Nachthorn	4'
11. Spitzflöit	2'
12. Nasatt	1½'
13. Zimbel	II

Pedal

14. Wooden Untersatz	16'
15. PosaunBass	16' or 8'

Rückpositiff/Pedal coupler
Coupler for both[58] manuals
Drum
Tremulant for entire organ
Tremblant fort for Rückpos.
Birdsong

3.
A Proposal for an Instrument of 15 stops.

[Werck]

1. Gentle Gedact	8'
2. Principal	4'
3. Spitzflöit	4'
4. Gentle Octave	2'
5. Gentle Schwiegel or Schweitzerpfeiff	1'
6. Very high Zimbel, containing a little Quint	III

In the Brust

7. Sordun or Rancket	16'
8. Geigend Regal	4'

4.
Stoplist for a very small organ: 10 or 11 stops.

1. Rohrflöit or Gedact with bass in the Pedal by transmission	8'
2. Principal	4'
3. Blockflöit	4'
4. Nachthorn	4'
5. Octava	2'
6. Octava	2'
7. NasattQuinta	1½'
8. Very little Zimbel instead of a Mixtur	II or III
9. Krumbhorn	8'
10. Pedal Untersatz of wood	16'

---

58. i.e., the stops in the Brust are played from the Werck.

DE ORGANOGRAPHIA.

Köndte er aber durchs gantze Manual durchgehen/ vnd hernacher zum Pedal abgesondert werden: were es desto besser.

Ein Clavier/ doch daß vff beyden seiten die Register halbirt/ biß ins c̄ etc. damit man den Choral drauff führen kan/ mit vnterschiedlichen Stimmen.

Tremulant.

Vom C biß ins c̄ oder f̄/ welches besser. Pedal vom C biß ins h.

Der Organist sol hinter dem Wercke sitzen/ daß das Werck fornen herauß kömpt.

Weil man eine Quintadeen von 8.füssen darzu setzen/vnd den Baß auch absondern/ so kan mans in acht nemen.

5.

Disposition einer Orgel von 16. vnd 48. Stimmen.

1. Vnter Baß von dicke Dañenholtz 16.fi.
2. Gedactflöite   16.fuß
3. Sordun oder Posaun   16
4. Krumbhorn   8
5. Trommet oder starck Regal   8
6. Principal   8
7. Gemßhorn   8
8. Quintadeen   8
9. Octava offen   4
10. Klein Blockflöit   4
11. Gemßhorn   4
12. Nachthorn   4
13. Quinta   3
14. Superoctava   2
15. Klein Zimbel
16. Mixtur 4.5.6. Pfeiffen oder mehr.

Gibt im OberPositiff eben so viel Stimmen/ doch alle in der Octava höher.

OberPositiff.

Vntersatz	8. fuß
Gedactflöit	8
Sorduen	8
Krumbhorn	4
Regal	4
Principal	4
Gemßhorn	4
Quintadeena	4
Superoctava	2
SuperBlockflöitlein	2
S. Gemßhörnlein	2
S. Nachthörnlein	2
Nasatt	anderthalb
Siefflöit	1
Klein Zimbel	
Mixtur.	

Summa 48. Stimmen vnd noch darüber.

1. Tremulant
2. Stern Zimbelglöcklin
3. Kuckuck
4. Vogelgesang
5. Hümmelchen
6. Bock
7. Trummel.

[The Pedal Untersatz] could, however, extend throughout the entire manual compass, and then be brought to the pedal by transmission; that would be all the better.

A single keyboard, but with each stop divided down to c', with stopknobs on both sides, so that a cantus firmus can be performed on it with a different registration.

Tremulant.

[Compass] from C up to c''', or to d''', which would be better.

The organist should sit behind the instrument, allowing it to extend further forward.

One might consider adding a Quintadeen 8' and bringing its bass to the pedal by transmission.

5.
Stoplist of an Organ with 16 and 48 stops.[59]

1. UnterBass of thick firwood	16'
2. Gedactflöite	16'
3. Principal	8'
4. Gemsshorn	8'
5. Quintadeen	8'
6. Octave, open	4'
7. Little Blockflöit	4'
8. Gemsshorn	4'
9. Nachthorn	4'
10. Quinta	3'
11. Superoctava	2'
12. Little Zimbel	
13. Mixtur IV, V, VI or more ranks	
14. Sordun or Posaun	16'
15. Krumbhorn	8'
16. Trommet or loud Regal	8'

The same number of stops appears in the OberPositiff, each of them speaking an octave higher.

OberPositiff

1. Untersatz	8'
2. Gedactflöit	8'
3. Principal	4'
4. Gemsshorn	4'
5. Quintadeena	4'
6. Superoctava	2'
7. SuperBlockflöitlein	2'
8. S[uper] Gemsshörnlein	2'
9. S[uper] Nachthörnlein	2'
10. Nasatt	1½'
11. Sieffloit	1'
12. Little Zimbel	
13. Mixtur	
14. Sorduen	8'
15. Krumbhorn	8'
16. Regal	4'

A total of 48 stops,
as well as:

1. Tremulant
2. Zimbelstern
3. Cuckoo
4. Birdsong
5. Bagpipe (drone)
6. Tremblant fort
7. Drum

---

59. Although Praetorius does not expressly state it, the presence of three strong 16' stops suggests that the same sixteen stops are intended to appear in the pedal as well, producing (together with the OberPositiff) a total of 48 stops. Praetorius's title suggests that he envisions 16 basic stops with transmissions to create an Oberpositiff and Pedal.

Disposition einer Orgel von
18. Stimmen.

Im OberWercke
9. Stimmen.

1. Principal von 8. fuß
2. Koppel oder Blockflöite / oder lieblich Gedact von 8. fi.
3. Nachthorn 4. ft.
4. Octava von 4. ft.
5. Gemßhorn lieblich von 2. fuß
6. Quinta von drittehalb fuß
7. Mixtur von 2. fi. Pfeiffen starck.
8. Untersatz von Holtz uff 16. fuß
9. Trommeten uff 8. fuß Thon/ vnnd 8. fuß lang

Im RückPositiff
9. Stimmen.

1. Principal von 4. fuß
2. Koppelflöiten von 4. fuß
3. Quintadeen 8. fuß
4. Assat uff die Quinten anderthalb fi.
5. Querpfeiffe lieblich von 4. fuß
6. Cymballen lieblich/
7. Ziflitt von 1. fuß
8. Schallmeyen von 4. fuß
9. Krumbhorn von 8. fuß
   Tremulant.
2. Coppeln / etc.

7.
Disposition einer Orgel von
22. Stimmen.

OberWerck zum Manual.

1. Principal 8. fuß
2.) Groß Quin- (Im Man.) 16
3.) tadeena (Im Ped. abg.) fi.
4. Gedacte Flöit: Oder Rohrflöit lieblich 8. fuß
5. Octava enger Mensur 4. fuß
6. Nachthorn oder Quintadeena 4. fuß
7. Nasatt Quinta 3. fuß
8. Mixtur, 4.5.6.7. Chöricht/ do man denn auch ein abgesondert Register zur 2. Chörichten Zimbel machen köndte.

Zum Pedal alleine im Oberwerck.

9. Gedacter starcker Untersatz 16. fuß
10. Posaunen Baß 16

Brust.

11. Klein Blockflöit 2. fuß
12. Siflöit oder Schwiegelpfeiff 1. fuß
13. Geigend Regal. 4. fuß

NB.

Wo nicht fleissige Organisten verhanden/ do sind viel Regal-vnd Schnarwercke nichts nütze / sonderlich von 4. füssen/ denn dieselbe wollen einen vnverdrossenen fleissigen Organisten haben/ der sich nicht verdriessen lest/ alle acht tage alle Schnarrwercke durch vnd durch zustimmen/ vnd in ihrem Stande zu erhalten: Inmassen ich dann in der Grüningischen Orgel bey den viertzehē Schnarrwercken solches ohne Ruhm mir nicht wenig angelegen seyn lassen.

Wolte man nun auch die Brust gantz aussen

6.
Stoplist of an Organ with 18 stops.

In the OberWerck
9 stops

1. Untersatz of wood at   16'
2. Principal at   8'
3. Koppel- or Blockflöite or gentle Gedact at   8'
4. Octava at   4'
5. Nachthorn   4'
6. Gentle Gemsshorn at   2'
7. Quinta   1½'
8. Mixtur 2' [?] ranks[60]
9. Trommet (both) 8' long and at 8' pitch

In the Rückpositiff
9 stops

1. Quintadeen   8'
2. Principal at   4'
3. Koppelflöit at   4'
4. Gentle Querpfeiffe at   4'
5. Assat[61] at the fifth   1½'
6. Ziflitt [i.e., Sifflet]   1'
7. Cymbal, gentle
8. Krumbhorn at   8'
9. Schallmey at   4'

Tremulant, 2 couplers, etc.

7.
Stoplist of an organ with 22 stops.

Oberwerck: [the primary] manual

1. Large Quintadeena, in the manual
2. and in the pedal by transmission   16'
3. Principal   8'
4. Stopped Flöit, or gentle Rohrflöit   8'
5. Octava, narrow scale   4'
6. Nachthorn or Quintadeena   4'
7. NasattQuinta   3'
8. Mixture IV-V-VI-VII, from which one might also make a stop by transmission for a two-rank Zimbel.

For the Pedal only, housed in the Oberwerck

9. Powerful stopped Untersatz   16'
10. PosaunenBass   16'

Brust[62]

11. Little Blockflöit   2'
12. Siflöit or Schwiegelpfeiff   1'
13. GeigendRegal   4'

N.B.

If no diligent organists are available, many Regals and [other] reed stops are worthless, especially at 4', since such stops need a willing organist who does not become annoyed by having to tune all the reeds every week and keep them in good condition. I have likewise devoted no small amount of effort to the thankless task of keeping the fourteen reed stops in the organ at Gröningen in tune.

---

60. The number of ranks is missing.
61. Probably a misspelling (or fanciful spelling) of "Nas[s]at;" see: Jacob Adlung, *Musica mechanica organœdi* (Berlin: Birnstiel, 1768), Vol. I, p. 73, "Assat."
62. played from the Oberwerck.

außen laſſen; So kan man das kleine Blockflöitlin von 2. füſſen ins Oberwercke/ vnd das Sifflöitlein von 1. Fuß ins Rückpoſitiff bringen.

RückPoſitiff.

1. SchweizerPfeiff zum Principal fornen an   4. fuß
2. Quintadeena   8
3. Gembßhorn oder Spitzflöit   4
4. Holflöit oder Querflöit   4
5. Klein Octava
6. Holquinten oder Scharffquinten anderthalb
7. Zimbeln   2. Chörich
8. Trommeten   8
9. Krumbhorn   8. fuß

Wiewol man eins vnter dieſen beyden Schnarrwercken auch auſſen laſſen köndte.

Coppeln vnd Tremulanten, wie in den vorigen Diſpoſitionibus.

N B.

Dieweil ich in Tomo Tertio, welcher jetzo gleich auch beym Drucker/ viel andere vnd mehrere Sachen tractiret, als in Indice Generali Syntagmatis muſici nuper præmiſſo angedeutet worden: So habe ich den titulum Tomi Tertij allhier mit einzuſetzen nicht vndienlich erachtet.

TOMUS TERTIUS.

Begreifft vnd helt in ſich drey Theil.

Im erſten wird die Signification vnnd Bedeutung der Namen/ Wie auch Beſchreibung faſt aller vnd jeder Lateiniſcher/Italiäniſchen/Engliſcher/Frantzöſiſcher/ vnd jetziger zeit in Deutſchland gebräuchlicher Geſänge vnd Lieder/ als Madrigalien, Canzonē, Villanellen, &c. befunden vnd erkläret wird.

Im andern ſeind allerley nothwendige Erinnerungen vnd Obſervationes, 1. bey den Ligaturen; 2. Noten. 3. beym b ♮ vnd ✕. 4. bey den Numeris vnter den Pauſen; 5. bey den Virgulis; 6. Modis. 7. beym Tact, ſignis vnnd characteribus. 8. Variationibus in Tactu; 9. Auch wie die Cantiones zu Transponiren, 10. die Parteyen vnd Stimmen füglich zu nennen; 11. Die Chori recht zu vnterſcheyden; 12. Vnd die Vniſoni vnd Octaven zu gebrauchen ſeyn;

Im dritten iſt der Verſtand vnd Interpretation 1.2.3. vieler Lateiniſchen vnnd Italiäniſchen terminorum vnd Vocabeln, welche in jetziger art der Muſic zum öfftern

If one wanted to omit the Brust entirely, one might bring the little Blockflöit 2' into the Oberwerck and the little Sifflöit 1' into the Rückpositiv.

RückPositiff

1. Quintadeena 8'
2. SchweitzerPfeiff as the Principal, in the façade 4'
3. Gemsshorn or Spitzflöit 4'
4. Holflöit or Querflöit 4'
5. Little Octava 2'
6. Holquint or Scharffquint 1½'
7. Zimbel II
8. Trommeten 8'
9. Krumbhorn 8'

Although one could also omit one of these two reeds.

Couplers and Tremulants as in the previous stoplists.

N. B.

Since various other matters have been discussed in Volume Three, which is now at the Printer, as indicated in the recently issued General Index of the Syntagma musicum; I consider it useful to insert here a notice concerning Volume Three.

VOLUME THREE
contains three parts.

In the first part may be found an explanation of the meaning of the names as well as a description of almost all the Latin, Italian, English, and French songs such as madrigals, canzonas, villanelles, etc., as well as those now in use in Germany at the present time.

The second [part] explains everything necessary to know about: 1) ligatures; 2) notes; 3) flats, naturals and sharps; 4) numbers below the rests; 5) *Virgulis*,[63] 6) modes, 7) time [signatures] and note values; 8) upbeats and downbeats; 9) also how to transpose compositions; 10) how to label parts and voices properly; 11) the correct differentiation of choirs; 12) how to use unisons and octaves

In the third [part] may be found an explanation and interpretation of: 1., 2. & 3. many Latin and Italian terms that frequently occur in today's music; 4. a

---

63. small strokes near the notes.

tern vorfallen: 4. Aller Musicalischer Instrumenten kürtzere abtheilung 5. vnnd eigendliche benennung: 6. vom Basso Generalisten continuo; 7. Wie alle vnd jede Concertgesänge per Choros gar leichtlich; 8. vnd die in meinen Polyhymnys vff vnterschiedliche Arten vnd Maniren gesetzte Cantiones vor sich anzuordnen; 9. auch die Knaben vnd andere im singen vff jetzige Italiänische Manier zu Informiren seyn / zu vernehmen.

ENDE.

Noch

brief classification of all musical instruments, 5) and their true meaning; 6) figured bass or continuo; 7) how easily to arrange all sorts of concertos, 8) and those in my *Polyhymnia,* in various ways; 8) how to train boy [choristers] and others in the current Italian manner of singing.

THE END.

ORGANOGRAPHIA.

Noch hab ich etlicher Orgeln Dispositiones allhier mit anhengen wollen/

Als:

1. Zu Sondershausen: So der Hoch- vnd Wolgeborne Graff vnnd Herr/ Herr Graff zu Schwartzenburgk/ durch M. Gotfried Fritschen/ Churf. Sächsischen Orgelmachern zu Dreßden: Anno 1616. hat 36. Stimmen.

Im Oberwerck.
11. Stimmen.

1. Schön Principal — 8. fuß
2. Höltzern Principal eng vnnd lieblich — 8. fuß
3. Quintadenna — 8. fuß
4. Scharff Octav — 4. fuß
5. Nachthorn offen/ weiter Mensur/ ist sehr lieblich — 4. fuß
6. Quinta — 3. fuß
7. Nasatt lieblich — 3. fuß
8. Mixtur — 6. fach
9. Zimbel — 2. fach
10. Quintadehn Sub Baß — 16. fuß
11. Dolcian oder Rancket — 16. f. Holtz

Pedal Bässe in den Thormen/ 8. Stimmen.

12. Principal Sub Baß von reinem Zinn in 16. fuß darinnen sind die 3. vntersten Pfeiffen / als C.D.E. doppeld klingend gesetzt / also daß die grosse Principal Pfeiffen vff beyden seiten an der grösst vnd lenge einander gleich respondiren.
13. Höltzern-Sub Baß — 16. fuß
14. Rohrflött-Baß — 16. fuß
15. Zimbel Baß.
16. Posaunen — 16. fuß
17. Trommet — 8. fuß
18. Singend Cornett.
19. Allerley Vogelgesang.

Brust Positiff
6. Stimmen.

20. Gemßhorn — 4. fuß
21. Octav — 2. fuß
22. Blockflött — 2. fuß
23. Quintadetz.
24. Schwiegelpfeiff — 1. fuß
25. GeigenRegal — 4. fuß

Rück Positiff/
7. Stimmen.

26. Principal — 4. fuß
27. Grob Gedackt flöyt — 8. fuß
28. Klein Gedackt — 4. fuß
29. Querflöyt — 4. fuß
30. Octävlin — 2. fuß
31. Quintlein.
32. Zimbeln.
33. Ranckes/ oder BärPfeiffe — 8. fuß
34. Vmblauffender Stern/
35. Rechte Heerpaucken
Zween Tremulanten.
Zwelff Blaßbälge.
Vom C. biß ins f̄ vnd doppelte Semitonia ins g̅.

Auch

I have decided to append a number of other
organ stoplists here, namely:

1. At Sondershausen: [the organ] the high- and nobly-born Lord, the Count of Schwartzenburg [had built] by the Electoral Saxon Organbuilder, Master Gottfried Fritzsche of Dresden, in the year 1616. It has 36 stops.

In the Oberwerck
11 stops

1. Quintadehn Sub Bass[64]	16'
2. Beautiful Principal	8'
3. Wooden Principal, narrow [scale] and gentle	8'
4. Quintadenna	8'
5. Scharff Octav	4'
6. Nachthorn, open, wide-scale; it is very gentle	4'
7. Quinta	3'
8. Nasatt, gentle	3'
9. Mixtur	VI
10. Zimbel	II
11. Dolcian or Rancket, wooden	16'

Pedal Stops in the [side] Towers

12. Principal Sub Bass of pure tin, at 16'. Its 3 lowest pipes, C, D & E, are doubled (both speaking); thus the large Principal pipes on both sides correspond precisely in size and height.

13. Wooden Sub Bass	16'
14. Rohrflött-Bass	16'
15. Zimbel Bass	
16. Posaunen	16'
17. Trommet	8'
18. Singend Cornett	[4'? 2'?]
19. Various Birdsongs	

BrustPositiff[65]
6 stops

20. Gemsshorn	4'
21. Octav	2'
22. Blockflött	2'
23. Quintadetz	[2'][66]
24. Schwiegelpfeiff	1'
25. GeigenRegal	4'

RückPositiff
7 stops

26. GrobGedacktflöyt	8'
27. Principal	4'
28. Little Gedackt	4'
29. Querflöyt	4'
30. Little Octave	2'
31. Little Quint	[1½']
32. Zimbeln	
33. Ranckett or BärPfeiffe	8'
34. Revolving [Cymbel]Stern	
35. Genuine military drums	

Two tremulants
Twelve bellows
[Manual compass?:] C – f'''[?] and doubled semitones for G♯[67]

---

64. "Bass" suggests that this stop was made available separately in the pedal, by transmission.
65. presumably played from the Oberwerck.
66. See: Jacob Adlung, *Musica mechanica organœdi* (Berlin: Birnstiel, 1768), Vol. I, p. 131, "Quinta decima" and "Quintetz."
67. i.e., one for G♯, the other for A♭.

II.

Auch hab ich an selben Orte ein sehr fein Orgelwercklin gesehen/ welches gar subtiel sauber vnd kleinlich in gestalt eines kleinen Schäpleins oder Contors gearbeitet/ also daß man nimmermehr vermeinen solte so viel Stimmen darin verhanden seyn könten: ist vor etlichen siebenzig Jahren von einem Münche gefertiget worden. Dasselbe hat vierzehen Stimmen/ 2. Manual vnd 1. Pedal.

Die Pfeiffen zum Pedal liegen vnten/ zu beiden Manualen oben.

Zum Obern Clavir
5. Stimmen.

1. Regal — 8. fuß
2. Gedact lieblich — 4. fuß
3. Principal — 2. fuß
4. Octav — 1. fuß
5. Zimbel.
  Vogelgesang.

Zum vntern Clavir
4. Stimmen.

6. Quintadehn oder Nachthorn sehr lieblich — 4. fuß
7. Klein Gedact — 2. fuß
8. Octävlin — 1. fuß
9. Zimbel.

Im Pedal 5. Stimmen.

10. SubBaß von holtz Gedact — 8. fuß
11. Posaunen — 8. fuß
12. Gedact — 4. fuß
13. Principal — 2. fuß
14. Schweitzer Bäßlein in der Octav repetirende.

Trummet:
Tremulant: vnd noch andere extraordinarii Stimmen.

III.

Disposition der Orgel zu S. Gothart in Hildesheim: von Meister Henning/ welcher anfangs ein Tischer gewesen/ vnd durch Gottes gnad so weit kommen/ daß er nebens dem grossen 32. füssigen Orgelwerck im Stifft S. Blasii zu Braunschweig/ sub num. XIII. noch viel andere herrliche/ liebliche vnnd wolklingende Orgeln verfertigt.

Ober Werck zum Manual vnnd Pedal 12. Stimmen.

1. Groß præstant — 16. fuß
2. Octav — vff 8. fuß
3. Octav — 4. fuß
4. Quint — 3. fuß
5. Mixtur im Discant von 12. Chören.
6. Vntersatz Gedact im Pedal — 16. fuß
7. Gedact offt auch Manualiter — 16. f.
8. Hollflot — 8. fuß
9. Coppelflot — 4. fuß
10. Gemshorn — 2. fuß
11. Dolcian im Manual — 16. fuß
12. Trommet im Manual — 8. fuß

Im Rück Positiff
11. Stimmen.

13. Principal — 8. fuß
14. Octava — 4. fuß
15. Quintadehna — 8. fuß
16. Zimbeln doppelt
17. Hollflot — 8. fuß
18. Holl-

II.

At the same place [i.e., Sondershausen] I also saw a very fine little organ fashioned very cunningly, neatly and painstakingly in the form of a small chest, so that no one would ever imagine that so many stops would fit inside it. It was constructed some seventy years ago[68] by a monk, and has fourteen stops, 2 manuals and pedal. The pedal pipes lie underneath, while those of both manuals lie above.

For the upper keyboard,
5 stops

1. Gedact, gentle — 4'
2. Principal — 2'
3. Octav — 1'
4. Zimbel
5. Regal — 8'
   Birdsong

For the lower keyboard,
4 stops

6. Quintadehn or Nachthorn, very gentle — 4'
7. Little Gedact — 2'
8. Octävlin
9. Zimbel — 1'

In the Pedal
5 stops

10. SubBass of wood stopped — 8'
11. Gedact — 4'
12. Principal — 2'
13. Little Schweitzer Bass, repeating at the octave
14. Posaunen — 8'

Drum, Tremulant and other supplementary stops.

III.

The stoplist of the organ at St. Gotthart in Hildesheim, [built] by Master Henning.[69] He was at first a carpenter, but by the grace of God has progressed so far that he has built, in addition to the great 32' organ in the Stiftskirche of St. Blasius in Braunschweig (under no. XIII above), many other magnificent, lovely and finesounding organs as well.

OberWerck—manual
and pedal. 12 stops

1. Gross præstant — 16'
2. Gedact [fl]öit in manual and pedal — 16'
3. Untersatz, stopped, in pedal — 16'
4. Octav — 8'
5. Hollfloit — 8'
6. Octav — 4'
7. Coppelfloit — 4'
8. Quint — 3'
9. Gemshorn — 2'
10. Mixtur in the treble — XII
11. Dolcian in the manual — 16'
12. Trommet in the manual — 8'

In the RückPositiff
11 stops

13. Principal — 8'
14. Hollfloit — 8'
15. Quintadehna — 8'
16. Octava — 4'
17. Hollfloit — 4'

---

68. i.e., before the Lutheran Reformation.
69. Master Henning Hencke (c. 1550-c. 1620) built three new organs in Hildesheim: St. Lambert (1590), St. Michael (1599), and St. Godehard (1612-1617).

ORGANOGRAPHIA.

18. Hollfloit	4. fus
19. Quer floit	4. fus
20. Quintfloit	3. fus
21. Assat	2. fus
22. Krumbhorn	8. fus
23. Cornet	4. fus
Vogelgeschrey	
Kuckuck. Drommel.	
5. Blasbälge.	

NB.

Es hat aber dieser Meister Henning eine gar sonderliche Art von Blasbälgen im brauch/ die den andern Spaenbälgen/ viel mehr aber den Läddern bälgen weit vorgehen/ vnnd haben nur ein einige falten so eines Schuchs/ das ist einer halben Ellen hoch in die höh/ auffgehet: Vnd sich gleich als 2. dicke (drey finger breit) Eichene Bretter zusamen schleust/ daß man also nichts mehr davon siehet: vnd also weder von der Lufft noch von Meusen schaden nemen kan. Die Leng ist gemeiniglich 8. oder neunzehalb schuch lang/ vnnd fünffzehalb schuch breit/ zu den grossen Orgeln aber 9. schuch lang/ vnnd 5. oder sechstehalb schuch breit.

IV.

Orgel im Kloster Riddageshausen von 31. Stimmen/ welche der jetzige Abt/ Herr Heinricus durch den Fürstl. Erzbischoffl. Magdeb. Orgelmacher/ Heinricum Compenium verfertigen lassen.

Im Oberwerck/ 11. Stimmen.

1. Principal von reinem Zinn/ etwas weiter mensur	8. fus
2. Grosse Rohrfloit durchs gantze Manual	16. fus
3. Abgesonderter Bas im Pedal allein/ von vorgedachter Rohrfloit	16. fus
4. Gedacte Rohrfloit lieblich vff	8. fus
5. Gros Gemshorn	8. fus
6. Octava	4. fus
7. Spitz floit oder flachfloit	4. fus
8. Quinta scharff	3. fus
9. Nasath lieblich	3. fus
10. Mixtur vnten 5. fach/ mitten 6. oben 8. ach: die gröste von 4. füssen.	

In der Brust 4. Stimmen mit einem Abzuge.

12. Blockflöitlin	2. fus
13. Nachthorn	4. fus
14. Rancket oder Krumbhorn	8. fus
15. Geigend Regälchen	4. fus

Rück Positiff 10. Stimmen.

16. Principal	4. fus
17. Quintadehna	8. fus
18. Groshölzern Gedact	8. fus
19. Rohrflöitlin	4. fus
20. Gemshörnlin	2. fus
21. Hollquintlin	anderthalb fus
22. Sisfloit	1. fus
23. Zimbeln einfach gar klein/	
24. Trommeten gedempft	8. fus
25. Sorduen von holz Dolcianen Art	16. fus

Pedal Bässe/ 6. Stimmen.

18. Quer[fl]oit   4'
19. Quintfloit   3'
20. Assat   2' [70]
21. Zimbel   II
22. Krumbhorn   8'
23. Cornet   4'
    Birdsong
    Cuckoo
    Drum
    5 bellows

NB.

This Master Henning is using a very special type of bellows that far surpasses other wedge-bellows, to say nothing of leather bellows.[71] It has only a single fold that rises about a foot (i.e., a half an ell) high. And when it is closed down between two heavy oak planks (three finger-widths thick), none of it is visible. Then it is impervious to damage by either weather or mice. It is ordinarily 8 or 8½ feet wide; in large organs, however, it is 9 feet long and 5 or 5½ feet wide. (There are also those who make only 2 folds in bellows; that is also very good.)

IV.

The organ in the Monastery at Riddagshausen,[72] which the present Lord Abbot, Heinricus, had built by the organbuilder to the Prince-Archbishop of Magdeburg, Heinrich Compenius, has 31 stops.

In the Oberwerck,
11 stops[73]

1. Large Rohrfloit in the manual, full-compass   16'
2. The abovementioned Rohrfloit, as a separate stop in the pedal alone   16'
3. Principal of pure tin, rather wide scale   8'
4. Stopped Rohrfloit, gentle   8'
5. Large Gemshorn   8'
6. Octava   4'
7. Spitz[fl]oit or Flachfloit   4'
8. Quinta, penetrating   3'
9. Querflöit[74]   3'
10. Mixtur 4', 5 ranks in the bass, 6 ranks in the middle, 8 ranks in the treble

In the Brust,
4 stops with a pull-down[75]

12. Nachthorn   4'
13. Little Blockflöit   2'
14. Rancket or Krumbhorn   8'
15. Little Geigend Regal   4'

Rück Positiff,
10 stops

16. Large wooden Gedact   8'
17. Quintadehna   8'
18. Principal   4'
19. Little Rohrflöit   4'
20. Little Gemshorn   2'
21. Nasath[76]   1½'
22. Sifloit   1'
23. Very little Zimbel   I
24. Sorduen of wood, like a Dolcian   16'
25. Trommeten, muted   8'

---

70. Probably a misspelling (or fanciful spelling) of "Nas[s]at;" see: Jacob Adlung, *Musica mechanica organœdi* (Berlin: Birnstiel, 1768), Vol. I, p. 73, "Assat."
71. Perhaps Praetorius is speaking of ordinary kitchen bellows.
72. Riddagshausen was incorporated into the City of Braunschweig in 1934.
73. Praetorius lists only 10, however; thus the specification as it stands has 30 stops, not 31.
74. The Errata, p. 236, correct the original "Nasath lieblich" to "Querflöit"; it is thus possible that "3'" should read "4'".
75. i.e., played from the Oberwerk keyboard; as with other instrument described by Praetorius that have Brustwerks, this one had only 2 manuals.
76. The Errata, p. 236, correct "Hollquintlin" to "Nasath."

26. Ein starcker offner vntersatzter sub-
Baß von Holtz   16. fuß
27. Iula   8. fuß
7 | 28. Nachthorn oder Bawrbäß-
lein   2. oder 1. fuß
29. Starcker Posaunen Baß   16. fuß
8 { 30. Posaun oder Trommet   8. fuß
9 { 31. Singend Cornetbäßlein   2. fuß
    Summa 31. Stimmen.
    Vber diese.
1. Zimbelglöcklein mit eim Stern.
2. Trummel.
3. Vogelgesang.

Vier ventile { 1. Zum OberWerck.
            2. Brust.
            3. Rückpositiff.
            4. Pedal.

1. Tremulant zum gantzen Werck.
2. Backtremulant zum Rückpositiff allein / vnd daß die Regal vnnd Schnarwercke / auch zum Tremulanten gebraucht werden können.
1. Coppel zum Rückpositiff vnd Pedal.
2. Spaenbälge starck vnd wol verwart. Mit einer doppelten Windladen newer Invention, da die ventile sich von einander kehren / damit man zu allen sachen mit dem Gesichte reichen vnd sehen kan.

      Pedal-Clavir.
F₅ G̃
D E B ♩ ♫ ff ♮ b ✻
C F G A H c d e f g a ḥ ṫ ḅ ḝ

V.
Eine andere.

Ohngefehrliche Disposition eines Orgelwercks von 34. oder 35. Stimmen nach Art der Dreßdnischen vnnd Schöningischen: Dergleichen vielleicht zu Barait im Voigtlande von mehr gedachtem Churf. Sächs. Orgelmacher Gottfried Fritschen / diesen Sommer wird gefertiget werden.

Oberwercke.
13. Stimmen.

Drey principal-Pfeiffen so im Augenschein kommen. {
1. Posaunen von holtz gantz vbergüldet. Am laut Trommetten art / vff 8. fuß Thon. Vnnd ist das erste principal.
2. Das ander principal Zinnern Octav offen von 4. fuß Thon.
3. Das dritte principal Zinnern Principal von 8. fuß Thon.

4. Zimbel 2. fach.
5. Mixtur 6. fach.
6. Gedacter SubBaß lieblich durchs gantze Manual, mit einem abgesonderten Baß zum Pedal allein.
7. Vnd gibt zwo Stimmen   16. fuß
8. Höltzern Principal enger Mensur vff rechte Blockflöten art   8. fuß
9. Quintadehna   vff 8. fuß
10. Spitzflöyt lieblich   4. fuß
                        11. Nacht-

Pedal, 6 stops

26. A powerful open Untersatz-Subbass of wood	16'
27. Jula	8'
28. Nachthorn or Bawrbässlein	2' or 1'
29. Powerful PosaunenBass	16'
30. Posaun or Trommet	8'
31. Little singing Cornetbass	2'

A total of 31 [30] stops,
In addition to which are:

1. Cymbelstern with a [revolving] star
2. Drum
3. Birdsong

Four ventils
{
1. For the OberWerck;
2. For the Brust;
3. For the Rückpositiff;
4. For the Pedal.
}

1. Tremulant for the entire organ.
2. Tremblant fort for the Rückpositiv alone, and so that the Regals and the reed stops may also be used with a tremulant.
3. Rückpositiff/Pedal coupler
4. Wedge bellows, strong and stoutly bound.

With a double windchest of a new type, in which the pallets are independent from each other, so that one can easily see directly into and reach into all the compartments.

The Pedal Keyboard

F♯ G♯
D E B♭ c♯ d♯ f♯ g♯ b♭ c♯
C F G A B c d e f g a b c''' d''' e'''[77]

V.
Another

hypothetical stoplist for an organ of 34 or 35 stops, similar to those at Dresden and Schöningen. The Electoral Saxon Organbuilder Gottfried Fritsche will perhaps finish building [an organ] of this sort this summer at Bayreuth in the Vogtland.

Oberwerck
13 stops

Three ranks of Principalia that are visible.
{
1. Posaune of wood, completely gilt. Like a trumpet in its tone, at 8' pitch. It is the first of the Principalia.
2. The second of the Principalia [is an] open Octav of tin, at 4' pitch.
3. The third of the Principalia is a tin Principal at 8' pitch.
}

4. Gentle stopped Subbass of full manual compass, with a Bass by transmission independently to the pedal.	
5. and [The above] produces two stops	16'
6. Wooden Principal of narrow scale, much like a Blockflöte	8'
7. Quintadehna	8'
8. Gentle Spitzflöyt	4'
9. Very gentle Nachthorn, open and of wide scale	4'
10. Penetrating Quint	3'

---

77. c''' d''' e''' is Praetorius's correction (p. 236); the original is not fully legible. His correction makes sense only if it indicates the compass of the manuals, not the pedal.

11. Nachthorn / offen weiter Mensur gar lieblich 4.fuß
12. Quinta scharff 3.fuß
13. Rancket od' Sorduen vff 16.f.thon.

BrustPositifflin.
6.Stimmen.

Auch 3. principalia.
- 14. Geigend Regal von holtz gantz vergüldet vff 4.fuß
- 15. Schön Zinern Schwiegel oder Hohlflöten vff 1.f.
- 16. Gembßhorn still oder klein Gedact/auch von schönem Zinn 4.fuß

17. Superoctavlin scharff vff 2.f.th.
18. Blockflöttlin 2.fuß
19. Klein Quintadeen/an stadt der Zimbeln.

RückPositiff.
11.Stimmen.

Auch 3. Principalia.
- 20. Kleine Trommeten / von Holtz gantz vergüldet müssen aber blind seyn/dieweil man von fornen zum stimmen nit kommen kan: es were denn daß ein Chor oder Poer Kirche vnter die Orgel von deren man zu dē förder Pfeiffen des RückPositiffs kommen könte.
- 21. Schön Zinnern Superoctava Querpfeiffen Art 2.fuß.
- 22. Schön Zinnern Principal 4.fuß

23. Grosse Coppel: oder liebliche flöten vff 8.fuß
24. Klein Quintadehn 4.fuß
25. Querflöten 4.fuß
26. Gembshörnlein oder gedact flötlein 2.fuß
27. Nasatt Quinta lieblich anderthalb fuß.
28. Zimbeln klein einfach
29. Rancket oder BärPfeiffen 8.fuß
30. Krumbhörner 8.fuß

Bässe im Pedal
5.Stimmen.

3. Principalia.
- 31. Groß Posaunen Baß 16.fuß.
- 32. Starcker SubBaß gedact Zinnern 16.fuß
- 33. Grob principal Baß Zinnern von 16.fuß

34. Cornet Bäßlin.
35. Vogelgesang/durchs gantze Pedal.

Extraordinarii Stimmen.
36. Vmblauffender Stern mit Zimbel glöcklin.
37. Kuckuck: Nachtigal.
1. Coppel zu beyden Manualen.
2. Coppel zum Pedal vnnd RückPositiff.

Wolte man drey manual Clavir haben/ so könte man noch drey BrustPositiff machen.

1. Tremulant zum gantzen Wercke durch vnd durch.
2. Tremulant zum RückPositiff absonderlich

11. Mixtur	VI	23. Large Coppel[flöte], or gentle flute	8'
12. Zimbel	II	24. Little Quintadehn	4'
13. Rancket or Sorduen	16'	25. Querflöten	4'

Little BrustPositiff
6 stops

Also 3 Principalia.
{ 14. Wooden Geigend Regal, completely gilt 4'
15. Beautiful tin Schwiegel or Hollflöeten 1'
16. quiet Gembsshorn or little Gedact, also of beautiful tin 4' }

17. Penetrating little Superoctav 2'
18. Little Blockflött 2'
19. Little Quintadetz in place of the Zimbel.

RückPositiff
11 stops

Also 3 Principalia.
{ 20. a little Trommeten of wood, entirely gilt. The pipes would have to be dummies, however, since they could not be reached from the front to tune them, unless there were a [elevated] choir or balcony beneath the organ[78] from which the façade pipes of the Rückpositiv would be accessible.
21. Beautiful tin Superoctava, like a Querpfeiffe 2'
22. Beautiful tin Principal 4' }

26. Little Gembshorn or little stopped flute 2'
27. Nasatt Quinta, gentle 1½'
28. Little Zimbel I
29. Rancket or BäerPfeiffen 8'
30. Krumbhörner 8'

Pedal Basses
5 stops.

3 Principalia
{ 31. Large Posaunen Bass 16'
32. Powerful stopped SubBass of tin 16'
33. Heavy Principal Bass, of tin 16' }

34. Little Cornet Bass [4'? 2'?]
35. Birdsong throughout the entire Pedal

Auxiliary Stops
36. Revolving star with little bells
37. Cuckoo: Nightingale

[Couplers]
1. Coupler between both manuals
2. RückPositiff/Pedal coupler

If three manuals are desired, it would be possible to make one for the Brustpositiff.

[Tremulants]
1. A tremulant for the entire organ
2. A separate tremulant for the Rückpositiff alone, otherwise called the "Bock".[79]

---

78. The organs at the Predigerkirche in Erfurt (Compenius, 1649) and Wenzelskirche in Naumburt (Hildebrandt, 1746) are examples of this arrangement.
79. i.e., Tremblant fort.

sonderlich / wird sonsten der Bock genant.
- 9. oder 11. Blasbälge.

Clavier zum Manual.

F̧ Ģ ȩ
D E B ♮
C F G A H C♯ D e ꝛc. bis in f̄ od f̄

Zum Pedal.

Ḑ F̧ Ģ B ♮ f̄
C D E F G A H C♯ D e f ꝛc. bis
ins c̄ d̄ ē

Es gefelt mir auch gar wol/ daß man zu einer jeden Laden / ein absonderlich Ventil mache/ damit 1. nicht ein jeder/ so vff die Orgel gelauffen kömpt wisse/ sich drein finden könne/ ob er gleich die Register ziehet. 2. Daß der Wind nicht so bald alle Laden erfüllet / wenn man nicht vff allen Claviren schlagen wil.

VI.

Noch ein Disposition
Zu ein kleinen Wercklein
vff gar liebliche Art gerichtet/
Von 13. Stimmen.

Oberwerck.

1. Liebliche Rohrflöte   8. fuß
2. Nachthorn   4
3. Gemshorn Spitzflöte   4
4. Octävlin scharff   2
5. Krumbhorn   8

Unter Positiff.

6. Quintadehna   8
7. Blockflöit   4
8. Zimbel scharff gar klein   2.3. fach
9. Nasatquint   anderthalb fuß
10. Rancket: 16. oder. Bäer Pfeiff 8. fuß.
11. Klein Regal.

Pedal.

12. Untersatz   16
13. Sorduen / oder gar stille liebliche Posaunen   16. fuß

Coppel zu beyden Manualn/
Und was sonsten mehr bey andern Orgeln erinnert werden.

Wolte man es etwas schärffer haben/

[Either] 9 or 11 bellows.

Manual Keyboard

```
      F♯  G♯              e♭
   D   E   B♭   [C♯?] d♯
C  F  G   G   B♮  C   d   e   f   etc.
up to d''' or f'''
```

For the Pedal

```
   D♯   F♯  G♯  B♭  [C♯] d♯   f♯
C  D  E  F  G  A  B♮  C   d   e   f   etc.
up to c' d' e'
```

It also pleases me very much when a separate ventil is made for each chest, so that: 1. not everyone who jumps on the organbench will be able to make the organ sound, even if he pulls the stops. 2. the wind does not immediately fill all the chests if one does not want to play on all the manuals.

VI.

Another Stoplist
For a little Instrument
designed in a very lovely way, with 13 stops.

Oberwerck

1.	Gentle Rohrflöte	8'
2.	Nachthorn	4'
3.	Gemshorn Spitzflöte	4'
4.	Little Octave, keen	2'
5.	Krumbhorn	8'

UnterPositiff

6.	Quintadehna	8'
7.	Blockfloit	4'
8.	keen Zimbel, very little	II
9.	Nasatquint	1½'
10.	Ranckett	16'
	or BäerPfeiff	8'
11.	Little Regal	

Pedal

12.	Untersatz	16'
13.	Sorduen, or a very quiet, gentle Posaunen	16'

A manual coupler

Other things to be mentioned about other organs

If a more penetrating tone is desired, a

ben/ so kan man ein lieblich principal von 4. Füssen darzu setzen.

Es müssen aber alle Stimmen/ auff die enge Mensuren gerichtet/ vnnd gar lieblich intoniret werden.

NB.
Was sonsten etwa allhier nicht erinnert worden/ dasselbe wird in dem tractätlin vom Verdingnis/ Bawen/vnd Lieferung einer Orgel vielleicht angedeutet werden.

INDEX

gentle Principal 4' may be added. All the stops, however, must be of narrow scale, and very gently voiced.

[See pp. 233-4 for the stoplist of the organ at St. Lambrecht in Lüneburg]

Nota bene
Matters that have not been mentioned here will perhaps be explained in the little treatise on *Contracting for organs, construction and delivery*.[80]

[80]. This treatise survives as a manuscript, entitled *Kurtzer Bericht, waß beÿ überliefferung einer Klein und grosverfertigten Orgell zu observiren*, now in the Herzog August Bibliothek, Wolfenbüttel, Germany. For an English translation of the treatise, see: Vincent Panetta, "An Early Handbook for Organ Inspection: the 'Kurtzer Bericht' of Michael Praetorius and Esaias Compenius," in: *The Organ Yearbook*, 1990, pp. 5-33. See also: Vincent J. Panetta, Jr., "Praetorius, Compenius, and Werckmeister: A Tale of Two Treatises," in: *Church, Stage, and Studio: Music and Its Contexts in Seventeenth-Century Germany* (Ann Arbor: Research Press [c.1990]), pp. 67-85.

INDEX I.

Verzeichnüs derer Autorum vnnd Kunstmeister/ so in diesem II. Tomo Syntagmatis Musici angezogen werden.

Pontifices : Episcopi.

Vitellianus P. P.
Sylvester II. PP.
David.
Salomon.
Alexander M.
Stephanus Episcopus Rom.
Gilbertus Archiepisco. Rhemensis.

Impp. Reges, Duces, Com.

Constantinus III. Imp.
Constantinus VI. Copronymus Imp.
Carolus M. Imp.
Ludovicus Pius Imp.
Solymanus Turcarum Imp.
Franciscus I. R. Galliæ.
Fridericus D. Mantuæ.
Pipinus.
Balricus Co. Hungariæ.

Philosophi & Medici.

Plato.
Aristoteles.
Hippocrates.
Vitruvius.

Theologi.

Hieronymus.
Thomas Aquinas.
Guilielmus Perkinsus.
Navarrus.

Musici.

Orpheus.
Amphon.
Boëthus.
Guido Aretinus.
Henricus Glareanus.
Timotheus Milesius.
Sethus Calvisius.
Galilæus.
Christophorus Cornetto.
Martinus Agricola.
Ludovicus Lacconi.

Philologi.

Athenæus.
Plinius.
Suidas.
Adrianus Tornetus.

Poëtæ.

Virgilius.
Franciscus Petrarcha.

Melopoëtæ.

Orlandus di Lasso.
Lucas Marentius.
Carolus Luyton S. C. M. Organicen.
Hieronymus diruta Italus.
Ioannes Bussanus.

Historici

INDEX I.

An Index[1] of those authors and master craftsmen
who are cited in in this second volume of *Syntagma musicum*.

Rulers, Bishops	[page]
Vitellianus, Pope	[90]
Sylvester II, Pope	[92]
David	[Dedication, 82]
Solomon	[82]
Alexander the Great	[94]
Stephen, Bishop of Rome	[91]
Gilbertus, Archbishop of Rheims	[92]

Emperors, Kings, Dukes, Counts	
Constantine III, Emperor	[90]
Constantine VI Copronymus, Emperor	[91]
Charlemagne, Emperor	[91]
Louis the Pious, Emperor	[92]
Suleiman, Turkish Emperor	[83]
Francis I, King of France	[83]
Friderico, Duke of Mantua	[92]
Pepin	[91]
Balric (Daldrico), Count of Hungary	[92]

Philosophers and Physicians	
Plato	[58]
Aristotle	[85]
Hippocrates	[85]
Vitruvius	[Dedication, 91]

Theologians	
Jerome	[56, 78, 83]
Thomas Aquinas	[90]
William Perkins	[90]
Navarrus (Martín de Azpilcueta)	[90]

Musicians	
Orpheus	[56, 78, 86]
Amphion	[86]
Boëthius	[92]
Guido of Arezzo	[60, 90]
Heinrich Glarean	[33, 57-8]
Timotheus Milesius	[94, 95]
Sethus Calvisius (Seth Kalwitz)	[75, 79, 90, 91]
Galileo	[67]
Christophorus Cornetto	[66]
Martin Agricola	[45]
Ludovicus Lacconi (Zacconi)	[39, 49]

Philologists	
Athenæus	[58]
Pliny	[Dedication, 56]
Suida	[Dedication]
Adrianus Tornetus (Turnebus)	[Dedication]

Poets	
Vergil	[Dedication, 56]
Petrarch	[85]

Musicians	
Orlando di Lasso	[17]
Luca Marenzio	[65]
Carolus Luyton, S.C.M. Organicen	[63]
Girolamo Diruta, Italian	[85, 88]
Giovanni Bassano	[41]

1. partial and apparently arbitrary.

INDEX I.

Historici.
Lambertus Schaffenburgensis.
Ioh. Aventinus.
Marianus Scotus.
Volaterranus.
Polydorus Virgilius.
Platina.
Genebrardus.
Albertus Crantzius.
Aimonius.
Henricus Erfordiensis.
Bergomas.
Sabellicus.
Leander.
Majolus.
David Chytræus.
Sebastianus Virdungus.

Kunstmeister / Orgel- vnnd Instrumentmacher.

Bernhardus Teuto.
Ioannes Bossus.
Carolus Cassanus.
Hans Händer.
Nicolaus Faber Sacerdos.
Gregorius Kleng.
Fabian Peters von Schnerck.
Heinrich Traxdorff.
Friederich Krebs.
Nicolaus Mülner.
Conrad Rotenburger.
Henricus Crantzius.
Esaias Compenius.
Henricus Compenius.
P. F. Andreas Iesuita.
Ioannes Buchor.
Ioan. Deutlin.
Iulius Antonius.
Michael Hirschfeld.
Gottfried Fritschen.
Heinrich Glovaß.
Gottschalck Burchard.
Nicolaus Maaß.
David Becke.
Hans Schärer.
Martin Schott.
Sirtus Kergel.
Dominicus Citharista zu Praga.

INDEX II.

AB.
Abwechselung des Tactus moviret die affectus.   70

AC.
Accort was.   12.13
Accort Querflötten helt an der zahl achte.   13

Doppioni vnd Baßandli sechs.   13
Posaunen acht.   13
Racket sieben.   13
Fagotten acht.   13
Krumbhörner neun.   13
Corna Muse sechs.   13
Bombarden dreyzehen.   13

Dd   Block-

INDEX I.

Historians

Lambert of Aschaffenburg	[91]
Johannes Aventinus	[91, 92]
Marianus Scotus	[91]
Volaterranus	[90]
Polydore Vergil	[89, 90]
Platina	[90, 91]
Genebrardus	[90, 92]
Albert Kranz	[90]
Aimonius	[90]
Henricus Erfordiensis	[92]
Bergomas	[92]
Sabellicus	[92, 96]
Leander	[92]
Majolus	[92]
David Chytræus	[91]
Sebastian Virdung	[60, 76, 79]

Master Craftsmen/Organ- and Instrument-makers

Bernhardus Teuto (the German)	[93, 96]
Johannes Bossus	[16]
Carolus Cassanus	[17]
Hans Häyde	[67]
Nicolaus Faber Sacerdos	[98]
Gregorius Kleng	[98]
Fabian Peters von Sneek	[108]
Heinrich Traxdorff	[110]
Friedrich Krebs	[112]
Nicolaus Mülner	[112]
Conrad Rotenburger	[111]
Hinricus Crantius	[112]
Esaias Compenius	[138, 139, 142, 160, 185, 189]
Henricus Compenius	[172]
P.F. Andreas Jesuita	[110?]
Joannes Buchor (Hans Bucher)	[162]
Joan. Deutlin (Johann Deutlein)	[162]
Julius Antonius	[162]
Michael Hirschfeld (Hirschfelder)	[171]
Gottfried Fritzsche	[186, 189, 197]
Heinrich Glovatz	[163]
Gottschalck Burchard (Gottschaldt Burckart)	[164]
Nicolaus Maass	[167]
David Becke (Beck)	[181, 188]
Hans Schärer (Scherer)	[176, 187 note]
Martin Schott	[52]
Sixtus Kergel [Kärgel]	[55]
Dominicus Citternist at Prague	[55]

INDEX II.

AB

Varying the tactus moves the emotions.	70

AC

Consort: what [it is]	12, 13
Consort of traverse flutes contains eight [players]	13
Doppioni and Bassandli six	13
Trombones eight	13
Ra[n]ket seven	13
Bassoon eight	13
Krummhorns nine	13
Cornamuse six	13
Bombards thirteen	13

INDEX II.

    Blockflöiten ein vnd zwantzig. 13
Accort Blockflöiten koftet 80.thal. 34
Acherhorn. 78
AEolius Modus eine Quart niedriger tranſponiret. 63
AEqual Principal. 105.127
    Reſonantz lieblich. 127
    woher æqual genennet. 127
    gebrauch im Choral v. Mottet. 127
    geheimnüs deſſelben. 127
AEqual Gembshorn. 134
    Reſonantz lieblich. 134
    dienet zur Variation mit andern Stimmen. 134
    Menſur deſſelben. 134

AL.

Alabaſteriſche Orgel. 92
Alt Bombart. 3
    faſt einer Schalmeien gleich. 36
    hat einen Schlüſſel. 36
Alte Harffe. 77
    derer Form viererley. 77
    Dreyecket. 77
Alten vnnd newen Harffen vndterſcheid. 77
Alte Inſtrument / SackPfeiffe vnnd Leire. 100
Alte Orgelwercke dreyerley / Groß/ Mittel vnd Klein. 105
    woraus derſelbige vnterſcheid. 105
Alten Orgeln vndterſchiedene Nahmen. 104
Alte Orgeln wie geſtimmet. 104
Alter Orgeln Thon. 102
Alte Orgeln nach jhrer Chormeſſe zu hoch. 102
Alter vnnd jetziger Orgeln vndterſcheid. 106
Alter vnnd jetziger Clavier vndterſcheid. 112
Alte Orgel zu Halberſtadt wenn gebawet. 98
    wenn renoviret. 98
Alten Orgeln ſtercker ſchall vnnd laut. 100
    Vnanmütig zu hören vnnd warumb. 100
Altiſta wie hoch er ſingen könne. 17

AM.

Amboß. 79

AN.

Anblaſende Inſtrument. 2
Angehenge in Orgeln. 106

AP.

Applicatio der Finger bey etzlichen Organiſten nit viel werth. 44
Apffel Regal. 148.126
    woher genennet. 148
    Gröſſe vnd Form. 148
    Gebrauch vnd Reſonantz. 148

AR.

Arci violate lire Ital. 4.49
Arce violira. 4.49
Arpa. 4.6.56
Arpa Hybernica. 6.56
Arpichordum. 5.67
Art der alten Blaßbälge. 103

INDEX II.

Recorders twenty one	13
Consort of recorders costs 80 Thal[ers]	34
Acherhorn	78
Aeolian mode transposed a fourth lower	63
Aequal Principal	105, 127
sound is gentle	127
whence the name "aequal"	127
use in chant and motets	127
mysterious property in it	127
Aequal Gembshorn	134
sound is gentle	134
provides variety in combination with other stops	134
its scale	134

AL

Alabaster organ	92
Alto bombard	3
almost like a schalmey	36
has a clef	36
Antique harp	77
in various shapes	77
triangular	77
Distinction between antique and modern harps	77
Old instrument[s]: bagpipe and hurdy-gurdy	100
Three types of old organs: large, medium and small	105
the difference among them	105
Old organs [had] various names	104
Old organs, how tuned	104
Old organs, pitch	102
Old organs, their pitch too high	102
Difference between old and present-day organs	106
Difference between old and present-day keyboard	112
Old organ at Halberstadt: when it was built	98
when rebuilt	98
Old Organs: loud, powerful sound	100
unpleasant to hear; why	100
Alto, how high he can sing	17

AM

Anvil	79

AN

Instruments that are blown	2
Trackers in organs	106

AP

Fingering of some organists not worth much	44
ApfelRegal	148, 126
whence the name	148
size and shape	148
use and sound	148

AR

Arci violate lire, Italian	4, 49
Arce violira	4, 49
Arpa	4, 6, 56
Arpa Hybernica	6, 56
Arpichordum	5, 67
Description of old bellows	103

BA.

Bandoer. 28. 53
   In Engelland erfunden. 53
   Einer Cither gleich. 53
   Mit Stälenen vnnd Messings Seyten. 54
   Von 6. auch 7. Chören. 54
   wie gestimmet. 54
Bandörichen. 53
Barbytus. 5
Barem Stimm in Orgeln. 139
Barpfeiffen. 126. 146
   woher genennet. 147
   Intonation. 147
   Form vnd Grösse. 147
   Mancherley art. 147
Bassanelli. 3. 41
   woher der Nahme. 41
   Resonantz. 41
   Gebrauch. 41
   haben sieben Löcher. 42
   werden mit blossem Rohr geblasen. 41
   vmb ein Quart niedriger als Cammerthon gestimmet. 42
   wie hoch vnd niedrig am Thon. 24
   wie sie höher vnd niedriger können intoniren. 35
   Vnterste Clavis F. 42
Baß auff Subbaß Geigen / Octav Posaunen / Doppelfagotten / vnnd grossen Baß Bombarden wie zu Musiciren. 46
Baß Bombard. 3. 36
Baß Clavier in alten Orgeln. 99
Baßgeige mit vier Seiten. 48
Baßgeige sonderlicher Art. 45
   wie formiret. 45
   von wem erfunden. 45
   mit Eisern Wirbeln. 45
   dessen Gebrauch. 99
Bassisten so sonderlich tieff singen können. 17
Bawren vnd Bettler Leire. 79. 49. 5
Bawrfloiten Baß in Orgeln. 140. 141
   Intonation. 141
   Gebrauch im Choral. 140
Bawrfloitlin. 132

BE.

Bernhardus Teuto hat zu Venedig das Pedal erfunden. 96
Beröhrete Instrument. 10
Besaitete Instrument. 4. 43
   Sollen vmb ein Thon tieffer gestimmet werden. 15
Beschreibung Musicalischer Instrument. 9

BL.

Blasende Instrumenta. 2
   zweyerley. 2
   wie hoch vnd tieff zu bringen. 19
Blaßbälge bey den alten. 103
   fast den Schmiedebälgen gleich. 103
   mit Gewichte erfunden. 115
   Mit Roß: vnd Ochsenheuten vberzogen. 115
   Spaenbälge auff eine sondere newe art / so nur ein einige falte haben / vnd sehr gut seyn. 197. 198
Blechen Regal. 116

BA

Bandoer [Pandora]	28, 53
invented in England	53
resembles a cittern	53
with steel and brass strings	54
with 6, also 7 courses	54
how tuned	54
Bandörichen	53
Barbytus	5
Barem: a stop in organs	139
Barpfeiffen	126, 146
whence the name	147
sound	147
shape and size	147
many varieties	147
Bassanelli	3, 41
whence the name	41
sound	41
use	41
have seven holes	42
are blown by an exposed reed	41
tuned a fourth lower than chamber pitch	42
how high and low they sound	24
how they can be tuned higher or lower	35
lowest key is F	42
How to play the bass on the SubbassGeigen, OctavePosaune, Double Fagott, and great BassBombard	46
BassBombard	3, 36
Pedal keyboard in old organs	99
Bass viol with four strings	48
Bass viol of a special kind	45
its form	45
by whom discovered	45
with iron pins	45
its use	99
Basses who can sing especially low	17
Peasant- and beggar lyra	79, 49, 5
Pedal Bauerfloit in organs	140, 141
sound	141
use for cantus firmus	140
Bawrfloitlin	132

BE

Bernhard the German invented the pedal in Venice	96
Reed instrument[s]	10
Stringed instrument[s]	4, 43
Should be tuned a step lower	15
Description of musical instrument[s]	9

BL

Wind instruments	2
of two kinds	2
their compasses	19
Bellows in the past	103
almost like blacksmith's bellows	103
with weights	115
covered with horse- and ox-hides	115
Wedge bellows of a special new kind, that are single-fold, and are very good	179[1]
Plated-metal Regal	116

---

1. Praetorius reads "197, 198."

BO

Bock art einer Sackpfeiffen.	3.42
wie gestimmet.	42
Boëthius zu welcher zeit gelebet	90
Citherini Instrumenti erfinder.	92
Bombyces.	3.36
Bombard: Bombardoni.	36
woher der nahme.	36
desselben Intonation.	36
Im Tenore.	36
Im Nicolo.	36
Im Alto.	36
Baß Bombard groß.	37
desselben länge.	37
Bombardo piccolo.	37
Bombard in Orgeln.	126
Bordun.	139

BR.

Brumeisen.	5

Bu.

Buccina.	2.35

CA.

Campana.	4
Cammerthon für der Tafel vnnd in conviviis gebreuchlich.	15
Canal oder Windröhre.	106
Cæsaron Basista zu Rom.	17
Cappelle an K. Salomonis Hofe.	83

CH.

Chelys.	4.49
Chitarrone.	52
deren grösse.	52
Chiterra.	53
Chor: vnd Cammerthon.	14
Chorthon bey den alten vmb ein Thon niedriger.	14
Warumb.	15
Wird in Kirchen gebrauchet.	15
Chormesse.	121
Chormesse respondiret acht fuß thon.	121
Chorus Instrumentum.	76
hat zwo Röhren.	76
Chor der besäiteten Instrument.	19
Chor auff Lauten vnterschiedlich genennet.	50
Choro da Flauto Ital.	34
Chorist Fagott.	38
Intonation.	38
Wie hoch vnd niebrig am Thon.	23
Choral wercke.	102
wie gestimmet.	102
Choral wie auff alten Orgeln geschlagen.	100.101
Chor Principal.	122
Woher der Nahme vnnd woran erkant.	123

CI.

Cithara: Either.	5.6.28.54.56
jetzo anders als bey den alten.	54
fünfferley art.	28.54
I. Von 4. Choren.	28.54
gestimmet auff Italiänisch.	54
auff Frantzösisch.	54
II. Von 5. Choren vnd wie gestimmet.	28.55
III. Von 6. Choren/wird auff dreyerley

INDEX II.

BO
Buck, a kind of bagpipe	3, 42
how tuned	42
Boethius, when he lived	90
inventor of the instrument the Chiterini	92
Bombyces	3, 36
Bombard: Bombardoni	36
whence the name	36
its sound	36
in the tenor	36
in the nicolo	36
in the alto	36
Bass Bombard, large	37
its length	37
Bombardo piccolo	37
Bombard in organs	126
Bordun	139

BR
Jew's harp	5

Bu
Buccina	2, 35

CA
Bell[s]	4
Chamber pitch used for dinner music and at festivities	15
Conduit[s] or wind ducts	106
Cæsaron, bass at Rome	17
Chapel at King Solomon's court	83

CH
Chelys [i.e., lute]	4, 49
Chitarrone	52
its size	52
Chiterra	53
Choir and chamber pitch	14
Choir pitch among our forebears a step lower	14
Why	15
It is used in churches	15
Pitch for singing	121
Pitch for singing corresponds to 8' pitch	121
Chorus: an instrument	76
has two tubes	76
Choir of stringed instruments	19
Courses on lutes have different names	50
Consort of recorders [in] Italy	34
Chorist curtal	38
sound	38
range	23
Chant organs	102
how tuned	102
Chant, how played on old organs	100, 101
Chorprincipal [8']	122
Whence the name and how identified	123

CI
Cithara: cittern	5, 6, 28, 54, 56
different now that in antiquity	54
five kinds	28, 54
I. 4 courses	28, 54
Italian tuning	54
French tuning	54
II. 5 courses and how tuned	28, 55
III. 6 courses: tuned in three ways.	28, 55

INDEX II.

erley art gestimmet. 28.55
IV. Grosse 6.Chörichte. 29.55
vmb ein Quint tieffer. 55
fast 2.Ellen lang. 55
V. Von 12. Choren. 29.55
Resoniret gleich einem Clavicymbalo. 55
Citherlein klein Englisch. 29.55
wie gestimmet. 55
Cithara Hieronymi. 77
Cithara der alten vnser jetzige Harffe. 54
Cymbalum: Cymbeln. 4
Cymbalum Hieronymi. 78
dessen bedeutung. 78
Cymbelchen. 79
Cymbalum universale seu perfectum. 63

CL.

Clavichordum. 5.60
  Auß dem Monochordo erfunden. 60
  hat erstlich 20.claves gehabt. 60
  Fenget vom C. an. 61
  Ist das Fundament aller clavirten Instrument. 61
  Dienet für anfahende Schüler vnd warumb. 61
  Hat im genere Diaterrico nur 20.claves. 60
  In einer octav dreyerley Semitonia. 60
  Vermehrung der Clavir darinnen. 60

Sonderliches Clavichordi Beschreibung. 61
Im Clavichordo zu einer Seiten offt zwey/drey/vier Clavier. 61
Clavichordum, darinn etzliche dieses Enharmonicæ. 61
Clarien auff einem Trumscheid. 59
Claves der alten wie vnterschieden. 112
Clavier in alten Orgeln. 98.99.109. 110. 111.
  gebrauch. 99
Clavier vermehrung. 109.111
  Verenderung. 109
Clavier der alten von ♮ angefangen vnd warumb. 112.113
Clavicymbalen. 5.7.63
  dessen Resonantz. 63
  Seiten doppelt / drey vnnd vierfach. 63
Clavicymbali im Chorthon lieblicher Resonantz. 16
Clavicymbeln, Symphonien, Virginal &c. etwas imperfect vnnd warumb. 63
Clavicymbel, darinn das ♫ gedoppelt. 63
Clavicymbel mit 77.Claviren. 64
Clavicymbel, in welchen alle Semitonia gedoppelt. 64
  deroselben doppelter Abriß in Clavibus vnd Noten. 64
Clavicymbel, welches sieben mal kan transponirt vnd fortgerücket werden. 65

INDEX II.   209

IV. Size 6 courses	29, 55
a fifth lower	55
almost 2 yards long	55
V. of 12 courses	29, 55
sounds like a harpsichord	55
Cittern, little English	29, 55
how tuned	55
Cithara Hieronymi	77
Cithara of antiquity [is] our present-day harp	54
Cymbalum: cymbals	4
Cymbalum Hieronymi	78
its meaning	78
Little cymbals	79
Universal or perfect harpsichord	63

CL

Clavichord	5, 60
invented from the monochord	60
at first it had 20 keys	60
[compass] begins from C up	61
is the foundation of all keyboard instruments	61
serves beginning students, and why	61
in the diatonic genus it had only 20 keys	60
three semitones in an octave	60
increase in [number of] keys	60
Description of a special clavichord	61
In a clavichord there are often two, three, or four keys to one string	61
Clavichord in which several of these [keys] are enharmonic	61
Glarean on the Marine Trumpet	59
Variety in keyboards of the past	112
Keys in old organs	98, 99, 109, 110, 111
their use	99
Increase in keys	109
change	109
Old keyboards began at B♮, and why	112, 113
Harpsichords	5, 7, 63
their sound	63
strings doubled, tripled, and quadrupled	63
Harpsichords at choir-pitch [produce] a more gentle sound	16
Harpsichords, symphonies, Virginals, etc., are somewhat imperfect; and why	63
Harpsichord in which the d♯ is doubled	63
Harpsichord with 77 keys	64
Harpsichord in which all semitones are doubled	64
a sketch of this in symbols and notes	64[-5]
Harpsichord that can be transposed and shifted [upward] seven times	65

auff alle drey genera modulandi
gerichtet. 65
 deſſen gebrauch. 65
Clavicithorium. 5.67
 deſſen Reſonantz 67
 Spitz wie ein Clavicymbalum. 67
 gantz in die höhe gerichtet. 67
Claviorganum Inſtrument mit
Pfeiffen vnd Seiten. 5.67
Clavitympanum. 4
Claves erſtlich vier / darnach ſieben/
bald 14.vnd endlich 15. 90
Claves Chromaticæ worauß erfun-
den. 91
Claves Tetrachordi Synemme-
ni. 91
Clavicymbeln rein zu ſtimmen. 150
GO.
Comma. 66
Conſonantiæ worauß erfunden. 79
Concertium bey den alten nicht ge-
breuchlich. 14
Compendium eine ſloite jünger oder
gröber zu ſtimmen. 35
Contra Baſſo de Gamba. 44
 wird durch eine Quart geſtimet. 44
Contrapunctus Gloridus wie auff
Orgeln erfunden. 101
Coppelflöten in Orgeln. 134
Coppeln in Orgeln. 132
Corna Muſe. 3.41.42
 derer Reſonantz. 41
 ſeins Chorthon. 41
 hoher vnd niedriger thon. 24

Geben ſo viel Thon als Löcher. 40
 haben ein einfache Röhr. 41
 vnten zugedeckt. 41
 Am Reſonantz den Krumbhörnern
 gleich. 41
Corna muti,terti, Florti. 3.40
 wie hoch vnd niedrig am thon. 24
Cornetto Ital. Cornet, Cornu 3.35
 Recto,diretto. 35
 Curvo. 35.36
 Muto. 36
 Torto. 36
 wie hoch vnd niedrig. 22
 Gröber oder Jünger zu Stim-
 men. 35
Cornettino. 36
 wie hoch intoniret. 36
Cornon. 36
 wie intoniret. 36
 wie viel thon. 36
 wie ein S. formiret. 36
Cornett in Orgeln. 126.146
CR.
Crembalum. 5
Crepitaculum. 4
DA.
Darmſeiten verſtimmen ſich ehe als
Ertzſeiten. 6
DE.
Decken macht die Pfeiffen am Thon
tieffer vmb ein Octav/ Quint/ oder
Sext. 124
Der Griechen meinung von der Muſi-
ca. 83

Digni-

possessing all three genera of modulation	65
its use	65
Clavicyther	5, 67
its sound	67
tapered like a harpsichord	67
built vertically	67
Claviorganum: an instrument with pipes and strings	5, 67
Clavitympanum	4
Keys: first four, then seven, then 14, and finally 15	90
Chromatic keys: whence discovered	91
Keys from the tetrachord Synemmenon	91
Harpsichord, how to tune purely	150

CO

Comma	66
Consonances, whence discovered	79
Playing in concert not usual among our ancestors	14
An easy way to tune a flute higher or lower	35
Contra Bass de Gamba	44
tuned in fourths	44
Florid counterpoint, how discovered on organs	101
Coppelfloiten in organs	134
Coppeln in organs	132
Cornamuse	3, 41, 42
their sound	41
they are at choir pitch	41
[at] higher and lower pitches	24
produce as many pitches as holes	40
single bore	41
stopped at the bottom	41
Like krummhorns in their sound	41
Krummhorns	3, 40
at what pitches	24
Cornetto (Ital.), Cornet, Cornu	3, 35
straight	35
curved	35, 36
Muto	36
Torto	36
at what pitches	22
tuning higher or lower	35
Cornettino	36
how high pitched	36
Cornon	36
at what pitch	36
how many pitches	36
shaped like an S	36
Cornett in organs	126, 146

CR

Crembalum [Jew's harp]	5
Crepitaculum [triangle]	4

DA

Gut strings go out of tune more quickly than metal strings	6

DE

Caps make pipes lower in pitch by an octave, fifth, or sixth	124
The Greek opinion of musica	83

INDEX II.

DI.
Dignität der Orgeln.	82
Discant Clavier.	98.99
Gebrauch.	98.99
Discant Geige mit 4. Seiten.	48
h̄ in Orgeln/ Positiven/ Clavicymbeln zu dupliren.	63
Dispositiones der Orgeln zu Costnitz.	161
Ulm.	162
Dantzig.	162
Rostock.	163
Lübeck.	164.165.166
Stralsund.	167
zu Hamburg.	168.169
Lüneburgk.	170
Breßlaw.	171
Magdeburgk.	172.173.174
Bernaw.	176.177
Stendal.	176.177
Hall.	177
Brounschweigk.	178
Leipzig.	179.180
Torgaw.	180
Halberstadt.	181
Cassel.	183
Bückelburg.	185
Dreßden.	186
Grüningen.	188
Hessen.	189
Schöningen.	190
Andere mehr. M.P.C.	91.99.100
Sondershausen.	197
Kloster S. Gothard in Hildesheimb.	197
Kloster Rittagshausen.	198
Einer kostbarn Orgel.	198
Eines kleinen Wercklin.	199

DO.
Doeff Stimm in Orgeln.	127
Doppel Cither.	7
Doppel Corthol.	23
Doppel Fagott.	28
zweyerley.	38
Intonation.	38
wie hoch vnd niedrig.	23
Doppelte Harffe hat alle Semiton.	56
Doppioni.	3.39
hoher vnd niedriger thon.	23

Du.
Dudei art von Sackpfeiffen.	3.43
hat drey Stimmen.	43
Duiflott in Orgeln von wem erfunden.	140
Dulcian: Dulzaine.	3.38.39
woher der Nahme.	38
lieblicher als Bombard vnnd warumb.	38
Dulzflotten.	35
wie intoniret.	35
Dulcian in Orgeln.	126.136.147
Form vnd gebrauch.	147
Dulce suono.	38

E.
Echo auff dem Geigen Instrumēt.	70
Einstimmige Instrument.	7
Englischer Chorthon vmb etwas niedriger.	15
Enderung der Stimmen.	116
Erster Orgel art vñ eigenschafft.	93.94

INDEX II.

DI

Dignity of organs	82
Discant keyboard	98, 99
its use	98, 99
discant violin with 4 strings	48
d♯ to be split in organs, positivs, and harpsichords	63
Stoplists of organs at:	
Constance	161
Ulm	162
Danzig	162
Rostock	163
Lübeck	164, 165, 166
Stralsund	167
at Hamburg	168, 169
Lüneburg	170
Breslau	171
Magdeburg	172, 173, 174
Bernau	176, 177
Stendal	176, 177
Halle	177
Braunschweig	178
Leipzig	179, 180
Torgau	180
Halberstadt	181
Kassel	183
Bückeburg	185
Dresden	186
Gröningen	188
Hessen	189
Schöningen	190
others in addition MPC	91, 99, 100
Sondershausen	197
St. Godehard Monastery in Hildesheim	197
Riddagshausen Monastery	198
A sumptuous organ	198
A small instrument	199

DO

Doeff, a stop in organs	127
Double cittern	7
Double curtal	23
Double Fagott [curtal]	38
two kinds	38
pitch	38
sizes	23
Double harp with all semitones	56
Doppioni	3, 39
sizes	23

Du

Dudey, a kind of bagpipe	3, 43
has three drones	43
Duifloit in organs: by whom discovered	140
Dulcian, Dulzaine	3, 38, 39
whence the name	38
gentler than a bombard, and why	38
Dulzfloiten	35
how tuned	35
Dulcian in organs	126, 136, 147
form and use	147
Dulce suono	38

E

Echo on the Geigenwerck	70
Single-melody instrument[s]	7
English choir pitch is somewhat lower	15
Varieties of stops	116
Characteristics of the earliest organ	93, 94

hat 11. Claves ohne Semitonia. 94
hat drey Tetrachorda der Alten. 94
warumb nur 11. claves. 95
vmb eine octav ergrössert. 95
Eunuchi in Keyser vnd Catholischen Cappellen wie hoch singen können. 78
Exilent Plockfloit. 21

FA.
Fagotti, Fagott. 3.38
   wie hoch vnd niedrig. 23
   Lieblicher Resonantz als Bombarden. 38
   warumb. 38
Fagotten vnnd Dulcianen vndterscheid 38
Fagotten doppelt zweyerley. 38
Fagott contra wie niedrig am thon. 38
Fagott in Orgeln. 126.147
   Form vnd grösse. 147
   Gebrauch. 147
Falset Stimme. 12.19

FE.
Feld Pfeiffe. 35

FI.
Fides: Fidicula. 4
Fidicinia Instrumenta. 4.43
Fiffari: Querpfeiff. 3.35
Figural gesang durch die Orgel erfunden. 90
Figural gesang von der alten Harmonia durch aus anders. 90
Fistula. 3.33
Fistula Hieronymi. 78
   Form derselben. 78
   Bedeutung. 78
Fiedel. 48

FL.
Flachfloite in Orgeln. 126.136
   welcher genennet. 136
   deren Intonation. 136
   dreyerley art. 136
Flauti. 3.33
Floit das Fundament aller gelöcherten Instrument. 61
Floite. 3.7.33
   wie zu höher oder niedriger Intonation zu bringen. 34.35
   wie viel Löcher. 33
   Lauten im Chorthon lieblich. 16
   wie eine von der andern gestimet. 37
Floiten Chor. 34
Floiten in Orgeln. 125.139
   Zweyerley. 125
Flügel Instrument. 63

FV.
Fundament Instrument. 7
Fusston wie zu verstehen. 121
   Einem Organisten zu wissen von nöthen. 14
Füsse namen vnnd zahl den Orgelmachern im gebrauch. 19

GA.
Gantz Orgelwerck was bey den altē. 105
Gläserne Orgel. 92

GE.
Gedackte Stim in Orgeln. 139

Sechser-

had 11 keys without semitones	94
had the three ancient tetrachords	94
why only 11 keys	95
extended by an octave	95
Eunuchs, in imperial and Catholic chapels: how high they can sing	18
Exilent: [sopranino] Blockfloit	21

FA

Curtals (Fagotti, Fagott)	3, 38
their ranges	23
a more gentle sound than shawms	38
why	38
Difference between curtals and dulcians	38
Curtal's bore doubles back	38
Contra-curtal: how low in pitch	38
Fagott in organs	126, 147
shape and size	147
use	147
Falset voice	12, 19

FE

Fife	35

FI

Fides; Fidicula [violins]	4
Stringed instruments	4, 43
Fiffari: traverse flute	3, 35
Polyphony invented by means of the organ	90
Polyphony entirely different from ancient harmony	90
Fistula [recorder]	3, 33
Fistula Hieronymi	78
its shape	78
meaning	78
Fiedel [Fiddel]	48

FL

Flachfloite in organs	126, 136
whence its name	136
its voicing	136
three varieties	136
Recorders	3, 33
Recorder the basis for playing all fingerhole instruments	61
Recorder	3, 7, 33
how to tune it higher or lower	34, 35
how many fingerholes	33
Recorders gentle at choir pitch	16
Tuning them to each other	37
Recorder consorts	34
Flue pipes in organs	125, 139
Two kinds	125
Flügel/Instrument	63

FU

Foundation instruments	7
Pitch in feet: what it means	121
it is necessary for an organist to know this	14
Numbers in feet, as used by organ-builders	19

GA

"Whole organ;" what that meant in the past	105
Glass organ	92

GE

Stopped ranks in organs	139

INDEX II.

Sechserley art.	139	Räder an stadt der Tanganten.	68
Gedackter untersatz.	139	wie tieff am Thon.	68
Groß gedackter SubBaß.	139	Seiten von Stal und Messing.	68
dessen gebrauch.	140	Geigen Instrument eigentliche Beschreibung.	68
Gedackt sonderliche art.	140	Gebrauch.	69
Gedackte Quinta.	140	Lautenthon.	70
stehet eine quint vom Chorthon.	140	dienet zum Choral.	70
Gedackt Schnarwerck.	146	gibt einen Tremulant.	70
Gedackt gelinder als Principal unnd warumb.	38	Ein Sackpfeiffen/Schalmeyen uñ Leirenthon.	70
Gedackte Schnarwerck gelinder als Posaunen und warumb.	38	Cithern art zum Bassetum.	70
stehet eine Quint vom Chorthon.	38	gibt eine FeldMusicam mit Trommeten und Clarin.	71
Gedackt floitwerck.	125	Gembshorn.	126. 134
zweyerley.	126	am thon lieblich.	134
Gedackt von den Alten floiten genennet.	139	gebrauch.	134
Von den Niederländern Bordun.	139	Gembshorn Quinta.	134
Von andern Barem.	139	des Labij breite.	134
Gedackte wie und wenn erfunden.	114. 115	Gembshorn woher den Namen.	133
Geige.	44. 48	Geigen Regal.	146
hat 4. Seiten.	48	woher der Nahme.	146
wie zu stimmen.	48	gebrauch.	146
Geigelin.	48	Gelber Zinck.	3
hat drey Seiten.	48	Gemeine Leire.	5. 49
Geigen mit Messings unnd Stählen Seiten.	48	Gerader Zinck.	35
werden durch 5. gestimmet.	48	zweyerley.	35
Geigen Instrument: werck.	67	**GI.**	
Geigen Clavicymbel.	67	Gingrina.	37
Form und gestalt.	67	Gingrire proprium anserum.	37
Von wem erfunden.	67	G. In Orgeln / Positiven und Clavicymbeln zu doppeln und warum.	63
Invention woher genommen.	67	**GL.**	
		Glocken: glöcklein.	4. 79

Ee   Græci

INDEX II.

six varieties	139
Gedackt Untersatz	139
Great Gedackt Subbass	139
its use	140
Gedackt: an unusual variant	140
Gedackte Quint	140
built a fifth above choir pitch	140
Stopped reeds	146
Gedackts gentler than Principal, and why	38
Stopped reeds are gentler than Posaunes, and why	38
stands a fifth above choir pitch[2]	38
Stopped flutes	125
two types	126
Gedackt called "floiten" in the past	139
The Netherlanders call it "Bordun"	139
others call it "Barem"	139
How and when Gedackts were invented	114, 115
Violin	44, 48
has 4 strings	48
how to tune it	48
Little violin	48
has three strings	48
Violins with brass and steel strings	48
tuned by fifths	48
Geigen Instrument; -werck	67
Geigen Clavicymbel	67
form and shape	67
by whom invented	67
invention; whence derived	67
Wheels instead of tangents	68
how low they go	68
strings of steel and brass	68
Geigen Instrument: an actual description	68
its use	69
lute sound	70
serves to [bring out] the melody	70
can produce a tremolo	70
can sound like a hurdy-gurdy or shawm	70
use as a cittern for serenading	70
imitates military music with trumpets and clarions	71
Gemshorn	126, 134
gentle in tone	134
use	134
Gemshorn Quint	134
the width of its lip	134
Gemshorn: whence the name	133
GeigenRegal	146
whence its name	146
use	146
Yellow[3] Zinck	3
Common lyre	5, 49
Straight Zinck	35
two kinds	35

GI

Gingrina [Schalmei]	37
Gingrire proprium anserum	37
g♯: to be doubled in organs, positivs and harpsichords, and why	63

GL

Bells, little bells	4, 79

---

2. This entry appears to be a mistake.

3. Yellow because it is made of unstained wood.

GR.

Græci Musici.	66
Grave cymbalum.	63
Grobe Cymbel.	131
Grosse alte Orgelwercke.	97
Groß Baß Bombard.	37
desselben Länge.	37
wie hoch vnd niedrig.	22
Grosse Bock.	42
Grosse Flachfloit.	136
Groß Gembshorn.	134
Im Pedal zugebrauchen.	134
Grosse Holfloiten.	132
Bey den alten eine Quint tieffer als Chorthon gewesen.	132
Grosse Italiänische Leire.	4.49
derer structur.	49
mit 12. auch 14. Seiten.	49
Ist dem generi Chromatico vnd Diaterrico bequem.	49
Grosse Mixtur.	130
Bey den Alten von 30. auch 40. Chor starck.	130
Jetzo von 10. 12. selten 20. Chor starck.	130
Groß Octava.	129
Respondiret einem æqual Principal.	129
warumb klein Principal genennet.	129
Groß Principal.	105.122.127
Gebrauch im Manual vnnd Pedal zum langsamen tritt.	127
Groß Principalwerck woran erkät.	122
Grosse Quintadehna.	137
gebrauch im Manual vñ Pedal.	137
Grob Regal.	145
Materia.	145
Mensur.	145
Grosse Rohrfloit.	141
Besser als gedackt.	141
Groß Subprincipal Baß.	127
gebrauch im Pedal.	127
vnd warumb.	127
Grosse Schweitzer- Pfeiff in Orgeln.	128
Grosse Schwiegel.	133

Gu.

Guido Aretinus zu welcher zeit gelebt.	90

HA.

Hackebrett.	5.79
Halb Orgelwerck bey den alten.	105
Harffe.	4.56
woher der Nahme.	56
Bey den alten Cithara.	56
wiviel Seiten gehabt.	56
Formieret wie ein △	56
Jetzo dreyerley Art.	56
Einfache.	30.56
hat 24. Seiten ohne Semitonia.	56
Doppelte.	56
Claves zur lincken vnnd rechten hand.	56
Harpa.	4.56
Harpa doppia.	30.56
Harpa Irlandica.	5.30.56
hat 43. Seiten.	56

GR

Greek musicians	66
Gravecymbalum [harpsichord]	63
Low-pitched Cymbel	131
Large old organs	97
Large bass bombard	37
its length	37
ranges	22
Large bagpipe	42
Large Flachfloit	136
Large Gembshorn	134
to be used in the pedal	134
Large Holfloit	132
in the past it was a fifth lower than choir pitch	132
Large Italian lyra	4, 49
its construction	49
with 12 and also 14 strings	49
it is suited both to the diatonic and chromatic genus	49
Large mixture	130
in the past 30 or even 40 ranks large	130
now or 10, 12 or rarely 20 ranks large	130
Large Octava	129
corresponds to an 8′ Principal	129
why some call it "small Principal"	129
Large Principal	105, 122, 127
used in both manual and pedal at slow tempos	127
Large-principal organ; how recognized	122
Large Quintadehna	137
used in both manual and pedal	137
Grob Regal	145
made of [brass]	145
length	145
Large Rohrfloit	141
better than a Gedackt	141
Large pedal Subprincipal	127
used in the pedal	127
why	127
Large Schweitzerpfeiff in organs	128
Large Schwiegel	133

GU

Guido of Arezzo, when he lived	90

HA

Dulcimer	5, 79
Half organs in the past	105
Harp	4, 56
whence the name	56
in the past called "Cithara"	56
how many strings it had	56
shaped like Greek letter "Delta"	56
now of three kinds	56
single	30, 56
has 24 strings without semitones	56
double	56
notes for the left and right hand	56
Harpa	4, 56
double-harp	30, 56
Irish harp	5, 30, 56
has 43 strings	56

INDEX II.

Alle Semitonia. 56
Einen lieblichen Resonantz. 56
Alten vnnd newen Harffen vnterscheid. 77
Alten Harffen Form viererley. 77
dreyecket. 77
Harffenirender Resonantz. 59.67
Harmonia consonantiarum in der Natur gepflantzet. 47

HE.

HeerPaucke. 77.79
HeerPaucken gebrauch. 77
Heulen in Orgeln woher. 159

HI.

Hindersatz in alten Orgeln. 99.107
wie viel Pfeiffen darinn. 99.113
wie vnd wann zertheilet. 113.115
Hydraulicum Instrumentum. 91.92
dessen vnterscheid von der Orgel vnd anfang. 90.92
Hypodorius wird auß dem E Musiciret. 16
wird auß dem F. Musiciret. 63
Hypotonicus wird auß dem C. ins D. von den Italis transponiret vñ Musiciret. 16
Hypotonicus wie auff Floiten/Bombarden/Schalmeyen vnnd Krumbhörnern zu transponiren. 30.37

HO.

Holfloit in Orgeln. 126.131
derer Thon vnd woher. 131
woher der Nahme. 131
Hoher Thon worinn der beste. 14
Hoher Thon den Italis nicht annemlich. 16
Holquinten. 132
gebrauch. 132
Holquinten Baß. 132
Holschelle. 137
Holtzern Orgel. 138.189.190
Holtzern Pfeiffwerck ist mit andern Orgeln sowol am laut vnnd Arbeit als Fundament theilung nicht zu vergleichen. 141
Houtbois: Hoboyen. 36

Hu.

Himmelchen. 3.42
hat 2. Stimmen. 42

IA.

JägerHorn. 78

IN.

Instrument vnnd Instrumentist was eigentlich sey. 11.62
Instrumentorum Musicorum Beschreibung. 1
Instrumentorum Musicorum Abtheilung. 1
Instrumenta ἔμπνευστα. 2
zweyerley Art. 2
Instrumenta fidicinia. 4.8
Instrumenta inflatilia. 2.8
zweyerley Art. 2
ohne vnd mit Löchern. 2.3
Instrument mit Löchern dreyerley Art. 2.3
Instrumenta κρουστά, welche geschlagen oder geklopfft werden. 3.4

complete semitones	56
a gentle sound	56
difference between old and new harps	77
old harp took many forms	77
triangular	77
extraneous sound on the harp	59, 67
Sympathetic vibration rooted in nature	47

HE

Military drums	77, 79
Military drums: their use	77
Ciphers in organs: why	159

HI

Hindersatz in old organs	99, 107
How many pipes in them	99, 113
How and when split up	113, 115
Hydraulis	91, 92
distinct from the organ; origin	90, 92
Hypodorian performed on E	16
performed on F	63
Hypoionian transposed from C and performed on D	16
Hypoionian, how to transpose on recorders, bombards, schalmeis and krummhorns	30, 37

HO

Holfloit in organs	126, 131
Its sound; its origin	131
whence its name	131
Higher pitch: which is best	14
Italians find higher pitch unacceptable	16
Holquint	132
its use	132
Holquint in the pedal	132
Holschelle	137
Wooden organ	138, 189, 190
Wooden pipes: their proportions and sound not to be compared with other organs	141
Hautbois; hoboy	36

HU

Hümmelchen [bagpipe]	3, 42
has 2 drones	42
Jäger Horn	78

IN

Instrument and Instrumentist: what they actually are	11, 62
Musical instruments: a description	1[ff.]
Musical instruments: their classification	1[ff.]
Instrumenta εμπνευσα	2
two kinds	2
Instrumenta fidicinia	4, 8
Instrumenta inflatilia	2, 8
two kinds	2
without and with holes	2, 3
Instrument[s] with holes: three kinds	2, 3
Instrumenta κρωστα, that are struck or beaten	3, 4

ἄπνευτα. 3
ἄχορδα. 3.4
ἔγχορδα. 3.4
μενότονα. 7.11
πάντονα. 7
πολύτονα. 7
Instrumenta prima. 5
  A primis orta. 5
  Mixta. 5
  Multivoca. 7
  Omnivoca. 7
  Vnivoca. 7
  Tibicinia. 8
Instrumentum specialiter sic dictum: Instrument. 5
Instrumentenklang woher verursachet. 1
Instrument haben ihren ursprung aus dem Monochordo. 142
  können keinen Affectum exprimiren. 69
  leiden keine Moderation. 69
  werden nach ihrem Thon underschieden. 1
Instrument/welche uber ihren Natürlichen Thon können gezwungen werden. 6.7
  welche alle Stimmen repræsentiren. 6
In welchen der Thon leichtlich verstimmet. 6

Instrument in Engelland vnd Niederland vmb ein Tertl tieffer. 16
Instrumenten Eigentlicher Thon. 14
Instrumenten Thon respectu
  Latitudinis. 6.7
  Longitudinis. 6.7
  Profunditatis. 6.7
Instrumentalis Musica zu K. Davids zeiten wie zuverstehen. 83.84
  warumb zu grunde gangen. 84
Inventores der Orgeln/ Monochordi, Clavicymbali &c. sind vns verborgen. 90
Invention der Register. 116
In Græcia hat sich die Musica gar verlohren. 82

IR.
Irländische Harffe. 5.56
  hat 43. Seiten. 56
  lieblichen Resonanz. 56

IT.
Italiänische Leire. 4.49
  zweyerley art. 49
Itali haben keinen gefallen am hohen singen. 16

Iu.
Jungfrawen Regal. 145
Jungfrawen Baß. 145
  Mensur. 145
  woher der Nahme. 145
Jüdische Instrumenta. 83
Juden hören jetzo keine Orgeln vnnd warumb. 84

Kälber

απνευτα	3
αχορδα	3, 4
εγχορδα	3, 4
μενοτονα	7, 11
παντονα	7
πολυτονα	7
Instrumenta prima	5
A primis orta	5
Mixta	5
Multivoca	7
Omnivoca	7
Univoca	7
Tibicinia	8
Instrumentum specialiter sic dictum:	
Instrument	5
Instruments' sound: what causes it	1
[Stringed] keyboard Instruments	
arose from the monochord	142
cannot express affects	69
allow no change in dynamics	69
are distinguished by their sound	1
Instrument[s] that can be forced	
beyond their natural ranges	6, 7
that are able to play all parts/voices	6
[Instruments] whose pitch can easily	
be altered	6
Instruments in England and the Nether-	
lands a third lower	16
Instruments: their normal pitch	14

Instrument's sound with respect to:	
length	6, 7
breadth	6, 7
depth	6, 7
Instrumental music at the time of King	
David, how to understand	83, 84
why it has disappeared	84
Inventors of organs, monochords, harp-	
sichords, etc., are hidden from us	90
Invention of [organ] stops	116
In Greece music has	
totally disappeared	82

IR

Irish harp	5, 56
has 43 strings	56
a gentle sound	56

IT

Italian lyra	4, 49
two kinds	49
Italians find no pleasure in	
high[-pitched] singing	16

Iu.

JungfrauenRegal	145
Jungfrauen[Regal], pedal	145
scale	145
whence the name	145
Jewish instruments	83
Jews do not listen to organs; why	84

INDEX II.

KA.
Kälber Regal. 116

KE.
Kessel Paucke / Trummel. 79

KI.
Kirchen Musica. 82

KL.
Kleine Cither. 55
   wie gestimmet. 55
Kleine Flachsloit. 136
Klein Floiten Baß. 132
   Gebrauch im Choral. 132
Klein Gedackt. 139
Kleine Geige mit drey Seiten. 48
   gebrauch zur Variation. 139
Kleine Holsloite. 132
Kleine Italiänische Leire. 49
   hat 7. Seiten. 49
   Ist Triciniis bequem. 49
Kleine Mixtur. 131
   Niederländen scharp. 131
   wie disponiret. 131
Kleine Octav in Orgeln. 129
Klein Octaven Gembshorn. 134
   Gehöret ins Positiff. 134
   Gebrauch im Baß zum Choral. 134
Kleine Orgelwercke bey den alten. 97
Klein Päucklein. 77
Kleine Blockflotten. 34
   derer Lenge. 34
   wie viel Löcher. 34
   wie hoch vnd niedrig. 34
Kleine Principal. 127. 105
Kleine Principalwerck. 123
   woran zu erkennen. 123
Kleine Quintadehna. 137
   Gebrauch zur Variation. 137
Klein Regal. 146
Kleine Rohrsloit. 141
Kleine Schweitzerpfeiff in Orgeln. 128
Kleine Schwiegel. 133
Kleine Spitzsloit. 135
Klein vierecket Jnstrument. 62
   vmb ein 5. oder Octav höher gestimmet. 62
Kleine Zimbel. 131
Klein Zincken. 36
Klingende Zimbel. 131

KN.
Knopff Regal. 148
   woher der Nahme. 148

KO.
Köpfflin Regal. 126. 148
   Form vnd Grösse. 148
   Resonantz. 148
Kort Jnstrument. 39
   Gibt so viel Thon als Löcher. 40

KR.
Krumbhörner. 40
   wie viel Löcher. 40
   wie hoch vnd niedrig am Thon. 24
   wie eins vom andern gestimmet. 37
   Geben so viel Thon als Löcher. 40
Krumbhorn in Orgeln. 126. 145
Krumb Zincke. 35. 36

Ku.
Kuheschellen. 78

KA
KälberRegal	116

KE
Kettledrum, drum	79

KI
Church music	82

KL
Little cittern	55
how tuned	55
Little Flachfloit	136
Little pedal flute	132
use in chant	132
Little Gedackt	139
Little violin with three strings	48
used for variety	139[4]
Little Holfloite	132
Little Italian Lyra	49
Has 7 strings	49
suited to three-part pieces	49
Little Mixtur	131
[called] Scharp [by the] Netherlanders	131
how composed	131
Little Oktav in organs	129
Little Octave Gembshorn	134
belongs in the Positiff	134
used in the pedal for a cantus firmus	134
Little organs of the past	97
Little drum	77
Little recorder	34
their length	34
how many holes	34
their range	34
Little Principal	127, 105
Little Principal [organ]	123
how identified	123
Little Quintadehna	137
used for variety	137
Little Regal	146
Little Rohrfloit	141
Little Schweitzerpfeiff in organs	128
Little Schwiegel	133
Little Spitzfloit	135
Little rectangular spinet	62
tuned a fifth or an octave higher	62
Little Zimbel	131
Little cornett	36
Klingende Zimbel	131

KN
KnopfRegal	148
whence the name	148

KO
KöpfflinRegal	126, 148
shape and size	148
sound	148
Kort Instrument	39
produces as many pitches as [it has] holes	40

KR
Krummhorns	40
How many holes	40
range	24
how one is tuned from another	37
produce as many pitches as [they have] holes	40
Krummhorn in organs	126, 145
Curved Cornet	35, 36

Ku
Cow-bells	78

4. This belongs under the previous entry, "Little Gedackt."

LA.

Laute: Italis Linto. 4.6.7.49
  wieviel Sorten/vnd zu stimmen. 27
  Fundament der besetteten Instrument. 61
  Anfangs 4. Chor/ darnach 5. gehabt. 49
  jetzo 6.7.8.9.10.11. vñ mehr Chor. 50
  zum Generi chromatico bequem̃. 65
  wie die Chor Seiten vnterschiedlich zu nennen vnd zehlen. 50
Lauten groß vnnd klein in einander zu stimmen. 51
Lauten vnd Theorben vnterscheid. 50
Laut auff den Seiten kan nicht lange continuiret werden. 69

LE.

Leire der alten. 110
  Gebrauch. 100
  Italiänische Leire. 49
  zweyerley. 49
Leire der Bawren vnd Betler. 5.49
Lenge offen Pfeiffwercks. 124
Lenge gedacktes Pfeiffwercks. 124
Lerchen Pfeifflein. 78
Leviten haben ihre Psalmen vnd Lieder in Instrument gesungen. 90

LI.

Lyra, Italicè Lironi. 4.49
  Pagana. 5.49
  Rustica. 5.49
  de gamba 14. Seiten. 7.26
  de Bracio. 7.26.49
  wie zu stimmen. 26

hat 7. Seiten. 49
  Gebrauch. 49
Lironi perfecto Ital. 49
  hat 12.14. auch 16. Seiten. 49
  Gebrauch. 49
Lituus. 3.40

LO.

LockPfeifflin. 78

Lu.

Lufft in Instrumenten zweyerley. 2
  Natürlich.
  Menschlich. 2

MA.

Magas. 57
Maisenbeinlein. 78
Mandör/ Mandürichen/ Mandurichen. 28.53
  woher der Nahme. 53
  hat 4. oder 5. Seiten. 53
  wie gestimmet. 53
  wird mit einem Finger oder Federkeil geschlagen. 53
  dessen gebrauch in Franckreich. 53
Mangel in Orgeln. 159
Manual Clavir bey den alten Discant genennet. 97
  warumb. 90
  wieviel Claves gehabt. 97
Materia der Orgeln. 84

ME.

Menschlicher Stimme hohe vnd tieffe im Basso, Ten. Alt. vnd Cantu. 20
Mensur im flottwerck je enger je besser Resonantz. 143

Mittel

LA

Lute: Italian *Liuto*	4, 6, 7, 49
how many kinds; how to tune	27
foundation for stringed instruments	61
at first it had 4 courses, then 5	49
now 6, 7, 8, 9, 10 or more courses	50
suitable for the chromatic genus	65
how to label and count the various courses of strings	50
Lutes, how to tune large and small ones to each other	51
Lutes and theorbos: difference	50
Sound produced by strings does not last long	69

LE

The ancient hurdy-gurdy	[100]
use	100
Italian hurdy-gurdy	49
two kinds	49
Hurdy-gurdy of peasants and beggars	5, 49
Length of open [organ] pipes	124
Length of stopped [organ] pipes	124
Fowler's pipes	78
Levites sang their Psalms and hymns with instruments	90

LI

Lyra, Italian *Lironi* (hurdy-gurdy)	4, 49
Pagana	5, 49
Rustica	5, 49
de gamba, 14 strings	7, 26
de Bracio	7, 26, 49
how to tune	26
has 7 strings	49
use	49
Large lyra, Italian	49
has 12, 14, also 16 strings	49
use	49
Lituus	3, 40

LO

LockPfeifflin	78

Lu

Air for instruments of two kinds	2
natural	
human	2

MA

Magas [marine trumpet]	57
Maisenbeinlein	78
Mandora, Mandürichen, Mandurinichen	28, 53
whence the name	53
has 4 or 5 strings	53
how tuned	53
played with one finger or a feather quill	53
its use in France	53
Shortcomings in organs	159
Manual keyboard in the past called Discant	97
why	90
number of keys	97
Materials used to build organs	84

ME

Human voice, its bass, tenor, alto, and treble ranges	20
Scale in [organ] flue pipes: the narrower, the better the sound	143

MI.

Mittel OrgelWercke bey den Alten. 97
Mittel Principal. 122
  woran erkant. 122
Mixtur. 130
  Mancherley Art. 130
  gebrauch. 130
  Correspondiret dem æqual principal. 130
  Ist 4.5.6.7.8.9.Chor. 130
  kan für sich alleine nicht gebraucht werden. 131
Mixtur in alten Orgeln. 99.115

MO.

Moderation der Stimmen sonderlich in acht zu nehmen. 68
Moviret die affectus. 69
  wie geschaffen. 69
Monochordum. 60.142
  dessen Beschreibung. 60
  hat eine Seiten. 60
  gibt alle Consonantias. 60
  gründet auff die proportiones. 60
  wird durch den Circkel ausgetheilet. 60.142
Monochordum aller Musicalischen Instrument Mutter. 142
μονότονα Instrumenta. 7

Mu.

Multivoca Instrumenta. 7
Mundstück am Zincken. 35
Mundstück lenglich vnd schmal geben in Schnarwercken einen lieblichen Resonantz. 143
Muscowiterische Instrument. 79
Musica bey den alten. 100
Musica Figuralis durch die Orgeln erfunden. 90
Musica Orlandi di Lasso. 17
Musica von den Teutschen wieder in Italiam gebracht. 96
Musica vor zeiten in Italia zergangen. 96
Musica zu David vnd Salomons zeiten. 82.83
Musicalischer Instrument Beschreibung. 1
  Abtheilung. 1.10
  Erfindung. 1
  Thon. 1
  quo ad qualitativam generationem. 1
  quo ad qualitativam mensurationem. 6
  Respectu longitudinis. 6
  latitudinis. 6.7
  profunditatis. 6.7
Musicalischer Instrument Autores viel bey den alten vergessen. 89
Musicalischer Instrument beste Zier die Moderation. 68

NA.

Nachthorn in Orgeln. 132.138
  woher der Nahme. 138
  Intonation. 138
  Gebrauch. 138

Quin-

MI

Medium-sized organs of the past	97
Medium-principal	122
how recognized	122
Mixture	130
various kinds	130
use	130
corresponds to the 8' Principal	130
is 4, 5, 6, 7, 8, 9 ranks	130
cannot be used by itself	131
Mixtur in old organs	99, 115

MO

Changing vocal dynamics is especially to be kept in mind	68
It moves the emotions	69
How it is done	69
Monochord	60, 142
description of it	60
has one string	60
produces all the consonances	60
based on the proportions	60
divided using the compass	60, 142
Monochord is the mother of all musical instruments	142
μονοτονα instruments	7

Mu

Multivoca instruments	7
Mouthpiece on the cornett	35
Shallot: long and narrow produces a gentle sound in reeds	143

Moorish instrument[s]	79
Music in the past	100
Figural music invented by means of organs	90
Music [at the time of] Orlando di Lasso	17
Music brought back to Italy by the Germans	96
Italian music at one time perished	96
Music at the time of David and Solomon	82, 83
Description of	
musical instruments	1
classification	1, 10
invention	1
pitch	1
according to quality of generation	1
according to quality of measurement	6
with regard to length	6
[with regard to] breadth	6, 7
[with regard to] depth	6, 7
Inventors of musical instruments: much from antiquity is forgotten	89
The greatest virtue of musical instruments is change of dynamics	68

NA

Nachthorn in organs	132, 138
whence the name	138
pitch	138
use	138

… INDEX II.

Quintadehnen Mensur. 138
woher der Hornklang. 138
Nachthorn Baß. 138
Nahmen der Orgelwercke. 121
Nach dem Manual zu rechnen. 121
Nasath. 134
   woher der Nahme. 134
   Thon. 134
   Gebrauch. 134

NI.
Niederländische Coppelfloiten. 134
Niederländisch Nachthorn. 138
   dessen thon. 138
Niedriger thon worinn der beste. 14

NO.
Nola. 4

OC.
Octaven in Orgeln. 129
   Viererley art. 129
   Mensur. 129
   Gebrauch. 129
   gehöret in die AEqualwercke. 129
Octaven Gembshorn. 134
   gebrauch. 134
Octaven müssen rein gestimmet werden. 150
Octava nur drey Semitonia bey den alten. 60
Octaven Principal. 127
   Gebrauch. 127
   woran zuerkennen. 123

OF.
Offenfloitwerck. 125
   zweyerley. 125

OM.
Omnifona, omnivoca Instrumenta. 11

OR.
Organum Instrumentum Instrumentorum. 11
Organum pneumaticum. 2
   portatile. 2
Organisten sollen wissen die Stimmen zu vndterscheiden vnnd zu verendern. 14
Organisten requisita. 88
Orgel. 7
Orgeln dispositiones. 191.&c.
Orgeln dreyerley Art. 122
Orgel begreifft alle andere Instrumenta Musica. 85
Orgeln Encomium Hieronymi dirutæ Itali. 85
Orgeln in Teutschland nach dem gewöhnlichen Cammerthon gestimmet. 16
Orgeln im Sommer höher/ im Winter aber niedriger am Thon vnnd warumb. 34.74.75
Orgeln können nicht moderiret werden. 69
Orgeln menschlichem Leibe verglichen. 87
Orgel mit heissem wasser regiret. 92
   wenn vnd von wem gebawet. 92
Orgeln rechter thon. 14
Orgeln von wem erfunden. 89
   Vor 600. Jahren in Teutschland gebawet.

of Quintadena scaling	138
whence its horn-like timbre	138
Nachthorn in the pedal	138
Names of organs	121
Determined by the [lowest] pitch in the] manual	121
Nasat	134
whence the name	134
sound	134
use	134

NI

Netherlands Coppelfloiten	134
Netherlands Nachthorn	138
its sound	138
Lower pitch, why the best	14[-15]

NO

Nola [jingle]	4

OC

Octaves in organs	129
of four types	129
scale	129
use	129
belongs in unison instruments	129
Octave Gemshorn	134
use	134
Octaves must be tuned pure	150
Octave: had only three semitones in the past	60
Octave Principal	127
use	127
how to recognize it	123

OF

Open flue pipes	125
two types	125

OM

Omnisona, omnivoca instruments	11

OR

Organ the instrument of instruments	11
Organum pneumaticum	2
[Organum] portatile	2
Organists should know the various stops and how to change them	14
Organists, requirements for	88
Organ	7
Organ stoplists	191ff.
Organs, three kinds of	122
Organ comprises all other musical instruments	85
Organ encomium by the Italian, Girolamo Diruta	85
Organs in Germany are tuned according to the customary chamber pitch	16
Organs rise [in pitch] in summer but fall in winter; why	34, 74, 75
Organs cannot change their dynamics	69
Organs compared to the human body	87
Organ controlled by hot water	92
when and by whom built	92
Organs' proper pitch	14
Organs, by whom invented	89

INDEX II.

gebawet. 93
warumb ihren Sitz in der Kirchen. 87
woher den Nahmen. 86
zum Choral Gesang gebraucht. 90
zu was ende in Kirchē gebraucht. 90
zu welcher zeit in Teutschland vnnd Franckreich auffkommen. 91
zu welcher zeit erfunden. 90
Orgelwerck in Teutschland. 161
  Bamberg im Stifft. 111
  Bernaw. 176
  Braunschweig S. Egidien. 109
  S. Blasij. 178. 111
  Breßlaw. 172
  Bückelburgk. 185
  Cassel. 183
  Costnitz. 161
  Dantzig. 162
  Dreßden. 187
  Erffurd. 111
  Göttingen. 116
  Grüningen. 188
  Halberstadt. 181
  Hall. 177
  Hamburgk. 168. 169
  Hessem. 189
  Leipzig. 116. 179. 180
  Lübeck. 164. 165
  Lüneburgk. 170
  Magdeburgk. 172 ꝛc.
  Minden. 110
  dessen Clavier. 110
  Northausen. 116
  drey Manual Clavier. 116
  Nürnbergk. 110. 111
  Clavier. 110
  Rostock. 163
  Schöningen. 190
  Stendal. 176
  Stralsund. 167
  Torgaw. 181
  Venedig. 110
  Clavier. 110
Orgelwerck von Holtze. 138
Orgelwercke werden noch Füssen genennet. 121
Orlandi di Lasso Capellen von 90. Personen starck. 17
Ornamenc-Instrumenta. 7
Orpheoreum. 5. 6. 28. 54
  Ist wie ein Pandor. 54
  Seiten. 54
  wie gestimmet. 54
  Ist Cammerthon. 54

PA.

Padonnische Theorbe hat 8. Seitē. 52
Pandora. 5. 6. 7. 53
Pandurina. 53
πάντoνα Instrumenta. 7
Paucke. 4
Päucklin. 77
Pauolin. 140

PE.

Pedal wenn/ wo vnd von wem erfunden. 96
  wieviel Clavier erstlich gehabt. 96

built 600 years ago in Germany	93	three manuals	116
why they are found in churches	87	Nürnberg	110, 111
whence the name	86	keyboard	110
used for chant	90	Rostock	163
for what purpose used in church	90	Schöningen	190
at what time did they appear in Germany and France	91	Stendal	176
		Stralsund	167
at what time discovered	90	Torgau	181
Organs in Germany	161	Venice	110
Bamberg Cathedral	111	keyboard	110
Bernau	176	An organ of wood	138
Braunschweig: St. Aegidius	109	Organs are named according to [their size in] feet	121
St. Blasius	178, 111		
Breslau	172	Orlando di Lasso's chapel with 90 personnel	17
Bückeburg	185		
Kassel	183	"Ornament instruments"	7
Constance	161	Orpharion	5, 6, 28, 54
Danzig	162	is like a pandora	54
Dresden	187	strings	54
Erfurt	111	how tuned	54
Göttingen	116	is at chamber pitch	54
Gröningen	188		

PA

Halberstadt	181
Halle	177
Hamburg	168, 169
Hessen	189
Leipzig	116, 179, 180
Lübeck	164, 165
Lüneburg	170
Magdeburg	172f.
Minden	110
its keyboard	110
Nordhausen	116

Paduan Theorbo has 8 strings	52
Pandora	5, 6, 7, 53
Pandurina	53
παντονα instruments	7
Pauke [tympano: kettle-drum]	4
Päucklin	77
Päurlin	140

PE

Pedal: when, where, and by whom invented	96
how many keys it had at first	96

Pedal Clavier bey den alten. 99
Pedal von wem vnnd zu welcher zeit zu Venedig erfunden. 92
Pedal wird jetzo in Welschland vnnd Engeland nicht vielgebraucht. 96
Penoreon. 5.6.7.28.54
   Ist wie ein Pandoer. 54
   hat 9.Chor. 54

PF.

Pfeiff-floit in Orgeln. 140
   woher den Nahmen. 140
Pfeiffende Instrument. 2
Pfeiffen in alten Orgeln lenge vnnd dicke. 101.102
Pfeiffen in alten Orgeln disposition auff einem Chor. 102
Pfeiffen in alten Orgeln alle auff ein mal zusammen geklungen. 97
Pfeiffen in alten Orgeln Mixtur sehr vberheuffet. 102
Pfeiffen in der Dantzischer Orgeln. 37.42
Pfeiffen in Orgeln zweyerley. 125
Pfeiffen nach zu stimmen. 149
Pfeiffen so drey absonderliche Register haben. 79
Pfeiffen wieviel offtmals auff einem Clave. 114
Pfeiffwerck hat seinen rechten Thon vnd Fundament theilung aus dem Monochordo. 142

PI.

Piffari. 3.37

PL.

Plockfloite. 33
   wieviel Löcher. 33
   wieviel Thon. 33
   wieviel Thon extraordinar. 33
   Achterley Sort. 33.34
   derselben Intonation. 34
   wie tewr ein Stimwerck. 34
Plockfloite in Orgeln. 135
   derer Form vnd lenge. 135
   Auff Querfloiten Art. 135
PlockPfeiffe. 3
   Allerley Sorten wie hoch vnnd niedrig am Thon. 21
Plock Pfeiffe in Orgeln. 135

PO.

Pochetto. 48
Poeten Instrument. 78
Πολύτονα Instrumenta. 7
Pombard allerley Sort wie hoch vnd niedrig am Thon. 22
   wie eins vom andern gestimmet. 37
Pombard in Orgeln. 147
   Intonation vnd grösse. 147
   Form vnd Gebrauch. 147
Pommern vide Pombard.
Polnische Geigen. 44
   woher den Nahmen. 44
Positivum. Positiv. 2
Positiv / darinne alle Semitonia gedoppelt. 66
Positiv so zu einerley Pfeiffen drey absonderliche Register. 79
Posaune. 2.7.31
   Alt- Discant- Posaune. 31
   Tenor- Posaun. 31

Pedal keyboard in the past	99
Pedal: by whom and when it was discovered at Venice	92
Pedal is now seldom used in Italy and England	96
Penorcon	5, 6, 7, 28, 54
is like the pandora	54
has 9 courses [of strings]	54

PF

Pfeifferfloit in organs	140
whence its name	140
Pipe-instruments	2
Pipes in old organs: their length and thickness	101, 102
Pipes in old organs placed together as a single choir	102
Pipes in old organs all sounded together at once	97
Pipes in old organs: a great number in one Mixture	102
Pipes in the Danzig organs	37, 42[5]
Pipes in organs: of two kinds	125
Pipes: tuning to each other	149
Pipes that produce three separate registers	79
Pipes: number often found on a single key	114
Pipes derive their proper pitch and temperament from the monochord	142

PI

Piffaro	3, 37

PL

Blockflöte	33
how many [finger-]holes	33
how many pitches	33
how many extraordinary pitches	33
eight kinds	33, 34
their tuning	34
the cost of a consort	34
Blockfloite in organs	135
their shape and length	135
a variety like a Querfloit	135
Blockpfeiffe	3
various kinds; their pitches	21
BlockPfeiffe in organs	135

PO

Pochette	48
Instruments for poets	78
Πολυτονα instruments	7
Bombards of all kinds: their pitches	22
how one is tuned from another	37
Bombard in organs	147
their pitch and size	147
shape and use	147
Pommern: see "Bombarde"	
Polish violin	44
whence the name	44
Positivum, Positiv	2
Positiv with all the semitones duplicated in it	66
Positiv with three separate registers for each pipe	79
Sackbutt	2, 7, 31
alto/descant sackbutt	31
tenor sackbutt	31

---

5. There is no mention of Danzig's organs on these pages. The stoplist of the organ at St. Mary's Church, Danzig, is found on pp. 162-3.

Quart-Posaun.	31	Intoniret gleich einer Plockfloite.	35
Quint-Posaun.	32	Quer oft in Orgeln.	138
Octav-Posaun zweyerley Art.	32	Aus der Quintadehna erfunden.	138
Posaun wie hoch vnnd niedrig am Thon.	20	Intonation derselben.	138
wie vielerley Sorten.	20.31	zweyerley Art.	138
Posaun in Orgeln.	126	Querpfeiffe.	3.35
warumb stercker als Gedeckte Schnarrwerck.	38	thon derselben.	21
		wie hoch vnd niedrig.	22
Mancherley Mensur.	142	wieviel Löcher.	35
Posaun sonderlicher Art.	143	wieviel Thon.	35
Posaunen/ Trommetten vnnd Schalmeyen proportion in Orgeln.	142	**QuI.**	
		Quinta in Orgeln.	130
PR.		Quindez.	130
Præstantur in Orgeln.	106.126	Quintadehna.	136.137
Principal.	107.126	wenn erfunden.	137
woher der Nahme.	126	woher der Nahme.	137
viererley Art.	127	woher die Quinta.	125
warumb stercker als gedeckte.	38	Form vnd Proportion.	137
Principal Discant.	128	Intonation.	137
Pritschen auff dem Hafen.	78	dreyerley Art.	137
Proba im Stimmen.	153	Gebrauch.	137
Ob ein Regal just vnnd fleissig gemacht.	144	hat zwey vnterschiedliche Laut.	137
		Ist ein Octav tieffer als offen Pfeiffwerck.	137
PS.		zum Choral Baß bequem.	137
Psalterium.	4	Sonsten Quinta ad una genennet.	137
Psalterium decachordum.	76	Quint Fagott.	38
Ist zweyerley Art.	76	Quintfloit.	132
QuA.		Quinterna.	4.28.53
Quart Fagott.	38	hat 4. Chor.	53
wie hoch vnd niedrig.	23	wie gestimmet.	53
QuE.		Form vnd gestalt.	53
Querfloite.	3		
Querfloite sonst Dulzfloite.	35		

Ff 2   Gebrauch

Quart-sackbutt	31	voiced just like a Blockfloite	35
Quint-sackbutt	32 [31]	Quer[fl]oit in organs	138
Octave sackbutt of two kinds	32	developed from the Quintadena	138
Sackbutt: range[s]	20	its voicing	138
how many kinds	20, 31	two kinds	138
Posaune in organs	126	Querpfeiffe	3, 35
why more powerful than stopped reeds	38	its pitch	21 [22]
various dimensions	142	range	22
Posaune of an unusual sort	143	how many holes	35
Posaunes, Trommets and Schalmeis: their proportion in organs	142	how many pitches	35

PR

Præstants in organs — 106, 126
Principal — 107, 126
   whence the name — 126
   a variety of kinds — 127
   why louder than gedeckts — 38
Principal Discant — 128
Pot-and-sticks — 78
Tests in tuning — 153
   if a Regal is precisely and diligently made — 144

PS.

Psaltery [harp] — 4
Psalterium decachordum — 76
   two kinds — 76

QuA

Quart curtal — 38
   range — 23

QuE

Querfloite [traverse flute] — 3
Querfloite or Dulzfloite — 35

QuI

Quint in organs — 130
Quindetz — 130
Quintadena — 126, 137
   when invented — 137
   whence the name — 137
   whence the fifth — 125
   shape and proportion — 137
   pitch — 137
   three kinds — 137
   use — 137
   has two distinct sounds — 137
   is an octave lower than open pipes — 137
   suited for playing a pedal cantus firmus — 137
   Also called "Quint ad una" — 137
Quint-curtal — 38
Quintfloit — 132
Guitar — 4, 28, 53
   has 4 courses — 53
   how tuned — 53
   form and shape — 53

    Gebrauch. 53
Quinten im stimmen müssen schweben. 150
Quinten muß im stimmen etwas genommen vnd der Quarten zugelegt werden. 151

RA.
Racket. 3.39
  Neunfache Röhr. 39
  Resonantz. 39
Baß Racket. 39
  wie hoch vnnd niedrig am Thon. 24.40
  Lenge. 40
  Löcher. 40
  geben so viel Thon als Löcher. 40
  gebrauch. 40
  Im Baß anmütig zu hören. 40
Rancket in Orgeln. 126.147
  Grösse. 147
  Resonantz vnd Gebrauch. 147
RauschPfeiffe in Orgeln. 115.130
  derselben Baß. 130
  woher entstanden. 115.130
Rausch Quinta. 130
  warumb. 130

RE.
Rebecchino. 4.48
Recordor Instrumentum. 33
Regal. 3.7.72
  zweyerley. 72
  Besser als ein Clavicymbalum. 72
  gebrauch. 72
Regalwercks etliche arten. 73

Von Holtze. 73
Resonantz. 72.73
  woher der Nahme. 74
  sonderliche Art. 74
Verstimmen sich durch Hitze vnnd Kälte. 74.75
  warumb. 74.75
  woran gestimmet. 143
  wie zu stimmen. 148
Repetiren wz in Mixturen heisse. 131
Repetirende Zimbel. 131
Resonantz der Schnarrwercke rühret vom Mundstück her. 143

RO.
Rohrflöte. 126.141
  woher der Nahme. 141
  Gebrauch. 141
  zweyerley Art. 141
  Geben einen guten Bawrfloiten Baß. 141
Rohrschelle. 141
  woher der Nahme. 141
Röslichen. 4
Romanische Theorbe hat 6. Seiten Chor. 52

Ru.
RuckPositiff wenn erfunden. 115

SA.
Sackpfeiffe. 3.6.42.100
  Allerley Sorten: wie hoch vnd niedrig. 25
  derer Art. 42
  wie gestimmet. 42.43
  Mit zwey Stimmen. 43

use	53	sound	72, 73
Fifths must beat when tuning	150	whence the name	74
Fifths must beat flat and fourths must beat sharp	151	of a special kind	74
		heat and cold make them go out of tune	74, 75

RA

Rackett	3, 39	why	74, 75
nine-fold bore	39	how tuned	143
sound	39	how to tune	148
Bass Rackett	39	"Repeat:" what it means in mixtures	131
range	24, 40	Repeating Zimbel	131
length	40	Sound of reeds produced by their shallots	143
[finger]holes	40		
produce as many pitches as [finger]holes	40		

RO

use	40	Rohrfloite	126, 141
pleasant to listen to as a bass	40	whence the name	141
Ranket in organs	126, 147	use	141
size	147	two kinds	141
sound and use	147	produce a good Bauerfloit in the pedal	141
Rauschpfeiffe in organs	115, 130	Rohrschelle	141
in the pedal	130	whence the name	141
whence its origin	115, 130	Rattle	4
Rauschquinte	130	Roman theorbo has 6 courses of strings	52
why [so named]	130		

RE

Ru

Rebecchino	4, 48	Ruckpositiv, when discovered	116

SA

Recorder: instrument	33	Bagpipe	3, 6, 42, 100
Regal	3, 7, 72	a number of varieties: ranges	25
two meanings	72	kinds of them	42
better than a harpsichord	72	how tuned	42, 43
use	72	with two drones	43
Regals, a number of types	73		
of wood	73		

INDEX II.

jede vier Löcher. 43
Mit zwey Clavier Röhren. 43
Geben ein Bicinium. 43
Mit einem Blaßbalge. 43
Stimwerck derselben. 43
Sambuca 5
Satyrisch Pfeifflin. 83

SC.

Scala Musicalis durch die Orgel verbessert. 90
Schaffer Orgel. 3. 42
Schaffer Pfeiff.
   hat 2. Stimmen. 42
   Ist in den Obersten Löchern falsch vnd warumb. 42
Schalmeye. 3. 7. 36. 37
   Allerley Sort wie hoch vnd niedrig am Thon. 22
   Sind ein Thon höher als Zincken vnd Posaunen. 37
   Wie eine von der andern gestimmet. 37
Schalmeyen in Orgeln. 126. 145
Scharp in Orgeln. 131
   woher der Nahme. 131
Schellen. 4. 78
Scheitholtz. 57
   woher der Nahme. 57
   wie viel Seiten. 57
   wie gestimmet. 57
   wie geschlagen. 57
Schleiffladen. 108. 114
   Geben eine enderung in Stimmen. 108

Schlüssel Fiedel. 79
Schnarrwerck in Orgeln. 125
   Ist zweyerley. 126
   wenn erfunden. 116
   Viereckt zu Prag erfunden. 147
   Liebliches Resonantzes. 147
Schnarrwercken Stimmung. 148
Schreier Pfeiff. 42
   Gebrauch. 42
   wieviel Löcher. 42
   Resonantz vnd Thon. 42
Schryari. 3. 42
   wie hoch vnd niedrig am Thon. 24
   Geben so viel Thon als Löcher. 40
   Lenge. 42
   vnten offen. 42
Schwartzer Zinck. 3. 36
Schweben was bey den Orgelmachern bedeutet. 151
   woher der Nahme. 151
Schweinskopff Instr. 63
   Woher der Nahme. 63
Schweitzer Pfeiff. 35
   wie Intoniret. 35
   Kompt mit der Querpfeiff nicht vberein. 35
Schweitzer Pfeiff in Orgeln. 128
   woher den Nahmen. 128
   Resonantz. 128
   zweyerley art. 128
   Discant. 128
   Baß. 128
   Gebrauch. 128
   Oben gedeckt. 129

each with four [finger]holes	43
with two chanters	43
produce a bicinium	43
with a bellows	43
consort of them	43
Sambuca [dulcimer]	5
Panpipe	83

SC

Musical scale improved by means of the organ	90
Schafforgel	3, 42
Shepherd's pipe	[42]
has 2 drones	42
[notes from] upper holes are out of tune; why	42
Schalmei	3, 7, 36, 37
All varieties: ranges	22
are a step higher than cornetts and sackbutts	37
how one is tuned from another	37
Schalmei in organs	126, 145
Scharp in organs	131
whence the name	131
Bells (Schellen)	4, 78
Scheitholt	57
whence the name	57
how many strings	57
how tuned	57
how played	57
Slider chests	108, 114
produces a variety of stops	108
Keyed fiddle	79
Reeds in organs	125
two kinds	126
when invented	116
mitered invented at Prague	147
those having a gentle sound	147
Tuning reeds	148
SchreierPfeiff [Schryari]	42
use	42
how many holes	42
sound and pitch	42
Schryari	3, 42
ranges	24
produce only as many pitches as holes	40
length	42
open at the bottom	42
Cornetts [covered with] black [leather]	3, 36
Beating: what it means among organbuilders	151
whence the name	151
Pig's snout: Instr[ument]	63
whence the name	63
Swiss fife	35
its sound	35
not the same as the traverse flute	35
SchweitzerPfeiff in organs	128
whence the name	128
sound	128
two kinds	128
treble	128
bass	128
use	128
stopped at the top	129

zum langsamen Tact.	128	Sympathria der Seiten.	47
ohne Coleraturen.	128	der Pfeiffen in Orgeln.	47
Schwiegel.	34.77	Symphonia.	62

Schwiegel. 34.77
  wie hoch vnd niedrig am thon. 27.34
  wie lang. 34
  wieviel Löcher. 34
  Gebrauch. 34
Schwiegel in Orgeln. 133
  woher genennet. 133
  zweyerley Art. 133
  wenn erfunden. 133
  Resonantz. 133

SE.

Sedetz. 129
  wie eine müsse von der andern gestimmet werden. 19
Seiten aus Därmen oder Metall. 4.5
Semitonia aus dem genere Chromatico im Clavichordo augiret worden. 60
Semitonium Majus sol 5. Commata, Minus aber 4. halten. 66
Semitonia in Orgeln wenn erfunden. 95
  woraus erfunden. 90
Sexta bey den alten keine Consonantia. 101
Sexta Minor muß im stimmen rein seyn/ Major aber schweben. 152

SI.

Siebenderley Sorten vnd Bombarden. 13
Sesiott. 132

Symphonia. 62
Singel Corthol wie hoch vnd niedrig am Thon. 23
Singekugel. 79
Singen per choros. 90
Sistrum. 4

SO.

Soldaten Trummel. 35.77.79
Sonderliche Art einer Baß Geige. 45
Sordoni: Sordunt. 3.39
  derer Resonantz. 39
  Löcher. 39
  Länge. 39
  geben so viel Thon als Löcher. 40
  hoher vnd niedriger Thon. 23
Sordunen Baß. 39
  wie niedrig am Thon. 39
Sordunen in Orgeln. 126.146
Sorten von Stimmen. 12.13
  von Querflotten dreyerley. 13
  von Doppionen dreyerley. 13
  von Bassandlis dreyerley. 13
  von { Posaunen, Racket, Schriari } Viererley. 13
  von { Fagotten, Sordunen, Krumbhörnern, Corna Muse } fünfferley. 13
  Von Blockflotten achterley. 13.33
  Intonation. 146

Form

INDEX II.

for a slow tempo	128
without rapid embellishments	128
Tabor pipe [Schwiegel]	34, 77
range	21, 34
how long	34
how many holes	34
use	34
Schwiegel in organs	133
whence the name	133
two kinds	133
when invented	133
sound	133

SE

Sedetz	129
how one must be tuned from another	19[?]
Strings of gut or metal	4, 5
Semitones of the chromatic genus developed in the clavichord	60
A major semitone should contain 5 commas, a minor 4	66
Semitones in organs: when invented	95
how developed	90
Sixth not a consonance in ancient times	101
Minor sixth must be tuned pure; major, however, must beat	152

SI

Seven varieties of shawms	13
Siefloit	132
Sympathetic vibration of strings	47

of pipes in organs [?]	47[?]
Symphonia	62
Single Corthol, range	23
Jew's Harp (Singekugel)	79
Polychoral singing	90
Rattle [Sistrum]	4

SO

Military drum	35, 77, 79
Bass viol of a special kind	45
Sordoni, Sorduns	3, 39
their sound	39
holes	39
length	39
produce as many pitches as holes	40
at higher and lower pitches	23
Sordun Bass	39
its lowest pitch	39
Sorduns in organs	126, 146
Sizes of instruments	12, 13
of traverse flutes, 3	13
of Doppioni	13
of Bassanelli, 3	13
of Sackbutts, 4	13
of Racketts, 4	13
of Schryari, 4	13
of Curtals, 5	13
of Sorduns, 5	13
of Krummhorns, 5	13
of Cornamuses, 5	13
[of Shawms,	12, 13]
of Recorders, 8	13, 33
Pitch [of Sordun in organs]	146

INDEX II.

Form vnd Grösse.	146
Resonantz vnd Gebrauch.	146

SP.
Spaenbälge wenn angefangen zu machen.	116
Spielflotten in Orgeln.	126.135
woher der Nahme.	135
Spinetto.	5.62
wie gestimmet.	62
Spitzflott in Orgeln.	135
Vnterscheid von den Gembshörnern.	135
woher der Nahme.	135
zweyerley Art.	135
wenn sie erfunden.	135
Springladen.	107.108
wenn/ worauß vnd warumb erfunden.	107.108.114

ST.
Stamentien Pfeiffen.	34.77
Lenge.	34
wird vnten mit einem Finger regieret.	34
Stille Krumbhörner.	41.39
Stille Zincken.	36
Sanfft vnd lieblich zu hören.	36
Stimmen in Orgeln von 1. oder 2. fuß Thon von den Italis nicht groß geachtet.	140
Stimmung der gedackten.	150
der Pfeiffen.	149
der Regal.	149
nach den Proportionibus.	156.157
wie zu stimmen.	153
von welchē clave anzufangē.	153.156
dreyerley Art.	153.154
Storti.	40
Strohfiedel.	4.79
StrohPfeiffe.	78

Su.
SubBaß.	132
SubBaß de Gamba.	46
Gebrauch.	46
Suiflott oder Sieflit.	132
Super Gedacklein.	140
dienet zur Variation.	140
zum Discant.	140
Resonantz einer Plockflotten ehnlich.	140
Super octava.	129
Super octävlein.	129
Super Rohrflötlin.	141

TA.
Tabella universalis aller Instrumenten Intonatiō höhe vn tieffe rc.	18.19 vnnd den fünff folgenden Blättern.
Tabella Musicalischer Instrument abtheilung.	10
Tambuer de Biscaye.	29

TE.
Tenor Geige mit 4. Stieen.	48
Tenorista wie hoch singen könne.	17
Tertia bey den alten keine Consonantia.	101
Tertiæ Majores müssen rein gestimmet werden.	150
Müssen richter seyn im stimen.	151
Tertia minor muß in der Quinta vnrein seyn.	151

Testudo

INDEX II. 227

Shape and size ["]	146	three kinds	153, 154
Sound and use ["]	146	Storti	40
		Straw fiddle	4, 79
		Straw pipe	78

SP

Wedge bellows, when they began to be made	116
Spielfloiten[6] in organs	126, 135
whence the name	135
Spinet	5, 62
how tuned	62
Spitzfloit in organs	135
difference from Gemshorns	135
whence the name	135
two kinds	135
when invented	135
Spring chest	107, 108
when, from what, and why invented	107, 108, 114

Su.

SubBass	132
SubBass viol	46
its use	46
Suifloit or Sieflit	132
Super Gedäcktlein	140
provides variety	140
[played] in the treble	140
sound is similar to a Blockfloit	140
Super octava	129
Little Superoctave	129
Little Rohrflöte	141

ST

Stamentien Pfeiff [tabor-pipe]	34, 77
length	34
controlled underneath by a thumb-hole	34
Mute Krummhorn	41, 39
Mute Cornett	36
gentle and delicate sound	36
Organ stops at 1' or 2' not prized by the Italians	140
Tuning of Gedackts	150
of pipes	149
of Regals	149
tempered tuning	156, 157
how to tune	153
from which note to begin	153, 156

TA.

Universal Table of all instruments: pitch, range, etc.	18-19
and the five following leaves	
Table of musical instruments by categories	10
Basque Tambour	29 [79]

TE

Tenor Violin with 4 strings	48
Tenor, how high one can sing	17
Thirds not a consonance in the past	101
Major thirds must be tuned pure	150
must be guides when tuning	151
Minor thirds must be impure against their fifths	151

---

6. There is no mention of the Spielfloit on p. 126.

Testudo. 4.6.49
Tetrachorda durch die Orgel abgeschaffet. 90
Tetrachorda der Alten. 94
   Hypaton. 94
   Meson. 94
   Hyperbolæon. 94
   Synemmeνon. 91.94
   deſſen claves. 91
   wenn erfunden. 94

TH.

Theorbe. 4.6.27.52
   von 14. auch 16. Seiten. 52
   hat zwey Hälſe. 52
   Einer Baßlauten gleich. 52
   Seiten. 52
   wie geſtimmet. 27.52
   Gebrauch. 52
   Ohne Coleraturen. 52
   hat am langen Halſe 8. Seiten. 52
   wird ein Diſcant oder Tenor darein geſungen. 52
   wird von der Lauten vnterſchieden. 51
   Iſt zweyerley. 27.52
   Romaniſche hat 6. Seiten Chor. 52
   Padoaniſche hat 8. Seiten Chor. 52
Thon der Inſtrument aſpectu Longitudinis. 6
   Latitudinis. 6.7
   Profunditatis. 6.7
Thon zweyerley: Chor vnd Cammerthon. 14
Thon in welchen Inſtrumenten beſtendig. 6
   Sowol in Orgeln als andern Inſtrumenten vngleich. 14
Thon in tertia inferiore in Clavicymbeln vnd floiten lieblicher. 16
   In Italia vnd Catholiſchen Capellen ſehr gebreuchlich. 16
ThunBaß. 132
   woher der Nahme. 132

TI.

Tibia. 3
   utricularis. 3.6.42
   Transverſa.
   Trover 2. 3.35
Tieffe eines Baſſiſten in Fürſtlichen Capellen. 17
Tympaniſchiza. 5.57
   woraus erfunden. 57
   hat eine Seite/bißweilen mehr. 57.5
   Lenge. 59.5
   Reſonantz. 59.5
   Gebrauch im Ionico vnd Hypojonico modo. 58
Tympanum. 4.77
Tympanum Hieronymi. 77
Tintinnabulum. 4

TR.

Tremulant wenn erfunden. 117
Triangel. 4.78
Trigonia Pyramis. 57
Trigonus Inſtruments. 57
Trombone. 2
Trommel. 2.32

Trom-

Testudo (Lute)	4, 6, 49
Tetrachord done away with by the organ	90
The ancient tetrachords	94
Hypaton	94
Meson	94
Hyperbolæon	94
Synemmenon	91, 94
its notes	91
when invented	94

TH

Theorba	4, 6, 27, 52
has 14, also 16 strings	52
has two necks	52
similar to a bass lute	52
strings	52
how tuned	27, 52
use	52
[played] without divisions	52
has 8 strings on the longer neck	52
tenor or descant voice sung against it	52
distinguished from the lute	51
two kinds	27, 52
the Roman has 6 string courses	52
the Paduan has 8 string courses	52
Pitch of instruments in respect to length	6
width	6, 7
depth	6, 7
Pitch, two kinds: choir and chamber pitch	14
Which instruments stable in pitch	6
Pitch differs in organs as well as other instruments	14
Harpsichords and flutes more pleasant tuned a third lower	16
This is very common in Italy and in Catholic chapels	16
ThunBass	132
whence the name	132

TI

Tibia	3
utricularis [i.e., bagpipe]	3, 6, 42
transverse	[3]
traversa	3, 35
Low pitch of a bass in princely chapels	17
Tympanischiza [marine trumpet]	5, 57
whence developed	57
has one string, at times more	5, 57
length	5, 59
sound	5, 59
used for ionic and hypoionic modes	58
Tympanum	4, 77
Tympanum Hieronymi	77
Tintinnabulum	4

TR

Tremulant, when invented	117
Triangle	4, 78
Triangular pyramid	57
Trigonus Instruments (?)	57(?)
Trombone	2
Trommet	2, 32

Trometten an der Mensur erlengert.	33
Wie hoch vnd niedrig am Thon.	20
Sind ChorThon.	33
lang von Past.	33
Trommeten gleich einem Posthorn oder Schlangen.	33
Trommeten Krumbbogen.	33
Trommeten Baß im C ad modum Hypolonicum gestimmet.	33
Trommet in Orgeln.	126
Trummel.	4. 77
Trumpel.	78
Trumscheid.	57

T V.

Tuba.	2
Tuba Hieronymi.	77
Derer bedeutung.	77
Türcken achten keine Music.	83
Türckische Instrument.	79
Zum rechten Chor-Thon vnnd Chormaß ein Pfeifflin zu machen.	231. 232

VE.

Verenderung vnnd vermehrung der Stimmen in Alten Orgeln.	113
Vermehrung der Clavier im Clavi-Chordio.	60
Verstimmung der besaiteten Instrumēt.	144
Verstimmung der Schnarwercke/ woher im Winter vnd Sommer.	143
Verstimmen der Pfeiffen woher.	150
Vestigia der alten Harmoniæ.	100. 101

VI.

Violino.	4. 48
Viole de Gamba.	4
Woher den Nahmen.	44
Wie viel Sorten.	25
Haben 6. Säiten.	44
Wie gestimmet.	25. 44
Sind dreyerley Art.	45
Etliche mit 3. 4. vnd 5. Säiten.	45
Resonantz lieblich.	44
SubBass derselben.	46
Zum generi Chromatico bequē.	65
Viola, Vivola de bracio.	4. 48
Woher der Nahme.	48
Wie viel Sorten: vnd wie zu stimen.	26
Violino da Brazzo.	4. 48
Violetta picciola.	48
Viola de Bastarda.	4. 47
Woher der Nahme.	47
Gebrauch.	47
wie vnterschiedlich zustimmen.	26. 47
Hat gemeine Säiten/ Sechs: Stählene/ achte.	47
Violono.	44
Violuntze.	43
Vielstimmige Instrument.	7
Virginale.	5. 62
Erstlich aus dē Psalterio erdacht.	76
was in Engeland.	62

VN.

Vniversal Musici in Welschland.	11
Vnivoca Instrumenta.	7
Vn Tambour de Biscaye.	79
Vnterscheid zu reden von Fußthon vnd auff Fußthon.	125
Vnterscheid zwischen Chor vnnd CammerThon.	14

Trumpets' dimensions increased	33
range	20
sounds at choir pitch	33
long ones from strips of bark	33
Trumpets like a posthorn or a snake	33
Trumpets' crook	33
Trumpets' with a fundamental of C, tuned in hypoionian mode	33
Trumpet in organs	126
Drum (Trummel)	4, 77
Drum (Trumpel)	78
Marine Trumpet (Trumscheid)	57

TU

Tuba (trumpet)	2
Tuba Hieronymi	77
its meaning	77
Moors prize no music	83
Moorish instruments	79
How to make a small pipe to set correct pitch	231, 232

VE

Change and increase of stops in old organs	113
Extension of keyboards in the clavichord	60
Stringed instruments going out of tune	144
Why reeds go out of tune in winter and summer	143
Why pipes go out of tune	150
Vestiges of ancient harmony	100, 101

VI

Violin	4, 48
Viol di Gamba	4
whence the name	44
How many varieties	25
have 6 strings	44
how tuned	25, 44
there are three kinds	45
some with 3, 4, and 5 strings	45
tone is pleasant	44
sub-bass viols	46
suited to the chromatic genus	65
Viola, Vivola di bracio	4, 48
whence the name	48
how many kinds, and how to tune	26
Violino da Brazzo	4, 48
Violetta picciola	48
Viola de Bastarda	4, 47
Whence the name	47
Use	47
various ways of tuning	26, 47
has six ordinary strings and eight of steel	47
Violono	44
Violuntze	43
polyphonic instrument	7
Virginal	5, 62
originated from the psaltery	76
the English name	62

UN

Universal musicians in Italy	11
Univoca instruments	7
Tambour de Biscaye	79
Distinction in speaking of pitch of open and stopped pipes	125
Difference between choir and chamber pitch	14

V O.
Voces Muſicales durch die Orgel erfunden.	90
Vollſtimmige Inſtrument.	7
Vortheil eine Flöite jünger oder gröber zu Stimmen.	34

VV.
Wachtelbeinlin.	78
Waldflöit in Orgeln.	132
an welchem Ort gebreuchlich.	132
wird repetiret.	132
Was eigentlich Inſtrument vnnd Inſtrumentiſt ſey:	11
Was in lieſſerung der Orgeln in acht zu nehmen.	158

VV E.
Wäſterwälder Schäffer.	33
Wäſterwälder Trommet.	33
Weiber Leyre.	49
Wellbretter.	106
Wenn die Semitonia b. vnnd ♯ erfunden.	91

VV I.
Wie die Orgelmacher die Schnarwerck zur rechten Intonation bringen.	41
Wie viel Commata ein bund auff der Lauten vnd Viola de Gamba in ſich begreifft.	66
Windlade / darin Cancellen, Ventil vnd Stöhn Feddern.	106

VV O.
Wolff was im Stimmen.	155

ZI.
Zinck Schwartz vnd Krumb.	3. 36
Gelb vnd Gerad.	3. 35
Stille.	36
Wie viel Thon.	36
Wie Hoch vnnd Niedrig am Thon.	22
Jünger vnd gröber zu Stimmen.	35
Kleine Zincken.	36
Wie Intoniret.	36
Zincken in Orgeln.	126. 146
Zingel Corthol.	38
Zimbel.	131
Klingende Zimbel.	131
Repetirende Zimbel.	131
Zimbel-Baß.	131
Zimbel kan für ſich alleine nicht gebraucht werden.	131

VO
Church modes invented with the help of the organ — 90
Polyphonic instrument — 7
Advantage of tuning a recorder sharp or flat — 34

W
Fowler's pipe — 78
Waldflöit in organs — 132
    where in use — 132
    repeats — 132
How 'Instrument' and Instrumentist are to be understood — 11
What to consider when contracting for an organ — 158

WE
Wästerwälder shepherds — 33
Wästerwälder trumpet — 33
Women's lyre — 49
Rollerboards — 106
When the accidentals b♭ and e♭ were invented — 91

WI
How organbuilders voice reed stops properly — 41

How many commas a fret encompasses on the lute and viola di gamba — 66
Windchest, with channels, pallets and pallet-springs — 106

WO
Wolf: what it means in tuning — 155

ZI
Zinck, black and curved — 3, 36
    yellow and straight — 3, 35
    mute — 36
    range — 36
    ranges of various types — 22
    tuning sharp and flat — 35
    small Zincks — 36
    how tuned — 36
Zinck in organs — 126, 146
Zingel (i.e., single) Corthol — 38
Zimbel — 131
    Klingende Zimbel — 131
    Repeating Zimbel — 131
    Zimbel in the pedal — 131
Zimbel cannot be used by itself — 131

NB.

DJeweil in diesem Tomo Secundo/zum offtern des rechten Chor-Thons erwehnet: vnd ich befunden/ das an vielen örtern/ auch wol in sehr grossen vnd vornehmen Städten/vnd doselbst befindlichen herzlichen Orgelwercken/ die rechte Chormaß/ wornach sich die Menschen Stimmen/so wol als die Instrumenta richten müssen/ nicht: sondern der Tonus derselben entweder zu hoch oder zu niedrig: Vnd solches einer von den fürnembsten Defecten der Orgeln ist. So hab ich vff allerley Mittel vnd Wege gedacht/wie vnd welcher gestalt solchem abzuhelffen/vnd einem jeden/ so wol Orgelmachern als Organisten der rechte Tonus vnd Chormaß bekandt würde: Wornach ein Orgelmacher sich richten/ die Newe Orgeln nach demselben intoniren, die Alten aber Renoviren vnnd Corrigiren könte. Derowegen hierunter einen richtigen Abriß der rechten Chormaß setzen wollen; von dem c̄, so nach Orgelmacher Mensur ein halben Fuß Thon (wenn das grosse C. von 8. Fussen ist) bringet.

C 8 Fueß/   c 4 Fueß/   c̄ 2 Fueß/   c̿ 1. Fueß/   c̿ ½ Fueß/

Nach welcher Mensuer etliche Pfeifflin zur rechten Chormaß/ durch eine gantze Octav, gar just vnd rein können gearbeitet werden: Deren sich/neben den Orgelmachern/ auch die Organisten vnd Cantores zum anstimmen zugebrauchen.

Inmassen dan auch in folgendem Tractat von der **Orgeln Verdingnüß/ Baw vnd Lieferung** sol angezeiget werden: Welcher gestalt man mit gar geringer Müh/ auch ohne sonderbahren kosten/ eine Orgel/ so wol auch Clavi-Cymbel vnd Instrument entweder vmb einen Tonum oder Semitonium Höher oder Niedriger/zur rechten Chormaß bringen könne.

Welches alles dann ein jeder Orgelmacher (die ich wegen jhrer Kunst sehr liebe/venerire vnd jhnen alles Liebes vnd Guttes gönne vnd wünsche) im besten vnd nicht zum ergesten von mir auffnehmen vnd verstehen wolle.

Denn was ich an einem vnd anderm Ort/bevorab pag. 159. 160. erinnert/ desselben hat sich kein rechtschaffener Orgermacher/ Sondern allein die Hümpler vnd Stümpler/ die noch nicht eine Pfeiffe recht anzurichten gelernet/ vnnd flugs Meister spielen wollen/ anzunehmen. Sintemahl ich wol weiß/ was von dieser Kunst/ so auch in Warheit mit vnterhohe Künste zu rechnen/ zu halten sey: Darvon vielleicht an eim andern Ort weitleufftiger zu tractiren, sich gute gelegenheit offeriren könte.

Gg ij   Pfeiff-

N.B

he matter of correct pitch has often been mentioned hither and yon in this second volume. I have discovered that, even in splendid organs found in large and distinguished cities, the proper standard pitch adopted by both human voices and instruments is incorrect; their pitch is either too high or too low. This is one of the primary shortcomings in organs. Thus I have pondered all the ways and means by which this can be rectified; how to make the correct pitch known to one and all, both organbuilders as well as organists; how an organbuilder may be guided in setting the pitch of new organs, as well as renovating and correcting old ones. Therefore I have decided to place below an accurate sketch that provides organbuilders with the correct measurement for c''',[1] the six-inch-long pipe above an 8' C.

$$C = 8' \qquad c = 4' \qquad c' = 2' \qquad c'' = 1' \qquad c''' = \tfrac{1}{2}'$$

Following these measurements, an entire octave of pipes may be produced quite precisely and accurately at the correct pitch. This is to be used not only by organbuilders, but also by organists and cantors, for the purpose of tuning.

Furthermore, the treatise to follow concerning *Contracting for organs, construction and delivery*[2] will indicate how, with little effort or excessive cost, to shift an organ, harpsichord or *Instrument*[3] either a whole- or half-step higher or lower to the correct pitch.

I trust that all organbuilders (whom I greatly prize and admire for their art, and for whom I have nothing but the very best wishes) will accept all this in good faith and without resentment.

For what I have noted here and there, in particular on pp. 159-60, applies not to decent organbuilders, but rather only to bunglers and amateurs who have never learned how to produce a proper pipe, and merely want to play at mastery. Indeed, I know very well what to expect from this art, which is truly to be considered among the fine arts; perhaps I will treat this matter elsewhere in greater detail, should the opportunity arise.

---

1. The original print reads c"; the context suggests this is either a mistake or a fault in the type.
2. This treatise survives as a manuscript, entitled *Kurtzer Bericht, waß beÿ überlieffrung einer Klein und grosverfertigten Orgell zu observiren*, now in the Herzog August Bibliothek, Wolfenbüttel, Germany. For an English translation of the treatise, see: Vincent Panetta, "An Early Handbook for Organ Inspection: the 'Kurtzer Bericht' of Michael Praetorius and Esaias Compenius," in: *The Organ Yearbook*, 1990, pp. 5-33. See also: Vincent J. Panetta, Jr., "Praetorius, Compenius, and Werckmeister: A Tale of Two Treatises," in: *Church, Stage, and Studio: Music and Its Contexts in Seventeenth-Century Germany* (Ann Arbor: Research Press [c.1990]), pp. 67-85.
3. a virginal; see *Syntagma musicum II*, p. 62, as well as Theatrum Instrumentorum, Plate XIV.

Pfeifflin zur Chormaß.

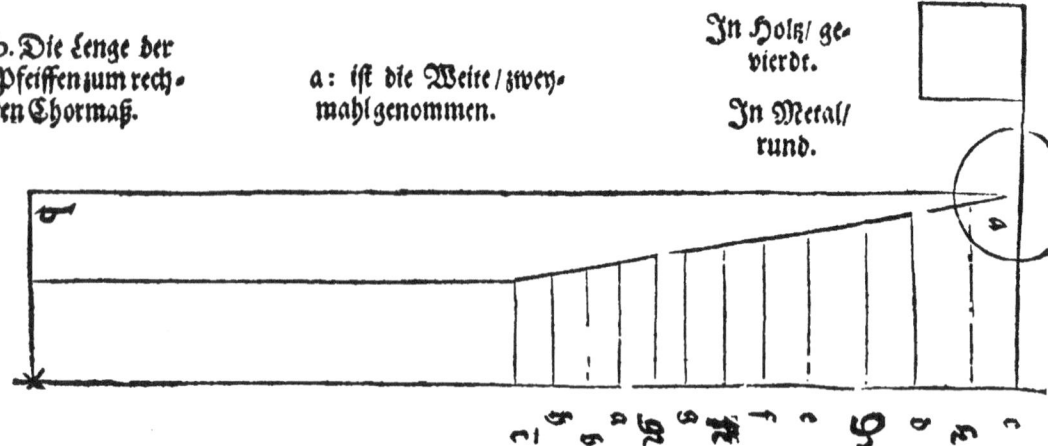

b. Die Lenge der Pfeiffen zum rechten Chormaß.

a: ist die Weite / zweymahl genommen.

In Holtz / gevierdt.

In Metall / rund.

Auch halte ich vor meine Wenigkeit kein besser Instrument, den rechten Thon zuerfahren / als eine Posaune / sonderlich die vor der zeit vnd noch / zu Nürnberg gefertiget seyn: Daß man nemblich den Zug vmb 2. Finger breit vom ende außziehe / so gibt es gar recht vnd just / in rechter Chormasse / das

alamire im Tenor.

Dieweil die Cornet, sonderlich / vnd auch die Flöiten leichtlich vberblasen / so wol / die Fagot vnd Dolcian, nach dem sie berühret seyn / bald Niedriger bald Höher intonirt werden können: Vnd man also sich darauff nicht zuverlassen hat. Derowegen dann auch in die Regalia, so vnter meine Hände gerahten / Ich ein Pfeifflin zur rechten Intonation des c. oder f. oder g. einrichten lassen / darmit man allzeit die Regalia oder andere Instrumenta pennata nach solchem Pfeifflein stimmen vnd einziehen könne. Dieweil man doch nimmermehr ein Pfeifflein mit dem Winde vnd anblasen des Mundes / so gewis intoniren kan / alß mit den BlaseBälgen des Regals / welche den
Wind allzeit gleich halten / vnd nicht falliren
können.

Ad fol.

A small pipe at the correct pitch

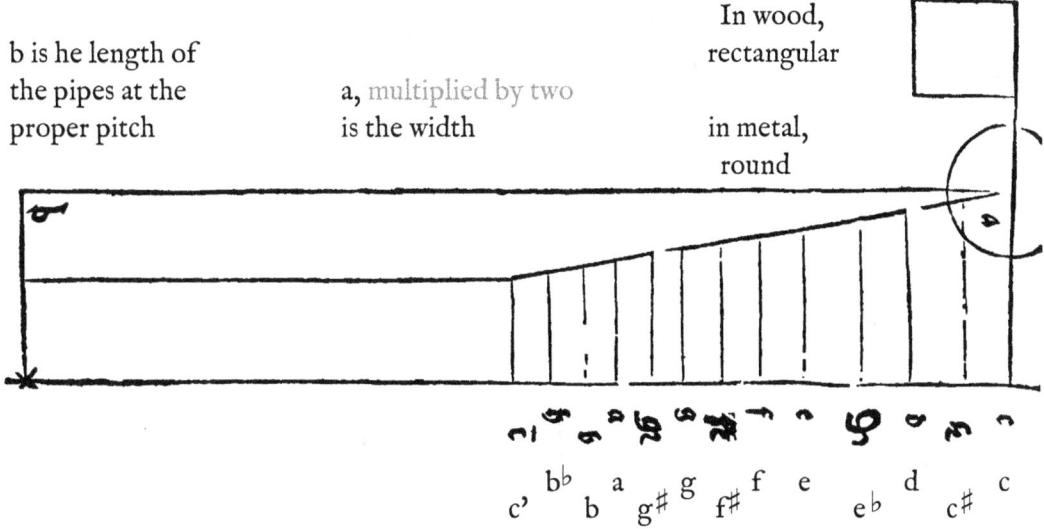

b is he length of
the pipes at the
proper pitch

a, multiplied by two
is the width

In wood,
rectangular

in metal,
round

c' bb a g f e d c
 b g# f# eb c#

In all modesty, I consider that there is no better instrument from which to determine the proper pitch than a trombone made in Nuremberg, both at present as well as in the past. Drawing out the slide two finger-widths from the end will produce tenor a la-mi-re, at just the proper pitch.

a la-mi-re in the tenor:

Since cornets in particular but also flutes, overblow easily, and bassoons and dolcians sound sharp or flat, depending on what fingerings are used, one cannot depend on them. Therefore I have also had a small pipe installed in the regals that have come into my hands, to sound the correct pitch for c or f or g. Regals and the various plucked stringed instruments can then always be tuned according to such a small pipe. For purposes of tuning, no pipe winded by human breath can ever be as precise as the bellows of a regal, which can supply steady wind without wavering.

Ad fol. 170. sol auch die Disposition nachfolgender Orgel/ referiret werden.

Orgel zu S. Lambrecht in Lüneburg / hat
60. Stimmen vnd drey Manual Clavier.

Mittel oder GroßWerck : zum Mitlern Clavier :
Hat 13. Stimmen.

1.	Principal.	16 Fueß.	22.	Feldpfeiff.	1½.
2.	Gedact.	16 Fueß.	23.	Zimbel.	
3.	Octava.	8. Fueß.	24.	Trummet.	8.
4.	Iula oder Spitzflöit.	8.	25.	Regal.	8.
5.	Querpfeiff.	8.	26.	Krumbhorn.	8.
6.	Octava.	4.	27.	Zinck halbirt.	8.
7.	Spillpfeiff.	4.			
8.	Flöite.	4.			

RückPositieff.
Hat 15. Stimmen.

9.	SpitzQuinta.	3.
10.	Octava.	2.
11.	Rußpfeiff.	
12.	Zimbel.	
13.	Mixtur.	

28.	Principal.	8.
29.	Quintadehna.	8.
30.	Gedact.	8.
31.	Blockflöit.	4.
32.	Holflöit.	4.
33.	Quintflöit.	3.
24.	Octava.	2.
35.	SedetzenQuint.	1½.
36.	Seiflöit.	1.
37.	Repetirend Zimbel.	
38.	Scharp.	
39.	Mixtur.	
40.	Regal.	
41.	Schalmey.	
42.	Baarpfeiff.	

OberWerck : zum Obern Clavier.
Hat 14. Stimmen.

14.	Principal.	8 Fueß.
15.	Hellpfeiff.	8.
16.	Querpfeiff.	8. Halbirt.
17.	Quintflöit.	3.
18.	Nasat.	3.
19.	Gedact.	2.
20.	Gemßhorn.	1.
21.	Waldflöitlin	1.

The stoplist of the following organ should be
inserted at p. 170.

The Organ at St. Lambrecht in Lüneburg
has 60 stops and three manual keyboards.[1]

Middle- or Great-Werck, on the Middle Manual,
has 13 stops.

1. Principal	16'
2. Gedact	16'
3. Octava	8'
4. Jula or Spitzflöit	8'
5. Querpfeiff	8'
6. Octava	4'
7. Spillpfeiff	4'
8. Flöite	4'
9. SpitzQuinta	3'
10. Octava	2'
11. Rauschpfeiff	
12. Zimbel	
13. Mixtur	

OberWerck, on the upper Manual, has 14 stops.

14. Principal	8'
15. Hellpfeiff	8'
16. Querpfeiff, half-compass	8'
17. Quintflöit	3'
18. Nasat	3'
19. Gedact	2'
20. Gemsshorn	1'
21. Little Waldflöte	1'
22. Feldpfeiff	½'
23. Zimbel	
24. Trummet	8'
25. Regal	8'
26. Krumbhorn	8'
27. Zinck, half-compass	8'

Rückpositieff
has 15 stops

28. Principal	8'
29. Quintadehna	8'
30. Gedact	8'
31. Blockflöit	4'
32. Holflöit	4'
33. Quintflöit	3'
34. Octava	2'
35. SedetzenQuint	1½'
36. Sciflöit [i.e., Sifflöit]	1'
37. Repeating Zimbel	
38. Scharp	
39. Mixtur	
40. Regal	
41. Schalmey	
42. Baarpfeiff	

---

1. Praetorius, however, lists only 59 stops; he gives no 4' stops on the Oberwerck. The Lambertikirche was torn down in 1859, together with this organ, built by Christian Bockelmann in 1610, of its time one of the largest instruments in Germany.

Pedal-Bässe:		Mixtur.	
17. Stimmen.		55. Posaunen.	16.
43. Principal-Baß	16. Fueß.	56. Krumhorn.	16.
44. Untersatz.	16.	57. Trommetten.	8.
45. Octava.	8.	58. Schalmey.	4.
46. Gedact.	8.	59. Cornet.	2.
47. Super-Octava.	4.		
48. Nachthorn.	4.	Tremulant.	
49. Spitz-Quint.	3.	1. ⎫ Ventiel ⎧ Oberwerck.	
50. Gemßhorn.	2.	2. ⎬ zum ⎨ Mittelwerck.	
51. BawrFlöit.	1.	3. ⎭ ⎩ Pedael.	
52. Rauschpfeiff.		1 Coppel zu beyden Manualen.	
53. Zimbel.		2. Coppel/ Pedal zu Rückpositiff.	

ERRATA IN II. TOMO.

Zweyerley Mängel sind leider alhier verhanden.

1. Der Erste vnd nicht der geringste ist: daß die Paginæ nicht allein auff etlichen örtern nicht numeriret, vnd die Zahl auff vielen Blettern außlauterm vnfleiß genzlich aussen gelassen / sondern auch vnrichtig gesetzet ist.

Wie vom Bogen C.ij an/ so mit 19 bezeichnet/ biß auff den Bogen F. welches der rechten Ordnung nach 41. sein solte/ gnugsamb befindlich. Welchen Errorem der günstige Leser/wegen des Indicis/ so auff die richtige vnd natürliche Ordnung der Bletter gerichtet/ vnbeschwehrt also bald zum anfang selber Corrigiren wolle/ vnd die Zahlen/so zwischen C ij vnd F seyn für Falsch vnd Nichtig halten.

Zahlen / so aussen gelassen : sind/

B.iij,13. L,81. L ij.facie 2.84.
L iij, 85. L iiij fac. 2. 88.   O iiij. fac. 2. 112.
A a, iij, 189.   A a. iiij fac. 2. 192.

Zahlen so verfälschet : sind/

C. 1. fac. 2. 28. für 18.   F, 30. pro 41.
F iij, fac. 2. 38. pro 46.   F iiij, f. 2. 48. pro 47.

G iiij f. 2.

Low stops in the Pedal
17 stops.

43. Principal-Bass	16'
44. Untersatz	16'
45. Octava	8'
46. Gedact	8'
47. Super-Octava	4'
48. Nachthorn	4'
49. Spitz-Quint	3'
50. Gemsshorn	2'
51. BawrFlöit	1'
52. Rauschpfeiff	
53. Zimbel	
54. Mixtur	
55. Posaunen	16'
56. Krumhorn	16'
57. Trommetten	8'
58. Schalmey	4'
59. Cornet	2'

Tremulant

1. ⎫ Ventils ⎧ Oberwerck
2. ⎬   for   ⎨ Middle-Werk
3. ⎭ the   ⎩ Pedal

1. Coupler between both manuals [?]
2. Rückpositiff/Pedal Coupler

ERRATA IN VOL. II

[Praetorius's corrections and additions have been entered at the appropriate places in the text.]

G iiij fac. 2. 54. pro 56.　　　　I iij, 62. pro 70.
K ij, 57. pro 75.　　　　K iij 88. pro 78.
N iiij, 105. pro 103.　　　　P iij, 114. pro 118.
Q iij, 128. pro 126.　　　　S j, 158. pro 138.

2. Der ander Mangel ist:

Das bißweilen nicht allein Wörter aussen gelassen / besondern auch die Buchstaben vnd Distinctiones verwechselt / versetzet oder gar mangeln. Von denen/ allein die vornembste alhier verzeichnet / die andern vnd geringere wolle der gutherzige Leser im lesen selber Corrigiren.

Pagina. 4. l. 6. sol heissen / Clavitympanum. l. 9. Tintinnabula.
p. 10. Arpichordum.　　　P. 14. l. 30. Bassanelli. Bombardoni.
pag. 36. l. 4. Cornetti Curvi.
pag. 42. SchäfferPfeiffen.
pag. 52. GeigenSaiten.　　　p. 54. Orpheoréon.
p. 56. ἁρπάζω.　　　p. 58. Saiten.
p. 59. l. 7. vnd bleiben die　　　p. 61. l. 17. vielen vnd offtern.
p. 66. l. 5. Commata.　　l. 13. nemen vnd geben kan.
p. 67. l. 15. da in einer Symphony.　　p. 74. l. 8. muß ich auch hinzusaß.
p. 75. l. 6. æs cyprium veró.　　p. 76. l. 12. Decachordum.
p. 78. l. 10. Cymbalum.　　p. 89. l. 17. Salaria.
p. 97. l. 3. bloß mit einer Stimm.
p. 100. l. 2. der gepreste Wind.
p. 108. davon im 14. Cap.
　　　l. 12. vnd durchstechen / sehr gut.
p. 113. l. 27. Canaal.
p. 120. l. 20. sich nach erfahrnen.　l. 23. beydes von.
p. 123. lin. 23. SubPrincipaln.
p. 125. l. 4. 5. durch der Quintadehnen engigkeit.
p. 129. l. 26. Ordnung / das Groß Octav,
p. 131. lin. 4. repetiret: auch wol in grossen.
p. 137. lin. ult. gearbeitet werden kan.
p. 144. lin. 7. contrahiret, vnd sich
p. 147. lin. 26. im starcken laut.
p. 150. lin. 6. denn je niedriger: l. 20. er sie gar zu sehr.
170. Do hinein gehört die Disposition der Orgel zu S. Lambrecht / so fol.
　　　zu befinden.

　　　　　　　　　　　　　　　　　　p. 18)

[Praetorius's corrections and additions have been entered at the appropriate places in the text.]

236

p. 189. lin. penultima.   Schloß Capell zu Schöningen/durch
p. 199. fac. 1. nach der 26. Zeilen Einzusetzen (etliche machen auch nur 2. falten an
  Blaßbälge/ welche auch gar gut seyn.)
  f. 2. lin. 13. pro Nasath, liß/Querflöit.
  lin. 28. pro Holquint/ liß Nasath.
pag. 200. Bock Tremulant.
p. 201. lin. 64. noch eins zum Brust Positiff.
p. 204. Dalricus Co. Vitruvius. Amphion. Boëthius. Guido Aretinus. Cornet. Ludovicus Zacconi. Adrianus Turnebus. Ioannes Bassanus.
p. 207. BA.──Baarpfeiffen. 126. 147   BE. Beschreibung M. Instrument. 1
p. 208. lin. 40. 341. Chormasse.
  209. lin. 29. in genere Diatonico.   lin. 39. Dieses Enharm.
  210. lin. 21. Concertiren.   lin. 27. Floridus.   lin. 40. torti, Storti.
  211. lin. 43. Doppel Fagot. 38.

Hierauff folget nun der Sechste Theil: darinnen aller Musicalischen/ so wol jetziger unserer zeit Instrumenten, alß auch etlicher wenig der Alten Instrumenten, so viel man darvon nachrichtung haben können/ eigentlicher Abriß vnd Abconterfeyung eines jeden insonderheit/ nach der Grösse/ Lenge/ Dicke/ gar eigentlich nach dem Maßstabe abgetheilet vnd gezeichnet zubefinden ist.

VI. Theil.
Sciagraphia, seu
Theatrum Instrumentorum.

[Praetorius's corrections and additions have been entered
at the appropriate places in the text.]

Hereupon follows Part Six, in which is to be found an accurate sketch and
depiction, drawn according to the scale provided, of all musical instruments, both
those of our present time as well as a limited number of old instruments,
to provide some report about them,
in particular their size, length,
and width.

Dieses ist die rechte Lenge vnd Maß eines halben Schuhes oder Fusses nach dem Maßstabe/ welches ein viertel von einer Braunschweigischen Ellen: Vnd nach diesem sind alle Abrisse nachgesetzter Instrumenten/vffn kleinen Maßstab/so alzeit mit darbey gesetzet/gerichtet.

    This is the precise length and measure of a half *Schuh* or foot, according to the ruler; [a *Schuh*] is a fourth of a Brunswick *Ell*.[1] All of the subsequent depictions of instruments have been prepared in conformity with this small ruler.

1. The rough equivalent of a modern "yard."

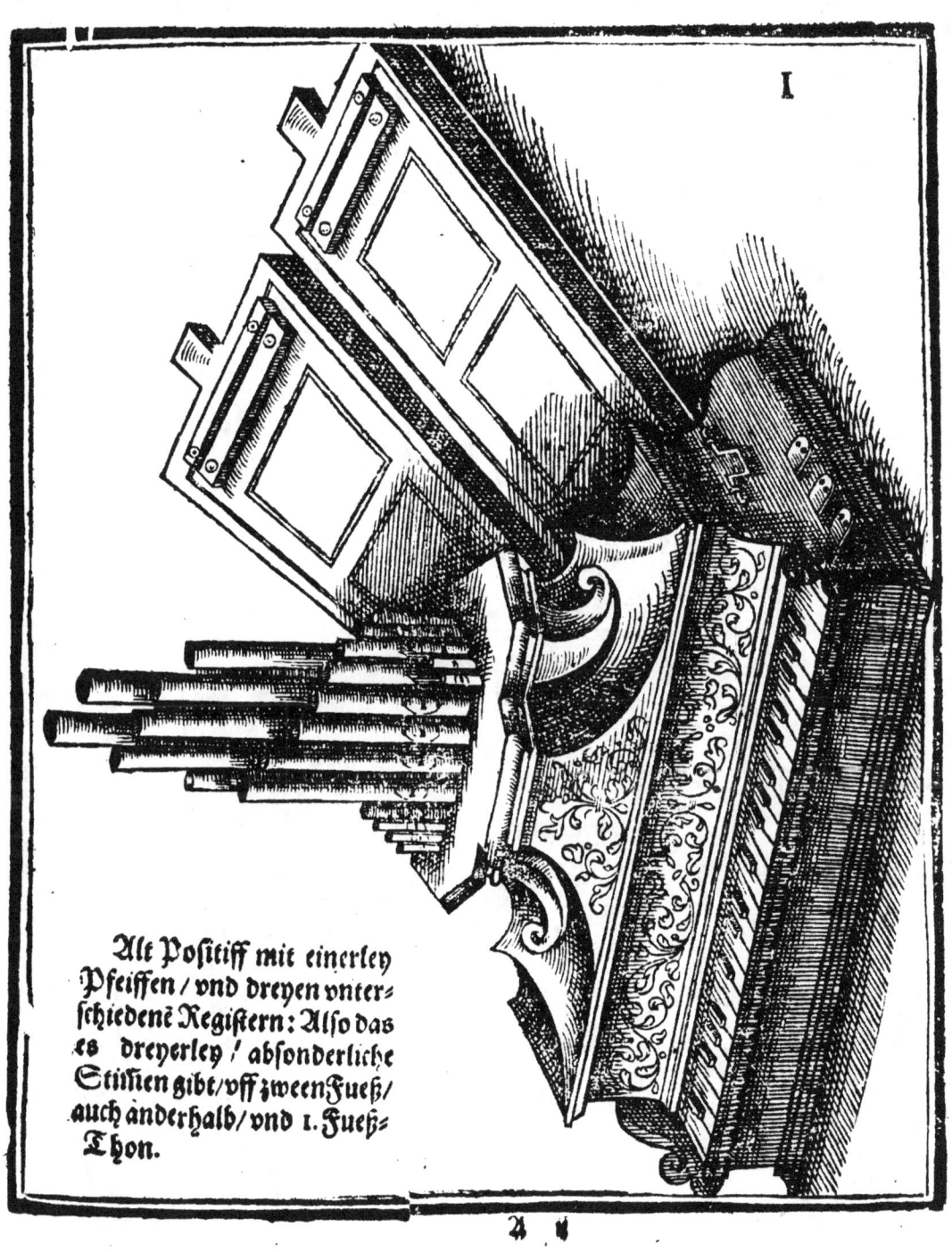

Plate I. An old positiv with a number of pipes and three different registers, producing three independent voices, at 2', 1½' and 1' pitch.

Plate II. Organ
(at the bottom of the page) "Here is where the Rückpositiv should be glued on."

Rückpositieff.

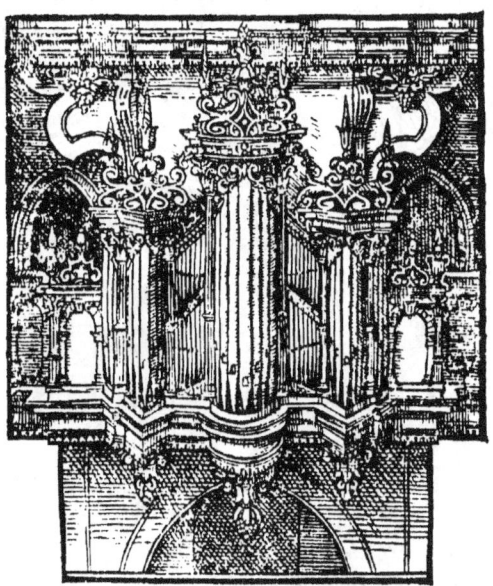

Dis Rückpositiefflin gehöret zu der II. Columna: vnd müssen vnten bey der Orgel angekleistert werden.

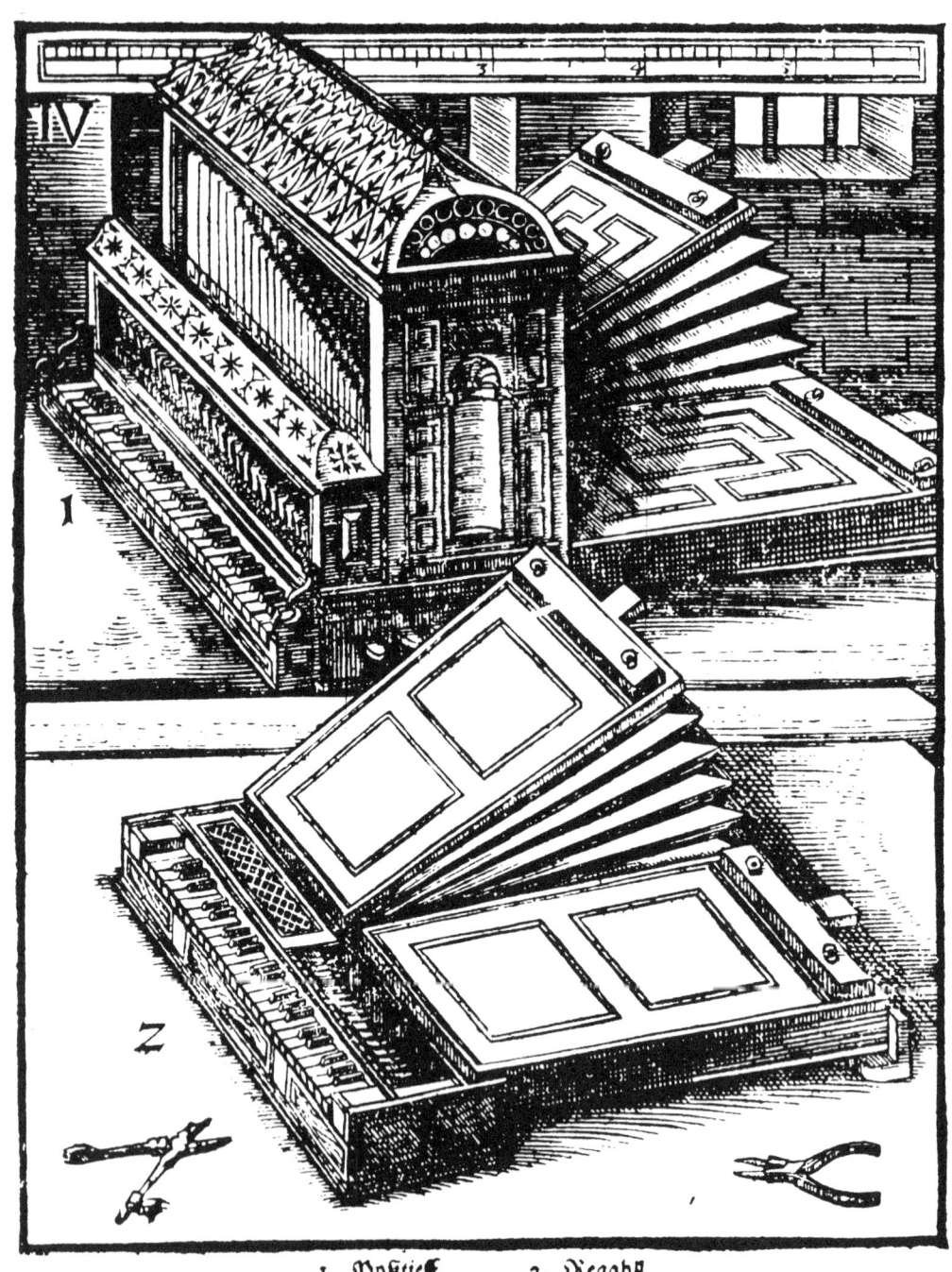

Plate IV: 1. Positiv. 2. Regal.

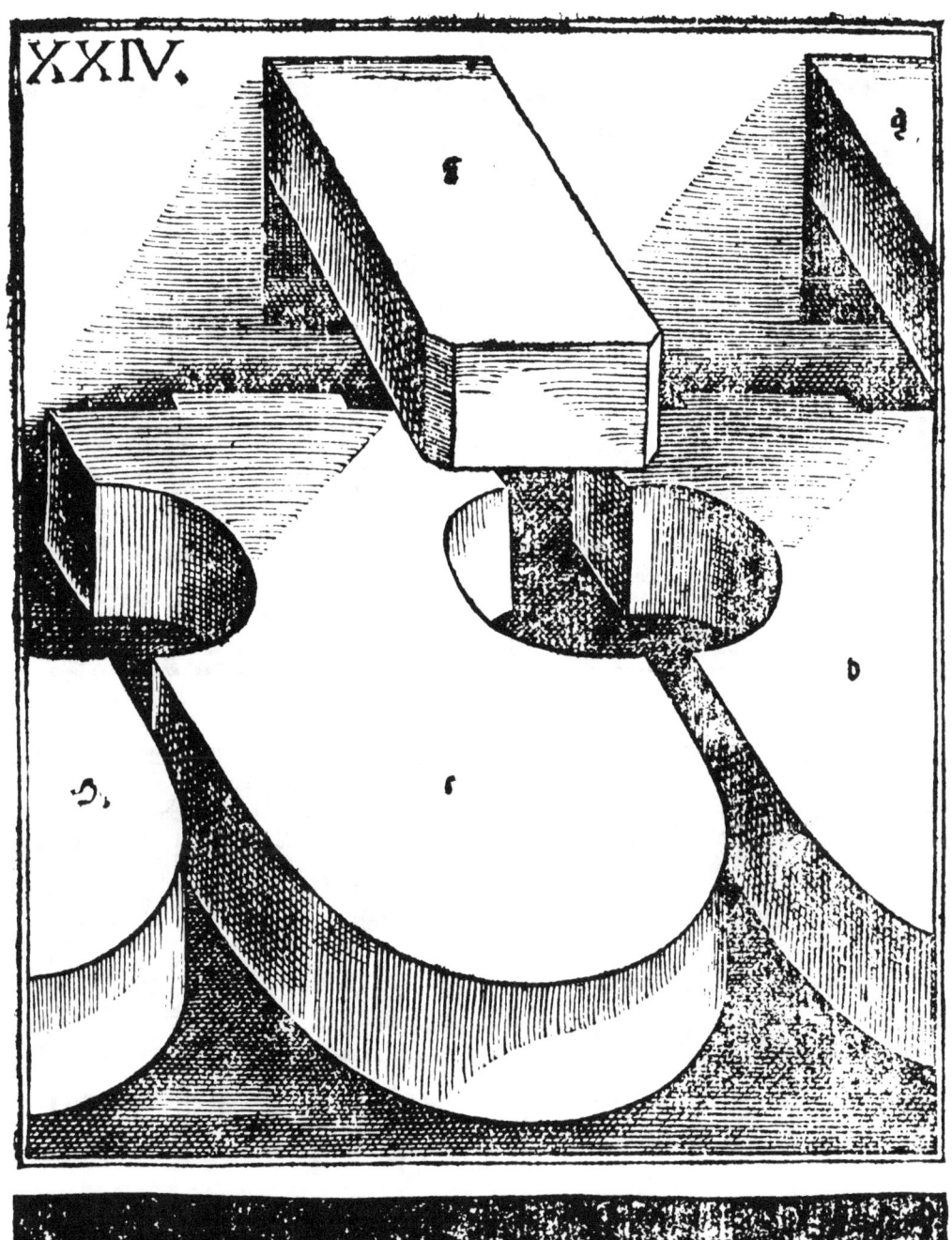

Plate XXXIV. Manual keyboard on the old organ in the Cathedral at Halberstadt.

Das I. vnd II. Discant-clavier.

Das III. Clavier.

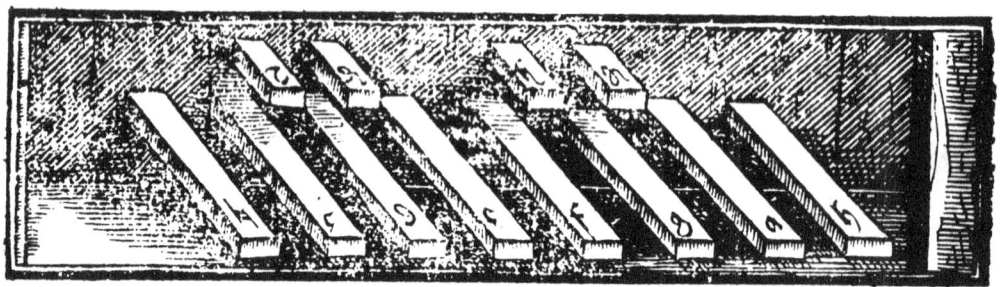

Das IV. Pedal-Clavier.

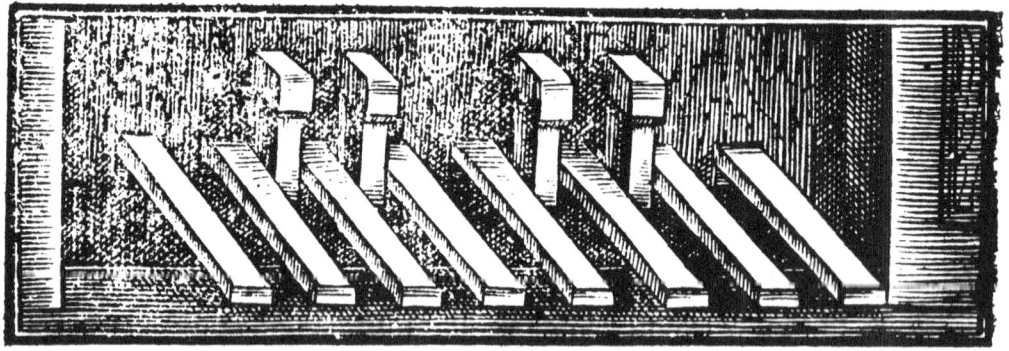

Diß sind die Manual- vnnd Pedal-Clavier, wie die in der gar grossen Orgel im Thumb zu Halberstadt vber einander liegen.

Plate XXV. (from top to bottom of page):

The first and second treble keyboards

The third keyboard

The fourth, for the pedal

These are the manual and pedal keyboards, as they lie one atop the other in the very large organ in the Cathedral at Halberstadt.

Blaßbälge vnd Calcanten, so zu d. zeit bey derselben Orgel gebraucht worden.

Plate XXVI. Bellows and bellows treaders as they were employed at the time of this organ [i.e., Halberstadt].

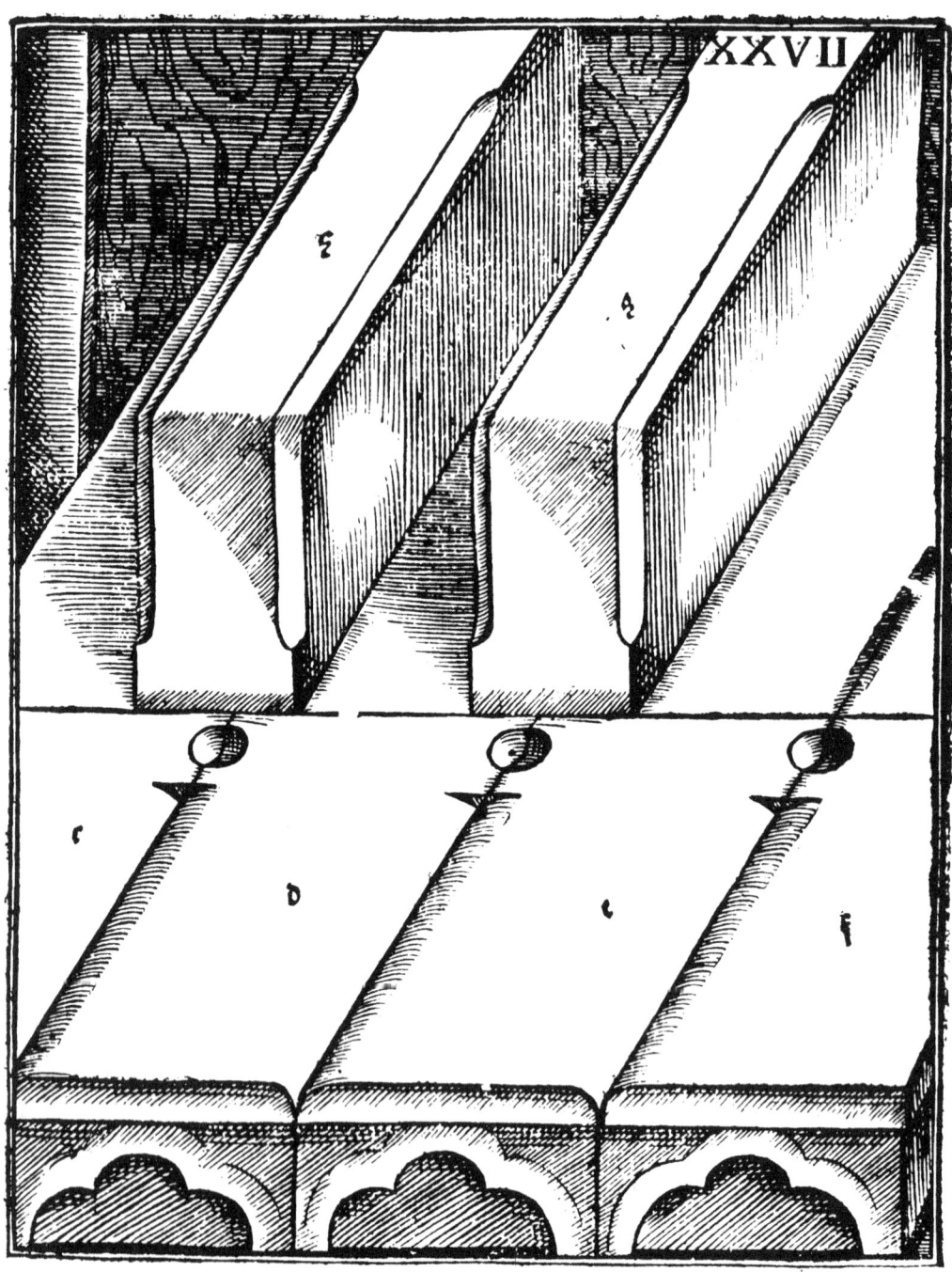

Plate XXVII. Keys of the Werck manual in the old organ at St. Aegidius in the city of Braunschweig.

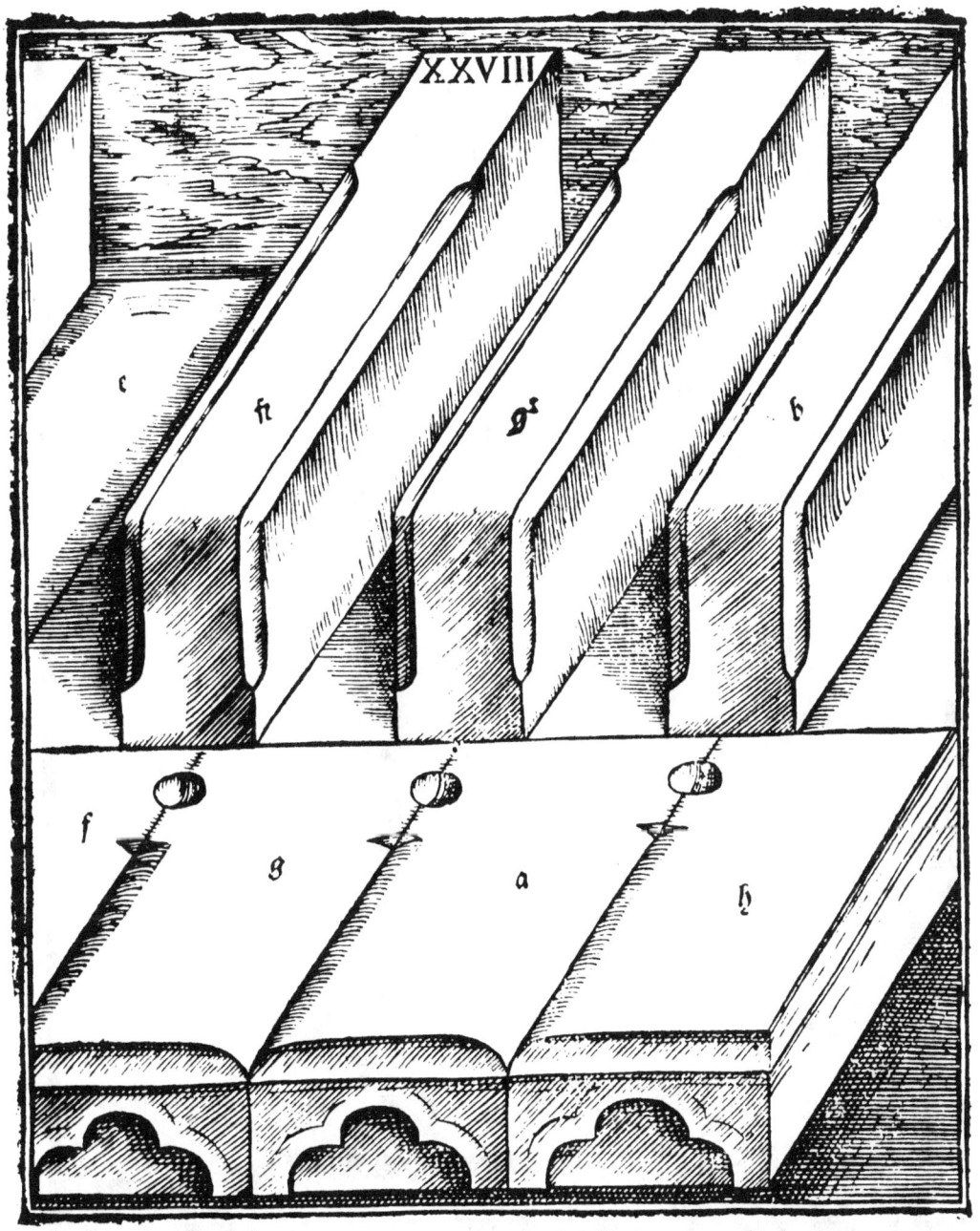

Plate XXVIII. Keys of the Rückpositiv in the same organ, St. Aegidius in Braunschweig.

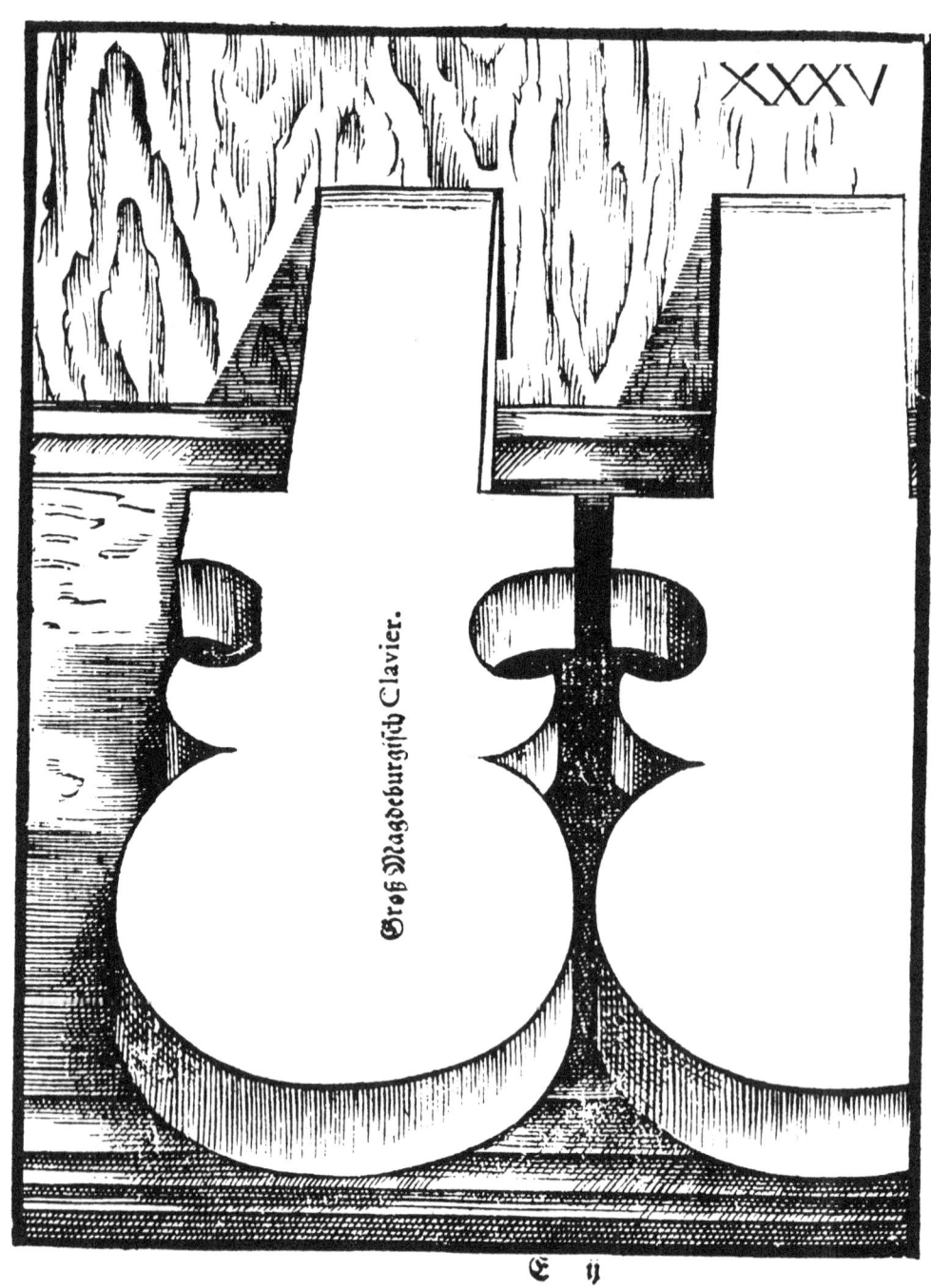

Plate XXXV. The large keyboard in Magdeburg Cathedral.

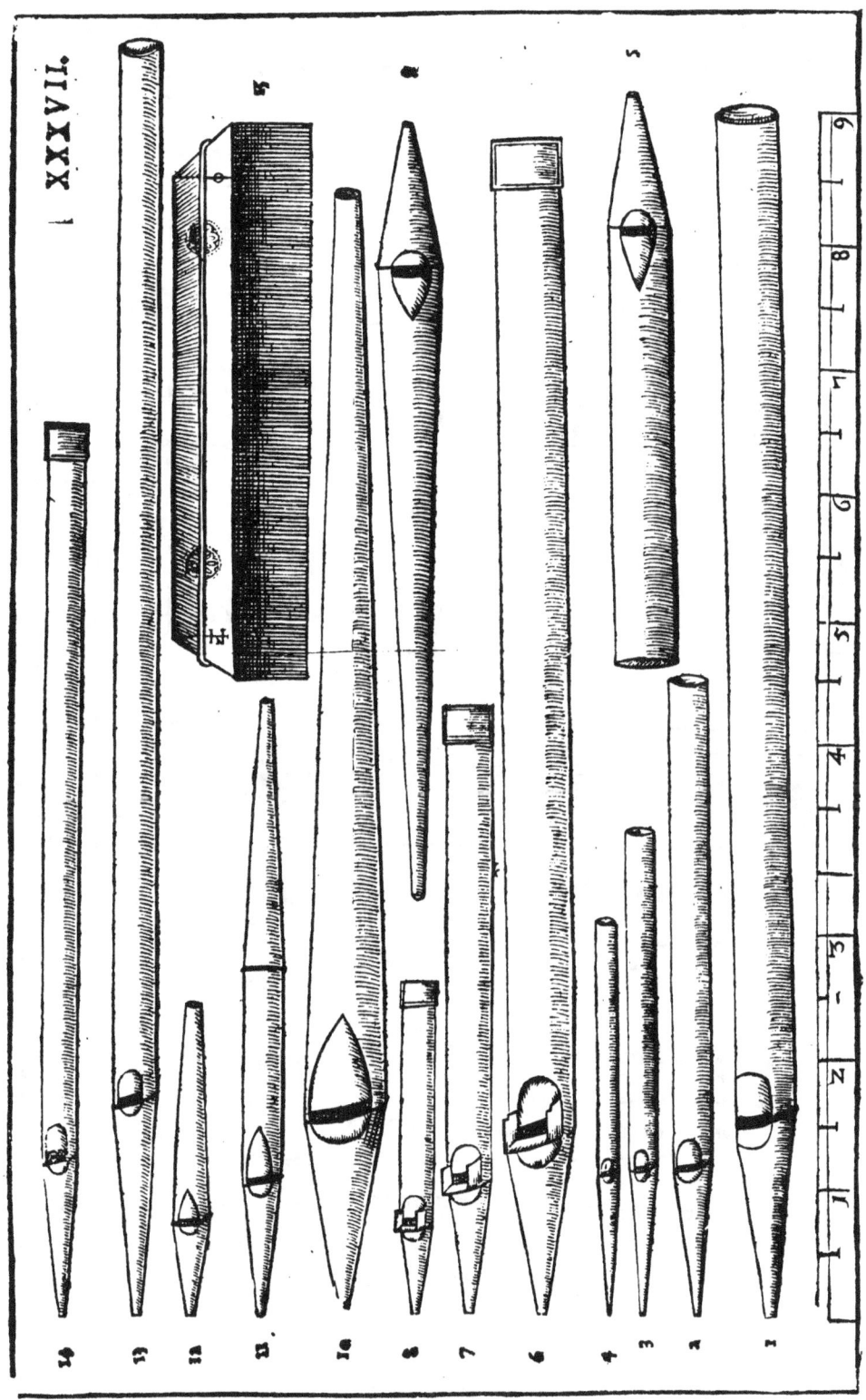

Plate XXXVII.

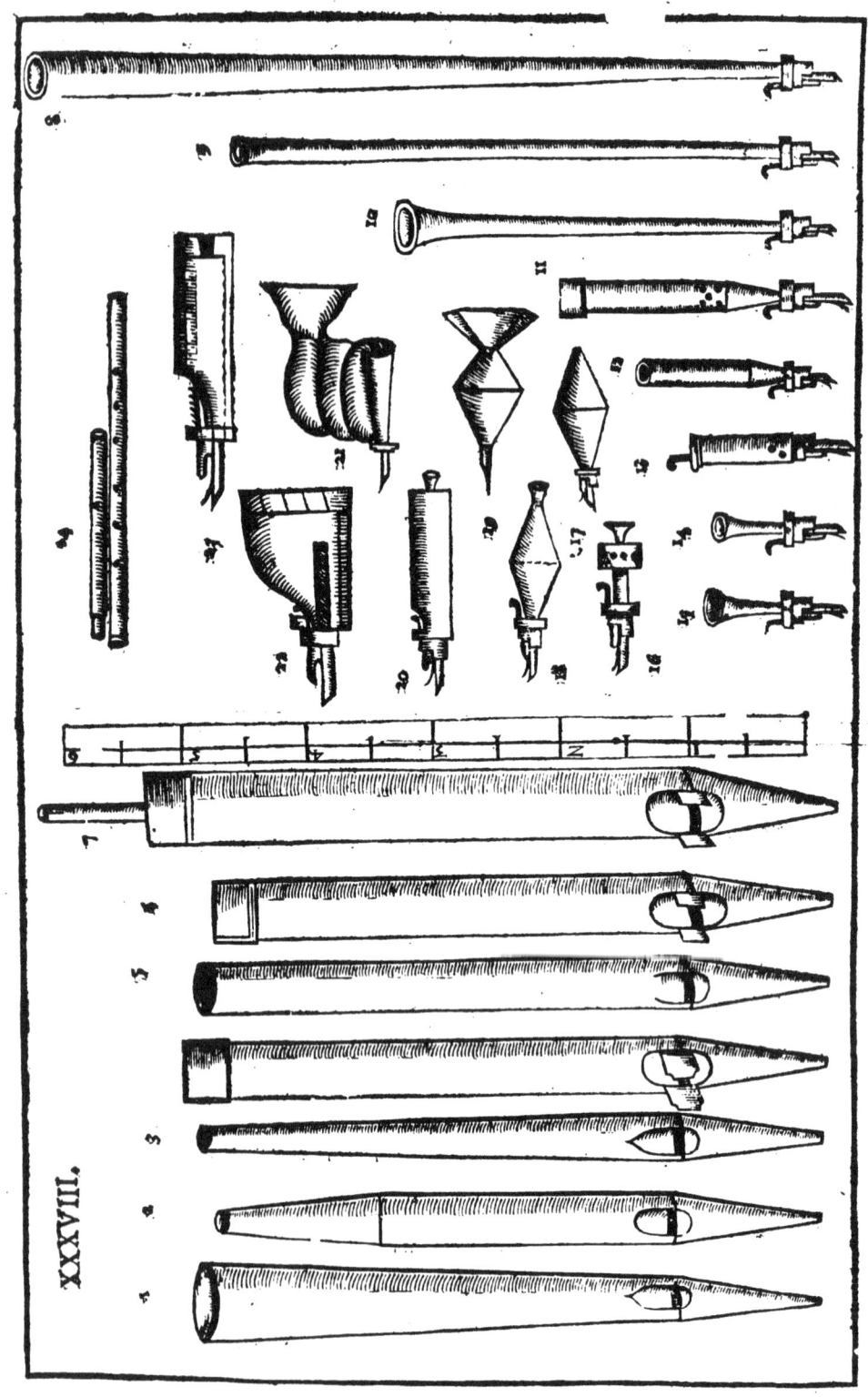

1. Dolcan. 4. Fuß. 2. Coppelflöt. 4. Fuß. 3. Flachflöt. 4. Fuß. 4. Klein Barduen. 8. Fuß. 5. Offenflöt. 4. Fuß. 6. Gleber. 8. Fuß. 7. Rohrflöt. oder Hohlflöt. 8. F. 8. Zcorna. 9. Krumbhorn. 8. Fuß. 10. Schalmey. 8. 4. Fuß. 11. Sorduen. 16. Fuß. 12. Zinck. Corner. Discant. 13. Flanckett. 8. 16. Fuß. 14. Brešing. Discabt. 8. Fuß. 15. Gemßhörnlein. 16. 17. 18. Krumbhorn. 19. 20. 21. 22. 23. Bass Pfeiffen Discant. Alt. 24. Duckflott.

Plate XXXVIII.

The University of Nebraska-Lincoln does not discriminate
based on gender, age, disability, race, color,
religion, marital status, veteran's status,
national or ethnic origin,
or sexual orientation.